The Classical Tradition
Part One

Edited by
John Bauschatz

University of Arizona

University Readers™
San Diego, CA

First published in the United States of America in 2009 by University Readers

13 12 11 10 09   1 2 3 4 5

Printed in the United States of America

ISBN: 978-1-934269-72-5

University Readers™
800.200.3908 I www.universityreaders.com

Contents

Homer's *Iliad* (Books 1 and 18)

𓏭𓏭𓏭𓏭𓏭𓏭𓏭𓏭𓏭𓏭𓏭𓏭𓏭𓏭𓏭

Translated by Ian Johnston

BOOK ONE
The Quarrel by the Ships

> *[The invocation to the Muse; Agamemnon insults Apollo; Apollo sends the plague onto the army; the quarrel between Achilles and Agamemnon; Calchas indicates what must be done to appease Apollo; Agamemnon takes Briseis from Achilles; Achilles prays to Thetis for revenge; Achilles meets Thetis; Chryseis is returned to her father; Thetis visits Zeus; the gods converse about the matter on Olympus; the banquet of the gods]*

Sing, Goddess, sing of the rage of Achilles, son of Peleus—
that murderous anger which condemned Achaeans
to countless agonies and threw many warrior souls
deep into Hades, leaving their dead bodies
carrion food for dogs and birds—
all in fulfilment of the will of Zeus.

Start at the point where Agamemnon, son of Atreus,
that king of men, quarrelled with noble Achilles.
Which of the gods incited these two men to fight?

That god was Apollo, son of Zeus and Leto.
Angry with Agamemnon, he cast plague down   10
onto the troops—deadly infectious evil.   [10]*
For Agamemnon had dishonoured the god's priest,
Chryses, who'd come to the ships to find his daughter,
Chryseis, bringing with him a huge ransom.

---

*   *[Note that the line numbers in square brackets refer to the Greek text]*

Homer, "Book One: The Quarrel by the Ships" and "Book Eighteen: The Arms of Achilles" from *Iliad*. Translation by Ian Johnston, 2008. Permission granted by translator.

In his hand he held up on a golden staff
the scarf sacred to archer god Apollo.
He begged Achaeans, above all the army's leaders,
the two sons of Atreus:

"Menelaus, Agamemnon, sons of Atreus,   20
all you well-armed Achaeans, may the gods
on Olympus grant you wipe out Priam's city,
and then return home safe and sound.
Release my dear child to me. Take this ransom.   [20]
Honour Apollo, far-shooting son of Zeus."

All the Achaeans roared out their support:

"Respect the priest. Take the generous ransom."

Displeased, Agamemnon dismissed Chryses roughly:

"Old man,
don't let me catch you by our hollow ships,
sneaking back here today or later on.   30
Who cares about Apollo's scarf and staff?
I'll not release the girl to you, no, not before
she's grown old with me in Argos, far from home,   [30]
working the loom, sharing my bed. Go away.
If you want to get home safely, don't anger me."

The old man, afraid, obeyed his words, walked off in silence,
along the shore by the tumbling, crashing surf.
Some distance off, he prayed to lord Apollo,
Leto's fair-haired child:

"God with the silver bow,
protector of Chryse, sacred Cilla,   40
mighty lord of Tenedos, Sminthean Apollo,
hear my prayer:* If I've ever pleased you
with a holy shrine, or burned bones for you—   [40]
bulls and goats well wrapped in fat—
grant me my prayer. Force the Danaans
to pay full price for my tears with your arrows."

So Chryses prayed. Phoebus Apollo heard him.
He came down from Olympus top enraged,
carrying on his shoulders bow and covered quiver,
his arrows rattling in anger against his arm.   50
So the god swooped down, descending like the night.
He sat some distance from the ships, shot off an arrow—
the silver bow reverberating ominously.

First, the god massacred mules and swift-running dogs,   [50]
then loosed sharp arrows in among the troops themselves.
Thick fires burned the corpses ceaselessly.

For nine days Apollo rained death down upon the troops.
On the tenth, Achilles summoned an assembly.
White-armed Hera put that thought into his mind,
concerned for the Danaans, seeing them die.   60
The men gathered. The meeting came to order.
Swift-footed Achilles rose to speak:

                    "Son of Atreus,
  I fear we're being beaten back, forced home,
  if we aren't all going to be destroyed right here,   [60]
  with war and plague killing off Achaeans.
  Come now, let's ask some prophet, priest,
  interpreter of dreams—for dreams, too, come from Zeus—
  a man who might say why Apollo is so angry,
  whether he faults our prayers and offerings,
  whether somehow he'll welcome sacrificial smoke   70
  from perfect lambs and goats, then rouse himself
  and release us from this plague."

Achilles spoke and took his seat.
Then Calchas, Thestor's son, stood up before them all,
the most astute interpreter of birds, who understood
present, future, past. His skill in prophecy,   [70]
Apollo's gift, had led Achaean ships to Troy.
He addressed the troops, thinking of their common good:

  "Achilles, friend of Zeus, you ask me to explain
  Apollo's anger, the god who shoots from far.
  And I will speak. But first you listen to me.   80

Swear an oath that you will freely help me
in word and deed. I think I may provoke
someone who wields great power over Argives,
a man who is obeyed by everyone.
An angry king overpowers lesser men.   [80]
Even if that day his anger is suppressed,
resentment lingers in his chest, until one day
he acts on it. So speak. Will you protect me?"

In response to Calchas, swift-footed Achilles said:

"Take courage. State what your powers tell you.   90
By Apollo, whom Zeus loves, to whom you, Calchas,
pray in prophesy to the Danaans, I swear this—
while I live to look upon the light of day,
no Achaean will raise violent hands against you,
no, not even if you name Agamemnon,   [90]
who claims he's by far the best Achaean."

Encouraged, the wise prophet then declared:

"Apollo does not fault us for prayers or offerings,
but for his priest, disgraced by Agamemnon,
who did not free his daughter and take ransom.   100
That's why the archer god has brought disaster,
and will bring still more. He won't remove
this wretched plague from the Danaans,
until we hand back bright-eyed Chryseis,
give her to her beloved father, freely,
without ransom, and offer holy sacrifice
at Chryse. If we will carry out all that,
we may change Apollo's mind, appease him."   [100]

So he spoke and sat back down. Then, Atreus' son,
wide-ruling, mighty Agamemnon, stood up before them,   110
incensed, spirit filled with huge black rage.
Eyes blazing fire, he rounded first on Calchas:

"Prophet of evil, when have you ever said
good things to me? You love to predict the worst,
always the worst! You never show good news.

Now, in prophecy to the Danaans,
you say archer Apollo brings us pain   [110]
because I was unwilling to accept
fine ransom for Chryses' daughter, Chryseis.
But I have a great desire to take her home.   120
In fact, I want her more than Clytaemnestra,
the wife I married. Chryseis is just as good
in her shape, physique, intelligence, or work.
Still, I'm prepared to give her back, if that's best.
I want the people safe, not all killed off.
But then you'll owe me another prize.
I won't be the only Argive left without a gift.
That would be entirely unfair to me.
You all can see my spoils are going elsewhere."   [120]

At that point, swift-footed Achilles answered the king: 130

"Noble son of Atreus, most acquisitive of men,
how can brave Achaeans give you a prize now?
There are none left for us to pass around.
We've divided up what we allotted,
loot from captured towns we devastated.
For men to make a common pile again
would be most unfair. Send the girl back now,
as the god demands. Should Zeus ever grant
we pillage Troy, a city rich in goods,
we'll give you three or four times as much."   140

Mighty Agamemnon then said in reply: [130]

"Achilles, you're a fine man, like a god.
But don't conceal what's in your heart.
You'll not trick me or win me with your words.
You intend to keep your prizes for yourself,
while the army takes my trophy from me.
That's why you tell me to give Chryseis back.
Let Achaeans give me another prize,
equal in value, something I'll enjoy.
If not, then I'll take a prize myself by force,   150
something from you or Ajax or Odysseus.
The man I visit is going to be enraged.

But let's postpone discussion of all this. [140]
Let's drag a black ship to the sacred sea,
select a crew, load oxen on for sacrifice,
and Chryseis, that fair-complexioned girl.
Let's have as leader some wise counsellor—
Idomeneus, Ajax, godlike Odysseus,
or you, Peleus's son, most eminent of all,
so with a sacrifice we may appease   160
the god who shoots from far away."

Scowling grimly, swift-footed Achilles interposed:

"You insatiable creature, quite shameless.
How can any Achaean obey you willingly—   [150]
join a raiding party or keep fighting
with full force against an enemy?
I didn't come to battle over here
because of Trojans. I have no fight with them.
They never stole my bulls or horses
or razed my crops in fertile Phthia,   170
where heroes grow. Many shady mountains
and the roaring sea stand there between us.
But you, great shameless man, we came with you,
to please you, to win honour from the Trojans—
for you, dog face, and for Menelaus.
You don't consider this, don't think at all.   [160]
You threaten now to confiscate the prize
I worked so hard for, gift from Achaea's sons.
When we Achaeans loot some well-built Trojan town,
my prizes never match the ones you get.   180
The major share of war's fury rests on me.
But when we hand around the battle spoils,
you get much larger trophies. Worn out in war,
I reach my ships with something fine but small.
So I'll return home now to Phthia.
It's far better to sail back in my curved ships.   [170]
I don't fancy staying here unvalued,
to pile up riches, treasures just for you."

To that, Agamemnon, king of men, shot back:

"Fly off home then, if that's your heart's desire.   190
I'll not beg you to stay on my account.
I have others around to honour me,
especially all-wise Zeus himself.
Of all the kings Zeus cherishes, it's you
I hate the most. You love constant strife—
war and combat. So what if you're strong?
Some god gave you that. So scurry off home.
Take ships and friends. Go rule your Myrmidons.   [180]
I don't like you or care about your rage.
But I'll make this threat: I'll take your prize,   200
fair-cheeked Briseis. I'll fetch her in person.
You'll see just how much I'm the better man.
And others will hate to speak to me as peers,
in public claiming full equality with me."
As Agamemnon spoke, Peleus' son, Achilles,
was overwhelmed with anguish, heart torn two ways,
debating in his shaggy chest what he should do: [190]
Should he draw out the sharp sword on his thigh,
incite the crowd, kill Atreus' son, or suppress his rage,
control his fury? As he argued in his mind and heart,   210
he slid his huge sword part way from its sheath.
At that moment, Athena came down from heaven.
White-armed Hera sent her. She cherished both men,
cared for them equally. Athena stood behind Achilles,
grabbed him by his golden hair,
invisible to all except Achilles. In astonishment he turned.
At once he recognized Pallas Athena,
the dreadful glitter in her eyes. Achilles spoke—   [200]
his words had wings.

         "Child of aegis-bearing Zeus,
why have you come now?* Do you wish to see   220
how overbearing Agamemnon is?
I'll tell you where all this is going to lead—
that arrogance will soon cost him his life."

Glittery-eyed Athena then spoke in reply:

"I came down from heaven to curb your passion,
if you obey. White-armed Hera sent me.
She loves you both alike, cares equally.
Give up this quarrel. Don't draw your sword.   [210]
Fight him with words, so he becomes disgraced.
For I say to you, and this will happen,   230
because of Agamemnon's arrogance
some day gifts three times greater than this girl
will be set down before you. Control yourself.
Obey."

      Swift-footed Achilles answered Athena:

"Goddess, men should follow your instructions,
though angry in their hearts. It's better so.
The person who's obedient to the gods,
the gods attend to all the more."

          Obeying Athena's words,
Achilles relaxed his huge fist on the silver hilt
and pushed the massive sword back in its scabbard.   240   [220]
Athena then returned to heaven, home of Zeus,
who bears the aegis, and the other gods.

Achilles turned again on Agamemnon, Atreus' son,
with harsh abuse, his anger still unabated:

"You drunken sot, dog-eyed, deer-timid coward,
you're never strong enough within yourself
to arm for war alongside other comrades,
or venture with Achaea's bravest on a raid.
To you that smells too much like death.
No. You'd much prefer to stroll around   250
throughout the wide Achaean army,
to grab gifts from a man who speaks against you.   [230]
A king who gorges on his own people!
You lord it over worthless men. If not,
son of Atreus, this would be your last offence.
I'll tell you, swear a great oath on this point,

by this sceptre, which will never sprout
leaves and shoots again, since first ripped
away from its mountain stump, nor bloom any more,
now that bronze has sliced off leaf and bark.
This sceptre Achaea's sons take in hand   260
whenever they do justice in Zeus' name.
An oath on this has power. On this I swear—
the time will come when Achaea's sons
all miss Achilles, a time when, in distress,   [240]
you'll lack my help, a time when Hector,
that man killer, destroys many warriors.
Then grief will tear your hearts apart,
because you shamed Achaea's finest man."

So the son of Peleus spoke, throwing to the ground   270
the sceptre with the golden studs. Then he sat down,
directly facing furious Agamemnon.

Then Nestor stood up, clear, sweet orator from Pylos.
Sweeter than honey the words flowed from his tongue.
In his own lifetime two generations of mortal men   [250]
had come and passed away, all those born and raised
with him so long ago in sacred Pylos.
Now he ruled a third generation of his people.
Concerned about their common good, he said:

"Alas, this is great sorrow for Achaeans.   280
Priam and Priam's children will be glad,
the hearts of other Trojans swell with joy,
should they find out about such quarrelling,
a fight between you two, among Danaans,
the very best for counsel or combat.
But listen. You are both younger men than I.   [260]
And I've been colleague of better men than you,
men who never showed me any disrespect,
men whose like I have not seen again,
and never will—like Peirithous, Dryas,   290
a shepherd to his people, Caeneus,
Exadios, god-like Polyphemus,
Theseus, son of Aegeus, all god-like men—
the mightiest earthborn men, the strongest.

And the enemies they fought against were strong,
the most powerful of mountain centaurs.
But they destroyed those creatures totally.
Associate of theirs, I came from Pylos,
a long way from that land, summoned personally.   [270]
I fought on my own behalf, by myself.   300
No man alive on earth could now fight them.
Yet they heard me and followed my advice.
So listen, both of you. That's what's best now.
Agamemnon, you're an excellent man,
but do not take Briseis from Achilles.
Let that pass. Achaea's sons gave her to him first.
And you, Peleus' son, don't seek to fight the king,
not as your enemy. The sceptre-bearing king,
whose powerful authority comes from Zeus,
never shares honours equally. Achilles,   310
you may be stronger, since your mother was divine,   [280]
but he's more powerful, for he rules more men.
But you, son of Atreus, check your anger.
Set aside, I urge you, your rage against Achilles,
who provides, in the middle of war's evils,
a powerful defence for all Achaeans."

Mighty Agamemnon then replied to Nestor:

"Old man, everything you say is true enough.
But this man wants to put the rest to shame,
rule all of us, lord it over everyone.   320
But some, I think, will not obey him.
So what if the gods, who live forever,   [290]
made him a spearman? Is that some reason
we should let him say such shameful things?"

Achilles, interrupting Agamemnon, shouted:

"I'd be called a coward, a nobody,
if I held back from any action
because of something you might say.
Order other men about. Don't tell me
what I should do. I'll not obey you any more.   330
But I will tell you this—remember it well—

I'll not raise my hand to fight about that girl,
no, not against you or any other man.
You Achaeans gave her to me, and now,
you seize her back again. But you'll not take
another thing from my swift black ship—   [300]
you'll get nothing else with my consent.
If you'd like to see what happens, just try.
My spear will quickly drip with your dark blood."

Thus the pair of them continued arguing.   340
Then they stood up, dissolving the assembly by the ships.
Peleus's son went back to his well-balanced ships and huts,
along with Patroclus, Menoetius' son, and friends.
Agamemnon dragged a swift ship down the shore,
chose twenty sailors, loaded on the oxen,
offerings for the god, and led on fair-cheeked Chryseis.   [310]
Shrewd Odysseus shipped on as leader. All aboard,
they set off, carving a pathway through the sea.
Atreus' son ordered troops to cleanse themselves.
The men bathed in the sea, washed off impurities.   350
They then made sacrificial offerings to Apollo—
hundreds of perfect bulls and goats—beside the restless sea.
Savoury smells curled up amid the smoke high into heaven.
The men thus occupied, Agamemnon did not
forget the challenge he'd made earlier to Achilles.
He called his heralds, Talthybius and Eurybates: [320]

"Go to Achilles' tent, Peleus's son,
take fair-complexioned Briseis by the hand.
Bring her to me. If he won't surrender her,
I'll come myself in force and take her.   360
For him that will be a worse disaster."

With these firm orders, he dismissed the men, who moved off,
heavy hearted, along the shore of the restless sea.
They reached the huts and ships of the Myrmidons.
There they found Achilles seated by his hut
and his black ship. As he saw them approach,

Achilles felt no joy. The two heralds, afraid,   [330]
just stood in silence, out of deference to the king.
In his heart Achilles sensed their purpose. He called them.

"Cheer up, heralds, messengers for gods and men.   370
Come here. I don't blame you, but Agamemnon.
He sends you both here for the girl Briseis.
Come, Patroclus, born from Zeus, fetch the girl.
Give her to these two to take away.
Let them both witness, before blessed gods,
mortal men, and that unfeeling king,   [340]
if ever there's a need for me again
to defend others from a shameful death.
That man's wits are foolish, disastrously so—
he's not thinking about past or future,   380
how Achaeans may fight safely by their ships."

Patroclus did as his dear comrade had requested.
He led out fair-cheeked Briseis from the hut
and gave her up to be led off. The heralds went back,
returning to Achaean ships, Briseis with them, but against her will.

                              Achilles then, in tears,
withdrew from his companions, sat by the shore,
staring at the wide gray seas. Stretching out his hands,   [350]
he cried aloud, praying repeatedly to Thetis,
his beloved mother.*

                    "Mother, since you gave me life—   390
if only for a while—Olympian Zeus,
high thunderer, should give me due honour.
But he doesn't grant me even slight respect.
For wide-ruling Agamemnon, Atreus' son,
has shamed me, has taken away my prize,
appropriated it for his own use."

                    As he said this, he wept.
His noble mother heard him from deep within the sea,
where she sat by her old father. Quickly she rose up,
moving above grey waters, like an ocean mist,
and settled down before him, as he wept. She stroked him,   400   [360]

then said:

"My child, why these tears? What sorrows
weigh down your heart? Tell me, so we'll both know.
Don't hide from me what's on your mind."

With a deep groan, swift-footed Achilles then replied.

"You know. Why should I tell you what you know?
We came to Thebe, Eëtion's sacred city,
sacked it, taking everything the city had.
Achaea's sons apportioned it all fairly
amongst themselves. Agamemnon's share
was fair-skinned Chryseis. Then Chryses arrived   410   [370]
at the swift ships of bronze-armed Achaeans.
Archer god Apollo's priest sought out his daughter.
He brought with him an enormous ransom,
carried in his hands the sacred golden staff
with the shawl of archer god Apollo.
He begged Achaeans, above all Atreus' two sons,
the people's leaders. All Achaeans called on them
to respect the priest, accept the splendid ransom.
But that didn't please Agamemnon in his heart.
He sent him roughly off with harsh abusive orders   420
The old man went away again, enraged.   [380]
He prayed to Apollo, who loved him well.
The god heard him and sent his deadly arrows
against the Argives. The troops kept dying,
one by one, as the god rained arrows down
throughout the wide Achaean army.
The prophet Calchas, understanding all,
told us Apollo's will. At once I was the first
to recommend we all appease the god.
But anger got control of Agamemnon.   430
He stood up on the spot and made that threat
which he's just carried out. So quick-eyed Achaeans
are sending Chryseis in fast ships back to Chryse,   [390]
transporting gifts for lord Apollo, and heralds came
to take away Briseis from my huts,
the girl who is my gift from Achaea's sons.
So now, if you can, protect your son.

Go to Mount Olympus, implore Zeus,
if ever you in word or deed have pleased him.
For often I have heard you boast in father's house   440
that you alone of all the deathless gods
saved Zeus of the dark clouds from disgraceful ruin,
when other Olympians came to tie him up,
Hera, Pallas Athena, and Poseidon.   [400]
But you, goddess, came and set him free,
by quickly calling up to high Olympus
that hundred-handed monster gods call Briareos,
and men all name Aigaion, a creature
whose strength was greater than his father's.*
He sat down beside the son of Cronos,   450
exulting in his glory. The sacred gods, afraid,
stopped tying up Zeus. So sit down right by Zeus,
clasp his knee, remind him of all that,
so he'll want to help the Trojans somehow,
corner Achaeans by the sea, by their ships' prows,
have them destroyed, so they all enjoy their king,   [410]
so the son of Atreus, wide-ruling Agamemnon,
himself may see his foolishness, dishonouring
Achilles, the best of the Achaeans."

Thetis, shedding tears, answered her son, Achilles: 460

"Oh my child, why did I rear you,
since I brought you up to so much pain?
Would you were safely by your ships dry-eyed.
Your life is fated to be short—you'll not live long.
Now, faced with a quick doom, you're in distress,
more so than any other man. At home,
I gave you life marked by an evil fate.
But I'll tell these things to thunder-loving Zeus.
I'll go myself to snow-topped Mount Olympus,   [420]
to see if he will undertake all this.   470
Meanwhile, you should sit by your swift ships,
angry at Achaeans. Take no part in war.
For yesterday Zeus went to Oceanus,
to banquet with the worthy Ethiopians.
The gods all journeyed with him. In twelve days,
when he returns and comes home to Olympus,

I'll go to Zeus' bronze-floored house, clasp his knee.
I think I'll get him to consent."

                                   Thetis spoke.
Then she went away, leaving Achilles there,
angry at heart for lovely girdled Briseis,   480
taken from him by force against his will.

Odysseus sailed to Chryse, bringing with him
the sacrificial animals as sacred offerings.
When they had sailed into deep anchorage,
they took in the sails and stowed them in the ship.
With forestays they soon set the mast down in its notch,
then rowed the ship in to its mooring place.
They threw out anchor stones, lashed stern cables,
and clambered out into the ocean surf.
They brought off the offerings to archer god Apollo.   490
Then Chryseis disembarked from the ocean ship.
Resourceful Odysseus led her to the altar,   [440]
placed her in her beloved father's hands, then said:

    "Chryses, I have been sent by Agamemnon,
    ruler of men, to bring your daughter to you,
    and then, on behalf of the Danaans,
    to make an offering to lord Apollo—   450
    all these sacrificial beasts—to placate the god,
    who now inflicts such dismal evil on us."   [410]

After saying this, he handed the girl over.   500
Chryses gave his daughter a joyful welcome back.
And then around the well-built altar, they arranged
the splendid sacrifice. They washed their hands,
and picked up the barley grain for sprinkling.
Raising his arms, Chryses prayed out loud on their behalf: [450]

    "Hear me, god of the silver bow, protector
    of Chryse, mighty lord of holy Cilla,
    sacred Tenedos. You heard me earlier,
    when I prayed to you. Just as you honoured me,
    striking hard against Achaeans then, so now,   510

grant me what I pray for—remove disaster,
this wretched evil, from the Danaans."

So Chryses spoke. Phoebus Apollo heard him.
Once they had prayed and scattered barley grain,
they pulled back the heads of sacrificial beasts,
slit their throats, flayed them, sliced the thigh bones out,
and hid them in twin layers of fat, with raw meat on top.   [460]
Old Chryses burned them on split wood, poured wine on them.
Young men beside him held out five-pronged forks.
Once the thighs were well burned, they sampled entrails,   520
then sliced up all the rest, skewered the meat on spits,
roasted it carefully, and drew off every piece.
That work complete, they then prepared a meal and ate.
No heart was left unsatisfied. All feasted equally.
And when the men had had their fill of food and drink,
young boys filled the mixing bowl with wine up to the brim,   [470]
and served it, pouring libations into every cup.
Then all day long young Achaean lads played music,
singing to the god a lovely hymn of praise,
honouring in dance and song the god who shoots from far.   530
Hearing them, Apollo felt joy fill his heart. At sunset,
as dusk came on, by the ship's stern they went to sleep.
But when early born, rose-fingered Dawn appeared,
they set off, once more back to the wide Achaean camp.
Far-shooting Apollo sent them favourable winds.
They raised the mast and then the sails. The wind blew,   [480]
filling out the body of the sail—on both sides of the prow
the purple waves hissed loudly as the ship sped on its way,
its motion carving a path through the ocean swell.
When they reached the broad Achaean army,   540
they hauled the black ship high up on the sand,
pushed long props tight beneath it, then dispersed,
each man returning to his own huts and ships.

Meanwhile, Achilles, divinely born son of Peleus,
sat down in anger alongside his swift ships. Not once
did he attend assembly where men win glory   [490]
or go out to fight. But he pined away at heart,
remaining idle by his ships, yearning
for the hue and cry and clash of battle.

Twelve days later, the company of gods came back   550
together to Olympus, with Zeus in the lead.
Thetis did not forget the promise to her son.
She rose up through the ocean waves at daybreak,
then moved high up to great Olympus. She found Zeus,
wide-seeing son of Cronos, some distance from the rest,
seated on the highest peak of many-ridged Olympus.
She sat down right in front of him. With her left hand,   [500]
she clutched his knees, with her right she cupped his chin,
in supplication to lord Zeus, son of Cronos:

"Father Zeus, if, among the deathless gods,   560
I've ever served you well in word or deed,
then grant my prayer will be fulfilled.
Bring honour to my son, who, of all men
will be fate's quickest victim. For just now,
Agamemnon, king of men, has shamed him.
He seized his prize, robbing him in person,
and kept it for himself. But honour him,
Zeus, all-wise Olympian. Give the Trojans
the upper hand, until Achaeans respect my son,
until they multiply his honours."   570   [510]

Thetis finished. Cloud gatherer Zeus did not respond.
He sat a long time silent. Thetis held his knees,
clinging close, repeating her request once more:

"Promise me truly, nod your head, or deny me—
since there's nothing here for you to fear—
so I'll clearly see how among the gods
I enjoy the least respect of all."

Cloud gatherer Zeus, greatly troubled, said:

                              "A nasty business.
What you say will set Hera against me.
She provokes me so with her abuse. Even now,   580
in the assembly of immortal gods,
she's always insulting me, accusing me   [520]
of favouring the Trojans in the war.
But go away for now, in case Hera catches on.

I'll take care of this, make sure it comes to pass.
Come, to convince you, I'll nod my head.
Among gods that's the strongest pledge I make.
Once I nod my assent, nothing I say
can be revoked, denied, or unfulfilled."

Zeus, son of Cronos, nodded his dark brows.   590
The divine hair on the king of gods fell forward,
down over his immortal head, shaking Olympus   [530]
to its very base. The conference over, the two parted.
Thetis plunged from bright Olympus back into the sea.

Zeus went inside his house. Their father present,
all the gods at once stood up from their seats.
No one dared stay put as he came in—all rose together.
Zeus seated himself upon his throne. Looking at him,
Hera sensed he'd made some deal with Thetis,
silver-footed daughter of the Old Man of the Sea.   600
At once she spoke up accusingly:

"Which god has been scheming with you, you crafty one?   [540]
You always love to work on things in secret,
without involving me. You never want
to tell me openly what you intend."

The father of gods and men replied:

                              "Hera,
don't hope to understand my every plan.
Even for my own wife that's dangerous.
What's appropriate for you to hear about,
no one, god or man, will know before you.   610
But when I wish to hide my thoughts from gods,
don't you go digging after them,
or pestering me for every detail."   [550]

Ox-eyed queen Hera then replied to Zeus:

"Most dread son of Cronos, what are you saying?
I have not been overzealous before now,
in questioning you or seeking answers.

Surely you're quite at liberty to plan
anything you wish. But now, in my mind,
I've got this dreadful fear that Thetis,   620
silver-footed daughter of the Old Man of the Sea,
has won you over, for this morning early,
she sat down beside you, held your knees.
I think you surely nodded your agreement
to honour Achilles, killing many soldiers,
slaughtering them by the Achaean ships."

Zeus, the cloud gatherer, spoke out in response: [560]

"My dear lady, you're always fancying things.
Your attention picks up every detail.
But you can't do anything about it,   630
except push yourself still further from my heart,
making matters so much worse for you.
If things are as they are, then that's the way
I want them. So sit down quietly.
Do as I say. If not, then all the gods
here on Olympus won't be any help,
when I reach out to set my hands on you,
for they're invincible."

                          Zeus finished speaking.
Ox-eyed queen Hera was afraid—so she sat down,
silently suppressing what her heart desired.   640
In Zeus' home the Olympian gods began to quarrel.   [570]
Then that famous artisan, Hephaestus, concerned
about his mother, white-armed Hera, spoke to them:

"A troublesome matter this will prove—
unendurable—if you two start fighting
over mortal men like this, inciting gods to quarrel. .
If we start bickering, we can't enjoy the meal,
our excellent banquet. So I'm urging mother,
though she's more than willing, to humour Zeus,
our dear father, so he won't get angry once again,   650
disturb the feast for us. For if Zeus,
the Olympian lord of lightning, was of a mind   [580]
to hurl us from our seats, his strength's too great.

But if you talk to him with soothing words,
at once Olympian Zeus will treat us well."

Hephaestus spoke, then stood up, passed a double goblet
across to his dear mother, saying:

"Stay calm, mother, even though you are upset.
If not, then, as beloved as you are,
I may see you beaten up before my eyes,   660
with me incapable of helping out,
though the sight would make me most unhappy.
It's hard to take a stand opposing Zeus.
Once, when I was eager to assist you,   [590]
Zeus seized me by the feet and threw me out,
down from heaven's heights. The entire day
I fell and then, right at sunset, dropped
on Lemnos, almost dead. After that fall,
men of Sintes helped me to recover."

As he spoke, the white-armed goddess Hera smiled.   670
She reached for her son's goblet. He poured the drink,
going from right to left, for all the other gods,
drawing off sweet nectar from the mixing bowl.

Then their laughter broke out irrepressibly,
as the sacred gods saw Hephaestus bustling around,   [600]
concerned about the feast. All that day they dined,
until sunset. No one's heart went unsatisfied.
All feasted equally. They heard exquisite music,
from Apollo's lyre and the Muses' beautiful song
and counter-song. When the sun's bright light had set,   680
the gods all went to their own homes. Hephaestus,
the famous lame god, with his resourceful skill,
had made each god a place to live. Olympian Zeus,
god of lightning, went home to his own bed,
where he usually reclined whenever sweet sleep   [610]
came over him. He went inside and lay down there,
with Hera of the golden throne stretched out beside him.

Notes to Book One

* *Smithean* is a special epithet given to Apollo. It seems to mean something like "killer of field mice." Chryse is a small coastal town near Troy, where *Chryses*, the father if *Chryses*, is a priest of Apollo.

* The *aegis* is a special divine shield, the sight of which has the power to terrify men and make them run away. Later in the poem Apollo uses it to terrify the Achaean soldiers.

* Achilles' mother, *Thetis*, is a minor sea goddess who married the mortal Peleus.

* The reference here is to an attempt by the Olympian gods to topple Zeus. Thetis brought the enormously powerful monster Briareos, one of the children of Gaia and Ouranos, to Zeus' aid.

* * * * *

BOOK EIGHTEEN
The Arms of Achilles

[Antilochus brings the news to Achilles of Patroclus' death; Achilles collapses in grief; Thetis hears his grief, talks to her sister Nereids, then visits Achilles, promises to bring him new armour from Hephaestus; Iris visits Achilles with a message from Hera; Achilles displays himself to the Trojans by the ditch and wall; Trojans debate what to do; Polydamas advises retreat; Hector opposes him; Achaeans take Patroclus' body back to the ships, begin their laments over Patroclus; Thetis visits Hephaestus, requests new armour for Achilles; Hephaestus makes new armour, especially a new shield; Thetis leaves with the armour]

As the men fought on like a blazing fire raging,
swift-footed Antilochus came to Achilles
with his news. He found Achilles by his beaked ship,
sensing in himself what had already happened,
speaking with a troubled mind to his own great heart:

"Why are long-haired Achaeans once again
retreating to their ships, being beaten back
across the plain in terror? I hope the gods
have not done something that will break my heart.
My mother told me once they'd do that,   10

when she told me that while I was alive
the best man of the Myrmidons would leave [10]
the sun's light at the hands of Trojans.
So it must be the case that the fine son
of Menoetius is dead, that reckless man.
I told him to return back to the ships,
once he'd saved them from consuming fire,
and not face up to Hector man to man."

As Achilles in his mind and heart was thinking this,
noble Nestor's son approached, shedding warm tears. 20
He told him the agonizing truth:

           "Son of warlike Peleus,
you must hear this dreadful news—something
I wish weren't so—Patroclus lies dead. [20]
Men are fighting now around the body.
He's stripped. Hector with his gleaming helmet
has the armour."

                 Antilochus finished speaking.
A black cloud of grief swallowed up Achilles.
With both hands he scooped up soot and dust and poured it
on his head, covering his handsome face with dirt,
covering his sweet-smelling tunic with black ash. 30
He lay sprawling—his mighty warrior's massive body
collapsed and stretched out in the dust. With his hands,
he tugged at his own hair, disfiguring himself.
The women slaves acquired as battle trophies
by Achilles and Patroclus, hearts overwhelmed
with anguish, began to scream aloud. They rushed outside
and beat their breasts around warlike Achilles. [30]
Then all the women's legs gave way, and they fell down.
Across from them, Antilochus lamented,
eyes full of tears, as he held Achilles by the hand. 40
Achilles' noble heart moaned aloud. Antilochus
feared he might hurt himself or slit his throat
with his own sword. Achilles gave a huge cry of grief.
His noble mother heard it from the ocean depths
where she was sitting by her ancient father.
She began to wail. Then around her gathered

all the divine daughters of Nereus deep in the sea—
Glauce, Thaleia, Cymodoce, Nesaea,
Speio, Thoe, ox-eyed Halië, Cymothoë,   [40]
Actaia, Limnoreia, Melite, Iaera,   50
Amphithoe, Agave, Doto, Proto,
Pherousa, Dynamene, Dexamene,
Amphinome, Callianeira, Doris, Panope,
lovely Galatea, Nemertes, Apseudes,
Callianassa. Also there were Clymene,
Ianeira, Ianassa, Maera, Orithyia,
Amatheia with her lovely hair, and others,
Nereus' daughters living in the ocean depths.
They filled the glistening cave, beating their breasts.   [50]
Thetis led them all in their laments:

                        "Sister Nereids, listen,   60
    so all of you, hearing what I say,
    will understand my heart's enormous sorrow.   [20]
    Alas, for my unhappy misery,
    that to my grief I bore the best of men.
    For when I gave birth to a fine strong boy
    to be an excellent heroic warrior,
    when he'd grown as tall as some young sapling,
    for I'd raised him like a lovely orchard tree,
    I sent him out in the beaked ships to Ilion,
    to war against the Trojans. But now,   70
    I'll never welcome him back home again,   [60]
    returning to the house of Peleus.
    While he's still alive and sees the sunlight,
    he lives in sorrow. When I go to him,
    I can provide no help. But I shall go
    to look on my dear child, to hear what grief
    has overtaken him while he remains
    detached from all the fighting."

                        With these words,
Thetis left the cave. Her sisters went with her in tears.
Around them sea waves parted, until they came   80
to fertile Troy. They emerged, climbing up on shore,
one after another, right where the Myrmidons
had dragged up their ships in close-packed formation

near swift Achilles. Then his noble mother moved   [70]
beside him, as he was groaning bitterly.
With a sharp cry, she cradled her son's head, then spoke.
As she grieved, she talked to him—her words had wings:

"My child, why are you crying? What sorrow now
has come into your heart? Speak out. Hide nothing.
Zeus has given you what you begged him to   90
when you stretched your hands out to him—
all Achaea's sons by their ships' sterns
are hemmed in there, desperate for your help,
suffering a terrible ordeal."

                    With a heavy groan,
swift-footed Achilles then answered Thetis:

                    "Yes, Mother,
Olympian Zeus has indeed accomplished
what I asked. But what pleasure's there for me,   [80]
when Patroclus, my beloved companion,
has been destroyed, the man I honoured
as my equal, above all my comrades.   100
I've lost him and the armour, which Hector took,
once he'd killed him, that massive armour,
so wonderful to look at, which the gods
gave as a priceless gift to Peleus
on that day they placed you in the bed
of a mortal man. If only you had stayed
among the eternal maidens of the sea
and Peleus had married a mortal wife.
But now there'll be innumerable sorrows
waiting for your heart, once your child is killed.   110
You won't be welcoming him back home again.   [90]
My own heart has no desire to live on,
to continue living among men,
unless Hector is hit by my spear first,
losing his life and paying me compensation
for killing Menoetius' son, Patroclus."

Through her tears, Thetis then answered Achilles:

"My son, from what you've just been saying,
you're fated to an early death, for your doom
comes quickly as soon as Hector dies."   120

Swift-footed Achilles answered her with passion:

"Then let me die, since I could not prevent
the death of my companion. He's fallen
far from his homeland. He needed me there   [100]
to protect him from destruction. So now,
since I'm not returning to my own dear land,
and for Patroclus was no saving light
or for my many other comrades,
all those killed by godlike Hector while I sat here
by the ships, a useless burden   130
on the earth—and I'm unmatched in warfare
by any other Achaean armed in bronze,
although in council other men are better—
so let wars disappear from gods and men
and passionate anger, too, which incites
even the prudent man to that sweet rage,
sweeter than trickling honey in men's throats,
which builds up like smoke inside their chests,   [110]
as Agamemnon, king of men, just now,
made me enraged. But we'll let that pass.   140
For all the pain I feel, I'll suppress the heart
within my chest, as I must. So now I'll go
to meet Hector, killer of the man I loved.
As for my own fate, let it come to me
when Zeus and the other deathless gods
determine. For not even strong Hercules,
the man lord Zeus, son of Cronos, loved the most,
escaped his death. He was destroyed by Fate
and by malicious Hera's anger, too.
And so for me. If a like fate has been set,   150   [120]
then once I'm dead, I'll just lie there. But for now,
let me seize great glory—let me make
so many Trojan and Dardan matrons weep,
and with both hands wipe tears from their soft cheeks,

and set them on to constant lamentation,
so that they'll know I've long refrained from war.
Don't keep me from battle. Though you love me,
you'll not convince me."

       Silver-footed Thetis
then said to Achilles:

"My child, what you say is true—
it's no bad thing to protect companions   160
when they're in trouble from complete disaster.
But now the Trojans have your lovely armour,   [130]
all your glittering bronze. It's on the shoulders
of Hector with the shining helmet—
he boasts about it. But I don't think
his triumph will last long, since his death
is coming closer. But you must not rejoin
Ares' conflict until with your own eyes
you see me in the morning here again.
I'll return at sunrise, and I'll bring you   170
lovely armour made by lord Hephaestus."

Saying this, Thetis turned away from her own son
to address her ocean sisters:

       "Now you must plunge   [140]
into the broad lap of Ocean and go find
the Old Man of the Sea in our father's house.
Tell him everything. I'll go to high Olympus,
to that famous artisan Hephaestus,
to see if he is willing to give my son
some splendid glittering armour."

            Thetis spoke.
Her sisters quickly plunged under the waves.   180
Then the silver-footed goddess Thetis went away
to fetch that lovely armour from Olympus
for her beloved son.

      As Thetis' feet carried her
towards Olympus, Achaeans were running back,

with a huge noise, fleeing man-killing Hector,
until they reached their ships beside the Hellespont.   [150]
But those well-armed Achaeans couldn't extricate
Achilles' comrade, dead Patroclus, from the spears,
for they'd been overtaken by Trojan warriors
and chariots once again, with Hector, Priam's son,   190
as furious as fire. Three times glorious Hector,
from behind, seized the corpse's feet, keen to drag it off,
shouting furiously to his Trojans. Three times,
the two Ajaxes, clothed in their full battle strength,
beat him from the corpse. But Hector kept on coming
without a pause, confident of his fighting power.
Sometimes he charged right at them in the frenzied crowd.
Sometimes he just stood there and gave a mighty yell,
but he never yielded any ground. Just as shepherds   [160]
are unable to drive off from their farmyard   200
a tawny ravenous lion by some carcass—
so the two warrior Ajaxes could not push Hector,
Priam's son, back from that body. And now Hector
would have seized that corpse, winning infinite glory,
if swift Iris with feet like wind had not come down,
speeding from Olympus to the son of Peleus,
with a message that he should arm himself for war.
Hera had sent her, unknown to Zeus and other gods.
Standing by Achilles, Iris spoke—her words had wings:

"Rouse yourself, son of Peleus, most feared of men.   210   [170]
Defend Patroclus. For on his behalf
a deadly conflict rages by the ships—
men are butchering each other, some trying
to protect the dead man's corpse, while others,
the Trojans, charge in to carry it away
to windy Ilion. The one most eager
to haul the body off is glorious Hector,
whose heart is set on hacking off the head
from its soft neck. He'll fix it on a stake
set in the wall. So get up. No more lying here.   220
Your heart will be disgraced if Patroclus
becomes a plaything for the dogs of Troy—
his mutilated corpse will be your shame."   [180]

Swift-footed godlike Achilles then asked her:

"Goddess Iris, which of the gods sent you
with this message to me?"

                       Swift Iris,
with feet like wind, then said to Achilles:

"Hera sent me, Zeus' glorious wife.
Cronos' son, who sits on high, doesn't know,
nor do any other immortal gods   230
inhabiting snow-capped Olympus."

Swift-footed Achilles then questioned Iris:

"But how can I rejoin that conflict?
Those men have my armour. My dear mother
has told me not to arm myself for war,
not until my own eyes see that she's come back.   [190]
She promised to bring me splendid armour
from Hephaestus. I don't know anyone
whose glorious equipment I could use,
with the exception of the shield of Ajax,   240
son of Telamon. But I expect he's out there
with his spear among the front-line warriors
in that conflict over dead Patroclus."

Wind-swift Iris then answered Achilles:

"We know well enough your lovely armour
is in Trojan hands. But you should go now,
just as you are, to the ditch. Show yourself
to Trojans. It may happen that the Trojans,
afraid of you, will pull back from battle,
giving Achaea's exhausted warlike sons   250   [200]
a breathing space. For rests in war are rare."

With these words, swift-footed Iris went away.
Then Achilles, loved by Zeus, moved into action.
Around his powerful shoulders Athena set
her tasselled aegis. Then the lovely goddess

wrapped his head up in a golden cloud, so from him
a fiery light blazed out. Just like those times when smoke
from a city stretches all the way to heaven,
rising in the distance from an island under siege
by an enemy, where men fight all day long   260
in Ares' hateful war, struggling for their city—
then at sunset, they light fires one by one,   [210]
beacons flaming upwards to attract attention
from those on near-by islands, so their ships will come
to save them from destruction—that's how the light
blazed then from Achilles' head right up to heaven.
He strode from the wall, then stood there by the ditch.
But recalling what his mother had said to him,
he didn't mingle with Achaeans. As he stood there,
he cried out. From far away, Pallas Athena   270
added her voice, too, causing great consternation
among the Trojans. As thrilling as a trumpet's note
when it rings clearly, when rapacious enemies   [220]
besiege a city—that's how sharp and piercing
Achilles' voice was then. When the Trojans heard it,
that brazen shout Achilles gave, all their hearts
were shaken. Their horses with the lovely manes
turned back the chariots, anticipating trouble
in their hearts. Charioteers were terrified, seeing
the fearful inextinguishable fire blazing   280
from the head of the great-hearted son of Peleus.
For Athena, goddess with the glittering eyes,
kept it burning. Three times godlike Achilles yelled
across that ditch. Three times Trojans and their allies
were thrown into confusion. At that moment,
twelve of their best men were killed by their own chariots   [230]
and their own spears. Achaeans then, with stronger hearts,
pulled Patroclus out of spear range and laid him on a cot.
His dear companions gathered mourning round him,
Achilles with them, shedding hot tears when he saw   290
his loyal companion lying on a death bed,
mutilated by sharp bronze. He'd sent him out to war
with chariot and horses, but never welcomed him
at his return.

                                 Then ox-eyed queen Hera
made the unwearied sun, against his will, go down   [240]
into the stream of Ocean. So the sun set.
Godlike Achaeans now could pause for some relief
from the destructive killing of impartial war.

For their part, once Trojans drew back from that harsh fight,
they untied swift horses from their chariots and then,   300
before they thought of food, called for a meeting.
There everyone stayed standing. No one dared sit down,
all terrified because Achilles had appeared,
after his long absence from that savage conflict.
The first to speak was Polydamas, Panthous' son,
a prudent man, the only one who weighed with care   [250]
the past and future. He was Hector's comrade,
both born on the same night. As a public speaker,
he was the better of the two, but Hector
far surpassed him with a spear. Bearing in mind   310
their common good, Polydamas addressed them:

"My friends, consider both sides of this issue.
For my part, I advise us to return
into the city—we should not stay here,
on the plain, waiting for dawn beside the ships.
Our walls are far away. While Achilles
kept up his anger at lord Agamemnon,
Achaeans were easier to fight against.
Personally, I was glad to spend the night
by their swift ships, hoping then we'd capture   320   [260]
those curved vessels. But now I really have
a dreadful fear of Peleus' swift-footed son.
He has a reckless heart—he's not a man
to rest content in the middle of the plain,
where Trojans and Achaeans have a share
of Ares' battle fury. No, he'll fight on
for our city and our women. So let's go back,
return into the city. Trust me when I say
that's how things will go. For now, sacred night
has stopped the swift-footed son of Peleus.   330
But if tomorrow he moves into action
fully armed and encounters us still here,

we'll recognize him well enough. Anyone
who gets away and makes it back to Ilion
will be a happy man. For dogs and vultures
will eat many Trojans. I don't want to hear
that such events have happened. If we all
follow my advice, although reluctantly,
tonight we'll collect our forces in one group.
Walls, high gates, and doors with fitted planks, 340
polished and bolted shut, will guard the city.
But in the morning early, we'll arm ourselves,
then take up our positions on the walls.
If Achilles comes from the ships keen to fight
for our walls, then he'll be disappointed.
He'll go back to his ships, once he's worn out [280]
his strong-necked horses with too much running,
scampering around below our city wall.
His heart won't let him force his way inside,
and he'll not lay waste our city, not before 350
our swift dogs eat him up for dinner."

With a scowl, Hector of the flashing helmet then replied:

"Polydamas, what you say displeases me—
you tell us to run back to the city
and stay inside it. Haven't you already
been cooped up long enough within those walls?
In earlier days, all mortal men would claim
that Priam's city was rich in gold and bronze.
But now those splendid treasures are all gone. [290]
Many goods from our own homes we've sold. 360
They went to Phrygia or fair Maeonia,
once great Zeus, in anger, turned against us.
But now, when crooked-minded Cronos' son
allows me to win glory by the ships,
hemming the Achaeans in beside the sea,
this is no time, you fool, to say such things
before the people. Not a single Trojan
will take your advice. I won't permit it.
But come, let's all follow now what I suggest.
You must take your dinner at your stations 370
all through the army, making sure you watch,

with every man awake. Any Trojan
too concerned about his property
should gather it up and give it to the men
for common use. Better that one of us
gets use from it than that Achaeans do.
Tomorrow morning early, right at dawn,
we'll fully arm ourselves with weapons,
then take keen battle to those hollow ships.
If indeed it's true that lord Achilles   380
is returning to that battle by the ships,
if he wants that, so much the worse for him.
I won't run from him in painful battle,
but stand against him, fighting face to face,
whether great victory goes to him or me.
In war the odds are equal, and the man
who seeks to kill may well be killed himself."

Hector spoke. The Trojans roared out in response.   [310]
The fools! Pallas Athena had robbed them of their wits.
They all applauded Hector's disastrous tactics.   390
No one praised Polydamas, who'd advised them well.
Then throughout the army they ate their dinner.

Meanwhile, Achaeans mourned Patroclus all night long
with their elegies. Among them, Peleus' son
began the urgent lamentations, placing
his murderous hands on the chest of his companion,
with frequent heavy groans, like a bearded lion,
when a deer hunter in dense forest steals its cubs—
the lion comes back later, then sick at heart   [320]
roams through the many clearings in the forest,   400
tracking the man's footprints, in hopes of finding him,
as bitter anger overwhelms the beast—just like that
Achilles, amid his groans, addressed his Myrmidons:

"Alas, what a useless promise I made then,
the day I tried to cheer Menoetius up
at home, telling him when I'd sacked Ilion,
I'd bring his splendid son back there to him,
in Opoeis, and with his share of trophies.
But Zeus does not bring to fulfilment

all things which men propose. Now both of us   410
share a common fate, to redden the same earth
right here in Troy. Old horseman Peleus   [330]
will not be welcoming me at my return
back to his home, nor will my mother Thetis.
For in this place the earth will cover me.
And now, Patroclus, since I'm journeying
under the earth after you, I'll postpone
your burial till I bring here Hector's head,
his armour, too, the man who slaughtered you,
you courageous man. I'll cut the throats   420
of twelve fine Trojan children on your pyre,
in my anger at your killing. Till that time,
you'll lie like this with me by my beaked ships,
and round you Trojan and Dardanian women
will keep lamenting night and day, shedding tears,   [340]
the very women we two worked hard to
win with our strength and our long spears, by looting
prosperous cities of mortal men."

After these words, godlike Achilles told his comrades
to place a large tripod on the fire, so they could wash   430
the blood clots from his comrade's corpse. On the blazing fire,
they set a cauldron with three legs, poured water in it,
then brought split wood to burn below the water.
Fire licked the cauldron's belly and made the water hot.
Once it had boiled inside the shining bronze,
they washed him, rubbed oil thickly over him,   [350]
and filled his wounds with ointment nine years old.
Then they placed Patroclus on a bed, covering him
with a fine woollen cloth from head to foot
and a white cloak on the cloth. Then all night long,   440
the Myrmidons around swift-footed Achilles
mourned Patroclus with their lamentations.

Then Zeus spoke to Hera, his sister and his wife:

"You've got what you wanted, ox-eyed queen Hera.
Swift-footed Achilles you've spurred into action.
From your own womb you must have given birth
to these long-haired Achaeans."

Ox-eyed queen Hera
then replied to Zeus: [360]

"Most dread son of Cronos,
what are you saying? Even a human man,
though mortal and ignorant of what I know,   450
can achieve what he intends for someone else.
And men say I'm the finest of all goddesses
in a double sense—both by my lineage
and my marriage to the ruler of the gods.
So why should I not bring an evil fortune
on these Trojans when they've made me angry?"

Thus these two conversed with one another then.

Meanwhile, silver-footed Thetis reached Hephaestus' home.
Made of eternal bronze and gleaming like a star,   [370]
it stood out among the homes of the immortals.   460
The crippled god had constructed it himself.
She found him working with his bellows, moving round,
sweating in his eager haste. He was forging
twenty tripods in all, to stand along the walls
of his well-built house. Under the legs of each one
he had fitted golden wheels, so every tripod
might move all on its own into a gathering of the gods
at his command and then return to his own house.
They were wonderful to look at. His work on them
had reached the stage where finely crafted handles   470
had still not been attached. He was making these,
forging the rivets. As he was working on them   [380]
with his great skill, silver-footed goddess Thetis
approached more closely. Noticing her, Charis,
lovely goddess with the splendid veil, came forward—
she was wife to the celebrated crippled god.
Taking Thetis by the hand, she called her name, and said:

"Long-robed Thetis, why visit our house now?
You're a welcome and respected guest, but to this point
you haven't come by very much. Do step inside.   480
Let me show you our hospitality."

With these words, the goddess led her inside the house.
She asked Thetis to sit in a silver-studded chair,
beautifully finished, with a footstool under it.   [390]
Then she called the famous artisan Hephaestus:

"Come here, Hephaestus. Thetis needs to see you."

The celebrated lame god then replied to Charis:

"Here's a fearful honoured goddess in my home,
the one who saved me when I was in pain,
after my great fall, thanks to my mother,   490
that shameless one, eager to conceal me,
because I was a cripple. At that time,
I would have suffered heartfelt agonies,
if Thetis and Eurynome, daughter
of circling Ocean stream, had not taken me
into their hearts. With those two, for nine years   [400]
I made many lovely things—brooches,
spiral bracelets, earrings, necklaces—
inside their hollow cave. The Ocean stream
flowed round me, always with the roar of surf.   500
No one else knew, neither god nor mortal man.
But Thetis and Eurynome—the ones
who rescued me—they knew.* And now Thetis
has come into my home. So I must give her
full recompense—fair-haired Thetis saved my life.
But Charis, show her now our hospitality.
I'll put away my bellows and my tools."

Huge god Hephaestus got up from the anvil block   [410]
with laboured breathing. He was lame, but his thin legs   510
moved quickly under him. He placed his bellows
far from the fire and collected all his work tools,
then stored them in a silver chest. With a sponge,
he wiped his face, both hands, thick neck, and hairy chest.
Then he pulled on a tunic and came limping out,
gripping a sturdy staff. At once he was helped along
by female servants made of gold, who moved to him.
They look like living servant girls, possessing minds,
hearts with intelligence, vocal chords, and strength.

They learned to work from the immortal gods.   520   [420]
These women served to give their master detailed help.
Hephaestus came limping up to Thetis and sat down
in a shining chair. Then, clasping her hand, he spoke:

"Long-robed Thetis, why have you come here,
to our house, an honoured welcome guest?
To this point, you haven't come here often.
But say what's on your mind. My heart tells me
I shall do it, if I can accomplish it,
if it's something that can be carried out."

Thetis answered him in tears:

        "Oh, Hephaestus,   530
is there any goddess on Olympus
who's suffered so much painful sorrow   [430]
in her heart to equal the unhappiness
that Zeus, son of Cronos, loads on me
more than any other god? Of all goddesses
living in the sea, he made me subject
to a mortal man, Peleus, son of Aeacus.
So I had to put up with a man in bed,
though much against my will. Now he lies there,
in his home, worn out by harsh old age.   540
And I have still more pain. He gave me a son
to bear and raise as an outstanding warrior.
The boy grew up as quickly as a sapling.
Then, when I had reared him like a tree
in a fertile garden, I sent him off
in the beaked ships to fight at Ilion
against the Trojans. I'll never welcome him   [440]
returning home to the house of Peleus.
And while he still lives to glimpse the sunlight,
he lives in sorrow. When I visit him,   550
I cannot help him. Achaea's sons chose for him
as his prize a girl, whom great Agamemnon
seized right out of his arms. In grief for her,
his heart has pined away. Then the Trojans
penned Achaeans in by their ships' sterns,
not letting them come out. The senior men

among the Argives pleaded with my son.
They promised splendid gifts. But he refused,   [450]
declining to protect them from disaster.
But then he sent Patroclus to the war,   560
dressing him in his own armour, providing
a force of many men. They fought all day
around the Scaean Gates, and that very day
would have utterly destroyed the city,
if Apollo had not killed Menoetius' son,
after he'd inflicted bloody carnage.
He killed him at the front, giving Hector
all the glory. That's why I've come here now,
asking at your knees if you'd be willing
to give my son, who is fated to die soon,   570
a shield, helmet, good leg armour fitted
with ankle clasps, and body armour, too.
His previous equipment was all taken   [460]
when Trojans killed his loyal companion.
Now my son lies in the dust, heart filled with pain."

The famous crippled god then answered Thetis:

"Cheer up. Don't let these things afflict your heart.
I wish I could hide him from distressful death,
when his cruel fate arrives, as surely
as I know there'll be fine armour for him—   580
such splendid armour that it will astound
all the many men who chance to see it."

With these words, Hephaestus left her there, going to start
his bellows. He directed them right at the fire,
then told them to start working. So the bellows,
twenty in all, started blowing on the crucibles,   [470]
each one emitting just the right amount of air,
sometimes blowing hard to help when he was busy,
sometimes gently, whatever way Hephaestus wished,
so his work could go ahead. He threw on the fire   590
enduring bronze and tin, precious gold and silver.
Next, he placed the great anvil on its block, took up
a massive hammer in one hand and in the other his tongs.

The first thing he created was a huge and sturdy shield,
all wonderfully crafted. Around its outer edge,
he fixed a triple rim, glittering in the light,   [480]
attaching to it a silver carrying strap.
The shield had five layers. On the outer one,
with his great skill he fashioned many rich designs.
There he hammered out the earth, the heavens, the sea,   600
the untiring sun, the moon at the full, along with
every constellation which crowns the heavens—
the Pleiades, the Hyades, mighty Orion,
and the Bear, which some people call the Wain,
always circling in the same position, watching Orion,
the only stars that never bathe in Ocean stream.*

Then he created two splendid cities of mortal men.   [490]
In one, there were feasts and weddings. By the light
of blazing torches, people were leading the brides
out from their homes and through the town to loud music   610
of the bridal song. There were young lads dancing,
whirling to the constant tunes of flutes and lyres,
while all the women stood beside their doors, staring
in admiration.

        Then the people gathered
in the assembly, for a dispute had taken place.
Two men were arguing about blood-money owed
for a murdered man. One claimed he'd paid in full,
setting out his case before the people, but the other   [500]
was refusing any compensation. Both were keen
to receive the judgment from an arbitration.   620
The crowd there cheered them on, some supporting one,
some the other, while heralds kept the throng controlled.
Meanwhile, elders were sitting there on polished stones
in the sacred circle, holding in their hands
the staffs they'd taken from the clear-voiced heralds.
With those they'd stand up there and render judgment,
each in his turn. In the centre lay two golden talents,
to be awarded to the one among them all
who would deliver the most righteous verdict.

The second city was surrounded by two armies,   630
soldiers with glittering weapons. They were discussing   [510]
two alternatives, each one pleasing some of them—
whether to attack that city and plunder it,
or to accept as payment half of all the goods
contained in that fair town. But those under siege
who disagreed were arming for a secret ambush.
Their dear wives and children stood up on the walls
as a defence, along with those too old to fight.
The rest were leaving, led on by Pallas Athena
and Ares, both made of gold, dressed in golden clothes,   640
large, beautiful, and armed—as is suitable for gods.
They stood out above the smaller people with them.
When the soldiers reached a spot which seemed all right
for ambush, a place beside a river where the cattle   [520]
came to drink, they stopped there, covered in shining bronze.
Two scouts were stationed some distance from that army,
waiting to catch sight of sheep and short-horned cattle.
These soon appeared, followed by two herdsmen
playing their flutes and not anticipating any danger.
But those lying in ambush saw them and rushed out,   650
quickly cutting off the herds of cattle and fine flocks
of white-fleeced sheep, killing the herdsmen with them.
When the besiegers sitting in their meeting place   [530]
heard the great commotion coming from the cattle,
they quickly climbed up behind their prancing horses
and set out. They soon caught up with those attackers.
Then they organized themselves for battle and fought
along the river banks, men hitting one another
with bronze-tipped spears. Strife and Confusion joined the fight,
along with cruel Death, who seized one wounded man   660
while still alive and then another man without a wound,
while pulling the feet of one more corpse from the fight.
The clothes Death wore around her shoulders were dyed red
with human blood. They even joined the slaughter
as living mortals, fighting there and hauling off
the bodies of dead men which each of them had killed.   [540]

On that shield Hephaestus next set a soft and fallow field,
fertile spacious farmland, which had been ploughed three times.
Many labourers were wheeling ploughs across it,

moving back and forth. As they reached the field's edge,   670
they turned, and a man came up to offer them
a cup of wine as sweet as honey. Then they'd turn back,
down the furrow, eager to move through that deep soil
and reach the field's edge once again. The land behind them
was black, looking as though it had just been ploughed,
though it was made of gold—an amazing piece of work!

Then he pictured on the shield a king's landed estate,   [550]
where harvesters were reaping corn, using sharp sickles.
Armfuls of corn were falling on the ground in rows,
one after the other. Binders were tying them up   680
in sheaves with twisted straw. Three binders stood there.
Behind the reapers, boys were gathering the crop,
bringing it to sheaf-binders, keeping them busy
Among them stood the king, a sceptre in his hand,
there by the stubble, saying nothing, but with pleasure
in his heart. Some distance off, under an oak tree,
heralds were setting up a feast, dressing a huge ox
which they'd just killed. Women were sprinkling white barley
on the meat in large amounts for the workers' meal.   [560]

Next, Hephaestus placed on that shield a vineyard,   690
full of grapes made of splendid gold. The grapes were black,
the poles supporting vines throughout were silver.
Around it, he made a ditch of blue enamel,
around that, a fence of tin. A single path led in,
where the grape pickers came and went at harvest time.
Young girls and carefree lads with wicker baskets
were carrying off a crop as sweet as honey.
In the middle of them all, a boy with a clear-toned lyre
played pleasant music, singing the Song of Linos,   [570]
in his delicate fine voice. His comrades kept time,   700
beating the ground behind him, singing and dancing.*

Then he set on the shield a herd of straight-horned cattle,
with cows crafted out of gold and tin. They were lowing
as they hurried out from farm to pasture land,
beside a rippling river lined with waving reeds.
The herdsmen walking by the cattle, four of them,
were also made of gold. Nine swift-footed dogs

ran on behind. But there, at the front of the herd,
two fearful lions had seized a bellowing bull.   [580]
They were dragging him off, as he roared aloud.   710
The dogs and young men were chasing after them.
The lions, after ripping open the great ox's hide,
were gorging on its entrails, on its black blood,
as herdsmen kept trying in vain to chase them off,
setting their swift dogs on them. But, fearing the lions,
the dogs kept turning back before they nipped them,
and stood there barking, close by but out of reach.

Then the famous crippled god created there a pasture
in a lovely valley bottom, an open ground
for white-fleeced sheep, sheep folds, roofed huts, and pens.   720

Next on that shield, the celebrated lame god made   [590]
an elaborately crafted dancing floor, like the one
Daedalus created long ago in spacious Cnossus,
for Ariadne with the lovely hair.* On that floor,
young men and women whose bride price would require
many cattle were dancing, holding onto one another
by the wrists. The girls wore fine linen dresses,
 the men lightly rubbed with oil wore woven tunics.
On their heads the girls had lovely flower garlands.
The men were carrying gold daggers on silver straps.   730
They turned with such a graceful ease on skilful feet,
just as a potter sits with a wheel between his hands,   [600]
testing it, to make sure that it runs smoothly.
Then they would line up and run towards each other.
A large crowd stood around, enjoying the dancing magic,
as in the middle two acrobats led on the dance,
springing, and whirling, and tumbling.

On that shield, Hephaestus then depicted Ocean,
the mighty river, flowing all around the outer edge.

When he'd created that great and sturdy shield,   740
he fashioned body armour brighter than blazing fire,   [610]
a heavy helmet shaped to fit Achilles' temples,
beautiful and finely worked, with a gold crest on top.
Then he made him leg guards of finely hammered tin.

When the famous lame god had made all the armour,
he took it and set it there before Achilles' mother.
Then, like a hawk, she sped down from Olympus,
carrying the gleaming armour of Hephaestus.

Notes to Book Eighteen

*   In some Greek myths, Hephaestus, child of Hera and Zeus, was born deformed in his legs. As a result Hera threw him away from Mount Olympus. He landed in the Ocean where Thetis and Eurynome, sea goddesses, raised him.

*   The phrase about not bathing in Ocean's stream refers to the fact that at the latitude of Greece, these stars do not disappear below the horizon.

*   The Song of Linos is a traditional harvest song.

*   Daedalus was a legendary craftsman of surpassing skill. He created the famous Labyrinth in Crete and, according to this comment, a dancing ground for Ariadne, a princess of Crete.

Homer's *Odyssey* (Books 8 and 9)

Translated by Stanley Lombardo

BOOK EIGHT

[Lines 1–286 of Book 8 are omitted. Odysseus is welcomed by Queen Arete and King Alcinous, who entertain him with feasting, dancing, and athletic competitions. Challenged by a young Phaeacian and aided by Athena, Odysseus throws the discus much farther than anyone else. Phaeacian dancers then perform for Odysseus, forming a ring around the bard Demodocus, for whom a lyre has been fetched.]

Then Demodocus swept the strings of his lyre
And began his song. He sang of the passion
Between Ares and gold-crowned Aphrodite,
How they first made love in Hephaestus' house,   290
Sneaking around, and how the War God Ares
Showered her with gifts and shamed the bed
Of her husband, Hephaestus. But it wasn't long
Before Hephaesus found out. Helios told him
That he had seen them lying together in love.   295
When Hephaestus heard this heart-wrenching news
He went to his forge, brooding on his wrongs,
And set the great anvil up on its block
And hammered out a set of unbreakable bonds,
Bonds that couldn't loosen, bonds meant to stay put.   300
When he had wrought this snare, furious with Ares,
He went to his bedroom and spread the bonds
All around the bedposts, and hung many also
From the high roofbeams, as fine as cobwebs,
So fine not even the gods could see them.   305
When he had spread this cunning snare
All around the bed, he pretended to leave
On a trip to Lemnos, his favorite city.

Ares wasn't blind, and when he saw Hephaestus
On his way out, he headed for the house   *310*
Of the glorious smith, itching to make love
To the Cytherean goddess. She had been visiting
Her father, Zeus, and was just sitting down
When Ares came in, took her hand, and said:

"Let's go to bed, my love, and lie down together.   *315*
Hephaestus has left town, off to Lemnos no doubt
To visit the barbarous Sintians."
This suggestion appealed to the goddess,
And they climbed into bed. They were settling in
When the chains Hephaestus had cunningly wrought   *320*
Fell all around them. They couldn't move an inch,
Couldn't lift a finger, and by the time it sank in
That there was no escape, there was Hephaestus,
Gimpy-legged and glorious, coming in the door.
He had turned back on his way to Lemnos   *325*
as soon as Helios, his spy, gave him the word.
He stood in the doorway, seething with anger,
And with an ear-splitting yell called to the gods:
"Father Zeus and all you blessed gods eternal,
Come see something that is as ridiculous   *330*
As it is unendurable, how Aprhodite,
Daughter of Zeus, scorns me for being lame
And loves that marauder Ares instead
Because he is handsome and well-knit, whereas I
Was born misshapen, which is no one's fault   *335*
But my parents', who should have never begotten me!
Come take a look at how these two
Have climbed into my bed to make love and lie
In each other's arms. It kills me to see it!
But I don't think they will want to lie like this   *340*
Much longer, not matter how loving they are.
No, they won't want to sleep together for long,
But they're staying put in my little snare
Until her father returns all of the gifts
I gave him to marry this bitch-faced girl   *345*
His beautiful, yes, but faithless daughter."
Thus Hephaestus, and the gods gathered
At his bronze threshold.

                                Poseidon came,
The God of Earthquake, and Hermes the Guide,
And the Archer Apollo. The goddesses   *350*
All stayed home, out of modesty; but the gods
Stood in the doorway and laughed uncontrollably
When they saw Hephaestus' cunning and craft.
One of them would look at another and snigger:
"Crime doesn't pay."
"The slow catches the swift.   *355*
Slow as he is, old Gimpy caught Ares,
The fastest god on Olympus."
"Ares has to pay the fine for adultery."
That was the general drift of their jibes.
And then Apollo turned to Hermes and said: *360*
"Tell me, Hermes, would you be willing
To be pinched in chains if it meant you could lie
Side by side with golden Aphrodite?"
And the quicksilver messenger shot back:
"I tell you what, Apollo. Tie me up   *365*
With three times as many unbreakable chains.
And get all the gods and goddesses, too,
To come here and look, if it means I can sleep
Side by side with golden Aphrodite."

The gods roared with laughter, except Poseidon   *370*
Who did not think it was funny. He kept
Pleading that Ares should be released,
And his words winged their way to Hephaestus:

"Let him go, and I will ensure he will pay you   *375*
  Fair compensation before all the gods."

And the renowned god, lame in both legs:

"Do not ask me to do this, Poseidon.
Worthless is the surety assured for the worthless.
How could I ever hold you to your promise
If Ares slipped out of the bonds and the debt?"   *380*
Poseidon the Earthshaker did not back off:

"Hephaestus, if Ares gets free and disappears
Without paying the debt, I will pay it myself."

And the renowned god, lame in both legs:

"I cannot refuse you. It wouldn't be right."   *385*

And with that the strong smith undid the bonds.
And the two of them, free at last from their crimp,
Shot out of there, Ares to Thrace,
And Aprhodite, who loves laughter and smiles,
To Paphos on Cyprus, and her precinct there   *390*
With its smoking altar. There the Graces
Bathed her and rubbed her with the ambrosial oil
That glistens on the skin of the immortal gods.
And then they dressed her in beautiful clothes,
A wonder to see.
                        This was the song   *395*
The renowned bard sang, and Odysseus
Was glad as he listened, as were the Phaeacians,
Men who are famed for their long-oared ships.

*[Lines 399–489 are omitted. Clothes and other gifts are presented to Odysseus.
Then Odysseus, who has not yet told the Phaeacians his name, is given a bath.]*

When the women had bathed him, rubbed him with oil,   *490*
And clothed him in a beautiful tunic and cloak,
Odysseus strode from the bath and was on his way
To join the men drinking wine.
                            Nausicaa,
Beautiful as only the gods could make her,
Stood by the doorpost of the great hall.   *495*
Her eyes went wide when she saw Odysseus,
And her words beat their way to him on wings:

"Farewell, stranger, and remember me
In your own native land. I saved your life."

And Odysseus, whose thoughts ran deep: *500*

"Nausicaa, daughter of great Alcinous,
So may Zeus, Hera's thundering lord,
Grant that I see my homeland again.
There I will pray to you, as to a god.
All of my days. I owe you my life."   505

And he took his seat next to Lord Alcinous.
 They were serving food and mixing the wine
When the herald came up leading the bard,
Honored Demodocus, and seated him on a chair
Propped against a tall pillar in the middle of the hall.   510
Odysseus, with great presence of mind,
Cut off part of a huge chine of roast pork
Glistening with fat, and said to the herald:

"Herald, take this cut of meat to Demodocus
For him to eat. And I will greet him   515
Despite my grief. Bards are revered
By all men upon earth, for the Muse
Loves them well and has taught them the songways."

The herald brought the cut of meat to Demodocus
And placed it in his hands, much to the bard's delight.   520
Then everyone reached out to the feast before them,
And when they had eaten and drunk to their hearts' content,
Odysseus spoke to Demodocus:

"I don't know whether it was the Muse
Who taught you, or Apollo himself,   525
But I praise you to the skies, Demodocus.
When you sing about the fate of the Greeks
Who fought at Troy, you have it right,
All that they did and suffered, all they endured.
It's as if you had been there yourself,   530
Or heard a first-hand account. But now,
Switch to the building of the wooden horse
Which Epeius made with Athena's help,
The horse which Odysseus led up to Troy
As a trap, filled with men who would   535
Destroy great Ilion. If you tell me this story
Just as it happened, I will tell the whole world

That some god must have opened his heart
And given to you the divine gift of song."

So he spoke, and the bard, moved by the god,   540
Began to sing. He made them see it happen,
How the Greeks set fire to their huts on the beach
And were sailing away, while Odysseus
And the picked men with him sat in the horse,
Which the Trojans had dragged into their city.   545
There the horse stood, and the Trojans sat around it
And could not decide what they should do.
There were three ways of thinking:
Hack open the timbers with pitiless bronze,
Or throw it from the heights to the rocks below,   550
Or let it stand as an offering to appease the gods.
The last was what would happen, for it was fated
That the city would perish once it enclosed
The great wooden horse, in which now sat
The Greek heroes who would spill Troy's blood.   555
The song went on. The Greeks poured out
Of their hollow ambush and sacked the city.
He sang how one hero here and another there
Ravaged tall Troy, but how Odysseus went,
Like the War God himself, with Menelaus   560
To the house of Deiphobus, and there, he said,
Odysseus fought his most daring battle
And won with the help of Pallas Athena.

This was his song. And Odysseus wept. Tears
Welled up in his eyes and flowed down his cheeks.   565

 A woman wails as she throws herself upon
 Her husband's body. He has fallen in battle
 Before the town walls, fighting to the last
 To defend his city and protect his children.
 As she sees him dying and gasping for breath   570
 She clings to him and shrieks, while behind her
 Soldiers prod their spears into her shoulders and back,
 And as they lead her away into slavery
 Her tear-drenched face is a mask of pain.

So too Odysseus, pitiful in his grief. 575
He managed to conceal his tears from everyone
Except Alcinous, who sat at his elbow
And could not help but hear his heavy sighs.
Alcinous acted quickly and said to his guests:

"Hear me, Phaeacian counselors and lords— 580
Demodocus should stop playing his lyre.
His song is not pleasing to everyone here.
Ever since dinner began and the divine bard
Rose up to sing, our guest has not ceased
From lamentation. He is overcome with grief. 585
Let the lyre stop. It is better if we all,
Host and guest alike, can enjoy the feast.
All that we are doing we are doing on behalf
Of the revered stranger, providing him
With passage home and gifts of friendship. 590
A stranger and suppliant is as dear as a brother
To anyone with even an ounce of good sense.
So there is no need, stranger, for you to withhold
What I am about to ask for, no need to be crafty
Or think of gain. Better to speak the plain truth. 595

Tell me your name, the one you were known by
To your mother and father and your people back home.
No one is nameless, rich man or poor.
Parents give names to all of their children
When they are born. And tell me your country, 600
Your city, and your land, so that our ships
May take you there, finding their way by their wits.
For Phaeacian ships do not have pilots.
Nor steering oars, as other ships have.
They know on their own their passengers' thoughts, 605
And know all the cities and rich fields in the world,
And they cross the great gulfs with the greatest speed,
Hidden in mist and fog, with never a fear
Of damage or shipwreck.
                            But I remember hearing
My father, Nausithous, say how Poseidon 610
Was angry with us because we always give
Safe passage to men. He said that one day

Poseidon would smite a Phaeacian ship
As it sailed back home over the misty sea,
And would encircle our city within a mountain.   *615*
The old man used to say that, and either the god
Will bring it to pass or not, as suits his pleasure.
But tell me this, and tell me the truth.
Where have you wandered, to what lands?
Tell me about the people and cities you saw,   *620*
Which ones are cruel and without right and wrong,
And which are godfearing and kind to strangers.
And tell me why you weep and grieve at heart
When you hear the fate of the Greeks and Trojans.
This was the gods' doing. They spun that fate   *625*
So that in later times it would turn into song.
Did some kinsman of yours die at Troy,
A good, loyal man, your daughter's husband
Or your wife's father, someone near and dear,
Or perhaps even a relative by blood?   *630*
Or was it a comrade, tried and true?
A friend like that is no less than a brother."

BOOK NINE

And Odysseus, his great mind teeming:

"My Lord Alcinous, what could be finer
Than listening to a singer of tales
Such as Demodocus, with a voice like a god's?
Nothing we do is sweeter than this—   *5*
A cheerful gathering of all the people
Sitting side by side throughout the halls,
Feasting and listening to a singer of tales,
The tables filled with food and drink.
The server drawing wine from the bowl   *10*
And bringing it around to fill our cups.
For me, this is the finest thing in the world.
But you have a mind to draw out of me
My pain and sorrow, and make me feel it again.
Where should I begin, where end my story?   *15*
Heaven has sent me many tribulations.

I will tell you my name first, so that you, too,
Will know who I am, and when I escape
The day of my doom, I will always be
Your friend and host, though my home is far. 20
I am Odysseus, great Laertes' son,
Known for my cunning throughout the world,
And my fame reaches even to heaven.
My native land is Ithaca, a sunlit island
With a forested peak called Neriton, 25
Visible for miles. Many other islands
Lie close around her—Doulichion, Samê,
And wooded Zacynthus—off toward the sunrise,
But Ithaca lies low on the evening horizon,
A rugged place, a good nurse of men. 30
No sight is sweeter to me than Ithaca. Yes,
Calypso, the beautiful goddess, kept me
In her caverns, yearning to possess me;
And Circe, the witch of Aeaea, held me
In her halls and yearned to possess me; 35
But they could not persuade me or touch my heart.
Nothing is sweeter than your own country
And your own parents, not even living in a rich house—
Not if it's far from family and home.
But let me tell you of the hard journey homeward 40
Zeus sent me on when I sailed from Troy.

From Ilion the wind took me to the Cicones
In Ismaros. I pillaged the town and killed the men.
The women and treasure that we took out
I divided as fairly as I could among all hands 45
And then gave the command to pull out fast.
That was my order, but the fools wouldn't listen.
They drank a lot of wine and slaughtered
A lot of sheep and cattle on the shore.
Some of the town's survivors got away inland 50
And called their kinsmen. There were more of them,
And they were braver, too, men who knew how to fight
From chariots and on foot. They came on as thick
As leaves and flowers in spring, attacking
At dawn. We were out of luck, cursed by Zeus 55
To suffer heavy losses. The battle-lines formed

Along our beached ships, and bronze spears
Sliced through the air. As long as the day's heat
Climbed toward noon, we held our ground
Against superior numbers. But when the sun   *60*
Dipped down, the Cicones beat us down, too.
We lost six fighting men from each of our ships.
The rest of us cheated destiny and death.

We sailed on in shock, glad to get out alive
But grieving for our lost comrades.   *65*
I wouldn't let the ships get under way
Until someone had called out three times
For each mate who had fallen on the battlefield.
And then Zeus hit us with a norther,
A freak hurricane. The clouds blotted out   *70*
Land and sea, and night climbed up the sky.
The ships pitched ahead. When their sails
Began to shred in the gale-force winds.
We lowered them and stowed them aboard,
Fearing the worst, and rowed hard for the mainland.   *75*
We lay offshore two miserable days and nights.
When Dawn combed her hair in the third day's light,
We set up the masts, hoisted the white sails,
And took our seats. The wind and the helmsmen
Steered the ships, and I would have made it home   *80*
Unscathed, but as I was rounding Cape Malea
The waves, the current, and wind from the North
Drove me off course past Cythera Island.

Nine days of bad winds blew us across
The teeming seas. On the tenth day we came   *85*
To the land of the Lotus-Eaters.
We went ashore,

And the crews lost no time in drawing water
And preparing a meal beside their ships.
After they had filled up on food and drink,
I sent out a team—two picked men and a herald—   *90*
To reconnoiter and sound out the locals.
They headed out and made contact with the Lotus-Eaters,
Who meant no harm but did give my men

Some lotus to eat. Whoever ate that sweet fruit
Lost the will to report back, preferring instead   95
To stay there, munching lotus, oblivious of home.
I hauled them back wailing to the ships.
Bound them under the benches, then ordered
All hands to board their ships on the double
Before anyone else tasted the lotus.   100
They were aboard in no time and at their benches,
Churning the sea white with their oars.

We sailed on, our morale sinking,
And we came to the land of the Cyclopes,
Lawless savages who leave everything   105
Up to the gods. These people neither plow nor plant,
But everything grows for them unsown:
Wheat, barley, and vines that bear
Clusters of grapes, watered by rain from Zeus.
They have no assemblies or laws but live   110
In high mountain caves, ruling their own
Children and wives and ignoring each other.

A fertile island slants across the harbor's mouth,
Neither very close nor far from the Cyclopes' shore.
It's well-wooded and populated with innumerable   115
Wild goats, uninhibited by human traffic.
Not even hunters go there, tramping through the woods
And roughing it on the mountainsides.
It pastures no flocks, has no tilled fields—
Unplowed, unsown, virgin forever, bereft   120
Of men, all it does is support those bleating goats.
The Cyclopes do not sail and have no craftsmen
To build them benched, red-prowed ship
That could supply all their wants, crossing the sea
To other cities, visiting each other as other men do.   125
These same craftsmen would have made this island
Into a good settlement. It's not a bad place at all
And would bear everything in season. Meadows
Lie by the seashore, lush and soft,
Where vines would thrive. It has level plowland   130
With deep, rich soil that would produce bumper crops
Season after season. The harbor's good, too,

No need for moorings, anchor-stones, or tying up.
Just beach your ship until the wind is right
And you're ready to sail. At the harbor's head   *135*
A spring flows clear and bright from a cave
Surrounded by poplars.
                                    There we sailed in,
Some god guiding us through the murky night.
We couldn't see a thing. A thick fog
Enveloped the ships, and the moon   *140*
Wasn't shining in the cloud-covered sky.
None of us could see the island, or the long waves
Rolling toward the shore, until we ran our ships
Onto the sandy beach. Then we lowered sail,
Disembarked, and fell asleep on the sand.   *145*
Dawn came early, with palmettoes of rose.
And we explored the island, marveling at it.
The spirit-women, daughters of Zeus,
Roused the mountain goats so that my men
Could have a meal. We ran to the ships,   *150*
Got our javelins and bows, formed three groups
And started to shoot. The god let us bag our game.
Nine goats for each of the twelve ships.
Except for my ship, which got ten.

So all day long until the sun went down   *155*
We feasted on meat and sweet wine.
The ships had not yet run out of the dark red
Each crew had taken aboard in large jars
When we ransacked the Cicones' sacred city.
And we looked across at the Cyclopes' land.   *160*
We could see the smoke from their fires
And hear their voices, and their sheep and goats.
When the sun set, and darkness came on
We went to sleep on the shore of the sea.
As soon as dawn brightened in the rosy sky,   *165*
I assembled all the crews and spoke to them:

'The rest of you will stay here while I go
With my ship and crew on reconnaissance.
I want to find out what those men are like,

Wild savages with no sense of right or wrong   *170*
Or hospitable folk who fear the gods.'

With that, I boarded ship and ordered my crew
To get on deck and cast off. They took their places
And were soon whitening the sea with their oars.
As we pulled in over the short stretch of water,   *175*
There on the shoreline we saw a high cave
Overhung with laurels. It was a place
Where many sheep and goats were penned at night.
Around it was a yard fenced in by stones
Set deep in the earth, and by tall pines and crowned oaks.   *180*
This was the lair of a huge creature, a man
Who pastured his flocks off by himself,
And lived apart from others and knew no law.
He was a freak of nature, not like men who eat bread,
But like a lone wooded crag high in the mountains.   *185*

I ordered part of my crew to stay with the ship
And counted off the twelve best to go with me.
I took along a goatskin filled with red wine,
A sweet vintage I had gotten from Maron,
Apollo's priest on Ismaros, when I spared both him   *190*
And his wife and child out of respect for the god.
He lived in a grove of Phoebus Apollo
And gave me splendid gifts: seven bars of gold,
A solid-silver bowl, and twelve jars of wine,
Sweet and pure, a drink for the gods.   *195*
Hardly anyone in his house, none of the servants,
Knew about this wine—just Maron, his wife,
And a single housekeeper. Whenever he drank
This sweet dark red wine, he would fill one goblet
And pour it into twenty parts of water,   *200*
And the bouquet that spread from the mixing bowl
Was so fragrant no one could hold back from drinking.
I had a large skin of this wine, a sack
Of provisions—and a strong premonition
That we had a rendezvous with a man of great might,   *205*
A savage with no notion of right and wrong.

We got to the cave quickly. He was out,
Tending his flocks in the rich pastureland.
We went inside and had a good look around.
There were crates stuffed with cheese, and pens   210
Crammed with lambs and kids—firstlings,
Middlings, and newborns in separate sections.
The vessels he used for milking—pails and bowls
Of good workmanship—were brimming with whey
My men thought we should make off with some cheese   215
And then come back for the lambs and kids,
Load them on board, and sail away on the sea.
But I wouldn't listen. It would have been far better
If I had! But I wanted to see him, and see
If he would give me a gift of hospitality.   220
When he did come he was not a welcome sight.

We lit a fire and offered sacrifice
And helped ourselves to some of the cheese.
Then we sat and waited in the cave
Until he came back, herding his flocks.   225
He carried a huge load of dry wood
To make a fire for his supper and heaved it down
With a crash inside the cave. We were terrified
And scurried back into a corner.
He drove his fat flocks into the wide cavern,   230
At least those that he milked, leaving the males—
The rams and the goats—outside in the yard.
Then he lifted up a great doorstone,
A huge slab of rock, and set it in place.
Two sturdy wagons—twenty sturdy wagons—   235
Couldn't pry it from the ground—that's how big
The stone was he set in the doorway. Then,
He sat down and milked the ewes and bleating goats,
All in good order, and put the sucklings
Beneath their mothers. Half of the white milk   240
He curdled and scooped into wicker baskets,
The other half he let stand in the pails
So he could drink it later for his supper.
He worked quickly to finish his chores,
And as he was lighting the fire he saw us and said: 245

'Who are you strangers? Sailing the seas, huh?
Where from, and what for? Pirates, probably.
Roaming around causing people trouble.'

He spoke, and it hit us like a punch in the gut—
His booming voice and the sheer size of the monster—   *250*
But even so I found the words to answer him:

'We are Greeks, blown off course by every wind
In the world on our way home from Troy, traveling
Sea routes we never meant to, by Zeus' will no doubt.
We are proud to be the men of Agamemnon,   *255*
Son of Atreus, the greatest name under heaven,
Conquerer of Troy, destroyer of armies.
Now we are here, suppliants at your knees,
Hoping you will be generous to us
And give us the gifts that are due to strangers.   *260*
Respect the gods, sir. We are your suppliants,
And Zeus avenges strangers and suppliants,
Zeus, god of strangers, who walks at their side.'

He answered me from his pitiless heart:

'You're dumb, stranger, or from far away,   *265*
If you ask me to fear the gods. Cyclopes
Don't care about Zeus or his aegis
Or the blessed gods, since we are much stronger.
I wouldn't spare you or your men
Out of fear of Zeus. I would spare them only   *270*
If I myself wanted to. But tell me,
Where did you leave your ship? Far
Down the coast, or close? I'd like to know.'

Nice try, but I knew all the tricks and said:

'My ship? Poseidon smashed it to pieces   *275*
Against the rocks at the border of your land.
He pushed her in close and the wind did the rest.
These men and I escaped by the skin of our teeth.'

This brought no response from his pitiless heart
But a sudden assault upon my men. His hands   280
Reached out, seized two of them, and smashed them
To the ground like puppies. Their brains spattered out
And oozed into the dirt. He tore them limb from limb
To make his supper, gulping them down
Like a mountain lion, leaving nothing behind—   285
Guts, flesh, or marrowy bones.
Crying out, we lifted our hands to Zeus
At this outrage, bewildered and helpless.
When the Cyclops had filled his huge belly
With human flesh, he washed it down with milk,   290
Then stretched out in his cave among his flocks.
I crept up close and was thinking about
Drawing my sharp sword and driving it home
Into his chest where the lungs hide the liver.
I was feeling for the spot when another thought   295
Checked my hand: we would die to a man in that cave,
Unable to budge the enormous stone
He had set in place to block the entrance. And so,
Groaning through the night, we waited for dawn.

As soon as dawn came, streaking the sky red,   300
He rekindled the fire and milked his flocks,
All in good order, placing the sucklings
Beneath their mothers. His chores done,
He seized two of my men and made his meal.
After he had fed he drove his flocks out,   305
Easily lifting the great stone, which he then set
Back in place as lightly as if he were setting
A lid upon a quiver. And then, with loud whistling,
The Cyclops turned his fat flocks toward the mountain,
And I was left there, brooding on how   310
I might make him pay and win glory from Athena.

This was the best plan I could come up with:
Beside one of the sheep pens lay a huge pole
Of green olive which the Cyclops had cut
To use as a walking stick when dry. Looking at it   315
We guessed it was about as large as the mast
Of a black ship, a twenty-oared, broad-beamed

Freighter that crosses the wide gulfs.
That's how long and thick it looked. I cut off
About a fathom's length from this pole   *320*
And handed it over to my men. They scraped it
And made it smooth, and I sharpened the tip
And took it over to the fire and hardened it.
Then I hid it, setting it carefully in the dung
That lay in piles all around the cave.   *325*
And I told my men to draw straws to decide
Which of them would have to share the risk with me—
Lift that stake and grind it in his eye
While he was asleep. They drew straws and came up with
The very men I myself would have chosen.   *330*
There were four of them, and I made five.

At evening he came, herding his fleecy sheep.
He drove them straight into the cave, drove in
All his flocks in fact. Maybe he had some
Foreboding, or maybe some god told him to.   *335*
Then he lifted the doorstone and set it in place,
And sat down to milk the goats and bleating ewes,
All in good order, setting the sucklings
Beneath their mothers. His chores done,
Again he seized two of my men and made his meal.   *340*
Then I went up to the Cyclops and spoke to him,
Holding an ivy-wood bowl filled with dark wine.

'Cyclops, have some wine, now that you have eaten
Your human flesh, so you can see what kind of drink
Was in our ship's hold. I was bringing it to you   *345*
As an offering, hoping you would pity me
And help me get home. But you are a raving
Maniac! How do you expect any other man
Ever to visit you after acting like this?'

He took the bowl and drank it off, relishing   *350*
Every last, sweet drop. And he asked me for more:

'Be a pal and give me another drink. And tell me
Your name, so I can give you a gift you'll like.
Wine grapes grow in the Cyclopes' land, too.

Rain from the sky makes them grow from the earth.
But this—this is straight ambrosia and nectar.'
So I gave him some more of the ruby-red wine.
Three times the fool drained the bowl dry,
And when the wine had begun to work on his mind,
I spoke these sweet words to him: 355

                              'Cyclops,   360
You ask me my name, my glorious name,
And I will tell it to you. Remember now,
To give me the gift just as you promised.
Noman is my name. They call me Noman—
My mother, my father, and all my friends, too.'   365

He answered me from his pitiless heart:

'Noman I will eat last after his friends.
Friends first, him last. That's my gift to you.'

He listed as he spoke and then fell flat on his back,
His thick neck bent sideways. He was sound asleep,   370
Belching out wine and bits of human flesh
In his drunken stupor. I swung into action,
Thrusting the stake deep in the embers,
Heating it up, and all the while talking to my men
To keep up their morale. When the olive-wood stake   375
Was about to catch fire, green though it was,
And was really glowing, I took it out
And brought it right up to him. My men
Stood around me, and some god inspired us.
My men lifted up the olive-wood stake   380
And drove the sharp point right into his eye,
While I, putting my weight behind it, spun it around
The way a man bores a ship's beam with a drill,
Leaning down on it while other men beneath him
Keep it spinning and spinning with a leather strap.   385
That's how we twirled the fiery-pointed stake
In the Cyclops' eye. The blood formed a whirlpool
Around its searing tip. His lids and brow
Were all singed by the heat from the burning eyeball
And its roots crackled in the fire and hissed   390

Like an axe-head or adze a smith dips into water
When he wants to temper the iron—that's how his eye
Sizzled and hissed around the olive-wood stake.
He screamed, and the rock walls rang with his voice.
We shrank back in terror while he wrenched   395
The blood-grimed stake from his eye and flung it
Away from him, blundering about and shouting
To the other Cyclopes, who lived around him
In caverns among the windswept crags.
They heard his cry and gathered from all sides   400
Around his cave and asked him what ailed him:

'Polyphemus, why are you hollering so much
And keeping us up the whole blessed night?
Is some man stealing your flocks from you,
Or killing you, maybe, by some kind of trick?'   405

And Polyphemus shouted out to them:

'Noman is killing me by some kind of trick!'

They sent their words winging back to him:

'If no man is hurting you, then your sickness
Comes from Zeus and can't be helped,   410
You should pray to your father, Lord Poseidon.'

They left then, and I laughed in my heart
At how my phony name had fooled them so well.
Cyclops meanwhile was groaning in agony.
Groping around, he removed the doorstone   415
And sat in the entrance with his hands spread out
To catch anyone who went out with the sheep—
As if I could be so stupid. I thought it over,
Trying to come up with the best plan I could
To get us all out from the jaws of death.   420
I wove all sorts of wiles, as a man will
When his life is on the line. My best idea
Had to do with the sheep that were there, big,
Thick-fleeced beauties with wool dark as violets.
Working silently, I bound them together   425

With willow branches the Cyclops slept on.
I bound them in threes. Each middle sheep
Carried a man underneath, protected by
The two on either side: three sheep to a man.
As for me, there was a ram, the best in the flock. 430
I grabbed his back and curled up beneath
His shaggy belly. There I lay, hands twined
Into the marvelous wool, hanging on for dear life.
And so, muffling our groans, we waited for dawn.

When the first streaks of red appeared in the sky, 435
The rams started to bolt toward the pasture.
The unmilked females were bleating in the pens,
Their udders bursting. Their master,
Worn out with pain, felt along the backs
Of all of the sheep as they walked by, the fool, 440
Unaware of the men under their fleecy chests.
The great ram headed for the entrance last,
Heavy with wool—and with me thinking hard.
Running his hands over the ram, Polyphemus said:

'My poor ram, why are you leaving the cave 445
Last of all? You've never lagged behind before.
You were always the first to reach the soft grass
With your big steps, first to reach the river.
First to want to go back to the yard
At evening. Now you're last of all. Are you sad 450
About your master's eye? A bad man blinded me.
Him and his nasty friends, getting me drunk,
Noman—but he's not out of trouble yet!
If only you understood and could talk,
You could tell me where he's hiding. I would 455
Smash him to bits and spatter his brains
All over the cave. Then I would find some relief
From the pain this no-good Noman has caused me.'

He spoke, and sent the ram off through the door.
When we had gone a little way from the cave, 460
I first untangled myself from the ram
And then untied my men. Then, moving quickly,
We drove those fat, long-shanked sheep

Down to the ship, keeping an eye on our rear.
We were a welcome sight to the rest of the crew,   465
But when they started to mourn the men we had lost
I forbade it with an upward nod of my head,
Signaling each man like that and ordering them
To get those fleecy sheep aboard instead,
On the double, and get the ship out to sea   470
Before you knew it they were on their benches
Beating the sea to white froth with their oars.
When we were offshore but still within earshot,
I called out to the Cyclops, just to rub it in:

'So, Cyclops, it turns out it wasn't a coward   475
Whose men you murdered and ate in your cave,
You savage! But you got yours in the end,
Didn't you? You had the gall to eat the guests
In your own house, and Zeus made you pay for it.'

He was even angrier when he heard this.   480
Breaking off the peak of a huge crag
He threw it toward our ship, and it carried
To just in front of our dark prow. The sea
Billowed up where the rock came down.
And the backwash pushed us to the mainland again,   485
Like a flood tide setting us down at the shore.
I grabbed a long pole and shoved us off,
Nodding to the crew to fall on the oars
And get us out of there. They leaned into it,
And when we were twice as far out to sea as before   490
I called to the Cyclops again, with my men
Hanging all over me and begging me not to:

'Don't do it, man! The rock that hit the water
Pushed us in and we thought we were done for.
If he hears any sound from us, he'll heave   495
Half a cliff at us and crush the ship and our skulls
With one throw. You know he has the range.'

They tried, but didn't persuade my hero's heart—
I was really angry—and I called back to him:

'Cyclops, if anyone, any mortal man,   *500*
Asks you how you got your eye put out.
Tell him that Odysseus the marauder did it,
Son of Laertes, whose home is on Ithaca.'

He groaned, and had this to say in response:

'Oh no! Now it's coming to me, the old prophecy.   *505*
There was a seer here once, a tall handsome man,
Telemos Eurymides. He prophesied well
All his life to the Cyclopes. He told me
That all this would happen some day,
That I would lose my sight at Odysseus' hands.   *510*
I always expected a great hero
Would come here, strong as can be.
Now this puny, little, good-for-nothing runt
Has put my eye out—because he got me drunk.
But come here, Odysseus, so I can give you a gift,   *515*
And ask Poseidon to help you on your way.
I'm his son, you know. He claims he's my father.
He will heal me, if he wants. But none
Of the other gods will, and no mortal man will.'

He spoke, and I shouted back to him: *520*

'I wish I were as sure of ripping out your lungs
And sending you to Hell as I am dead certain
That not even the Earthshaker will heal your eye.'

I had my say, and he prayed to Poseidon,
Stretching his arms out to starry heaven: *525*
'Hear me, Poseidon, blue-maned Earth-Holder,
If you are the father you claim to be.
Grant that Odysseus, son of Laertes,
May never reach his home on Ithaca.
But if he is fated to see his family again,   *530*
And return to his home and own native land,
May he come late, having lost all companions,
In another's ship, and find trouble at home.'

He prayed, and the blue-maned sea-god heard him.
Then he broke off an even larger chunk of rock,   535
Pivoted, and threw it with incredible force.
It came down just behind our dark-hulled ship,
Barely missing the end of the rudder. The sea
Billowed up where the rock hit the water,
And the wave pushed us forward all the way   540
To the island where our other ships waited
Clustered on the shore, ringed by our comrades
Sitting on the sand, anxious for our return.
We beached the ship and unloaded the Cyclops' sheep,
Which I divided up as fairly as I could   545
Among all hands. The veterans gave me the great ram,
And I sacrificed it on the shore of the sea
To Zeus in the dark clouds, who rules over all
I burnt the thigh pieces, but the god did not accept
My sacrifice, brooding over how to destroy   550
All my benched ships and my trusty crews.

So all the long day until the sun went down
We sat feasting on meat and drinking sweet wine.
When the sun set and darkness came on
We lay down and slept on the shore of the sea.   555
Early in the morning, when the sky was streaked red,
I roused my men and ordered the crews
To get on deck and cast off. They took their places
And were soon whitening the sea with their oars.

We sailed on in shock, glad to get away alive   560
But grieving for the comrades we had lost."

Works and Days

𝍖𝍖𝍖𝍖𝍖𝍖𝍖𝍖𝍖𝍖𝍖𝍖𝍖𝍖𝍖

By Hesoid
Translated by Daryl Hine

Come, you Pierian[1] Muses, who give us the glory of music,   1
Tell me of Zeus, your progenitor, make praise-songs in his honor;
Through him, moreover, are humankind undistinguished or famous,
They are sung or unsung by the will of omnipotent great Zeus.
Easily making a man strong, easily he overthrows him,   5
Easily humbles the proud as he lifts up high the obscure, and
Easily straightens the crooked as well as deflating the puffed-up—
Zeus, who is deathless and thunders aloft and dwells in the highest.
Listen to me and behold, make straight your decisions with justice.
I would be happy to speak true facts to you, Perses,[2] my brother.   10
There is not only one Discord, for on earth she is twofold:
One of them nobody would find fault with on closer acquaintance;
One you would deprecate, for they have totally different natures.
Wickedly, one promotes all the evils of warfare and slaughter;
No one of humankind likes her; out of necessity, at the   15
Will of the blessed immortals, they treat grim Discord with honor.
There is, moreover, another, the firstborn daughter of dark Night.
Her did the high-throned scion of Cronus whose home is in heaven
Place at the roots of the earth; she is certainly better for mankind.
This is that Discord that stirs up even the helpless to hard work.   20

Seeing a man gets eager to work on beholding a neighbor
Who is exceedingly wealthy and makes haste plowing and sowing,
Putting his household in order; so neighbor competing with neighbor
Runs after riches, and therefore this Discord benefits mankind.
Every potter begrudges another, and artists do likewise;   25
Every beggarman envies a beggar, and poets are rivals.

Perses, be sure you deposit these things in your heart and your spirit,
Lest Discord, which *is* given to mischief, distract you from work and

You begin sneaking about, eavesdropping on feuds in the forum.
You have no business getting in fights and disputing in public,   30
Not if you haven't sufficient for life laid up in your storeroom,
Seasonal fruits of the earth, ripe grain of abundant Demeter.
When you have plenty of that, turn freely to fierce competition
For the possessions of others; no second chance will be yours to
Do so. Let us however decide our disputes by means of impartial   35
Judgments, for justice derives from Zeus and is bound to be perfect.
When we had split our inheritance, you grabbed most of it, making
Off with it, to enhance the repute of our bribe-hungry royal
Masters, who love to adjudge such cases as ours in their courtrooms.
Idiots! They don't know how much more is the half than the whole, nor   40
What is the use of a diet of mallow and asphodel,[3] Perses?

Plainly the gods keep secret from humankind the means of survival;
Otherwise, you in a day could easily do enough work to
Last you a whole year long, and without any further exertion.
Soon, very soon you would hang up over the fireplace your rudder;   45
Then would be finished the labors of oxen and hard-working donkeys.
No, Zeus kept it a secret because in his heart he was angry,
Seeing how devious-minded Prometheus once had fooled him;
Therefore did almighty Zeus plot sorrows and troubles for mankind.
He hid fire, which, however, then Iapetus's great-hearted son, to   50
Benefit humankind, pilfered from Zeus, the purveyor of counsel,
Hid in a hollowed-out stalk to baffle the lover of thunder.

Then cloud-gathering Zeus to Prometheus said in his anger:
"Iapetus's brat, since you're so much smarter than anyone else, you're
Happy to outwit me, and rejoice in the fire you have stolen—   55
For yourself a calamity, also for men of the future.
For I shall give them a bad thing, too, in exchange for this fire, which
Heartily all may delight in, embracing a homegrown evil."
Speaking, the father of gods and of mankind exploded in laughter.
Then he commanded Hephaestus,[4] the world-famed craftsman, as   60
    soon as
✳ Possible to mix water and earth, and infuse in it human
Speech, also strength, and to make it look like a goddess, and give it
Likewise a girl-like form that was pretty and lovesome. Athena
Would instruct her in handwork and weaving of intricate fabrics;
Furthermore, gold Aphrodite[5] should drip charm over her head to   65
Cause heartsore longing, emotional anguish exhausting the body.

Zeus gave instructions to Hermes, the sure guide, slayer of Argus,[6]
To put in her the heart of a bitch and a devious nature.
Then did the famed lame god manufacture at once from the earth a
Fair simulacrum of one shy maiden, according to Zeus's will.   70
Next to her skin did the godlike Graces and gracious Persuasion
Carefully place gold necklaces; round her adorable head the
Hours who are gorgeously coiffed wove garlands of beautiful spring
   flowers.
Hermes, our sure guide, slayer of Argus, contrived in her breast
Lies and misleadingly false words joined to a devious nature,   75
At the behest of the deep-voiced thunderer, Zeus; and the herald
God of the gods then gave her a voice. And he called her Pandora,
Seeing how all who inhabit lofty Olympus had given
Something to pretty Pandora, that giant bane to industrious mankind.

When he had finished this downright desperate piece of deception,   80
To Epimetheus Zeus then dispatched the slayer of Argus,
Famed swift messenger of the immortals, with her as a present.
But Epimetheus had forgotten Prometheus's warning,
Not to accept anything from Olympian Zeus, but to send it
Back where it came from, lest it become a disaster for mortals.   85
Once he'd accepted it, he, possessing the bane, recognized it.

Formerly dwelt on earth all the various tribes of the human
Race, on their own and remote from evils and difficult labor
And from distressing diseases that bring doom closer to each one.
For in misfortune do humans age rapidly, quicker than ever.   90
Using her fingers, the maid pried open the lid of the great jar,
Sprinkling its contents; her purpose, to bring sad hardships to mankind.
Nothing but Hope stayed there in her stout, irrefrangible dwelling,
Under the lip of the jar, inside, and she never would venture
Outdoors, having the lid of the vessel itself to prevent her,   95
Willed there by Zeus, who arranges the storm clouds and carries the aegis.[7]
Otherwise, myriad miseries flit round miserable mortals;
Furthermore, full is the earth of much mischief, the deep sea also.
Illnesses visiting humans dally and nightly at all hours
All by themselves bring terrible troubles aplenty to mortals   100
Silently, seeing their power of speech was suppressed by all-wise Zeus.
There is no way of escaping from Zeus's implacable mind-set.
If you prefer, an alternate story[8] I'll summarize also
Well and expertly, and lay it up in your mind and preserve it—

Namely, the common origin shared by immortals and mortals.   105
First, the immortals who dwell high up on the top of Olympus
Fashioned the firstborn race of articulate men, which was golden,
And it is said that they lived when Cronus was ruling in heaven.
Godlike, they lived like gods, and their hearts were entirely carefree,
Distant strangers to labor and suffering; neither did wretched   110
Age overtake them; instead, their members intact and unchanged, they
Took much pleasure in banquets and parties, apart from all evils
Till they died as if sleep overcame them. And everything worthwhile
Came to their hand, as the grain-growing earth bore fruit without tilling,
Plenty of good food crops unbegrudged; so they lived at their pleasure,   115
Peacefully minding their own business, amid numerous good things.
Wealthy in flocks were they and beloved of the blessed immortals.
After this whole first gold generation was finally buried,
Even today they are called pure spirits inhabiting earth and
Noble protectors of mankind, warding off evils from mortals,   120
Givers of wealth, which royal prerogative still is their business.

Afterward, those that inhabit Olympus fashioned a second,
Silver race, which was very inferior, worse than the first one,
For they did neither in growth nor intellect equal the golden.
Children were then brought up by their diligent mothers a hundred   125
Years and engaged in sheer infantile child's play there in their own homes.
But when maturing at last they came to the measure of manhood
They lived only the tiniest time, and moreover they suffered
Much in their folly; they could not keep themselves back from their
          wicked
Violence on one another; nor were they willing to serve the immortals   130
Or make sacrifice using the Blessed Ones' sacrosanct altars,
As it is lawful for humans to do and according to custom.
Thereupon, Zeus, son of Cronus, suppressed them all in his anger,
Seeing they did not worship the gods who inhabit Olympus.
And when this generation of silver in turn was interred   135
Under the earth, they were termed blessed spirits although they were mortal,
Second in time, yet everywhere honor is also their portion.

Zeus manufactured a new third race of articulate mankind,
But this bronze generation in no way equaled the silver,
For they were offspring of ash trees, mighty and frightful, and Ares'   140
Noisy employment concerned them and violent deeds. They ate no
Bread and appeared tough-minded as adamant, wholly unpolished;

All too great was their strength and their hands were invincible, growing
Out of their mighty shoulders to hang at the end of their stout limbs.
Bronze was their armor and brazen their arms, brass-bound were their   145
     dwellings;
Bronze were the tools which they worked with, as Iron had not been invented.
Dying by each other's hands, they went down to the underworld's cold rot,
Leaving no names to posterity. Black death took them despite their
Physical strength, and they quit altogether the luminous sunlight.
But when this bronze generation, however, was finally buried,   150
Zeus, son of Cronus, created a whole new fourth generation
Here on the fertile earth who were better and fonder of justice;
This was a godlike race of heroical men who were known as
Demigods, last generation before our own on the broad earth.
Horrible war with its frightening war cries wholly destroyed them,   155
Some who fought in the kingdom of Cadmus below seven-gated
Thebes where they strove in vain with each other for Oedipus's rich flocks,[9]
Others transported across the immense deep gulf of the sea on
Shipboard to Troy after well-coiffed Helen, the fairest of women.[10]
Some of them there death's ending completely enveloped in darkness.   160
Others, however, the son of Cronus decided to grant a
Dwelling place far from men at the furthermost ends of the earth, and
There they continue to live, their consciousness perfectly carefree,
There in the Isles of the Blessed, beside deep-eddying Ocean,[11]
Distant from the immortals; and Cronus was king of that kingdom   165
After the father of gods and of men freed him from his bondage;
Now from those heroes he gets high honor as is most befitting.
Fortunate heroes! Their plowlands are so fertile they yield a
Crop more delicious than honey that flourishes three times yearly.
Zeus then created a fifth and last generation of mankind   170
Such as to this day also inhabit the bountiful green earth.
How I would wish to have never been one of this fifth generation!
Whether I'd died in the past or came to be born in the future.
Truly of iron is this generation, and never by day will
They intermit hard labor and woe; in the night they will also   175
Suffer distress, for the gods will give them unbearable troubles.
Nevertheless, there will always be good mixed in with the evil.
Zeus will destroy this race of articulate mankind, however,
When they have come to exhibit at birth gray hairs at their temples
And when fathers will differ from children and children from fathers,   180
Guests with their hosts will differ and comrades will differ with comrades.
And no more will a brother, as previously, be beloved.

When they grow old, people will show no respect to their elders;
Harshly upbraiding them, they use words that are horribly cruel,
Wretches who don't acknowledge the face of the gods and who will not   185
Payback ever the cost of their upbringing to their old parents,
Thinking that might means right; and they devastate each other's cities.
There will be nothing like gratitude for oath-keepers and just men,
Nor for the good man; rather, they'll only respect evildoers,
Monsters of violence. Might will be right, all shame will be lost and   190
All inhibition. The wicked will try to ruin the good man,
Shamelessly uttering falsehoods, wickedly bearing false witness.
Noisy, discordant Envy, malicious, delighting in mischief,
Hateful-faced will accompany all us unfortunate humans.
Self-respect and upright Indignation will go on their way to Olympus,   195
Quitting the broadly trod earth and concealing their beautiful forms in
Mantles of white, preferring the company of the immortals,
Wholly abandoning mankind, leaving them sorrow and grievous
Pain for the human condition, till there's no ward against evil.
Now I shall tell you a fable for kings who have understanding.   200
A hawk spoke to a speckle-necked nightingale cruelly, as he
Lifted her up to the clouds while gripping her tight in his talons.
Piteously she, transfixed by his crooked claws, was lamenting
When the imperious hawk addressed her in arrogant parlance,
"Why, little lady, such shrieks? One stronger than you now has got you;   205
Where you are going, I'll take you myself, though you are a songstress,
For as I please I'll make you my dinner or give you your freedom.
Witless is one who attempts to strive against those who are stronger.
When he is stripped of the prize it is injury added to insult."
Thus said the fast-flying hawk, that bird with the generous wingspan.   210
Pay more attention to Justice and curb high-handedness, Perses;
Violence ill suits men who are lowly; not even the noble
Man can lightly endure it; it weighs on a person who's fallen
Into affliction. It's better to take your way on the other
Road which conduces to right. For outrage surrenders to justice   215
When they arrive at discrete ends. Fools understand this the hard way.
Oath every step of the way keeps up with dishonest misjudgments.
There is a tumult when Justice is dragged where men who are venal
Hijack her, those who impose false judgments with crooked injustice.
Weeping, she visits a city and seeks out haunts of the people,   220
Dimly enveloped in mist, she's bringing misfortune to humans.
Those who have driven her out do not behave to her rightly.
Others deliver correct just judgments to stranger and fellow

Countryman, never transgressing a bit the way of the righteous;
Theirs is a stalwart city and flourishing people within it.   225
Peace that cherishes children is over the land, and all-seeing
Zeus never ever allots them cruel and terrible warfare.
Neither disasters nor famines befall men just in their dealings;
At their convivial banquets they eat the fruits of their labors.
Earth bears plentiful food for them; plenty of oaks on the mountains   230
Bear on their summit plentiful acorns, and bees in their center.
Beautifully woolly their sheep are, fraught with luxuriant fleece. Their
Women at term give birth to fine children resembling their fathers.
Always they flourish with all good things, but they never on shipboard
Venture; the grain-growing plowland provides them produce in plenty.   235

Zeus, son of Cronus, who sees far and wide, metes justice to those who
Care for evil and violence, foster criminal actions;
Time and again whole cities are lost on account of one wicked
Man who is sinful and dreams up deeds of presumptuous daring.
Zeus, son of Cronus, from heaven inflicts great suffering on them,   240
Famine and pestilence at once, making the populace perish;
Women do not give birth, so that households diminish in number,
All through the plans of Olympian Zeus, who likewise at other
Times devastates broad armies of men and their fortifications,
And in his wrath Cronus's son sinks ships in the midst of the sea, too.   245

Princes, behold for yourselves how just is this heavenly justice,
For the immortals are closer than you suppose to the actions of humans,
Closely observing how some of us, steeped in crooked injustice,
Grind one another right down, not minding the gods' indignation,
For on the bountiful earth there are thrice ten thousand immortal   250
Spies in the service of Zeus to watch over men who are mortal.
They watch just judgments and villainous deeds at the same time.
Dimly enveloped in mist, they wander all over the broad earth.
Maidenly Justice moreover exists, Zeus's virginal daughter,
Honored, respected among those gods who inhabit Olympus.   255
Should anyone by dishonest speech disrespect and offend her,
She will immediately sit down next to her father, the son of
Cronus, and tattle to him of unjust men's hearts, till the people
Pay for the mindless follies of rulers who, consciously wicked,
Like to subvert just judgments with sentences woefully crooked.   260
Rulers, be careful of matters like this; make straight your pronouncements,
Greedy for gifts though you are, and rescind your dishonest decisions.

He's only harming himself who's bent upon harming another;
Evil designs do the most harm always to workers of evil.
Zeus's all-seeing omniscient eye can see even these if it wishes,   265
Noticing also what sort of justice a city contains. But
Anyway may neither I nor my son be "just" among men if
Rascals pretend to be "just"; men more in the wrong get
Better decisions. But all-wise Zeus would, I hope, not permit it.
Brother Perses, lay up in your heart these things that I tell you: 270
Paying attention to righteousness, forget about force altogether.
Zeus, son of Cronus, ordained one rule of behavior for humans
But quite another for fishes and animals, likewise for birds, who
Commonly eat one another; there's no fair play in such creatures.
Men received justice, by far best quality ever conceived; to   275
That man who argues a just cause truthfully, knowing its justice,
Zeus the far seeing will give great blessings, prosperity, good luck,
But for someone who knowingly bears false witness, committing
Perjury, injuring justice, and doing permanent damage,
Surely his progeny will be left in the shadows hereafter,   280
Whereas the race of the faithful man will be better hereafter.
Perses, you idiot, knowing a thing or two will instruct you.
Wickedness may be obtained too easily and in abundance,
Smooth is the road to her dwelling; indeed she lives very nearby
But in the way of access to virtue, immortals have placed the   285
Sweat of our brows, and the pathway there is both lengthy and steep and
Rough and uneven at first; when at last one comes to the summit,
Then it is easy enough, though difficult still up to that point.
Best of all is the man who, considering every thing himself,
Now understands what things are thereafter and finally better;   290
Similarly he is wise who listens to expert advisers.
One who's unable to think for himself or listen to others,
Storing their words in his heart, that person is perfectly useless.
You on the other hand, Perses, remember forever my earnest
Precepts, and work, you descendant of Zeus, work hard, so that hunger   295
Loathes you and shuns you, and may rich-garlanded, honored Demeter
Kindly befriend you and fill your granary yearly with foodstuffs.
Hunger is always the boon best friend of a man who is shiftless.
Even the gods are disgusted, like men, with a chap who is lazy,
Living in idleness, like drones lacking a stinger to sting with,   300
Wholly exhausting the labors of bees by being voracious,
Shirking all work. But care for your labors and put them in order,
So may your granaries fill up quickly with seasonal produce.

Men by the work of their hands get plenty of sheep and are wealthy;
Someone who does hard work is a favorite of the immortals, 305
Also of mortals, for both of them hate sincerely the idle.
Labor is far from disgraceful. Indeed, unemployment's disgraceful,
And if you work hard, those who are idle will quickly begin to
Envy your wealth, for honor and worth are attendant on riches.
No matter what your condition, to work hard always is better. 310
If you can tear your misguided mind from another's possessions,
Turn your attention to work; yes, mind your own business, I tell you.
Modesty's no bad companion for one who is needy.
Modesty can at the same time bother and benefit mankind.
Modesty goes with misfortune as arrogance goes with good fortune. 315
Things are not there to be taken, no, wealth god-given is better.
If one gets hold of immense good fortune by physical force or
Steals it away with a lying tongue, as is often the case when
Lust for profit deceives the intelligence given to mankind
And when immodesty shamelessly casts out modesty wholly, 320
Readily heaven obscures that man and diminishes his house;
Only the shortest while does good fortune attend the dishonest.
Equally bad is the man who does wrong to a supplicant or a
Guest, or who guiltily goes upstairs to the bed of his brother,
Furtively lying in lust with that brother's wife, which is sinful, 325
Or who irrationally offends against fatherless children,
Or who disputes with his aged father on age's unhappy
Threshold, assailing the old man mercilessly with severe words.
With such a man even Zeus is irate, at last for the wicked
Doings of mortals exacting an ultimate harsh retribution. 330
See you exclude such deeds from your idiot heart altogether,
And insofar as you can, make sacrifice to the immortals
Blandly, with ritual purity, likewise burning the fat meats.
Gladden the deathless gods with libations and incense at all times,
Both upon going to bed and at the return of the holy 335
Light, so they'll grant you a tranquil heart and a satisfied spirit;
So you can bid on your neighbor's plot and not he on your own land.
Summon your friend to a feast; pass over your enemy rudely;
Summon above all the neighbor living the nearest to your place,
For should something or other occur on your property sometime, 340
Neighbors will come as they are, while in-laws are putting their coats on.
A bad neighbor's a curse just as much as a good one's a blessing;
Anyone gets good value who has a respectable neighbor.
Hardly an ox would get lost but for malevolent neighbors.

Borrow fair measure from neighbors, and pay them back in proportion 345
With an identical measure, and more, just as much as you're able.
Thus, if you're ever in need, you'll have somebody you can depend on.
Do not procure base gain, for a gain that is base is a dead loss.
One who befriends you, befriend, and someone who visits you, visit;
Give to a person who gives, but not to a person who doesn't: 350
Everyone gives to the open-handed but none to the stingy.
Giving's a good wife; grasping's a bad wife, death is her dowry;
Therefore, the man who gives willingly gives magnificently and
Comes to rejoice in his own gift, taking delight in his bounty,
Whereas the man who, prompted by shamelessness, seizes another's 355
Goods, be they ever so small, his heart will be thoroughly frozen.
If you continue to add a little amount to a little,
And if you do so quite often, that little will soon be a whole lot:
He who augments what he has can ward off the furies of hunger.
None of the stuff that a man lays up in his house will distress him; 360
Everything's better at home, outdoors is a dangerous region.
It is a fine thing to take what's available; wanting what's not brings
Anguish of mind and a heartfelt grief, which I bid you consider.
Drink your fill of the cask newly broached and when nearly finished;
Ration the stuff in the middle, the dregs make a horrible mouthful. 365
See that the wages you promise a faithful retainer are paid soon.
And with a brother be sure to smile, and in front of a witness,
Certainly trust and distrust prove equally fatal to mankind.
Don't let a wily, wheedling woman who wiggles her bottom
Wholly befuddle your wits: her purpose is rifling your pantry. 370
One who believes in a woman believes in cheats and deceivers.
Let there be only one heir, his paternal inheritance's steward,
Who will fatten it up so that wealth will augment in the household.
You should be careful to die old if you are leaving a grandson;
Easily Zeus will provide inexhaustible wealth to your increase: 375
Greater attention to labor by many enlarges the profit.
If your desire for wealth is engrained in the depths of your being,
Do as I tell you, and work, work, work, never cease from your labors.

Just as soon as the Pleiades,[12] daughters of Atlas, have risen,
Gather your harvest; begin to plow when those sisters are setting. 380
For forty nights and days is this bright constellation occluded,
Till, when the year has in part completed its annual cycle,
They reappear in the heavens at sunrise: time then to sharpen your
    sickle.

This, it appears, is the rule that governs the plains and all those who
Live by the seashore, also all those who inhabit the glens and   385
Hillsides remote from the billowing sea, rich country to live in:
Straight from your bed, without troubling to dress, plow, sow, and nude
    harvest,
If you are eager to do the work of Demeter in due time,
So that everything reaches its seasonal growth, lest hereafter,
Being in want, you go begging next door and return empty-handed.   390
So have you recently come to me, too, you idiot Perses.
I will not give any more, no more than your usual portion.
Work, silly Perses, work, for the gods have assigned it to mankind,
Otherwise you and your children and wife will go to your neighbors,
Begging your living, bitter in heart, and they'll pay no attention.
Two, three times you'll be lucky, but if you should further harass them   395
You will not get what you want, though talking much vain and inane talk.
All of your eloquence comes to nothing, and so I beseech you,
Think about paying your pressing debts and escaping from hunger.
First of all, purchase a house and a woman, an ox for the plowing,   400
That is, a woman to own, not to marry, who'll follow the oxen.[13]
Tidily keep all the goods in your house shipshape and all ready,
Lest you must ask of another and he say no, so you live in
Want, and the seasons go by and your agriculture is ruined.
Do not postpone your work till tomorrow and after tomorrow;   405
Men who are idle at work don't fill up their barns with abundance,
Nor do men who procrastinate. Industry benefits labor.
Someone who puts off labor will evermore wrestle with ruin.
When the unbearable strength of the sun abates and its sweaty
Heat, and omnipotent Zeus sends mortals the downpours of Autumn,   410

Then the complexions of humans feel comfortable—quite an improvement!
Sirius[14] briefly by day floats over the heads of devoted
Men but is visible more in the nighttime. Wood that you cut when
Leaves are bestrewing the ground and growth is arrested is worm-free.
Do not forget woodcutting, this season's for plying the hatchet.   415
Chisel a mortar that's three feet long and a pestle of five feet;
Also an axle that's seven feet long will prove mighty handy,
Or, if you fashion it eight feet long, you can carve out a mallet.
Whittle a wheel two feet and a half for a wagon of two foot
Three. There is plenty of bent firewood. If you come on a tree fork   420
Fit for a plow, bring it home with you, when you have looked on the
    mountains

And in the fields for a holm oak, strongest for plowing with oxen,
After some hand of Athena's[15] has fastened it tight to the plowshare,
Pegging the business end to the handle. So keep in the house two
Plows you are working on, one with a natural bent and the other   425
Joined artificially, for that scheme is undoubtedly better:
If you should break one plow you can yoke up the ox to the other.
Handles of laurel and elm are most likely totally worm-free,
So is a plowshare of oak as well as a plow-tree of holm oak.
Get two oxen, two bulls about nine years of age, when their strength is   430
Still at its peak in the prime of their age: such are excellent workers,
Nor will they fight one another in plowland, smashing the plow to
Pieces, and bringing your hard agricultural labor to nothing.
Let them be followed by some energetic farmworker of forty
Years, who has broken his fast with a quarter loaf of eight slices[16]   435
And will attend to his work while driving the straightest of furrows,
Having no time for glancing askance at his comrades; he keeps his
Mind on his work, for better by far a grown man as a partner,
Who's better at scattering seeds and doesn't keep scattering double;
While immature young men are too often intrigued with each other.   440

Every year when you hear the shrill din of the cranes from the clouds, take
Note, for it signals the season to plow, indicating the rainy
Wintertime, gnawing the heart of the man who possesses no oxen.
Now's the appropriate time for feeding up long-horned cattle

Indoors, for it's easy to ask for a team and a wagon,   445
Easier still to refuse: "I've plenty of work for my oxen."
Thick are the wits of the man who says that his wagon's already
Finished; the fool doesn't know there are hundreds of planks in a wagon.
Make it your business to have these planks in your house for the future.

Then, when the time for plowing at last is apparent to mortals,   450
That is the hour to hurry, yourself and your servants together.
Whether in wet or in dry, to plow at the season of plowing,
Rouse yourself early, get up, so your field will soon be overflowing.
Turn up the soil in the spring; then summer won't be disappointing.
Sow your seed in the fallow land when it is looser and lighter.   455
Fallow land wards agricultural ruin off, charms little children.
Beg subterranean Zeus, pray to Demeter the holy
That the perfected and sacred grains of Demeter be weighty.
When you're beginning the plowing at first, then hold in your hand the

End of the tail of the plow, lay stripes on the backs of your oxen,   460
Pulling the peg by the straps. While walking a little behind, a
Serf with a mattock creates much trouble and woe for the birds by
Hiding the seed in the ground. Good husbandry, that is the best for
Men who are mortal, as rotten husbandry is the most evil.
So will the heads of your wheat hang down to the ground in their fullness,   465
If the Olympian gives you a good outcome; after all, then
Dusting your storage jars you'll be brushing off cobwebs, I hope that
You will rejoice when you've got your livelihood safe in your keeping;
So, well-provided, you'll come to misty spring. And you'll look to
Nobody else, but another may likely need your assistance.   470
Yet if you plow the excellent earth at the winter solstice,
Squatting you'll reap, and you'll harvest by hand but a pitiful handful,
Binding the dust-covered sheaves all askew. You'll not be too happy
Bringing them home in a basket, when not very many admire you.
Truly the purposes vary of Zeus, who carries the aegis,   475
All too difficult are they to fathom by men who are mortal.
If you insist upon plowing too late, one remedy there is:
After the cuckoo is heard for the first time loud in the oak tree's
Foliage, cheering mankind all over the earth, which is boundless,
If on the third day Zeus begins raining and doesn't let up till   480
Rain neither rises above cows' hooves nor is very much under,
Then one who's late with his plowing will rival him who was early.
Keep this advice, every bit of it, well in mind, and forget not
Either the mist-gray days of the spring or the rain-sodden season.

Pass by the blacksmith's forge with its cozy and comfortable clubroom   485
During the winter, when cold prevents a man doing his outdoor
Work, at the time when laborious men do most for their households,
Lest in its terrible helplessness one bad winter surprise you
Stricken with poverty, scratching a swollen foot with a hand that is skinny.
Every man unemployed who waits upon hope, though it's empty,   490
Lacking a livelihood, grimly meditates plenty of evil.
Hope is no good that accompanies men who are poverty stricken,
Men who relax at the club, whose living is highly uncertain.[17]
While it is still midsummer, be sure to instruct your domestics,
"It will not always be summer; it's time to build yourselves shelters."   495
Skip the whole month of Lenaion,[18] those harsh days ready to take the
Skin off an ox, and the frost which becomes so ruthlessly cruel
Every time that the north wind, Boreas, blows on the good earth.
When over horse-training Thrace[19] aloft, agitating the broad sea,

Boreas blows, he awakes both forest and earth in an uproar, 500
Falling upon many tall, leafy oaks and bristling fir trees
Growing in groves on the mountains; he brings them crashing to earth, and
All of the endless, immense great forest resounds with the impact.
Animals shudder and tuck their tails in between their hind legs,
Even the ones whose hide is covered with fur, for the north wind, 505
Cold as it is, blows through them although they are terribly hairy,
And it can penetrate even the hide of a bull, which can't stop it.
Also it blows through the goat's fine hairs, but the fleece of a sheep it
Cannot, because it is so close-packed that the powerful north wind
Can't penetrate it, which nonetheless easily bowls over old men. 510
Nor is it able to penetrate smooth-skinned virginal maidens
As they abide in the house beside their affectionate mothers,
Blissfully ignorant still of the doings of gold Aphrodite.
They, after carefully washing their delicate bodies in water,
Slickly anointed with oil, lie down in the innermost private 515
Room, on a wintry day when the boneless octopus gnaws his
Foot in his home without fire, in his wretchedly humid apartment.[20]
Nor does the sun indicate fresh pasturage for a beginning,
Wandering, rather, over the countries and cities of black men,
Shining, however more sluggishly, on all Hellenes at the solstice. 520
Then both the horned and the hornless inhabitants of the wild woodland
Flee through the thickets and groves with pathetically chattering teeth and
All of them have in their hearts and their minds one single desire, while
Searching for shelter, to find some large, hollow rock or some thickset
Covert, and like a three-legged[21] man whose back is so bent it appears 525
Broken, whose face is moreover directed perpetually downward,
Like this old man, beasts wander at random, avoiding the white snow.
Furthermore, take my advice, put on for your body's protection
A soft cloak and a tunic that comes all the way down to your ankles,
Woven of thickest woof on top of the thinnest of warp threads. 530
Wrap yourself up in this garb, your hairs will not quiver with cold and
Bristle and stand up on end all over your shivering body.
Tie on your feet boots made of the hide of an ox freshly slaughtered,
Make them close-fitting and snug with a lining of felt on the inside.
And when the season of cold is at hand, get out a few kid skins, 535
Sew them together with sinews of oxen in order to throw them
Over your back to protect you from rain; on top of your head a
Felt cap cunningly made to prevent you from getting your ears wet.
Cold is the dawn when the north wind briskly commences its blowing;
Daily at sunrise a luminous mist spreads over the earth from 540

Star-spangled heaven and covers the fields of fortunate mortals,
Moisture drawn up from the rivers that go on flowing forever;
High it is lifted above the earth by tempestuous windstorms.
Sometimes it rains toward evening, sometimes it turns very windy,
Driven by Boreas blowing from Thrace, who disperses the thick clouds.   545
Finish your labors beforehand, hastily make your way homeward,
Lest an umbrageous cloud from the sky should envelope you sometime,
Soaking your body with ice cold moisture and drenching your clothing.
This you should surely avoid; this month is the hardest and harshest,
Wintry and cruel to livestock, cruel to men in addition.   550
This is the season to give your cattle a half of their rations,
More to your workman: long are the nights, although kindly and useful.
Take good care of such things till the annual round is concluded
And days finally equal the nights in duration, when again will
Earth, who is mother of all, produce all her various first fruits.   555
Soon after Zeus has completed the wintry sixty days since the
Solstice, Arcturus,[22] forsaking the sacred river of Ocean,
First climbs brilliantly shining above the penumbra of evening.
Following after this star, King Pandion's daughter, the swallow[23]
Twittering shrilly emerges for men when the spring is beginning.   560
Pruning your vineyard is better before the swallow's appearance.
But when the snail with its portable domicile climbs up the plants from
Earth as it hides from the Pleiades—too late to dig up your vineyard,
Rather it's time to sharpen your sickle and rouse your serfs in the morning.
Shun comfy seats in the shade, shun lying abed until sunrise   565
During the season of harvest when sunlight burns your complexion:
Then you should busy yourself to bring home agricultural produce,
Getting up early to make quite sure that your livelihood's certain.
For early morning accounts for a good third part of your work day.
Morning advances a man on his way and advances his labor;   570
Morning's appearance advances so many men on their journey;
Morning's the hour for putting the yokes upon all of your oxen.

After the artichoke flowers and one-note grasshoppers sitting
Up in the leaves pour forth their melodious high-pitched singsong
Constantly under their wings in the wearisome heat of the summer,   575
Then are the goats at their fattest, and wine tastes best at the vintage,
Women are then their most wanton, but men are then very feeble,
Forasmuch Sirius scorches their heads and their knees in his ardor,
Also the skin dries out in the wearisome heat. At that time let
There be the shade of a rock and some wine from the vineyards of Biblis,[24]   580

Cakes that are moistened with fresh goat's milk when they're practically
   dried up,
Meat of a heifer that, fed in the woods, has not yet given birth,
Also of newborn kids. It is pleasant to drink of the bright wine,
Sitting at ease in the shade, one's appetite sated with good food,
Turning one's face in the western direction of cool-blowing Zephyr.   585
From the perennial spring that flows crystalline and unsullied,
Pour out three portions of water mixed with a fourth part of neat wine.
Set your domestics to winnow the sacred grain of Demeter,
Grinding it down at the first appearance of mighty Orion[25]
In a well-aerated place and over a well-polished threshing   590
Floor. When you've measured it, carefully put it up in bins built for storage.
When you have stored all your goods under lock and key in your own house,
Set about hiring a steward with no household of his own, and
Look for a maid with no child; one nursing a brat is a bother.

Also take care of the dog with the pointed teeth; don't begrudge him his   595
   rations,
Lest any burglar who sleeps by day should purloin your possessions.
Fodder and litter in plenty provide for your mules and your cattle.
Afterward, let your domestics unbend their knees, and release your two oxen.
Then when Orion and Sirius enter the center of heaven,
And when Arcturus is glimpsed through the roseate fingers of dawn,   600
Perses, it's time to snip all the bunches of grapes for the household,
Spread them outside in the sun ten days and ten nights altogether,
Cover them over for five days, then on the sixth day extracting
Into containers the gift of jolly and gay Dionysus.
But when the Pleiades set, and the Hyades,[26] also Orion,   605
Do not forget it is now full season for plowing and sowing;
May the good seed tuck snugly and generate under the topsoil.
If a desire for the comfortless dangers of seafaring grips you,
After the Pleiades, fleeing the crude, brute strength of Orion,
Tumble into the mist-covered sea, beware of the winds then,   610
Verily all of them gusting every which way in a tempest,
Then you should no longer keep ships out on the glistening water.
Take my advice, just remember that agriculture is safer.
Pull up your boat on the dry land, fill it with stones mighty tightly
On every side, to withstand the force of the wind when it's blowing   615
Wetly, and pull out the bilge plug, so the rain may not rot it.
Tidily stow all your tackle inside your house for the winter;
Put up the wings, that is, sails, of your seafaring ship very neatly,

Hang up your well-manufactured rudder to smoke in the fireplace.
See that you wait for the sailing season to make its appearance;   620
Thereupon drag out your swift ship down to sea, and aboard it
Place an appropriate cargo, and you'll sail home with a profit.
So it was, you great idiot Perses, my father and yours took
Ship more than once, as he lacked a respectable living on dry land,
Till on this spot he arrived after crossing the stretches of deep sea,   625
Leaving Aeolean Cyma[27] aboard a black vessel in flight from
Neither abundance nor riches nor blessed material plenty,
But that unbearable poverty Zeus has inflicted on humankind.
Our father settled near Helicon[28] Mount, in a miserable village,
Ascra: it's horrid in winter, obnoxious in summer, and never   630
Pleasant. So, Perses, remember your tasks, and especially sailing.
Though you admire a small craft, put all your freight in a big one,
Seeing the better the cargo, the better the profit compounded
Surely will be, if the wind holds back its malevolent blasts, and
If you would only convert your ridiculous leanings to commerce,   635
Eager to flee from debt and avoid insalubrious hunger.
Then I shall show you the measure and ways of the bellowing sea, though
I am no expert on nautical matters or nautical vessels,
For I have never by ship sailed over the breadth of the broad sea,
Ever, except to Euboea[29] from Aulis,[30] where the Achaeans   640
Waited all winter through great storms, till they had marshaled the people
Out of our own holy Hellas to Troy with its beautiful women.
Thence to the games that commemorate wise Amphidamas[31] I voyaged,
Coming at last unto Chalcis's widely advertised contests,
Games that the sons of that brave man had there established. I swear I   645
Bore off the poetry prize, a tripod with wrought-iron handles,
Which I devoted, of course, to the Muses of Helicon—there first
They had apprised me of clear-voiced music and poetry also.
That's the extent of my total acquaintance with nail-studded ships, but
Nevertheless, I can tell you the mind of Zeus, who is lord of the aegis,   650
Seeing the Muses have taught me to sing an incredible poem.
After the fiftieth day that follows the solstice of summer,
After the season of withering heat begins to be over,
That is the right time, Perses, for men to go sailing: you will not
Wreck at that season your boat, no seas will make off with your sailors,   655
Unless Poseidon, the earth shaker, acting with malice aforethought
Or Zeus, who is king of immortals, should want to destroy them:
For in their hands are the equal outcomes of good and of evil.
This is the season when winds are benign, and the sea is not harmful;

You can entrust yourself carelessly then to the care of the breezes;   660
Drag down your ship to the sea, and be sure there is everything on it.
Hurry in order to come as fast as you can to your homeland.
See you don't wait for the new wine, nor for the rains of the autumn,
Nor for the winter that follows the south wind's terrible tempests,
Stirring the sea up as they accompany copious rain squalls,   665
Zeus's autumnal gales that render the deep such a danger.
Spring is another occasion for laboring men to go sailing.
When for the first time leaves that unfold on the top of a fig tree
Look to a man the size of the footprints made by a crow, the
Sea then is open, and spring is a suitable season for sailing.   670
Not that I praise it, indeed; spring isn't my favorite sailing
Season, so snatched at, a time so hard to avoid a disaster.
Yet even then, in their ignorance, men sail, knowing no better,
Forasmuch property means more than life to unfortunate mortals.
Yes, it's a terrible thing to die in the midst of the billows.   675
Take, I beseech you, these matters to heart, as I counsel you, Perses.
Never put all of your livelihood down in the hold of a vessel;
Rather, reserving the bulk, entrust the remainder on shipboard.
It is a terrible thing to meet with disaster at sea, but
Even more terrible still to try overloading your wagon,   680
Breaking your axle in half and spilling and spoiling your cargo.
Measure is best in all matters; always observe due proportion.

Take to your dwelling a woman when you are the right age, not very
Much before thirty but not much later's the right age to marry
See that she's four years older than puberty; wed in her fifth year.   685
Marry a virgin to teach her all her respectable duties.
Most of all marry a woman who lives in your neighborhood, nearby.
Looking about you, be sure no neighbor makes fun of your marriage.
Surely a man can obtain nothing better at last than a woman
When she is good; if she's bad, there is nothing more thoroughly   690
     tiresome;
Keeping her eye on her dinner, she kippers[32] her husband (however
Strong) without smoke. She will give him a rude and uncomfortable old age.
Try to avoid the displeasure and wrath of the blessed immortals.
Do not consider your closest companion the same as a brother,
But if you do so, be sure that you aren't the first one to wrong him.   695
Do not prevaricate just for the sake of inventing a story.
Should he begin the offense with a word or a deed to insult you,
Do not forget to repay him doubly. But if he again will

Offer you friendship and wants to give satisfaction, receive him
Kindly. That man is a wretch who changes one friend for another   700
Any old time; but do not let your visage belie your emotions.
Do not be over hospitable, nor inhospitable neither,
Known as a friend of the wicked, nor as a detractor of good men.
Don't you go taunting a man with his poverty, though it's lamented,
Eating away at the heart: it's a gift of the blessed immortals.   705
Treasure most precious to mankind would be a tongue that is sober,
And the most beautiful pleasure is one enjoyed in proportion.
If you will speak any evil, you'll hear much more pretty quickly.
Do not be churlish and rude at a feast where guests are in plenty.
Pleasure is greatest in common, and your expense is much smaller.   710
Never at sunrise pour a libation of glistening wine to
Zeus or the other immortals with unwashed hands, or the gods will
Not be inclined to your prayers but spit them again in your own face.
One should not urinate facing the sun while standing erect, but
One should remember always to do it at sunset and sunrise.   715
Nor should you piss on the path or next to the path when out walking;
Nor should you do it when naked; nighttime belongs to the blessed.
Either a god-fearing man, wise, knowing, will squat when he pisses,
Or he will go to the inner wall of some fortified courtyard.
Don't go exposing your privates bespattered with sperm at the fireside,   720
Even inside your own house, so shamelessly; rather, avoid this.
When you return from a somewhat lugubrious funeral, do not
Aim to beget any children, but after a festival do it.
Do not cross over on foot the fair-running currents of ever-
Rolling rivers before you pray, as you gaze at the lovely   725
Waters and washing your hands in the clear and delectable liquid.
Someone who crosses a stream without washing his hands will encounter
Evil, divine retribution, and all sorts of troubles hereafter.
No one should clip off the dry tip next to the quick on his five-branched
Members[33] with glittering iron during the gods' celebrations.   730
Never position a ladle on top of a mixing bowl at a
Bibulous party; unmerited bad luck follows upon that.
When you are building a house, take care not to leave it unfinished.
Otherwise, raucous crows will be likely to perch on it, cawing.[34]
Don't take food or water for washing with out of a cauldron   735
Hallowed by none of the gods; such pots are extremely unlucky.
Do not permit any twelve-year-old boy to sit on an unmoved
Object: that isn't too good, depriving a male of his manhood;[35]
Nor any twelve-month-old child, for that has a similar outcome.

Do not perform your ablutions in bathwater used by a woman: 740
There is a nasty pollution attaching to that for a long time.
If you should happen upon some sacrifice that is still burning,
Do not make fun of the mystery: heaven takes vengeance on that, too.
Don't ever piss in the outlets of rivers that flow to the sea or
Piss into springs; on the contrary, see you strictly avoid it.   745
Do not relieve yourself therein; it isn't decent to do so.
Act in this way and evade the malicious talk of us humans.
Gossip, moreover, is evil, so light it is easily lifted,
Yet it is terribly painful and awfully hard to get rid of.
Nobody's talk is dispersed altogether as long as a lot of   750
People repeat it, for Gossip herself is some kind of a goddess.

Keeping the days that derive from Zeus in appropriate order,
Kindly inform your domestics about them, specifically that the
Thirtieth day of the month[36] is best for inspecting and handing
Out food. Wherever people correctly determine the truth, then   755
That is the calendar long ordained by the Giver of Counsel.[37]
Foremost, the first and the fourth and the seventh are days that are holy,
For on the seventh Latona[38] gave birth to Apollo, whose sword is
Gold. Furthermore, both the eighth and the ninth, two days in the final
Phase of the waxing moon, are propitious for human endeavors,   760
And the eleventh as well as the twelfth are alike very good days,
Either for shearing the sheep or for getting a generous crop in,
Though the twelfth day of the month is superior to the eleventh;
That is the day when the airborne spider is spinning her frail web
In broad daylight, the day when the shrewd ant garners her heap, and   765
Women on that day set up their looms to further their weaving.
Shun the thirteenth of the waxing month for beginning your sowing;
That is, however, the best time for setting your plants out,
And though the sixth of the midmonth isn't auspicious for planting,
Yet it is good for all male births, not so auspicious for females.   770
Neither when first they are born nor when they are given in marriage.
Nor in a month is the sixth day fit for the birth of a girl child,
Though it's a perfect occasion for castrating kids and mature rams,
Also a beautiful day for building a fence round a sheep pen.
This day favors the birth of a boy, who'll be fond of sarcastic   775
Talk and of lies and of devious murmurs and sly conversation.
Geld on the eighth of the month your boar and your bellowing bullock,
But on the twelfth you should rather castrate your hardworking donkey.
Then at noon on the glorious twentieth day will a sage be delivered;

Anyone born on this day will likely be terribly clever. 780
Fine is the tenth for the birth of a male, but the fourth of the midmonth
Favors a female. This too is a day to domesticate sheep and
Shambling short-horned cattle, along with a sharp-toothed dog and
Hardworking donkeys. So take them in hand. But beware, should it be the
Fourth of the month as it waxes and wanes, for a heartbreaking sorrow 785
Gnaws at the mind then: a day that is overabundantly fateful.
Bring home blithely your bride on the fourth of the month, but consult the
Avian omens for what is best in the business of marriage.
Stay off the fifth, which is difficult, terrible, dreary, and painful,
For on the fifth they say that the Furies attended the birth of 790
Oath,[39] who was borne by Discord to make all perjurers suffer.
Following careful inspection, scatter Demeter's devoted
Grain on the well-smoothed area, in the midmonth on the seventh.
Then let the woodcutter cut stout beams for construction of houses,
Many ships' timbers as well, adapted for shipbuilding rightly. 795
But on the fourth of the month undertake the construction of trim ships.
The ninth day in the midst of the month will get better at evening,
But the first ninth of the month is perfectly harmless for humans
This is an excellent day for planting the seed and for childbirth,
Whether for females or males; for the day's never totally evil. 800
Few people know that of days of the month twenty-seventh is best for
Opening jars[40] and the yoking of oxen and mules and swift horses,
Also for dragging a swift ship fitted with multiple benches
Down to the glistening sea. Few label this day by its real name.
Open a jar on the fourth in the midst of the month, of all days the 805
Holiest. Not many know that the best time of day of the twenty-
First is the coming of dawn; the evening is not so propitious.
These are the days that are notably profitable to us earthlings;
Others, like dice miscast, are unlucky, productive of nothing.
Everyone praises a different day, but few understand that 810
Sometimes a day is a stepmother, other times more like a mother.
Happy and lucky in days like these is a man understanding
All of these matters, who does his work and displeases no deathless
God, and is learned in bird lore,[41] never committing a trespass.
 Personification; oaths were, of course, as essential to law then as now.

NOTES

1. From Pieria in Macedonia, one of the many homes of the Muses, like Mount Helicon and Mount Parnassus, nearer Hesiod's home.
2. Otherwise unknown. Note on pronunciation: a last or next to last *e* is sounded, as in *Perses* and as in many feminine names, such as *Phoebe* and *Hermione*.
3. Weeds, greens.
4. Vulcan in Latin, the god of workmanship.
5. Venus in Latin, the goddess of love.
6. A many-eyed monster, which Hermes killed. It became a peacock. We still say "argus-eyed."
7. Stock epithet whose meaning is obscure: "who carries the goatskin"? "Who follows the lapwing or snipe that presages a storm"? We say "under the aegis of."
8. There is no earlier source for this account of human history in Greek, as there is nothing earlier than Hesiod, but parallel versions exist in Persian, Sanskrit, Babylonian, and Hebrew (for instance, Daniel 2:31ff).
9. The sons of King Oedipus fought over their patrimony in front of Thebes, which was founded by Cadmus.
10. When Helen was abducted by the Trojan prince Paris, her husband Menelaus marshaled the armies of Greece to reclaim her, thus launching the Trojan war. This and the preceding reference are to stories current before Hesiod's day, part of his poetic patrimony, also the material of poetry long afterward.
11. An alternative abode of the dead, usually reserved for heroes, distinct from the underworld, the house of Hades, or Tartarus. In Hesiod's time the known world was surrounded by the stream of Ocean, the father of waters.
12. A constellation, the seven sisters, whose name is derived from the Greek verb "to sail," as their rising signaled the sailing season.
13. Slavery was, of course, common in Hesiod's day, as it was in many societies until quite recently.
14. The dog-star, conspicuous at high summer, in hot weather.
15. A skilled workman.
16. They did not, of course, have sliced bread then, but broke it off the whole loaf.
17. Hesiod and his like, as far as we can tell from the poem and only from the poem, were free, landowning, modest agriculturalists, neither serfs nor gentleman farmers.
18. Midwinter.
19. North and northeast, roughly the Balkans and Romania.
20. A rare example of Hesiod's flight of fancy.
21. That is, supporting himself on a stick; a reference to the riddle of the Sphinx to Oedipus.
22. A star, "the bear-warden" which rises in early spring.

23. In another old story, Pandion's daughter Philomela was turned into a swallow. See Ovid, *Metamorphoses,* book 6.

24. In Thrace or on Naxos, or a varietal; not to be confused with Byblos in Phoenicia.

25. Another constellation, "the hunter," very visible even today.

26. The "rainy" constellation.

27. A small town on the northern coast of Asia Minor, or Aeolis.

28. One of the haunts of the Muses, near Ascra, a village that Hesiod put on the map.

29. The long island stretching down the east coast of Greece.

30. The small port on the mainland from which Greeks (Achaeans) embarked for Asia and Troy.

31. A prominent citizen, otherwise unknown, of Chalcis, the capital of Euboea.

32. That is to say, cures him or smokes him; smoking, an age-old method of preserving fish and meat, is the source of this metaphor.

33. An example of metonymy rather than metaphor; cutting the finger- or toenails.

34. In many cultures, crows are ominous, particularly of death.

35. Only a speculative anthropologist could begin to explain this and some of the other ritual dos and don'ts in Hesiod, but they are superstitions of the same sort as not spilling salt or stepping on a crack—equally inexplicable.

36. Wholly ignorant of the week, Hesiod divided the thirty-day month into three decades. Thus, "the first ninth" is the ninth day of the first ten-day division, and so forth. He also counted by the waning and waxing moon.

37. One of the titles of Zeus.

38. Latin name of Leto; see index.

39. Grain, as well as oil and wine, was stored in jars in the ancient world.

40. Some think that Hesiod here was preparing the transition to a work on ornithomancy, the existence of which ancient opinion denies.

Politeia *of the Spartans*

॒॒॒॒॒॒॒॒॒॒॒॒॒॒॒॒॒॒

By Xenophon
Translated by J. M. Moore

I

I was reflecting one day on the fact that, although Sparta has one of the smallest populations, it has become the most powerful and famous of all Greek states, and I wondered how this could have come about. However, when I examined the way of life of the Spartiates, I ceased to be surprised. None the less I do admire Lycurgus, the man who established the laws under which they flourished; I consider him a remarkably wise man. Not merely did he not imitate other states, but he adopted opposite institutions to the majority with outstandingly successful results.

Let us begin our survey at the very beginning, with the begetting of children. In other cities, the girls who are to become mothers, and are brought up in the approved fashion, are reared on the simplest possible diet, and with a minimum of luxury foods; they either drink no wine at all, or only drink it diluted. Girls are expected to imitate the usually sedentary life of craftsmen, and to work their wool sitting quietly. How could one expect girls brought up in such a way to produce outstanding offspring? Lycurgus felt that slave girls were perfectly capable of producing garments, and that the most important job of free women was to bear children; he therefore decreed that women should take as much trouble over physical fitness as men. Moreover, he instituted contests of speed and strength for women parallel to those for men, on the grounds that if both parents were strong the offspring would be more sturdy. He saw that, generally, husbands spent a disproportionate amount of time with their wives when they were first married, and decreed the opposite here too, for he made it disgraceful for a man to be seen entering or leaving his wife's apartment. Thus their desire would inevitably be heightened when they did meet, and any offspring which might result would therefore be stronger than if the parents were surfeited with each other. Furthermore, he did not allow men to take wives as and when they wished, but decreed that marriage should take place at the period of physical prime, thinking that this also was likely to produce fine children. He realised that old men with young wives tend to be particularly jealous, and again made the opposite customary, for he made it possible for an old man to introduce to his wife a man whose appearance and character he approved and so have children. Further, if a man did not wish to live with a wife, but wanted children worthy of note, Lycurgus made it legal for him to select a woman who was noble and the mother of fine children, and, if he obtained the husband's consent, to have children by her. He approved many such arrangements, for the women wish to run two households, and the men to get more brothers for their children—brothers who will share in the honour and position of the family, but will make no financial claims. Lycurgus thus took the opposite position to the rest of the Greeks on the begetting of children; it is up to the observer to decide whether he managed to make the Spartans outstanding in stature and strength.

II

Having discussed the subject of birth, I wish to turn to the educational systems of Sparta and the rest of Greece. Outside Sparta, those who claim to educate their children best put servants in charge of them as *paidagogoi* as soon as the children can understand what is said to them, and immediately send them to teachers to learn to read and write, to study the arts, and to practise gymnastics. Moreover, they soften their children's feet by giving them shoes, and weaken their bodies by changes of clothes; their diet is limited only by their capacity. Instead of leaving each man to appoint a slave *paidagogos* privately for his children, Lycurgus put in charge of all of them a man who was drawn from the same class as those who hold the major offices of state; he is called the *Paidonomos,* and Lycurgus gave him authority to assemble the children, inspect them and punish any faults severely. This official was also given a group of young men provided with whips for floggings where necessary; the result is considerable respect and obedience there. Instead of softening their feet with shoes, Lycurgus decreed that they should harden them by going barefoot; he believed that if this were their practice, they would climb more easily, go downhill more sure-footedly, and that a man would leap, jump up and run more swiftly barefoot than wearing shoes, as long as his feet were accustomed to it. Instead of pampering them in matters of dress, he decreed that they should habitually wear one garment all the year round to make them more tolerant of heat and cold. He laid down each Eiren's contribution at such a level that nobody should be burdened by overeating or be without experience of going short. He thought that those brought up under such a regime would be better able to labour on without food if the situation demanded it, and to hold out longer on the same rations if ordered to do so; they would miss delicacies less, be less interested in food altogether, and live a healthier life. He thought that food which tended to produce slimmer figures would make them grow taller, rather than that which produces fat. To prevent their being too distressed by hunger, while he did not make it possible for them to take whatever they wanted without trouble, he did permit them to steal something to alleviate their hunger. As I am sure everyone realises, he did not allow them to feed themselves through their own resourcefulness because he lacked the means of providing for them. Obviously, a man who intends to steal must stay awake at night, and deceive and lie in ambush during the day, and if he is to succeed he must also have spies out. It is clear then that he included this element in their education to make the boys more resourceful in obtaining the necessities of life, and more suited for war. Someone may ask why, if he thought theft a good thing, he decreed a severe flogging for anyone who was caught. My answer is that this is parallel to the way in which punishment is always handed out for not carrying out well what one is taught—those who are caught they punish for stealing badly. Lycurgus made it honourable to steal as many cheeses as possible from the altar of Artemis Orthia, and detailed others to whip the thieves in the process, wishing to demonstrate in this way that a brief moment's pain can bring the joy of enduring fame. This shows that where speed is needed the idler gains nothing except a mass of trouble. To prevent the children being without control even if the supervisor left them, Lycurgus laid it down that any citizen who was present could give the boys whatever instructions seemed necessary, and punish any misconduct. By this means he produced more respect in the boys; in fact, adults and boys alike respect nothing more than the men who are in charge of them in order that they might not be without someone in charge even when there was no adult present, he put the keenest of the Eirens in charge of each company; therefore boys at Sparta are never without someone to control them.

It seems that I must say something also about affection for boys since this too is relevant to education. Elsewhere there are varying practices: in Boeotia, men and boys live together as if they were married; in Elis, they attract a young man by favours;[1] again, there are states where men are absolutely forbidden even to speak to boys in these circumstances. Lycurgus yet again took a totally different course; if an honourable man admired a boy's character, and wished to become his friend in all innocence, and spend time with him, he approved, and thought this a very fine form of education. If, however, a man was clearly physically attracted to a boy, he classed this as a heinous disgrace, and so ensured that in Sparta there is no more physical love between men and boys than there is between parents and children or brother and brother. I am not surprised that some find this difficult to believe, for many cities tolerate love between men and boys.

Such, then, are the educational systems of Sparta and of the other Greek States; which of them produces men who are more obedient, respectful and self-controlled is again for the reader to decide.

III

When a boy begins to grow up, the other Greeks release him from his *paidogogos* and no longer send him to school; no one controls him, and he is totally his own master. Lycurgus again chose the opposite. Realising that at this age pride is greatest, insolence

---

1 Or possibly: 'in Elis they win short periods with young men by favours'

at its height and temptations towards pleasures most insistent, he selected this period in which to subject them to the most demanding regime, and arranged for them to have as little free time as possible. By adding the provision that if anyone should avoid this stage of the training he should be deprived of all future privileges, he ensured that not merely those appointed by the state but also those who cared for each individual would take care that the boys did not, by shrinking from these duties, utterly destroy their standing in the city. Apart from this, because he wanted modesty to be firmly implanted in them, he decreed that they should keep their hands inside their cloaks in public, walk in silence, and not look about them, but keep their eyes fixed on the ground in front of their feet. Here it has become clear that in self-control as well as other fields men are stronger than women—you would be more likely to hear a stone statue speak than them, more likely to catch a wandering glance from a bronze figure, and would think them even more modest than the pupil of the eye.[2] At the common meals you have to be content if you can even get an answer to a question.

Such, then, was his care for those who were growing up.

IV

He took by far the greatest care about those who had just reached manhood, thinking that if they became the sort of people they ought to be, they would have a very great influence for good in the city. He realised that the greater the rivalry involved, the better choruses are to listen to and athletic contests to watch; therefore, he thought that if he could induce a spirit of competition among the young in the field of virtue, this would bring them to the highest levels of manliness. I will explain how he brought it about. The Ephors pick three men in their prime who are called *Hippagretai;* each of these chooses a hundred men, giving his reasons for choosing some and rejecting others. Those who do not achieve this honour are at odds with those who rejected them and with those selected instead of them, and keep a close watch on each other for any lapse from the accepted standards of honour. This is the strife most favoured by the gods and most beneficial to the city, since it demonstrates what a good man ought to do; each group individually aims at being outstanding, and collectively they protect the city with all their might if the need arises. The are compelled to take care of their physical fitness, for this strife leads to scuffles wherever they meet; however, any passer-by has the right to separate the combatants. If such an order is disobeyed, the *Paidonomos* takes the offender to the Ephors, who punish him severely, wishing to ensure that passion never becomes stronger than obedience to the laws.

---

2 Accepting a reading found only in ancient quotations, this sentence contains an untranslatable (and very frigid) play on words; the Greek word translated 'pupil' normally means 'maiden'—hence Xenophon plays on the modesty of a 'maiden' who has no chance of being anything but modest, and also gives a strict parallel to the other two illustrations.

The men who have reached maturity, who also fill the highest offices in the state, are relieved by the other Greeks of the duty of preserving their fitness, although they are still required to undertake military service. Lycurgus, on the other hand, established the principle that hunting was the noblest occupation for them, unless prevented by public duties, so that they, no less than the young men, should be able to stand the strain of campaigning.

V

After this description of the occupations laid down by Lycurgus for each stage of a Spartan's development, I will now try to describe the type of life which he arranged for everyone. The Spartiates were in the habit of living at home like the other Greeks, and he realised that this led to considerable neglect of duty; he therefore instituted public messes, believing that this would be the most effective check on disobedience. He specified a quantity of food which would not be too much nor leave them short; however, many unexpected additions come from huntings and rich men sometimes contribute wheat cakes instead. The result is that as long as they are together their table is never without food, and yet is not extravagant. He stopped anything involving compulsory drinking, which harms the body and fuddles the wits, but permitted each to drink when he was thirsty, believing this to be the least harmful and most pleasant form of drinking. When men live together like this, how could anyone ruin himself or his family through gluttony or drunkenness? In other cities it is usually contemporaries who meet, and in their company there is the minimum of restraint; Lycurgus mingled the age groups in Sparta so that the younger learn from their more experienced elders.[3] It is customary for noble deeds in the city to be recounted in the messes, with the result that there is the minimum of insolence, drunkenness, wickedness or foul talk there. The custom of eating in public has a further beneficial consequence, in that men are compelled to walk home; they know that they will not spend the night where they eat, and must be careful not to stumble through drink; they must walk during the night as they do by day, and men of military age may not even use a torch.

Lycurgus realised that the same food gives someone who is working a good colour, health and strength, but makes an idle man fat, flabby and feeble. He did not neglect this either, but, noticing that even when someone works hard of his own free will in doing his duty, he clearly stays satisfactorily fit, he required the senior members of each gymnasium to ensure that the rations were not out of proportion to the exercise under-taken.[4] In my judgement he was again right; it would be difficult to find a healthier or

---

3 There appears to be an omission in this sentence; a suggested restoration has been incorporated in the translation.

4 The text of this sentence is uncertain; the translation contains a possible free interpretation.

physically more well-developed people than the Spartans, for they exercise their legs, arms and necks equally.

VI

Another field in which Lycurgus' institutions differed from the normal was that of authority; in other cities each man controls his own children, servants and property, but Lycurgus, because he wished the citizens to benefit from each other without doing any harm, gave fathers equal authority over all children, whether their own or those of others. When a man realises that such men have the authority of fathers, he will inevitably control those he has authority over as he would wish his own sons to be controlled.[5] If a boy tells his father that he has been beaten by another man, it is a disgrace for his own father not to beat him too—to such an extent do they trust each other not to give improper commands to the children. Lycurgus made it possible for someone to use another man's servants in case of need, and established a similar system of sharing hunting dogs; those who need dogs invite the owner to join them, and if he has not time himself, he lends his pack with pleasure. Similarly with horses, when someone is ill, needs a carriage, or has to get somewhere quickly, if he sees a horse, he takes it, uses it carefully and returns it. Another unique custom concerns hunting parties which are caught out late and need food but, have none prepared; they open sealed caches of food which others, according to Lycurgus' rule, have left ready after eating, take what they need, and reseal them.[6] Because they share in this way, even those who are not well off have some part in all the resources of the country when they need something.

VII

There is yet another respect in which Lycurgus' institutions are unique in Greece. In other states, everyone, I suppose, makes as much money as he can; one farms, another is a ship-owner, another is a merchant, and others follow trades for their living. In Sparta Lycurgus forbad the free citizens to have anything to do with making money, and ordered them to devote themselves solely to activities which ensure liberty for cities. Anyway, what need was there to worry about wealth in a society where the establishment of equal contributions to the messes and a uniform standard of living excluded the search for wealth in order to obtain luxury? They do not even need wealth for clothes, since, for them, adornment is not rich fabrics but bodily health. Money is not even to be acquired to spend on the other members of one's mess; he made working physically to help one's companions more honourable than spending money to this end, showing that the former involves the use of character, the latter of wealth.

---

5   The text of this sentence is uncertain; the translation contains a possible free interpretation.

6   Freely translated to make the sense clear.

He prevented the acquiring of money by dishonesty. First, he established a currency such that even ten minas could not be brought into the house without the knowledge of the master and servants—it would take up a lot of space, and need a wagon to move it. There are also searches for gold and silver, and if any is found, the possessor is punished. Why, then, should anyone devote himself to making money when the pains of possessing it must outweigh the pleasure to be had from spending it?

VIII

Everyone knows the outstanding obedience of the Spartans to their rulers and laws; in my view, however, Lycurgus did not even try to instil this discipline until he had secured agreement among the leading men of the state. I deduce this from the fact that in other cities the most powerful citizens do not even wish to give the impression that they are afraid of the magistrates, thinking that this is illiberal, while in Sparta the leading citizens show the greatest respect for the magistrates, and pride themselves on being humble, and running rather than walking in answer to a summons. They think that if they set an example of exaggerated obedience the rest will follow; this has proved to be the case. It is likely that these same people helped to establish the power of the Ephorate. They realised that obedience was of vital importance in the city, in the army and in the home, and they thought that the greater the power of the office, the more likely it was to over-awe the people. Ephors have the right to inflict punishments at will, to require immediate payment of fines, to depose magistrates during their term of office, to imprison them, and even to put them on trial for their lives. Since they have so much power, they do not always allow office-holders to complete their year of office as they see fit, as is done in other cities, but, like tyrants or presidents of the games, they punish an offender as soon as the offence is detected. Among many other excellent ways in which Lycurgus encouraged the citizens to obey the laws willingly, one of the finest seems to me the fact that he did not deliver his laws to the people before going to Delphi with the leading citizens, and asking the oracle whether it would be more desirable and better for Sparta to be governed under his proposed laws. Only when the reply was that it would be better in every way did he deliver his laws; thus he made it not merely illegal but sacrilegious to disobey laws sanctioned by Delphi.

IX

Another aspect of Lycurgus' institutions which may properly be a source of wonder is his establishment of the principle that a noble death is preferable to living in dishonour. Investigation shows that fewer of those who believe this are killed than of those who choose to retreat from danger. In fact, one is more likely to avoid an early death through courage than cowardice, for courage is easier, more pleasant, more resourceful and stronger. Manifestly glory goes particularly with valour, for all wish somehow to be the allies of the brave. It is proper not to omit the means by which Lycurgus achieved this; he made it clear that the reward for the brave would be happiness, for the cowardly misery. In other cities the coward suffers nothing more than the stigma of cowardice—he goes to the same market-place as the brave man, sits with him, and attends the same gymnasium if he wishes. In Sparta anyone would think it a disgrace to take a coward into his mess or be matched against him in a wrestling bout. When teams are being selected for the *sphairai* contests, such a man is often not picked, and in the chorus he is relegated to the most ignominious position; he must give way to others in the street, and rise even for younger men when seated. He must keep the unmarried women of his family at home, and answer to them for the disadvantages his cowardice inflicts on them;[7] he must endure a house without a wife, and yet pay the penalty for being a bachelor. He must not go about the city looking cheerful, nor must he imitate those who are without reproach; if he does, he must submit to a beating from his betters. When such disabilities are attendant on cowardice, I am not surprised that Spartans prefer death to such a deprived and disgraceful existence.

X

The provision by which Lycurgus required men to practise virtue even into old age seems to me good. By placing selection for the *Gerousia* toward the very end of life he ensured that they would not neglect the virtues of an upright life even in old age. The protection he offered to good men past their prime is also worthy of admiration; by putting the members of the *Gerousia* in charge of capital trials he made old age more honourable than the strength of youth. The contest for the *Gerousia* is correctly regarded as the most important that a man can enter. Gymnastic contests are noble, but they depend on the body; selection for the *Gerousia* depends on nobility of character Just as the character is more important than the body, so rivalries hinging on it are worth more effort than physical contests.

Another admirable feature of Lycurgus' institutions was based on his realisation that where the encouragement of virtue is left to individual initiative the result is not sufficient to promote the good of the state; he therefore decreed that all citizens must practise all the virtues in public life. Just as individually those who practise virtue surpass those who disregard it, so it is reasonable that Sparta is outstanding above all cities in virtue because she is the only one where nobility is consciously practised in public life. For is it not also noble that, where other cities punish a man for wronging someone, Lycurgus decreed no less severe penalties for a man who openly did not live as nobly as possible? His principle, it seems, was that if someone enslaves people, deprives them of something or steals, then only those who are directly harmed are wronged, but that wickedness and cowardice are a betrayal of the whole city. It

---

7   Or: 'answer to them for the fact that they are unmarried'.

therefore seems to me right that they should receive the severest punishment. He laid down an inflexible requirement to practise all political virtue. Those who carried out their legal duties were given an equal share in the life of the states. He did not take into account physical infirmity or poverty; if anyone shrank from fulfilling what was required of him, Lycurgus decreed that he should no longer even be considered one of the *Homoioi*. It is obvious that these laws are very old, for Lycurgus is said to have lived at the time of the sons of Heracles. Old as they are, they are very strange to the other Greeks; it is a most extraordinary phenomenon that they all praise such practices, but no city is willing to imitate them.

XI

The aspects I have discussed up to now are blessings common to times of peace and war; I will now demonstrate how Lycurgus' arrangements are superior to those of other states for military purposes. First, the Ephors proclaim, the age-groups to be called up, listing cavalry and infantry, and then also craftsmen, with the result that the Spartans have a sound supply of everything which is available in the city while on campaign as well. All equipment that the army needs centrally is specified, to be produced on wagons or baggage animals; in this way omissions are least likely to be overlooked. He devised the following costume for battle: red cloaks, thinking that this was least effeminate and most warlike and bronze shields since they are quickest to polish and slow to tarnish. He also allowed those who were grown up to wear their hair long, on the basis that they would thus appear taller, more noble, and more terrifying.

Having equipped them in this way, he divided infantry and cavalry into six regiments. Each infantry regiment has one commanding officer, four company commanders, eight section officers and sixteen junior officers. At the word of command, each regiment forms up in platoons two,[8] three or six abreast. The prevalent impression that Spartan formation under arms is extremely complicated is the opposite of the truth; the front rank man in the Spartan formation is in command, and each file is self-sufficient.[9] The formation is so easy to understand that anyone who can recognise another man cannot go wrong, for some are designated to lead, others to follow. Deployments are ordered by the junior officers orally, acting as heralds, and the depth of the line of battle is established as they deploy. There is nothing remotely difficult to learn in this. However, to fight on with whoever is at hand after the line has been disrupted is a secret not easily mastered except by those trained under the system of Lycurgus. The Spartans also carry out with considerable ease manoeuvres which instructors in tactics think very difficult. When they are marching in column, obviously with every platoon following the one in front, if an enemy force appears in front of them, the word is passed to the junior officers to deploy

---

8   This number is missing from the text; two is the most likely restoration, though single file is possible.

9   There is some doubt about the exact text here which renders the sense doubtful.

to the left, and so down the column until the line is drawn up facing the enemy. If the enemy appears from the rear when the Spartans are in this formation, each file takes up reverse order so that the best men always face the enemy. The fact that the leader thus finds himself on the left is not regarded as a disadvantage, but on occasions as a positive gain; should the enemy attempt an encircling movement they would do so not on the unprotected side but on the shield side. If it seems right at any time or for any reason for the commander to have the right wing, they reverse the stations of the army by countermarching until the commander is on the right wing and the rearguard on the left. If the enemy appear on the right flank while the Spartans are in column, they just swing each company to face them head on, like a trireme; thus the rear ranks occupy the right wing. They are no more disturbed by an enemy appearing on the left, but run forward,[10] or swing the companies to face them; this time the rear company will be on the left.

XII

A word about the type of camp approved by Lycurgus. Because he realised that the corners of a square were useless, he used a circular camp except where a hill provided security, or there was a wall or river in the rear. By day sentries were stationed by the arms dumps looking inwards, for they watch out for friends, not enemies. Cavalry keep watch for the enemy from points where they have as wide a view as possible to detect an enemy approach. By night the Skiritai were assigned to the outposts around the main force, though now this duty may also be undertaken by mercenaries if there happen to be any present. One must be quite clear that the rule that spears should always be carried has the same purpose as the banning of slaves from the arms dumps, and the fact that those who leave their posts for necessary purposes go only so far from their companions and their weapons as they must to avoid giving offence; the common basis is safety. They change the sites of their camps frequently to harm the enemy and help their friends. It is laid down that all Spartans must take exercise all the while they are on campaign, with the result that they improve their own splendid physique and appear more dignified than other men. The exercise area and running track must not exceed in size the area covered by the camp so that no one may get far from his arms. After exercise the senior officer present has the order given to sit down; this is a form of inspection; after this comes the order to break their fast, and to relieve the outposts quickly. There follow amusements and a period of relaxation before the evening exercise. The order is then given for the evening meal, and, after singing a hymn to the gods to whom they have sacrificed with good omens, to rest by their arms.

There is no cause for surprise in the length of my account; it would be very difficult to find anything meriting attention in military matters which the Spartans have overlooked.

----

10   There is some doubt about the exact text here which renders the sense doubtful.

XIII

I will now describe the power and the honour which Lycurgus decreed for the king on campaign. First, the king and his entourage are maintained at public expense when in the field. The regimental commanders eat with the king, so that, since they are always present, they may take a larger part in any necessary deliberations. Three others of the *Homoioi* also eat with them and see to their every need, so that nothing may distract them from concentrating on matters connected with the war.

But I will go back to the beginning, to the moment when the king leaves the city with the army. First, he sacrifices in Sparta to Zeus the Leader and to the gods associated with him. If the omens here are good, the fire-bearer takes fire from the altar and leads the way to the frontiers of the state. There the king sacrifices again to Zeus and Athena; when the omens from both are good, then he crosses the frontier. The fire from these sacrifices is carried in front, and never put out, and sacrificial victims of all sorts follow. Whenever the king sacrifices, he starts the rites before dawn, wishing to obtain the favour of the gods before the enemy. There are present at the sacrifice the regimental and the company commanders and the section officers, the commanders of foreign detachments and of the baggage train, and any of the commanders of the detachments from individual cities who wish to be present. Two of the Ephors are also present, but take no part unless the king invites them to do so; needless to say, by watching each man's conduct they exercise a restraining hand on all. When the sacrifice is over, the king summons everyone and issues the orders for the day. Watching this, one might think that the other Greeks were amateurs in military matters, and the Spartans the only true professionals. When the king is leading the army, if no enemy appear, nobody marches in front of him except the Skiritai and cavalry outriders. If they expect a battle, the king takes the first company of the first regiment and wheels to the right until he takes up his position between two regiments and two regimental commanders. The senior member of the king's council arranges the necessary supporting troops. The council consists of the *Homoioi* who share the king's mess, prophets, doctors, *aulos*-players, the commanders of the army and any volunteers present. There is therefore no problem about making the necessary arrangements, for nothing is unforeseen. Other Lycurgan provisions affecting battles seem to me useful: when a goat is sacrificed with the enemy already in sight, it is the custom that all the *aulos*-players present should play and all the Spartans wear garlands; all armour must be polished. Young men are also permitted to go into battle with their hair oiled, looking cheerful and impressive. Words of encouragement are spoken by the junior officers, for not even a whole platoon can hear the words of the junior officer of the next platoon. The regimental commander is responsible for seeing that the process is effectively carried out. When they decide that it is time to camp, the king is in charge, and indicates the site; however, he has no authority to despatch embassies, whether to friends or enemies. All are subject to the king's authority when they have any business to transact. Lawsuits are referred by the king to the *Hellanodikai* applications for money to the treasurers, and any booty which is brought in is handed over to the auctioneers. With this system, the king is left with no duties on campaign except those of a priest in the religious field and a general in human affairs.

XV*

I would also like to describe the agreement which Lycurgus made between king and state. The royal authority at Sparta is the only one which remains to-day unchanged in its original form; investigation would show that all other constitutions have undergone modifications and are even now in the process of change. He laid it down that the king should make all public sacrifices for the state because of his divine descent, and should lead the army on any foreign campaign. He granted the king the choice parts of the sacrificial victims, and set aside enough land in many of the surrounding cities to ensure that he was not without adequate means, and yet was not too rich. So that the kings should eat in public, he established a state *sussition* for them; he also honoured them with a double portion at meals, not so that they should eat twice as much but so that they should have the means of honouring anyone they wished. He also gave them the right of choosing two companions each for their *sussition,* who are called *Puthioi.* They also received the right to take one pig from each litter, so that a king would never be without victims should he need to consult the gods. A spring near their houses provides a plentiful supply of water; those without such an amenity will realise its manifold uses. Everyone stands when the king enters except Ephors seated on their official thrones. Oaths are exchanged every month, the Ephors swearing on behalf of the city, the king for himself. The king swears to rule according to the established laws of the city, the city to maintain the royal authority unimpaired as long as the king keeps his oath. Such are the honours the king receives in Sparta during his lifetime; they do not greatly exceed the position of a private citizen. Lycurgus did not wish to encourage a tyrannical attitude in the kings, nor to make the people envy their power. The honours given to a king after death by Lycurgus' legislation are intended to demonstrate that kings of Sparta are honoured not as men but as heroes.

XIV

If someone were to ask me whether I felt that the laws of Lycurgus still remained un-changed, I could not confidently say yes. I know that in the past the Spartans preferred to stay in Sparta in moderate prosperity rather than expose themselves to the flattery and corruption involved in governing other cities. In the past they were afraid of being proved to have gold, but there are those now who even pride themselves on possessing

---

* Chapter XIV appears to be an intrusion in its present position, and may well be a later addition to the main treatise; it is therefore printed at the end.

some. In the past the purpose of the expulsion of foreigners and the ban on foreign travel was to prevent citizens from being infected with idleness by foreigners; now I understand that the apparent leaders of the state are eager to govern foreign cities for the rest of their lives. There was a time when they worked to be worthy to lead, but now they are far more interested in ruling than in being worthy of their position. This is the reason why whereas formerly the Greeks used to come to the Spartans and ask them for leadership against reputed wrongdoers, now many are encouraging each other to prevent a revival of Spartan power. There is, however, no cause for surprise that such reproaches are being cast at them; they obviously do not obey either the gods or the laws of Lycurgus.

The Constitution of the Athenians
(Sections 42–69)

By Aristotle
Translation by J. M. Moore

XLII

The constitution of the present day is as follows. Full citizenship belongs to men both of whose parents were citizens, and they are inscribed on the list with their fellow demesmen when they are eighteen years old. When they are being registered, the members of the deme vote under oath first on whether they appear to have reached the legal age, and, if they do not, they are returned to the status of children, and secondly on whether a man is free and born as the laws prescribe. If they decide that he is not free, he appeals to the dikasterion; while the demesmen select five of their number as accusers; if it is decided that he has no right to be registered as a citizen the city sells him into slavery, but if he wins his case, the demesmen are required to register him. Then the Boule reviews those who have been registered, and if it is decided that a man is younger than eighteen, the demesmen who registered him are fined. When the Ephebes have been approved, their fathers meet by tribes and choose under oath three members of the tribe over forty years old whom they consider best and most suitable to take charge of the Ephebes, and from them the people elect one for each tribe as guardian, and they elect a controller from the rest of the citizen body for all of them. These men take the Ephebes, and after visiting the temples they go to the Peiraeus and take up guard duties, some at Munichia and others at Akte. The people also elect two trainers for them, and two men to teach them to fight in armour, and to use the bow, the javelin and the catapult. The guardians receive a drachma each for their maintenance and the Ephebes four obols. Each guardian receives the allowances for the members of his tribe and buys what is necessary for them all centrally (for they live together by tribes), and takes care of everything else for them. This is how they spend the first year of their training. At the beginning of the second at a meeting of the *Ekklesia* held in the theatre they demonstrate to the people their knowledge of warfare and receive a shield and spear from the city. For the year thereafter they patrol the countryside and man the guard posts. For their two years service they wear the military cloak, and are exempt from all duties. They cannot prosecute or be prosecuted so that there may be no reason for their leaving their post; the only exception is to deal with matters of inheritance or an *epikleros,* or to take up a priesthood hereditary in a man's family. After this two years, they join the main citizen body.

XLIII

That is how citizens are registered and Ephebes trained. The holders of all routine offices in the state are selected by lot except for the treasurer of the military funds, the controllers of the Theoric Fund and the supervisor of the water supply. These are elected, and hold office from one Penathenaic festival to the next. All military officials are also elected.

The *Boule* of 500 members is selected by lot, 50 from each tribe. Each tribe acts as Prytany in an order decided by lot, the first four for thirty-six days each, the last six for thirty-five, for they work by a lunar year. The Prytanies eat together in the Tholos at the city's expense, and summon meetings of the *Boule* and *Ekklesia;* the *Boule* meets every day except for holidays, the *Ekklesia* four times in every prytany. They publish the agenda and place for each meeting of the *Boule,* and also draw up the agenda for the *Ekklesia.* In each prytany the *Ekklesia* meets for one plenary session, in which there-must be a vote on whether all office-holders have performed their duties well; there must also be discussions of the corn supply and the safety of Attica; those who wish to bring impeachments do so at this meeting, lists of confiscated property are read out, and also claims to inheritances and to marry *epikleroi,* so that nobody may be ignorant of any unclaimed estates. In the sixth prytany, in addition to the business already discussed, they put to the vote the question of whether an ostracism should be held, and hear accusations against informers, whether Athenians or metics (with a limit of three of each), and allegations against anyone who has failed to fulfil an undertaking made to the city. The second meeting must hear petitioners, and anyone who wishes may appear as a suppliant on any subject he chooses, private or public, and address the people on it. The other two meetings deal with other matters, amongst which the law prescribes the consideration of three motions about sacred matters, three concerning heralds and embassies, and three about secular matters. On occasions they also consider matters without a preliminary vote. Heralds and ambassadors report to the Prytanies first, and despatches are delivered to them.

XLIV

One man is picked as chairman of the Prytanies by lot, and holds office for a night and a day; he cannot preside for longer, nor can the same man serve twice. He holds the keys of the sanctuaries where the treasure and the public records are kept; he holds the city's seal, and must remain in the Tholos with one third of the Prytanies selected by him. When the Prytanies summon a meeting of the *Boule* or *Ekklesia,* he casts lots for nine chairmen, one from each tribe except the one supplying the Prytany; he casts lots again among the nine for the man who will actually preside, and he hands over the agenda to them. The nine take over, and are responsible for good order, put forward topics for discussion, assess the voting, and control everything else. They also have the right to adjourn the meeting. An individual may not preside at a meeting more than once in a year, nor be one of the nine chairmen more than once in each prytany.

They elect *strategoi,* cavalry commanders and other military officers in the *Ekklesia* in accordance with the will of the people; the elections are held on the first meeting after the sixth prytany when the omens are favourable. There must also be a preliminary resolution to hold the elections.

XLV

In former times the *Boule* had powers of punishment by fine, imprisonment or execution. Once when the *Boule* had handed Lusimachos over to the public executioner and he was already sitting waiting for the sentence to be carried out, Eumelides of Alopeke saved him, saying that no citizen ought to be executed without a vote of the *dikasterion.* When *dikasterion* heard the case, Lusimachos was acquitted and was nicknamed 'the man who escaped the rod'. The people deprived the *Boule* of all powers of fine, imprisonment or execution, and passed a law that if the *Boule* condemned a man or punished him, the *Thesmothetai* were to bring the condemnations or punishments before the *dikasterion* and their decision should be final

The *Boule* conducts the investigations into the conduct of the great majority of the magistrates, particularly those who handle money; their decision is not final, but subject to appeal to the *dikasterion.* Private citizens can bring a charge of acting illegally against any office holder they wish; he has a right of appeal to the *dikaster-ion* if condemned by the *Boule.* It also considers the credentials of the following year's *Boule* and of the nine Archons; in the past, their decision was final, but now there is a right of appeal to the *dikasterion* for those disqualified

In these matters, then, the *Boule* does not have the final decision, but it holds a preliminary discussion on everything that is to come before the people, nor can the people vote on anything that has not been previously discussed by them and put on the agenda by the Prytanies. Anyone who violates this law is liable to a prosecution for an illegal proposal.

XLVI

The *Boule* is in charge of the completed triremes, the tackle stores and the tackle stores and the ship sheds, and builds new triremes or quadriremes, whichever the people vote to construct, and tackle and ship sheds for them, but the people elect the naval architects for the ships. If the *Boule* do not hand them over to the new *Boule* completed, they cannot receive the usual reward, for they receive the reward under the next *Boule*. The triremes are constructed under the supervision of a board of ten members of the *Boule*. The *Boule* inspects all public buildings, and if it decides that someone has committed an offence, it reports him to the people, and hands him over to the *dikasterion* if they find him guilty.

XLVII

The *Boule* also joins the other magistrates in most areas of the administration. First, there are ten Treasurers of Athena, one picked by lot from each tribe; in accordance with Solon's law (which is still in force) they must be *pentakosiomedimnoi*, but the man picked by lot holds; office even if he is very poor. These officers take over in front of the *Boule* the image of Athena and the Victories, and the other ceremonial equipment and the money. Then there are the ten *poletai* picked by lot, one from each tribe. They let out all the public contracts, sell the right to work the mines, and left the rights of collecting taxes with the treasurer of military affairs and those in charge of the Theoric Fund; this is done in front of the *Boule*. They confirm the position of anyone elected by the *Boule,* and matters concerning mining leases which have been sold, both those where rights of exploitation have been sold for a period of three years and those where special agreements cover a period of ten years. They sell the property of those exiled by the Areopagus and of other exiles before the *Boule* and the nine Archons confirm the transaction. They list on whitened boards taxes sold for a period of a year with the name of the buyer and the price. They hand the boards over to the *Boule*. They list separately on ten boards those who have to pay their instalments every prytany, on three boards those who have to pay three times a year, and on a separate list those who pay once a year in the ninth prytany. They also list the properties and. houses confiscated and sold in the *dikasterion,* for they are responsible for their sale. The price of a house must be paid in five years, of land in ten; these payments are made in the ninth prytany. The King Archon produces a list of the leases of the sacred estates on whitened boards; they are leased for a period of ten years, and the rent is payable in the ninth prytany. For this reason a great deal of money is collected in this prytany. Lists of the payments due are deposited with the *Boule,* and the state secretary keeps them; when a payment is due, he takes from the pigeon holes the list of those whose payments are due on this particular day, and whose entry must be cancelled after payment and hands it over to the Receivers; the other lists are stored separately so that nothing may be prematurely cancelled.

XLVIII

There are ten Receivers, one picked by lot per tribe; they take the list, and in front of the *Boule* in its chamber erase the record of the money that has been paid, and return the records to the state secretary. If anyone fails to pay an instalment, his name is recorded there, and he has to pay double the arrears under penalty of imprisonment. The *Boule* has the legal right to exact the money or imprison the defaulter. On one day they receive all the payments and divide the money among the magistrates, and on the next they bring a record of their actions on a board and read it out in the chamber. They also pose the question in the *Boule* whether anyone knows of any malpractice by a magistrate or a private citizen in the division; if anyone is suspected, there is a vote on the case.

The members of the *Boule* select ten of their number by lot as auditors to check the accounts of the magistrates every prytany. They also select by lot one man from each tribe for the *euthuna* and two assistants for each of them. They are required to sit each market-day[1] by the statue of the eponymous hero of their tribe, and if any-one wishes to bring a charge, whether of public misdemeanour or private malfeasance, against any of those who have undergone the *euthuna* in the *dikasterion* within three days of that hearing, he records on a whitened board the names of the accuser and the defendant, the charge, and the fine which he considers suitable, and hands it to the representative of his tribe. The latter takes it and reads it, and if he considers the charge justified, he hands a private suit to the deme justices who prepare cases for the relevant tribe for the courts, while if it is a public offence, he reports the matter to the *Thesmothetai*. If the *Thesmothetai* take it over, they reopen the examination of this man before the *dikasterion,* and the decision of the jury is final.

XLIX

The *Boule* also reviews the horses, and if a man appears to have a good horse but to be maintaining it badly, deprives him of his maintenance allowance. Horses which cannot keep up, or will not remain in line but run away, are branded with a wheel on the jaw, and are disqualified. They also review the mounted skirmishers to find who seem to be suitable for this, and anyone they vote against loses his horse. They also review the infantry attached to the cavalry, and anyone voted against loses his pay. The cavalry are enrolled by a board of ten elected by the people for this purpose; the names of those enrolled are handed to the cavalry commanders and the commanders of the tribal cavalry units who receive the list and bring it before the *Boule*. They open the document in which the names of the cavalrymen are recorded, and erase the names of those previously enrolled who swear that they are prevented by physical disability from

---

1 The word translated as 'market-day' may not be the correct restoration of a damaged part of the papyrus, but no convincing alternative has yet been suggested.

serving as cavalry. Then they call those newly enrolled, and if anyone swears that he is physically or financially incapable of serving, they dismiss him. Those who do not take this oath are subject to a vote by the *Boule* as to their suitability for cavalry service; if they are approved, they are enrolled. If not they are dismissed.

The *Boule* used to take decisions about the models and the robe, but this is now done by a *dikasterion* selected by lot, for it was felt that the *Boule* was swayed by personal feelings. The *Boule* joins the treasurer of military affairs in supervising the making, affairs in supervising the making of the statues of Victory and the prizes for the Panathenaia.

The *Boule* also reviews the incapable; for there is a law that anyone with property of less than three minae who suffers from a physical disability which prevents his undertaking any employment should come before the *Boule*, and if his claim is approved he should receive two obols a day subsistence from public funds. There is a treasurer selected by lot to handle this.

The *Boule* also cooperates with the other magistrates in most of what they do

L

Those then are the areas of administration handled by the *Boule.*

A board of ten are also selected by lot to take care of the sanctuaries; they are given thirty minae by the Receivers, and repair the temples most in need of attention. There are ten city commissioners of whom five hold office in the Peiraeus and five in the city itself. They see that the girls who play the flute, the harp or the lyre are not hired for more than two drachmae; if more than one man wishes to hire the same performer, they cast lots, and allocate her to the winner. They ensure that the dung collectors do not deposit dung within ten stades of the walls, and see that no building either obstructs or has balconies overhanging the streets; they also prevent the construction of waste pipes with outfalls from above into the street, or windows with shutters opening into the road. With assistants provided by the state, they remove the corpses of those who die in the streets.

LI

Ten superintendents of the markets are selected by lot, five for the Peiraeus and five for the city. They are required by law to supervise goods for sale to ensure that merchandise is pure and unadulterated. Ten inspectors of weights and measures are similarly selected, five for the city and five for the Pelraeus to ensure that honest weights and measures are used by those who are selling. There used to be ten commissioners in charge of the corn supply, picked by lot, of whom five were allocated to the Pelraeus and five to the city, but there are now twenty for the city and fifteen for the Pelraeus. They ensure first that there is no sharp practice in the selling of unprepared corn in the market, secondly that the millers should sell their barley flour at a price corresponding to that of unmilled barley, and thirdly that the bakers should sell loaves at a price corresponding to the price of wheat, and containing the full weight which the commissioners have laid down as the law requires them to do. They also pick by lot ten commissioners of trade to supervise trading and ensure that two-thirds of the corn imported is brought to the city.

LII

The Eleven whose duty it is to take care of prisoners are selected by lot. They execute thieves, kidnappers and who confess their guilt, while is they deny the charge, they bring them before the *dikasterion* and if they are acquitted let them go, and if not put them to death after their trial. They report to the *dikasterion* land and houses listed as belonging to the city, and hand over to the *poletai* any that is judged to be public property. It is also part of their duties to bring summary indictments before the *dikasterion* though the *Thesmotheiai* also introduce some similar indictments.

Five men are picked by lot to introduce cases which are to be settled within a months each of whom covers two tribes. Cases falling in this category include failure to pay a dowry which is owed, failure to repay a loan made at an interest of a drachma per mina, or a loan of capital made to finance the opening of a business in the market; prosecutions for assault, cases involving friendly loans, cooperative ventures, slaves, animals, trierarchies and banking matters. These officials introduce within the month cases of these classes, while the Receivers handle cases involving tax-farming, with the power to make a final decision in cases up to ten drachmae; they refer the remainder to the *dikasterion* for settlement with in the month.

LIII

The Forty are picked by lot, four from each tribe, and other suits are brought before them. They used to be a board of thirty, and travel round the demes to try cases, but after the tyranny of the Thirty their numbers were increased to forty. They can make the final decision in cases involving up to ten drachmae, but anything above that they hand over to the Arbitrators. These officials then take the case, and if they cannot bring about a settlement, give a decision; if the decision satisfies both sides and they accept it, the case is ended. If one party appeals to the *dikasterion* the Arbitrators place the depositions, the challenges and the relevant laws in boxes, one for each side in the case, seal the boxes, add the decision of the Arbitrator written on a tablet, and hand everything over to the four members of the Forty who handle the cases of the tribe of the defendant. They take them over, and bring the case before the *dikasterion* cases of less than 1,000 drachmae before a jury of 201 members, those over 1,000 before 401 jurors. At the hearing it is forbidden to use laws, challenges or depositions other than those used in front of the, Arbitrator and sealed in the boxes. The Arbitrators are men in their sixtieth year; their age is known from the Archons and the eponymous heroes. There are ten eponymous heroes for the tribes, and forty-two for the age-groups; the Ephebes' names are recorded together with the Archon under whom they were enrolled and the eponymous hero of the previous year's Arbitrators; this used to be done on whitened boards, but they now use a bronze plaque which is set up in front of the chamber of the *Boule* by the statues of the eponymous heroes. The Forty take the list under the name of the last of the eponymous heroes, and allot to those on the list the cases for arbitration and cast lots to decide which each will decide. The man selected is required to arbitrate as directed, for the law provides that if any man fails to serve as an Arbitrator when his age-group is performing this duty he shall lose his citizen rights, unless he happens to hold public office that year or to be abroad; only these categories are exempt.

Information can be laid before the Arbitrators as a body if anyone is wronged by an individual Arbitrator, and the penalty laid down by law for anyone condemned under this procedure is loss of citizen right; there is a right of appeal. They also use the names of the eponymous heroes for military service; when they send an age-group on campaign, they publish a notice saying that the groups from one Archon and eponymous hero to another are called up for service.

LIV

The following offices are also filled by lot : five commissioners of roads, whose duty it is to employ the slaves provided by the city to repair the road. Ten Auditors and ten assistants for them, to whom all those who have held public office must submit their accounts; this is the only body which audits the accounts of those subject to the *euthuna* and submits the results to the *dikasterion*. If they detect anyone who has been guilty of embezzlement, the jury condemns him for theft of public money, and he is sentenced to pay ten times the amount stolen; if they demonstrate that anyone has taken bribes and the jury convicts him, they assess the size of the bribe, and again he pays ten times this amount. If they condemn him for maladministration, they assess the amount, and this is what he pays as long as he pays up before the ninth prytany; if not, the sum is doubled. Fines of ten times the amount involved in the offence are not doubled.

They cast lots for the officer called Clerk to the Prytanies, who is in charge of the Prytanies, who is in charge of the documents, keeps the decrees which have been passed, checks the transcription of everything else, and attends meeting of the *Boule*. In earlier days this official was elected and they used to elect the most famous and reliable men; their names are recorded on the inscribed texts of alliances, and grants of *proxenia* and citizenship; now they are selected by lot. They also pick another man by lot to look after laws; he attends the *Boule* and also checks all transcriptions. The people elect the clerk whose duty it is to read out documents in the *Ekklesia* and *Boule,* and this is his only duty.

Ten sacred officials are elected who are called 'those in charge of expiation'; they make sacrifices ordered by oracles, and if good omens are required they see to it with the prophets. Another ten religious officials are selected by lot, called 'those in charge of annual rites'; they offer certain sacrifices and are in charge of all four- yearly festivals except for the Panathenala. The four-yearly festivals are: 1. the mission to Delos (which is also celebrated every six years); 2. the Brauronla; 3. the Heracleia; 4. the Eleusinia; 5. the Panathenaia; none of these festivals occurs in the same place. The Hephaistia was added to the group in the Archonship of Kephisophon.

An Archon is appointed for Salamis and a demarch for the Pelraeus by lot; they celebrate the Dionysia in each place, and appoint the *choregoi* in Salamis the name of the Archon is recorded.

LV

The holders of the above offices are selected by lot, and their duties are those listed above. As to the so-called nine Archons, I have already described their original ways of appointment; to-day, six *Thesmothetai* and their secretary and also the Archon, the King Archon and the Polemarch are appointed by lot from each tribe rotation. Their qualifications for office are checked first in the *Boule* of 500, except for the secretary, whose qualifications are checked only in the *dikasterion* as happens for other office holders–for all officials, whether selected by lot or elected, have their qualifications checked before they take up office; the nine Archons have to go before both the *Boule* and the *dikasterion*. In the past a man who was disqualified by the *Boule* could not hold office, but now there is an appeal to the *dikasterion* and the final decision is taken there. When they are checking qualifications, they ask first: 'Who is your father, and what is your deme? Who was your father's father, and who was your mother, and her father and his deme?' Then they ask whether the candidate is enrolled in a cult of Apollo Patroos and Zeus Herkeios, and where the shrines are, then whether he has family tombs and where they are; whether he treats his parents well, pays his taxes, and has gone on campaign when required. When these questions have been asked, the candidate is required to call witnesses to his answers. When he has produced the witnesses, the question is put: 'Does anyone wish to bring any charge against this man?' If an accuser appears, the accusation and defence are heard, and then the matter is put to the vote by a show of hands in the *Boule* or a ballot if the hearing is in the *dikasterion*. If no one wishes to bring an accusation, the vote is held immediately. In former times, only one ceremonial vote was cast,[2] but now everyone is required to vote on candidates, so that if a criminal has managed get rid of all his accusers it is still in the power of the jurors to disqualify him. After this investigation, the candidates go to the stone on which are the parts of the sacrificial victim, and standing on it they swear to administer their office

---

2   That is, where no charge was brought, a single, formal vote of acquittal was all that was required.

justly and in accordance with the laws, and not to take bribes in connection with their office, and if they do, to dedicate a golden statue. At this stone also the Arbitrators give their decisions on oath and witnesses swear[3] to their depositions. After taking the oath the candidates go to the Acropolis, and repeat the same oath there; after that they take up their office.

LVI

The Archon, the King Archon and the Polemarch each have two assessors of their own choice, and these men have their credentials checked in the *dikasterion* before they take up their positions, and are subject to the *euthuna* in respect of their tenure.

As soon as the Archon takes up office, he proclaims that every man shall hold and control until the end of the year such property as he held before he took office. Then he appoints for the tragedians three *choregoi* who are the richest of all the Athenians; formerly he appointed five for the comedians, but now the tribes provide for them. Then he receives the *choregoi* appointed by the tribes, those for the men's and the boys' choruses and the comedies at the Dionysia, and for the men's and boys' choruses at the Thargella; those for the Dionysia are each provided by one tribe, but two tribes combine, for the Thargella, each of the tribes serving in turn. The Archon then arranges exchanges of property, and presents any claims for exemption which may arise if a man claims either to have performed this liturgy before, or to be exempt on the grounds of having performed another liturgy after which his period of exemption has not yet passed, or not to be of the required age—for the *choregoi* of the boys' chorus must be over forty years old. The Archon also appoints *choregoi* for Delos, and a chief of the sacred embassy to take the young people on the thirty-oared vessel. He is also in charge of the procession to Asclepius when the initiated hold a vigil, and the procession at the Great Dionysia. In arranging the latter he is aided by ten assistants who used to be elected by the people and meet the cost of the procession out of their own pockets, but now are picked by lot, one from each tribe, and receive a hundred minae for their expenses. The Archon also organises the processions at the Thargelia and to Zeus Soter; he organises the contests at the Dionysia and the Thargelia. These are the festivals which he organises. Some civil and criminal proceedings come before the Archon; he holds a preliminary hearing, and then introduces them into the *dikasterion*. They include cases of illtreating parents, in which the prosecutor is immune from penalty; accusations of offences against orphans, which are brought against the guardians, and of offences against *epikleroi*, which are brought against the guardians and the people living with the *epikleroi*; accusations of mismanaging the estate of an orphan, which are also brought against the guardians; charges of insanity where it is alleged that a man is wasting his substance because he is of unsound mind, and requests for the

---

3   See note on this translation in the commentary.

appointment of officials to divide up property where a person is unwilling to share out what is held in common; requests, to constitute or decide a wardship, for production in court, for enrolment as a guardian, and claims to estates and *epikleroi*. He also looks after orphans, *epikleroi,* and widows who declare themselves pregnant after the death of their husbands. He has the power to fine offenders or bring them before the *dikasterion.* He rents out the houses of orphans and *epikleroi* until they are fourteen years old, and takes security for the leases; he exacts maintenance from guardians who do not provide it for children in their care.

LVII

These matters are the province of the Archon. The King Archon supervises the Mysteries together with assistants elected by the people, two of whom are elected from the whole citizen body, one from the family of the Eumolpidai, and one from the Kerukes. Secondly he has charge of the festival of Dionysus called the Lenaia, which involves a procession and contest. The King Archon and his assistants jointly arrange the procession, but the contest is in his hands alone. He also arranges all torch-races and virtually all the traditional sacrifices. Cases of impiety come before him and disputes over priesthoods. He also decides all disputes about religious matters which arise between the clans or the priests; all cases of homicide come before him, and he it is who proclaims the exclusion of an individual from customary ceremonies. Charges of murder or wounding where a man deliberately kills or injures someone are heard before the Areopagus, as are cases of poisoning which result in death, and cases of arson; these are the only cases decided by that body. Charges of unintentional homicide, conspiracy to kill, and the killing of a slave, metic or foreigner are heard by the Court of the Palladion. Where a man admits to having killed someone but claims that his action was lawful, as for example where a man admits to having killed someone but claims that his action was lawful, as for example if he caught an adulterer in the act, or killed unwittingly in war or in the course of the games, the case is heard in the Delphinion. If a man has retired into exile in a situation where reconciliation is possible and is then accused of killing or wounding someone, his case is heard in the court of Phreatto, and he pleads his case from a boat anchored near the shore. Except for cases brought before the Areopagus, all these cases are tried by *Epheiai* selected by lot; the case is brought before the court by the King Archon, and the hearing is held in a sacred area out of doors; during the case the King Archon does not wear his crown. At all other times the defendant is excluded from all sanctuaries, and is even barred by law from the Agora, but for the trial he enters the sacred area and makes his defence. When the offender is not known, the proceedings are held against 'the guilty party'. The King Archon and the Tribal Kings also proceed against inanimate objects and animals.

LVIII

The Polemarch makes the sacrifices to Artemis the huntress and to Enualios, and arranges the funeral games in honour of those who have fallen in war, and makes the offerings to Harmodius and Aristogeiton. He hears only private suits which involve metics, tax-exempt metics and *proxenoi*; it is his duty to take them and divide them into ten groups, and to assign by lot one group to each of the ten tribes, and the jurors of the tribe must then bring them before the Arbitrators. The Polemarch himself introduces cases where a man is accused of disregarding his patron or not having one, and also cases involving inheritance and *epikleroi* of the metics; in other respects, the Polemarch performs for the metics the same duties as the Archon performs for citizens.

LIX

The *Thesmothetai* are responsible first for announcing the days on which the *dikasteria* will sit, and then for allotting the magistrates to the courts; the latter bring cases to court as the *Thesmothetai* direct. They bring impeachments and motions for the deposition of magistrates before the *Ekklesia,* and they introduce all accusations brought in the *Ekklesia,* indictments for illegal proposals and accusations of having proposed laws against the interests of the state, indictments against the chairmen or president, and the *euthunai* of the *strategoi.* They hear cases where the prosecutor has to make a deposit, including charges of wrongly claiming citizen rights, or using bribery to this end, which arises when a man uses bribery to escape a charge of wrongly claiming to be a citizen, charges of malicious prosecution, bribery, false entry in the lists of state debtors, falsely witnessing a summons, failure to erase the name of a debtor who has paid, non-registration of a debtor, and adultery. They also introduce the investigations into the credentials of all candidates for office, the appeals of those whose registration has been refused by their demes, and condemnations sent for confirmation by the *Boule.* They also introduce private suits involving trade or the mines, and cases where a slave is accused of slandering a free man. They allocate courts to the magistrates by lot for public and private suits. They validate international agreements and introduce cases arising under them, and also charges of bearing false witness in the Arepagus.

The selection of the jurors by lot is done by all the nine Archons tighter with the secretary of the *Thesmothetai,* each handling his own tribe.

LX

Such then is the position of the nine Archons.

Ten commissioners are also selected by lot to run the games, one from each tribe. When they have passed the preliminary examination, they hold office for four years, and they organise the procession at the Panathenaia, the musical contest, the athletics and the horse races, and they arrange the making of Athena's robe and the vases for prizes in conjunction with the *Boule;* they also give olive oil to the athletes. This oil comes from the sacred olives, and the Archon collects three-quarters of a pint per tree from the owners of the land in which they grow. In the past the city used to sell the fruit, and if anyone dug up or cut down one of the sacred olives, he was tried before the Areopagus and the penalty for those found guilty was death. Ever since the owner of the land has paid the contribution of oil, the law has remained in force, but the penalty has been allowed to lapse. The oil is now levied as a tax on the property, not collected from the trees themselves. The Archon collects the oil due in his year of office, and hands it over to the Treasurers for storage on the Acropolis; he is not allowed to take his seat in the Areopagus until he has handed over the full amount to the stewards. At other times the stewards keep the oil on the Acropolis, but at the time of the Panathenaia they measure it out to the commissioners of the games, who give it to the winning contestants. The prizes for those who win the musical contests are of silver and gold, for those who win the contests in manliness, shields, but for those who win the athletic events and the horse races, olive oil.

LXI

All military offices are also filled by election. There are ten *strategoi* who once were elected one from each tribe, but are now elected from the whole people. They are allocated by show of hands, one to the hoplites, to command on any expedition, and one to patrol Attica and to fight any enemy who invades the country; two are stationed in the Peiraeus, one in Munichia and one in Akte—their duty is to guard the Peiraeus; one is in charge of the symmories, and enrols the trierarchs, arranges any exchanges of property for them, and introduces cases where there are disputes to the *dikasteria;* the remainder are despatched to deal with any situation that may arise. There is a vote in every prytany on their conduct of their office, and if the people vote against a man, he is tried in the *dikasterion* and if condemned., the jury assesses the appropriate penalty or fine, while if he is acquitted he resumes his position. When in command of troops, they have the power to imprison anyone for insubordination to discharge him, and to impose a fine, though this last is not usual.

Also elected are ten regimental commanders, one for each tribe; they lead their fellow tribesmen, and appoint the subordinate officers. Two cavalry commanders are also elected from the whole citizen body; they lead the cavalry, divided into two units of five tribes each. They have the same authority over their men as the *strategoi* have over the hoplites, and are likewise subject to a monthly vote on their conduct. They also elect ten tribal commanders, one per tribe, to command the cavalry just as the regimental commanders command the hoplites. They elect a cavalry commander for Lemnos to command the cavalry there, and a steward for the 'Paralos' and another for the 'Ammonis'

LXII

The magistrates chosen by lot were formerly divided into two groups, those who, with the nine Archons, were selected from whole tribes, and those were selected from the demes in the Theseum. However, when corruption affected the choices of the demes, the selection of the latter officers was transferred to the whole tribe also, except that members of the *Boule* and the guards are still selected by demes.

The citizens receive the following fees for public services: at ordinary meetings of the *Ekklesia* a drachma, but nine obols for the plenary session; jurors receive three obols, while members of the *Boule* receive five, and the Prytanies a sixth for their maintenance. The nine Archons receive four obols each for maintenance and have a herald and *aulos*-player to maintain and the Archon of Salamis gets a drachma a day. The commissioners of the games receive their meals in the Prytanelon in the month of Hecatombalon during the Panathenaia, starting from the fourth day of the month. The sacred commissioners to Delos receive a drachma a day from Belos, and the officers sent out to Samos, Scyros, Lemnos or Imbros receive money for maintenance.

Military offices may be held repeatedly but no other office may be held more than once, except that a man may sit in the *Boule* twice.

LXIII

The allocation of *dikasiai* to the *dikasteria* is conducted by the nine Archons for their respective tribes, and the secretary of the *Thesmothetai* handles the tenth tribe. There are ten entrances into the *dikasteria*, one for each tribe, twenty allotment machines, two for each tribe, one hundred boxes, ten for each tribe, and other boxes into which are thrown the tickets of the *dikasiai* who have been successful in the ballot. There are two urns by the entrance to each court, and staves equal to the number of *dikasiai* required; the same number of ballot balls are thrown into the urns as there are staves, and the balls have letters written on them starting with the eleventh of the alphabet, *Λ*, the number of letters corresponding with the number of courts to be filled. Those over thirty years of age may sit as *dikastai* as long as they are not public debtors and have not lost their citizen rights. If a man who is disqualified sits, information is laid against him and he is brought before the *dikasterion;* if he is found guilty, the jury assess whatever penalty or fine seems to them appropriate, and if it is a fine, he must be imprisoned until he has paid the previous debt on the grounds of which he was indicted and the additional fine imposed by the *dikasterion.* Each *dikastes* has a ticket of boxwood with his name, his father's name and his deme written on it, together with one of the first ten letters of the alphabet, those up to K; the *dikastai* of each tribe are divided into ten roughly equal sections under the ten letters. The *Thesmothetes* draw lots for the letters which are to be placed by each court, and his servant puts the relevant letter up in each case.

LXIV

The ten boxes stand in front of the entrance for each tribe, and the letters up to K are inscribed on them. When the *dikastai* throw their tickets into the box which has the same letter on it as is on their ticket, the servant shakes the boxes and the *Thesmothetes* draws one ticket from each. The man drawn is called the ticket-inserter, and inserts the tickets from the box into the column over which is the same letter as there is on the box. This man is selected by lot to prevent malpractice if the same man should always make the draw. There are five columns of slots in each allotment machine. When the Archon has put the cubes into the machines, he draws lots for each tribe according to the allotment machines. The cubes are bronze, some white, some black; he puts in as many white cubes as *dikastai* are needed, one per five columns, and black cubes in the same proportion. When the Archon takes out the cubes, the herald calls the men who have been selected; the ticket-inserter is included in their number. When a man has been called, he steps forward and draws a ball from the urns, and holds it out with the letter upwards, and shows it first to the presiding Archon. The Archon then puts the man's ticket into the box on which is the letter which is on the ball, so that he shall go to the court which he has drawn by lot, not the one he wishes to sit in, and it may not be possible for anyone to arrange to have the jury he wishes. There are beside the Archon as many boxes as there are courts to be manned, each with the letter on it which has been allocated to the relevant court.

LXV

When the *dikastes* has shown his ball to the servant, he goes inside the inner door. The servant gives him a staff of the same colour as that of the court whose letter was the same as the one on his ball, so that he is compelled to sit in the court to which he has been allotted. If he goes into a different court, the colour of the staff gives him away, for a colour is painted on the lintel of the entrance of each court. He takes his staff and goes into the court whose colour corresponds to-his staff and whose letter is the same as that on his ball, and when he enters he receives an official token from the man selected by lot to distribute them. The *dikastai* then take their seats with their ball and staff having got into court in the manner described above. The ticket-inserters return their tickets to those who have been unsuccessful in the ballot. The public servants from each tribe hand over the boxes of each tribe, one for each court, in which are the names of the members of each tribe who are sitting in each court. They hand them over to those who have been selected by lot to return them to the *dikastai* in each court, so that they may summon them by using their tickets, and so give them their pay. There are five of these officials.[4]

---

4   The number is missing in the text; cf. lxvi,3 and Commentary.

LXVI

When all the courts have their requisite juries, two allotment machines are set up in the first court, with bronze cubes on which are the colours of the courts and other cubes on which the names of the Archons are written. Two *Thesmothetai* picked by lot separately put the cubes in the machines, one putting the colours into one machine, the other the names of the Archons into the other. The herald announces whichever magistrate is picked first as allocated to the court which is drawn first, and the second to the second, and so on, so that no magistrate may know where he is to preside but each will preside over the one he draws by lot.

When the *dikastai* have arrived and been allocated to their courts, the presiding magistrate in each court draws one ticket from each box, so that he has ten, one from each tribe, and puts these tickets into an empty box, and draws five of these, and of the five drawn one super vises the water clock and the other four the voting, so that nobody may interfere either with the man in charge of the clock or those in charge of the voting, and there may be no chicanery in these matters. The remaining five of the ten drawn receive instructions detailing how and where the jury will receive their pay in the court itself; this is done separately by tribes after they have fulfilled their duties, so that they may receive it in small groups and not cause trouble because there are a lot of people crowded together.

LXVII

After these preparations, they call the cases. If they are dealing with private cases, they call four, one from each of the categories defined by law, and the litigants take an oath to speak to the point; when they deal with public cases, they summon the litigants, but deal with only one case.

There are water clocks with narrow tubes attached; they pour the prescribed amount of water into them, and this decides the length of time allowed for the speeches. They allow ten measures for cases involving over 5,000 drachmae, with three measures for the supporting speech, seven measures for those up to 5,000, with two for the supporting speech, and five and two for those under 1,000; six measures are allowed for the deciding of disputed claims, and second speeches are not allowed. The man in charge of the water clock cuts off the flow of water when the clerk is going to read out a decree, law, piece of evidence or contract. If however, parts of the day's hearing have been allocated to each side, then he does not cut it off, but an equal period of time is allowed to the prosecutor and the defendant. The standard of division is the length of the day in the month of Poseideon …

The following section of the papyrus is so badly mutilated that the text cannot be reconstructed; the only section of which something may be made is:

... The day is divided into proportionate parts ... for contests where the penalty laid down on conviction is imprisonment death, exile, loss of citizen rights or confiscation of property. ...

There follows a further mutilated section of papyrus.

LXVIII

The majority of the juries are of five hundred members ... but when it is necessary for public suits to have a jury of 1,000, two juries are combined in the *Heliaia*. The votes are cast votes are cast with tokens of bronze which have a pipe through the middle, half of them pierced and half blocked. At the conclusion of the speeches, those chosen to supervise the voting give each member of the jury two tokens, one pierced and one blocked, showing them clearly to the litigants so that the jury do not receive either two pierced tokens or two blocked ones. Then the designated official takes the staffs, in return for which each *dikastes* when he casts his vote deceives a bronze tag with the number three on it, for when he hands it in he receives three obols; this is to ensure that all vote, for no one can receive a tag without voting. There are two containers in the court, one of bronze and one of wood; they can be taken apart so that nobody can introduce votes into them fraudulently before the voting begins. The *dikastai* cast their votes in them, the bronze container counting while the wooden is for the vote which is not used. The bronze one has a lid with a hole in it through which only one token can pass, so that the same man may not insert two tokens into it. When the jury are about to vote, the herald first asks whether the contestants wish to protest at any of the evidence, for protests cannot be lodged after voting has commenced. Then he makes a second announcement: 'The pierced token for the first speaker, the solid for the second.' The *dikastes* takes the tokens from the stand, holding the pipe in the token so that he does not show the litigants which is pierced and which Is not; he places the token that counts in the bronze container and the other in the wooden one.

LXIX

When the voting is complete the servants take the container which counts and pour out the contents onto frame a frame which has as many holes in it as there are votes so that it may be easy to add up the tokens which county both the pierced and solid ones. Those selected by lot for the task count them up on the board, separating the solid from the pierced, and the herald announces the number of votes cast, the pierced for the prosecutor and the solid for the defendant Whichever gets more votes wins, while if the votes are equal the verdict goes to the defendant. If it is necessary, they then assess a penalty by voting in the same way; for this the *dikastai* return their tags and take back their staffs. Each side is allowed half a measure of water for their speeches at this stage.

When the *dikastai* have fulfilled their duties as required by law, they take their fees in the part of the building assigned to them.

Oedipus the King

回回回回回回回回回回回回回回

By Sophocles
Translated by Ian Johnston

TRANSLATOR'S NOTE

In the following text the numbers in square brackets refer to the Greek text; the numbers without brackets refer to the English text. The asterisks indicate links to explanatory notes inserted by the translator.

BACKGROUND NOTE

Sophocles (495 BC-405 BC) was a famous and successful Athenian writer of tragedies in his own lifetime. Of his 120 plays, only 7 have survived. Oedipus the King, also called Oedipus Tyrannos or Oedipus Rex, written around 420 BC, has long been regarded not only as his finest play but also as the purest and most powerful expression of Greek tragic drama.

Oedipus, a stranger to Thebes, became king of the city after the murder of king Laius, about fifteen or sixteen years before the start of the play. He was offered the throne because he was successful in saving the city from the Sphinx, an event referred to repeatedly in the text of the play. He married Laius' widow, Jocasta, and had four children with her, two sons, Eteocles and Polyneices, and two daughters, Antigone and Ismene.

DRAMATIS PERSONAE

OEDIPUS: king of Thebes
PRIEST: the high priest of Thebes
CREON: Oedipus' brother-in-law
CHORUS of Theban elders
TEIRESIAS: an old blind prophet
BOY: attendant on Teiresias
JOCASTA: wife of Oedipus, sister of Creon
MESSENGER: an old man
SERVANT: an old shepherd
SECOND MESSENGER: a servant of Oedipus

Sophocles, "Oedipus the King." Translation by Ian Johnston. Permission granted by the translator.

ANTIGONE: daughter of Oedipus and Jocasta, a child
ISMENE: daughter of Oedipus and Jocasta, a child
SERVANTS and ATTENDANTS on Oedipus and Jocasta

[The action takes place in Thebes in front of the royal palace. The main doors are directly facing the audience. There are altars beside the doors. A crowd of citizens carrying branches decorated with laurel garlands and wool and led by the PRIEST has gathered in front of the altars, with some people sitting on the altar steps. OEDIPUS enters through the palace doors]

OEDIPUS: My children, latest generation born from Cadmus,
    why are you sitting here with wreathed sticks
    in supplication to me, while the city
    fills with incense, chants, and cries of pain?[1]
    Children, it would not be appropriate for me
    to learn of this from any other source,
    so I have come in person—I, Oedipus,
    whose fame all men acknowledge. But you there,
    old man, tell me—you seem to be the one
    who ought to speak for those assembled here.   10   [10]
    What feeling brings you to me—fear or desire?
    You can be confident that I will help.
    I shall assist you willingly in every way.
    I would be a hard-hearted man indeed,
    if I did not pity suppliants like these.

PRIEST: Oedipus, ruler of my native land,
    you see how people here of every age
    are crouching down around your altars,
    some fledglings barely strong enough to fly
    and others bent by age, with priests as well—   20
    for I'm priest of Zeus—and these ones here,
    the pick of all our youth. The other groups
    sit in the market place with suppliant sticks
    or else in front of Pallas' two shrines,   [20]
    or where Ismenus prophesies with fire.[2]
    For our city, as you yourself can see,
    is badly shaken—she cannot raise her head
    above the depths of so much surging death.
    Disease infects fruit blossoms in our land,
    disease infects our herds of grazing cattle,   30

makes women in labour lose their children.
And deadly pestilence, that fiery god,
swoops down to blast the city, emptying
the House of Cadmus, and fills black Hades   [30]
with groans and howls. These children and myself
now sit here by your home, not because we think
you're equal to the gods. No. We judge you
the first of men in what happens in this life
and in our interactions with the gods.
For you came here, to our Cadmeian city,   40
and freed us from the tribute we were paying
to that cruel singer—and yet you knew
no more than we did and had not been taught.[3]
In their stories, the people testify
how, with gods' help, you gave us back our lives.
So now, Oedipus, our king, most powerful   [40]
in all men's eyes, we're here as suppliants,
all begging you to find some help for us,
either by listening to a heavenly voice,
or learning from some other human being.   50
For, in my view, men of experience
provide advice which gives the best results.
So now, you best of men, raise up our state.
Act to consolidate your fame, for now,
thanks to your eagerness in earlier days,
the city celebrates you as its saviour.
Don't let our memory of your ruling here   [50]
declare that we were first set right again,
and later fell. No. Restore our city,
so that it stands secure. In those times past   60
you brought us joy—and with good omens, too.
Be that same man today. If you're to rule
as you are doing now, it's better to be king
in a land of men than in a desert.
An empty ship or city wall is nothing
if no men share your life together there.

OEDIPUS: My poor children, I know why you have come—
    I am not ignorant of what you yearn for.
    For I well know that you are ill, and yet,   [60]
    sick as you are, there is not one of you   70

whose illness equals mine. Your agony
comes to each one of you as his alone,
a special pain for him and no one else.
But the soul inside me sorrows for myself,
and for the city, and for you—all together.
You are not rousing me from a deep sleep.
You must know I've been shedding many tears
and, in my wandering thoughts, exploring
many pathways. After a careful search
I followed up the one thing I could find   80
and acted on it. So I have sent away
my brother-in-law, son of Menoeceus,
Creon, to Pythian Apollo's shrine,   [70]
to learn from him what I might do or say
to save our city. But when I count the days—
the time he's been away—I now worry
what he's doing. For he's been gone too long,
well past the time he should have taken.
But when he comes, I'll be a wicked man
if I do not act on all the god reveals.   90

PRIEST: What you have said is most appropriate,
  for these men here have just informed me
  that Creon is approaching.

OEDIPUS: Lord Apollo,   [80]
  as he returns may fine shining fortune,
  bright as his countenance, attend on him.

PRIEST: It seems the news he brings is good—if not,
  he would not wear that wreath around his head,
  a laurel thickly packed with berries.[4]

OEDIPUS: We'll know soon enough—he's within earshot.

[Enter CREON. OEDIPUS calls to him as he approaches]

  My royal kinsman, child of Menoeceus,   100
  what message from the god do you bring us?

CREON: Good news. I tell you even troubles
　　　difficult to bear will all end happily
　　　if events lead to the right conclusion.

OEDIPUS: What is the oracle? So far your words
　　　inspire in me no confidence or fear.　　　　　　　　　[90]

CREON: If you wish to hear the news in public,
　　　I'm prepared to speak. Or we could step inside.

OEDIPUS: Speak out to everyone. The grief I feel
　　　for these citizens is even greater　　　　　　　110
　　　than any pain I feel for my own life.

CREON: Then let me report what I heard from the god.
　　　Lord Phoebus clearly orders us to drive away
　　　the polluting stain this land has harboured—
　　　which will not be healed if we keep nursing it.

OEDIPUS: What sort of cleansing? And this disaster—
　　　how did it happen?

CREON:　　　　　　　　　　　By banishment—　　　　[100]
　　　or atone for murder by shedding blood again.
　　　This blood brings on the storm which blasts our state.

OEDIPUS: And the one whose fate the god revealed—　　　120
　　　what sort of man is he?

CREON:　　　　　　　　　　Before you came, my lord,
　　　to steer our ship of state, Laius ruled this land.

OEDIPUS: I have heard that, but I never saw the man.

CREON: Laius was killed. And now the god is clear:
　　　those murderers, he tells us, must be punished,
　　　whoever they may be.

OEDIPUS:　　　　　　　　　And where are they?
　　　In what country? Where am I to find a trace
　　　of this ancient crime? It will be hard to track.

CREON: Here in Thebes, so said the god. What is sought
    is found, but what is overlooked escapes. 130 [110]

OEDIPUS: When Laius fell in bloody death, where was he—
    at home, or in his fields, or in another land?

CREON: He was abroad, on his way to Delphi—
    that's what he told us. He began the trip,
    but did not return.

OEDIPUS: Was there no messenger—
    no companion who made the journey with him
    and witnessed what took place—a person
    who might provide some knowledge men could use?

CREON: They all died—except for one who was afraid
    and ran away. There was only one thing 140
    he could inform us of with confidence
    about the things he saw.

OEDIPUS: What was that?
    We might get somewhere if we had one fact— [120]
    we could find many things, if we possessed
    some slender hope to get us going.

CREON: He told us it was robbers who attacked them—
    not just a single man, a gang of them—
    they came on with force and killed him.

OEDIPUS: How would a thief have dared to do this,
    unless he had financial help from Thebes? 150

CREON: That's what we guessed. But once Laius was dead
    we were in trouble, so no one sought revenge.

OEDIPUS: When the ruling king had fallen in this way,
    what bad trouble blocked your path, preventing you
    from looking into it?

CREON: It was the Sphinx—   [130]
  she sang her enigmatic song and thus forced us
  to put aside something we found obscure
  to look into the urgent problem we now faced.

OEDIPUS: Then I will start afresh, and once again
  shed light on darkness. It is most fitting   160
  that Apollo demonstrates his care
  for the dead man, and worthy of you, too.
  And so, as is right, you will see how I
  work with you, seeking vengeance for this land,
  as well as for the god. This polluting stain
  I will remove, not for some distant friend,
  but for myself. For whoever killed this man
  may soon enough desire to turn his hand   [140]
  in the same way against me, too, and kill me.
  Thus, in avenging Laius, I serve myself.   170
  But now, my children, as quickly as you can
  stand up from these altar steps and take
  your suppliant branches. Someone must call
  the Theban people to assemble here.
  I'll do everything I can. With the god's help
  this will all come to light successfully,
  or else it will prove our common ruin.

[OEDIPUS and CREON go into the palace]

PRIEST: Let us get up, children. For this man
  has willingly declared just what we came for.
  And may Phoebus, who sent this oracle,   180
  come as our saviour and end our sickness.   [150]

[The PRIEST and the CITIZENS leave. Enter the CHORUS OF THEBAN ELDERS]

CHORUS: Oh sweet speaking voice of Zeus,
  you have come to glorious Thebes from golden Pytho—
  but what is your intent?
  My fearful heart twists on the rack and shakes with fear.
  O Delian healer, for whom we cry aloud
  in holy awe, what obligation
  will you demand from me, a thing unknown

or now renewed with the revolving years?
Immortal voice, O child of golden Hope,   190
speak to me!

First I call on you, Athena the immortal,
daughter of Zeus, and on your sister, too,   [160]
Artemis, who guards our land and sits
on her glorious round throne in our market place,
and on Phoebus, who shoots from far away.
O you three guardians against death,
appear to me!
If before now you have ever driven off
a fiery plague to keep away disaster   200
from the city and have banished it,
then come to us this time as well!

Alas, the pains I bear are numberless—
my people now all sick with plague,
our minds can find no weapons   [170]
to serve as our defence. Now the offspring
of our splendid earth no longer grow,
nor do our women crying out in labour
get their relief from a living new-born child.
As you can see—one by one they swoop away,   210
off to the shores of the evening god, like birds
faster than fire which no one can resist.

Our city dies—we've lost count of all the dead.
Her sons lie in the dirt unpitied, unlamented.   [180]
Corpses spread the pestilence, while youthful wives
and grey-haired mothers on the altar steps
wail everywhere and cry in supplication,
seeking to relieve their agonizing pain.
Their solemn chants ring out—
they mingle with the voices of lament.   220
O Zeus' golden daughter,
send your support and strength,
your lovely countenance!

And that ravenous Ares, god of killing,
who now consumes me as he charges on

with no bronze shield but howling battle cries,
let him turn his back and quickly leave this land,
with a fair following wind to carry him
to the great chambers of Amphitrite[5]
or inhospitable waves of Thrace.   230
For if destruction does not come at night,
then day arrives to see it does its work.
O you who wield that mighty flash of fire,   [200]
O father Zeus, with your lighting blast
let Ares be destroyed!

O Lyceian lord,[6] how I wish those arrows
from the golden string of your bent bow
with their all-conquering force would wing out
to champion us against our enemy,
and the blazing fires of Artemis, as well,   240
with which she races through the Lycian hills.
I call the god who binds his hair with gold,
the one whose name our country shares,   [210]
the one to whom the Maenads shout their cries,
Dionysus with his radiant face—[7]
may he come to us with his flaming torchlight,
our ally against Ares,
a god dishonoured among gods.

[Enter OEDIPUS from the palace]

OEDIPUS: You pray. But if you listen now to me,
    you'll get your wish. Hear what I have to say   250
    and treat your own disease—then you may hope
    to find relief from your distress. I shall speak
    as one who is a stranger to the story,
    a stranger to the crime. If I alone
    were tracking down this act, I'd not get far   [220]
    without a single clue. That being the case,
    for it was after the event that I became
    a citizen of Thebes, I now proclaim
    the following to all of you Cadmeians:
    Whoever among you knows the man it was   260
    who murdered Laius, son of Labdacus,
    I order him to reveal it all to me.

And if the murderer's afraid, I tell him
to avoid the danger of the major charge
by speaking out against himself. If so,
he will be sent out from this land unhurt—
and undergo no further punishment.
If someone knows the killer is a stranger, [230]
from some other state, let him not stay mute.
As well as a reward, he'll earn my thanks. 270
But if he remains quiet, if anyone,
through fear, hides himself or a friend of his
against my orders, here's what I shall do—
so listen to my words. For I decree
that no one in this land, in which I rule
as your own king, shall give that killer shelter
or talk to him, whoever he may be,
or act in concert with him during prayers,
or sacrifice, or sharing lustral water.[8] [240]
Ban him from your homes, every one of you, 280
for he is our pollution, as the Pythian god
has just revealed to me. In doing this,
I'm acting as an ally of the god
and of dead Laius, too. And I pray
whoever the man is who did this crime,
one unknown person acting on his own
or with companions, the worst of agonies
will wear out his wretched life. I pray, too,
that, if he should become a honoured guest
in my own home and with my knowledge, 290 [250]
I may suffer all those things I've just called down
upon the killers. And I urge you now
to make sure all these orders take effect,
for my sake, for the sake of the god,
and for our barren, godless, ruined land.
For in this matter, even if a god
were not prompting us, it would not be right
for you to simply leave things as they are,
and not to purify the murder of a man
who was so noble and who was your king. 300
You should have looked into it. But now I
possess the ruling power which Laius held
in earlier days. I have his bed and wife— [260]

she would have borne his children, if his hopes
to have a son had not been disappointed.
Children from a common mother might have linked
Laius and myself. But as it turned out,
fate swooped down onto his head. So now I
will fight on his behalf, as if this matter   310
concerned my father, and I will strive
to do everything I can to find him,
the man who spilled his blood, and thus avenge
the son of Labdacus and Polydorus,
of Cadmus and Agenor from old times.[9]
As for those who do not follow what I urge,
I pray the gods send them no fertile land,
no, nor any children in their women's wombs—   [270]
may they all perish in our present fate
or one more hateful still. To you others,
you Cadmeians who support my efforts,   320
may Justice, our ally, and all the gods
attend on us with kindness always.

CHORUS LEADER: My lord, since you extend your oath to me,
I will say this. I am not the murderer,
nor can I tell you who the killer is.
As for what you're seeking, it's for Apollo,
who launched this search, to state who did it.

OEDIPUS: That is well said. But no man has power   [280]
to force the gods to speak against their will.

CHORUS LEADER: May I then suggest what seems to me   330
the next best course of action?

OEDIPUS: You may indeed,
and if there is a third course, too, don't hesitate
to let me know.

CHORUS LEADER: Our lord Teiresias,
I know, can see into things, like lord Apollo.
From him, my king, a man investigating this
might well find out the details of the crime.

OEDIPUS: I've taken care of that—it's not something
    I could overlook. At Creon's urging,
    I have dispatched two messengers to him
    and have been wondering for some time now340
    why he has not come.

CHORUS LEADER: Apart from that,
    there are rumours—but inconclusive ones   [290]
    from a long time ago.

OEDIPUS: What kind of rumours?
    I'm looking into every story.

CHORUS LEADER: It was said
    that Laius was killed by certain travellers.

OEDIPUS: Yes, I heard as much. But no one has seen
    the one who did it.

CHORUS LEADER: Well, if the killer
    has any fears, once he hears your curses on him,
    he will not hold back, for they are serious.

OEDIPUS: When a man has no fear of doing the act,   350
    he's not afraid of words.

CHORUS LEADER: No, not in the case
    where no one stands there to convict him.
    But at last Teiresias is being guided here,
    our god-like prophet, in whom the truth resides
    more so than in all other men.

[Enter TEIRESIAS led by a small BOY]

OEDIPUS: Teiresias,   [300]
    you who understand all things—what can be taught
    and what cannot be spoken of, what goes on
    in heaven and here on the earth—you know,
    although you cannot see, how sick our state is.
    And so we find in you alone, great seer,   360
    our shield and saviour. For Phoebus Apollo,

in case you have not heard the news, has sent us
an answer to our question: the only cure
for this infecting pestilence is to find
the men who murdered Laius and kill them
or else expel them from this land as exiles.
So do not withhold from us your prophecies   [310]
in voices of the birds or by some other means.
Save this city and yourself. Rescue me.
Deliver us from this pollution by the dead.   370
We are in your hands. For a mortal man
the finest labour he can do is help
with all his power other human beings.

TEIRESIAS: Alas, alas! How dreadful it can be
to have wisdom when it brings no benefit
to the man possessing it. This I knew,
but it had slipped my mind. Otherwise,
I would not have journeyed here.

OEDIPUS: What's wrong? You've come, but seem so sad.

TEIRESIAS: Let me go home. You must bear your burden   380   [320]
to the very end, and I will carry mine,
if you'll agree with me.

OEDIPUS: What you are saying
is not customary and shows little love
toward the city state which nurtured you,
if you deny us your prophetic voice.

TEIRESIAS: I see your words are also out of place.
I do not speak for fear of doing the same.

OEDIPUS: If you know something, then, by heaven,
do not turn away. We are your suppliants—
all of us—we bend our knees to you.   390

TEIRESIAS: You are all ignorant. I will not reveal
the troubling things inside me, which I can call
your grief as well.

OEDIPUS: What are you saying?   [330]
    Do you know and will not say? Do you intend
    to betray me and destroy the city?

TEIRESIAS: I will cause neither me nor you distress.
    Why do you vainly question me like this?
    You will not learn a thing from me.

OEDIPUS: You most disgraceful of disgraceful men!
    You'd move something made of stone to rage!   400
    Will you not speak out? Will your stubbornness
    never have an end?

TEIRESIAS: You blame my temper,
    but do not see the one which lives within you.
    Instead, you are finding fault with me.

OEDIPUS: What man who listened to these words of yours
    would not be enraged—you insult the city!   [340]

TEIRESIAS: Yet events will still unfold, for all my silence.

OEDIPUS: Since they will come, you must inform me.

TEIRESIAS: I will say nothing more. Fume on about it,
    if you wish, as fiercely as you can.   410

OEDIPUS: I will. In my anger I will not conceal
    just what I make of this. You should know
    I get the feeling you conspired in the act,
    and played your part, as much as you could do,
    short of killing him with your own hands.
    If you could use your eyes, I would have said
    that you had done this work all by yourself.

TEIRESIAS: Is that so? Then I would ask you to stand by   [350]
    the very words which you yourself proclaimed
    and from now on not speak to me or these men.   420
    For the accursed polluter of this land is you.

OEDIPUS: You dare to utter shameful words like this?
    Do you think you can get away with it?

TEIRESIAS: I am getting away with it. The truth
    within me makes me strong.

OEDIPUS: Who taught you this?
    It could not have been your craft.

TEIRESIAS: You did.
    I did not want to speak, but you incited me.

OEDIPUS: What do you mean? Speak it again,
    so I can understand you more precisely.

TEIRESIAS: Did you not grasp my words before,   430
    or are you trying to test me with your question?   [360]

OEDIPUS: I did not fully understand your words.
    Tell me again.

TEIRESIAS: I say that you yourself
    are the very man you're looking for.

OEDIPUS: That's twice you've stated that disgraceful lie—
    something you'll regret.

TEIRESIAS: Shall I tell you more,
    so you can grow even more enraged?

OEDIPUS: As much as you desire. It will be useless.

TEIRESIAS: I say that with your dearest family,
    unknown to you, you are living in disgrace.   440
    You have no idea how bad things are.

OEDIPUS: Do you really think you can just speak out,
    say things like this, and still remain unpunished?

TEIRESIAS: Yes, I can, if the truth has any strength.

OEDIPUS: It does, but not for you. Truth is not in you—   [370]
    for your ears, your mind, your eyes are blind!

TEIRESIAS: You are a wretched fool to use harsh words
    which all men soon enough will use to curse you.

OEDIPUS: You live in endless darkness of the night,
    so you can never injure me or any man   450
    who can glimpse daylight.

TEIRESIAS: It is not your fate
    to fall because of me. It's up to Apollo
    to make that happen. He will be enough.

OEDIPUS: Is this something Creon has devised,
    or is it your invention?

TEIRESIAS: Creon is no threat.
    You have made this trouble on your own.

OEDIPUS: O riches, ruling power, skill after skill   [380]
    surpassing all in this life's rivalries,
    how much envy you must carry with you,
    if, for this kingly office, which the city   460
    gave me, for I did not seek it out,
    Creon, my old trusted family friend,
    has secretly conspired to overthrow me
    and paid off a double-dealing quack like this,
    a crafty bogus priest, who can only see
    his own advantage, who in his special art
    is absolutely blind. Come on, tell me   [390]
    how you have ever given evidence
    of your wise prophecy. When the Sphinx,
    that singing bitch, was here, you said nothing   470
    to set the people free. Why not? Her riddle
    was not something the first man to stroll along
    could solve—a prophet was required. And there
    the people saw your knowledge was no use—
    nothing from birds or picked up from the gods.
    But then I came, Oedipus, who knew nothing.

Yet I finished her off, using my wits
rather than relying on birds. That's the man
you want to overthrow, hoping, no doubt,
to stand up there with Creon, once he's king.   480   [400]
But I think you and your conspirator in this
will regret trying to usurp the state.
If you did not look so old, you'd find
the punishment your arrogance deserves.

CHORUS LEADER: To us it sounds as if Teiresias
has spoken in anger, and, Oedipus,
you have done so, too. That's not what we need.
Instead we should be looking into this:
How can we best carry out the god's decree?

TEIRESIAS: You may be king, but I have the right   490
to answer you—and I control that right,
for I am not your slave. I serve Apollo,   [410]
and thus will never stand with Creon,
signed up as his man. So I say this to you,
since you have chosen to insult my blindness—
you have your eyesight, and you do not see
how miserable you are, or where you live,
or who it is who shares your household.
Do you know the family you come from?
Without your knowledge you've become   500
the enemy of your own kindred,
those in the world below and those up here,
and the dreadful feet of that two-edged curse
from father and mother both will drive you
from this land in exile. Those eyes of yours,
which now can see so clearly, will be dark.
What harbour will not echo with your cries?   [420]
Where on Cithaeron[10] will they not soon be heard,
once you have learned the truth about the wedding
by which you sailed into this royal house—   510
a lovely voyage, but the harbour's doomed?
You've no idea of the quantity
of other troubles which will render you
and your own children equals. So go on—

keep insulting Creon and my prophecies,
for among all living mortals no one
will be destroyed more wretchedly than you.

OEDIPUS: Must I tolerate this insolence from him?   [430]
  Get out, and may the plague get rid of you!
  Off with you! Now! Turn your back and go!   520
  And don't come back here to my home again.

TEIRESIAS: I would not have come, but you summoned me.

OEDIPUS: I did not know you would speak so stupidly.
  If I had, you would have waited a long time
  before I called you here.

TEIRESIAS: I was born like this.
  You think I am a fool, but to your parents,
  the ones who made you, I was wise enough.

OEDIPUS: Wait! My parents? Who was my father?

TEIRESIAS: This day will reveal that and destroy you.

OEDIPUS: Everything you speak is all so cryptic—   530
  like a riddle.

TEIRESIAS: Well, in solving riddles,   [440]
  are you not the best there is?

OEDIPUS: Mock my excellence,
  but you will find out I am truly great.

TEIRESIAS: That quality of yours now ruins you.

OEDIPUS: I do not care, if I have saved the city.

TEIRESIAS: I will go now. Boy, lead me away.

OEDIPUS: Yes, let him guide you back. You're in the way.
  If you stay, you'll just provoke me. Once you're gone,
  you won't annoy me further.

TEIRESIAS: I'm going.
   But first I shall tell you why I came.   540
   I do not fear the face of your displeasure—
   there is no way you can destroy me. I tell you,
   the man you have been seeking all this time,
   while proclaiming threats and issuing orders   [450]
   about the one who murdered Laius—
   that man is here. According to reports,
   he is a stranger who lives here in Thebes.
   But he will prove to be a native Theban.
   From that change he will derive no pleasure.
   He will be blind, although he now can see.   550
   He will be a poor, although he now is rich.
   He will set off for a foreign country,
   groping the ground before him with a stick.
   And he will turn out to be the brother
   of the children in his house—their father, too,
   both at once, and the husband and the son
   of the very woman who gave birth to them.
   He sowed the same womb as his father
   and murdered him. Go in and think on this.   [460]
   If you discover I have spoken falsely,   560
   you can say I lack all skill in prophecy.

[Exit TEIRESIAS led off by the BOY. OEDIPUS turns and goes back into the palace]

CHORUS: Speaking from the Delphic rock
   the oracular voice intoned a name.
   But who is the man, the one
   who with his blood-red hands
   has done unspeakable brutality?
   The time has come for him to flee—
   to move his powerful foot
   more swiftly than those hooves
   on horses riding on the storm.   570
   Against him Zeus' son now springs,   [470]
   armed with lightning fire and leading on
   the inexorable and terrifying Furies.[11]

   From the snowy peaks of Mount Parnassus[12]
   the message has just flashed, ordering all

to seek the one whom no one knows.
Like a wild bull he wanders now,
hidden in the untamed wood,
through rocks and caves, alone
with his despair on joyless feet,   580
keeping his distance from that doom
uttered at earth's central navel stone.   [480]
But that fatal oracle still lives,
hovering above his head forever.

That wise interpreter of prophecies
stirs up my fears, unsettling dread.
I cannot approve of what he said
and I cannot deny it.
I am confused. What shall I say?
My hopes flutter here and there,
with no clear glimpse of past or future.   590
I have never heard of any quarrelling,
past or present, between those two,
the house of Labdacus and Polybus' son,[13]
which could give me evidence enough
to undermine the fame of Oedipus,
as he seeks vengeance for the unsolved murder
for the family of Labdacus.

Apollo and Zeus are truly wise—
they understand what humans do.
But there is no sure way to ascertain   600
if human prophets grasp things any more
than I do, although in wisdom one man   [500]
may leave another far behind.
But until I see the words confirmed,
I will not approve of any man
who censures Oedipus, for it was clear
when that winged Sphinx went after him
he was a wise man then. We witnessed it.
He passed the test and endeared himself
to all the city. So in my thinking now   610   [510]
he never will be guilty of a crime.

[Enter CREON]

CREON: You citizens, I have just discovered
    that Oedipus, our king, has levelled charges
    against me, disturbing allegations.
    That I cannot bear, so I have come here.
    In these present troubles, if he believes
    that he has suffered any injury from me,
    in word or deed, then I have no desire
    to continue living into ripe old age
    still bearing his reproach. For me   620
    the injury produced by this report
    is no single isolated matter—   [520]
    no, it has the greatest scope of all,
    if I end up being called a wicked man
    here in the city, a bad citizen,
    by you and by my friends.

CHORUS LEADER: Perhaps he charged you
    spurred on by the rash power of his rage,
    rather than his mind's true judgment.

CREON: Was it publicized that my opinions
    convinced Teiresias to utter lies?   630

CHORUS LEADER: That's what was said. I have no idea
    just what that meant.

CREON: Did he accuse me
    and announce the charges with a steady gaze,
    in a normal state of mind?

CHORUS LEADER: I do not know.   [530]
    What those in power do I do not see.
    But he's approaching from the palace—
    here he comes in person.

[Enter OEDIPUS from the palace]

OEDIPUS: You! How did you get here?
    Has your face grown so bold you now come
    to my own home—you who are obviously
    the murderer of the man whose house it was,   640
    a thief who clearly wants to steal my throne?
    Come, in the name of all the gods, tell me this—
    did you plan to do it because you thought
    I was a coward or a fool? Or did you think
    I would not learn about your actions
    as they crept up on me with such deceit—
    or that, if I knew, I could not deflect them?
    This attempt of yours, is it not madness—   [540]
    to chase after the king's place without friends,
    without a horde of men, to seek a goal   650
    which only gold or factions could attain?

CREON: Will you listen to me? It's your turn now
    to hear me make a suitable response.
    Once you know, then judge me for yourself.

OEDIPUS: You are a clever talker. But from you
    I will learn nothing. I know you now—
    a troublemaker, an enemy of mine.

CREON: At least first listen to what I have to say.

OEDIPUS: There's one thing you do not have to tell me—
    you have betrayed me.

CREON: If you think being stubborn   660
    and forgetting common sense is wise,
    then you're not thinking as you should.   [550]

OEDIPUS: And if you think you can act to injure
    a man who is a relative of yours
    and escape without a penalty
    then you're not thinking as you should.

CREON: I agree. What you've just said makes sense.
    So tell me the nature of the damage
    you claim you're suffering because of me.

OEDIPUS: Did you or did you not persuade me   670
    to send for Teiresias, that prophet?

CREON: Yes. And I'd still give you the same advice.

OEDIPUS: How long is it since Laius ... *[pauses]*

CREON: Did what?
    What's Laius got to do with anything?

OEDIPUS: ... since Laius was carried off and disappeared,
    since he was killed so brutally?   [560]

CREON: That was long ago—
    many years have passed since then.

OEDIPUS: At that time,
    was Teiresias as skilled in prophecy?

CREON: Then, as now, he was honoured for his wisdom.

OEDIPUS: And back then did he ever mention me?   680

CREON: No, never—not while I was with him.

OEDIPUS: Did you not investigate the killing?

CREON: Yes, of course we did. But we found nothing.

OEDIPUS: Why did this man, this wise man, not speak up?

CREON: I do not know. And when I don't know something,
    I like to keep my mouth shut.

OEDIPUS: You know enough—   [570]
    at least you understand enough to say ...

CREON: What? If I really do know something
    I will not deny it.

OEDIPUS: If Teiresias
   were not working with you, he would not name me   690
   as the one who murdered Laius.

CREON: If he says this,
   well, you're the one who knows. But I think
   the time has come for me to question you
   the way that you've been questioning me.

OEDIPUS: Ask all you want. You'll not prove
   that I'm the murderer.

CREON: Then tell me this—
   are you not married to my sister?

OEDIPUS: Since you ask me, yes. I don't deny that.

CREON: And you two rule this land as equals?

OEDIPUS: Whatever she desires, she gets from me.   700   [580]

CREON: And am I not third, equal to you both?

OEDIPUS: That's what makes your friendship so deceitful.

CREON: No, not if you think this through, as I do.
   First, consider this. In your view, would anyone
   prefer to rule and have to cope with fear
   rather than live in peace, carefree and safe,
   if his powers were the same? I, for one,
   have no natural desire to be king
   in preference to performing royal acts.
   The same is true of any other man   710
   whose understanding grasps things properly.
   For now I get everything I want from you,   [590]
   but without the fear. If I were king myself,
   I'd be doing many things against my will.
   So how can being a king be sweeter to me
   than royal power without anxiety?
   I am not yet so mistaken in my mind
   that I want things which bring no benefits.

Now I greet all men, and they all welcome me.
Those who wish to get something from you   720
now flatter me, since I'm the one who brings
success in what they want. So why would I
give up such benefits for something else?
A mind that's wise will not turn treacherous.   [600]
It's not my nature to love such policies.
And if another man pursued such things,
I'd not work with him. I couldn't bear to.
If you want proof of this, then go to Delphi.
Ask the prophet if I brought back to you
exactly what was said. At that point,   730
if you discover I have planned something,
that I've conspired with Teiresias,
then arrest me and have me put to death,
not just on your own authority,
but on mine as well, a double judgment.
Do not condemn me on an unproved charge.
It's not fair to judge these things by guesswork,
to assume bad men are good or good men bad.   [610]
In my view, to throw away a noble friend
is like a man who parts with his own life,   740
the thing most dear to him. Give it some time.
Then you'll see clearly, since only time
can fully validate a man who's true.
A bad man is exposed in just one day.

CHORUS LEADER: For a man concerned about being killed,
my lord, he has spoken eloquently.
Those who are unreliable give rash advice.

OEDIPUS: If some conspirator moves against me,
in secret and with speed, I must be quick
to make my counter plans. If I just rest   750
and wait for him to act, then he'll succeed   [620]
in what he wants to do, and I'll be finished.

CREON: What do you want—to exile me from here?

OEDIPUS: No. I want you to die, not just run off—
so I can demonstrate what envy means.

CREON: You are determined not to change your mind
    or listen to me?

OEDIPUS: You'll not convince me,
    for there's no way that I can trust you.

CREON: I can see that you've become unbalanced.[14]

OEDIPUS: I'm sane enough to defend my interests.   760

CREON: You should be protecting mine as well.

OEDIPUS: But you're a treacherous man. It's your nature.

CREON: What if you are wrong?

OEDIPUS: I still have to govern.

CREON: Not if you do it badly.

OEDIPUS: Oh Thebes—
    my city!

CREON: I have some rights in Thebes as well—   [630]
    it is not yours alone.

[The palace doors open]

CHORUS LEADER: My lords, an end to this.
    I see Jocasta coming from the palace,
    and just in time. With her assistance
    you should bring this quarrel to a close.

[Enter JOCASTA from the palace]

JOCASTA: You foolish men, why are you arguing   770
    in such a silly way? With our land so sick,
    are you not ashamed to start a private fight?
    You, Oedipus, go in the house, and you,
    Creon, return to yours. Why blow up
    a trivial matter into something huge?

CREON: Sister, your husband Oedipus intends
    to punish me in one of two dreadful ways—   [640]
    to banish me from my fathers' country
    or arrest me and then have me killed.

OEDIPUS: That's right.
    Lady, I caught him committing treason,   780
    conspiring against my royal authority.

CREON: Let me not prosper but die a man accursed,
    if I have done what you accuse me of.

JOCASTA: Oedipus,
    for the sake of the gods, trust him in this.
    Respect that oath he made before all heaven—
    do it for my sake and for those around you.

CHORUS LEADER: I beg you, my lord, consent to this—
    agree with her.   [650]

OEDIPUS: What is it then
    you're asking me to do?

CHORUS LEADER: Pay Creon due respect.
    He has not been foolish in the past, and now   790
    that oath he's sworn has power.

OEDIPUS: Are you aware
    just what you're asking?

CHORUS LEADER: Yes. I understand.

OEDIPUS: Then tell me exactly what you're saying.

CHORUS LEADER: You should not accuse a friend of yours
    and thus dishonour him with a mere story
    which may not be true, when he's sworn an oath
    and therefore could be subject to a curse.

OEDIPUS: By this point you should clearly understand,
    when you request this, what you are doing—
    seeking to exile me from Thebes or kill me.   800

CHORUS LEADER: No, no, by sacred Helios, the god   [660]
    who stands pre-eminent before the rest,
    may I die the most miserable of deaths,
    abandoned by the gods and by my friends,
    if I have ever harboured such a thought!
    But the destruction of our land wears down
    the troubled heart within me—and so does this,
    if you two add new problems to the ones
    which have for so long been afflicting us.

OEDIPUS: Let him go, then, even though it's clear   810
    I must be killed or sent from here in exile,
    forced out in disgrace. I have been moved   [670]
    to act compassionately by what you said,
    not by Creon's words. But if he stays here,
    he will be hateful to me.

CREON: You are obstinate—
    obviously unhappy to concede,
    and when you lose your temper, you go too far.
    But men like that find it most difficult
    to tolerate themselves. In that there's justice.

OEDIPUS: Why not go—just leave me alone?

CREON: I'll leave—   820
    since I see you do not understand me.
    But these men here know I'm a reasonable man.

[Exit CREON away from the palace, leaving OEDIPUS and JOCASTA and the CHORUS on stage]

CHORUS LEADER: Lady, will you escort our king inside?

JOCASTA: Yes, once I have learned what happened here.   [680]

CHORUS LEADER: They talked—
    their words gave rise to uninformed suspicions,
    an all-consuming lack of proper justice.

JOCASTA: From both of them?

CHORUS LEADER: Yes.

JOCASTA: What caused it?

CHORUS LEADER: With our country already in distress,
    it is enough, it seems to me, enough
    to leave things as they are.

OEDIPUS: Now do you see   830
    the point you've reached thanks to your noble wish
    to dissolve and dull my firmer purpose?

CHORUS LEADER: My lord, I have declared it more than once,   [690]
    so you must know it would have been quite mad
    if I abandoned you, who, when this land,
    my cherished Thebes, was in great trouble,
    set it right again and who, in these harsh times
    which now consume us, should prove a trusty guide.

JOCASTA: By all the gods, my king, let me know
    why in this present crisis you now feel   840
    such unremitting rage.

OEDIPUS: To you I'll speak, lady,   [700]
    since I respect you more than I do these men.
    It's Creon's fault. He conspired against me.

JOCASTA: In this quarrel what was said? Tell me.

OEDIPUS: Creon claims that I'm the murderer—
    that I killed Laius.

JOCASTA: Does he know this first hand,
    or has he picked it up from someone else?

OEDIPUS: No. He set up that treasonous prophet.
　　What he says himself sounds innocent.

JOCASTA: All right, forget about those things you've said.　　850
　　Listen to me, and ease your mind with this—
　　no human being has skill in prophecy.
　　I'll show you why with this example.　　　　　　　　　　[710]
　　King Laius once received a prophecy.
　　I won't say it came straight from Apollo,
　　but it was from those who do assist the god.
　　It said Laius was fated to be killed
　　by a child conceived by him and me.
　　Now, at least according to the story,
　　one day Laius was killed by foreigners,　　　　　　860
　　by robbers, at a place where three roads meet.
　　Besides, before our child was three days old,
　　Laius fused his ankles tight together
　　and ordered other men to throw him out
　　on a mountain rock where no one ever goes.
　　And so Apollo's plan that he'd become　　　　　　　　[720]
　　the one who killed his father didn't work,
　　and Laius never suffered what he feared,
　　that his own son would be his murderer,
　　although that's what the oracle had claimed.　　　　860
　　So don't concern yourself with prophecies.
　　Whatever gods intend to bring about
　　they themselves make known quite easily.

OEDIPUS: Lady, as I listen to these words of yours,
　　my soul is shaken, my mind confused …

JOCASTA: Why do you say that? What's worrying you?

OEDIPUS: I thought I heard you say that Laius
　　was murdered at a place where three roads meet.　　　[730]

JOCASTA: That's what was said and people still believe.

OEDIPUS: Where is this place? Where did it happen?　　880

JOCASTA: In a land called Phocis. Two roads lead there—
one from Delphi and one from Daulia.

OEDIPUS: How long is it since these events took place?

JOCASTA: The story was reported in the city
just before you took over royal power
here in Thebes.

OEDIPUS: Oh Zeus, what have you done?
What have you planned for me?

JOCASTA: What is it,
Oedipus? Why is your spirit so troubled?

OEDIPUS: Not yet,   [740]
no questions yet. Tell me this—Laius,
how tall was he? How old a man?   890

JOCASTA: He was big—his hair was turning white.
In shape he was not all that unlike you.

OEDIPUS: The worse for me! I may have just set myself
under a dreadful curse without my knowledge!

JOCASTA: What do you mean? As I look at you, my king,
I start to tremble.

OEDIPUS: I am afraid,
full of terrible fears the prophet sees.
But you can reveal this better if you now
will tell me one thing more.

JOCASTA: I'm shaking,
but if you ask me, I will answer you.   900

OEDIPUS: Did Laius have a small escort with him   [750]
or a troop of soldiers, like a royal king?

JOCASTA: Five men, including a herald, went with him.
A carriage carried Laius.

OEDIPUS: Alas! Alas!
    It's all too clear! Lady, who told you this?

JOCASTA: A servant—the only one who got away.
    He came back here.

OEDIPUS: Is there any chance
    he's in our household now?

JOCASTA: No.
    Once he returned and understood that you
    had now assumed the power of slaughtered Laius,   910
    he clasped my hands, begged me to send him off   [760]
    to where our animals graze out in the fields,
    so he could be as far away as possible
    from the sight of town. And so I sent him.
    He was a slave but he'd earned my gratitude.
    He deserved an even greater favour.

OEDIPUS: I'd like him to return back here to us,
    and quickly, too.

JOCASTA: That can be arranged—
    but why's that something you would want to do?

OEDIPUS: Lady, I'm afraid I may have said too much.   920
    That's why I want to see him here in front of me.

JOCASTA: Then he will be here. But now, my lord,
    I deserve to learn why you are so distressed.   [770]

OEDIPUS: My forebodings now have grown so great
    I will not keep them from you, for who is there
    I should confide in rather than in you
    about such a twisted turn of fortune.
    My father was Polybus of Corinth,
    my mother Merope, a Dorian.
    There I was regarded as the finest man   930
    in all the city, until, as chance would have it,
    something really astonishing took place,
    though it was not worth what it caused me to do.

At a dinner there a man who was quite drunk
from too much wine began to shout at me,
claiming I was not my father's real son.   [780]
That troubled me, but for a day at least
I said nothing, though it was difficult.
The next day I went to ask my parents,   940
my father and my mother. They were angry
at the man who had insulted them this way,
so I was reassured. But nonetheless,
the accusation always troubled me—
the story had become well known all over.
And so I went in secret off to Delphi.
I didn't tell my mother or my father.
Apollo sent me back without an answer,
so I didn't learn what I had come to find.
But when he spoke he uttered monstrous things,   [790]
strange terrors and horrific miseries—   950
it was my fate to defile my mother's bed,
to bring forth to men a human family
that people could not bear to look upon,
to murder the father who engendered me.
When I heard that, I ran away from Corinth.
From then on I thought of it just as a place
beneath the stars. I went to other lands,
so I would never see that prophecy fulfilled,
the abomination of my evil fate.
In my travelling I came across that place   960
in which you say your king was murdered.
And now, lady, I will tell you the truth.   [800]
As I was on the move, I passed close by
a spot where three roads meet, and in that place
I met a herald and a horse-drawn carriage.
Inside there was a man like you described.
The guide there tried to force me off the road—
and the old man, too, got personally involved.
In my rage, I lashed out at the driver,
who was shoving me aside. The old man,   970
seeing me walking past him in the carriage,
kept his eye on me, and with his double whip
struck me on my head, right here on top.
Well, I retaliated in good measure—   [810]

I hit him a quick blow with the staff I held
and knocked him from his carriage to the road.
He lay there on his back. Then I killed them all.
If that stranger was somehow linked to Laius,
who is now more unfortunate than me?
What man could be more hateful to the gods?   980
No stranger and no citizen can welcome him
into their lives or speak to him. Instead,
they must keep him from their doors, a curse   [820]
I laid upon myself. With these hands of mine,
these killer's hands, I now contaminate
the dead man's bed. Am I not depraved?
Am I not utterly abhorrent?
Now I must fly into exile and there,
a fugitive, never see my people,
never set foot in my native land again—   990
or else I must get married to my mother
and kill my father, Polybus, who raised me,
the man who gave me life. If anyone
claimed this came from some malevolent god,
would he not be right? O you gods,
you pure, blessed gods, may I not see that day!   [830]
Let me rather vanish from the sight of men,
before I see a fate like that roll over me.

CHORUS LEADER: My lord, to us these things are ominous.
    But you must sustain your hope until you hear   1000
    the servant who was present at the time.

OEDIPUS: I do have some hope left, at least enough
    to wait for the man we've summoned from the fields.

JOCASTA: Once he comes, what do you hope to hear?

OEDIPUS: I'll tell you. If we discover what he says
    matches what you say, then I'll escape disaster.   [840]

JOCASTA: What was so remarkable in what I said?

OEDIPUS: You said that in his story the man claimed
    Laius was murdered by a band of thieves.

If he still says that there were several men,   1010
then I was not the killer, since one man
could never be mistaken for a crowd.
But if he says it was a single man,
then I'm the one responsible for this.

JOCASTA: Well, that's certainly what he reported then.
He cannot now withdraw what he once said.
The whole city heard him, not just me alone.   [850]
But even if he changes that old news,
he cannot ever demonstrate, my lord,
that Laius' murder fits the prophecy.   1020
For Apollo clearly said the man would die
at the hands of an infant born from me.
Now, how did that unhappy son of ours
kill Laius, when he'd perished long before?
So as far as these oracular sayings go,
I would not look for confirmation anywhere.

OEDIPUS: You're right in what you say. But nonetheless,
send for that peasant. Don't fail to do that.   [860]

JOCASTA: I'll call him here as quickly as I can.
Let's go inside. I'll not do anything   1030
which does not meet with your approval.

[OEDIPUS and JOCASTA go into the palace together]

CHORUS: I pray fate still finds me worthy,
demonstrating piety and reverence
in all I say and do—in everything
our loftiest traditions consecrate,
those laws engendered in the heavenly skies,
whose only father is Olympus.
They were not born from mortal men,
nor will they sleep and be forgotten.   [870]
In them lives an ageless mighty god.   1040

Insolence gives birth to tyranny—
that insolence which vainly crams itself
and overflows with so much stuff

beyond what's right or beneficial,
that once it's climbed the highest rooftop,
it's hurled down by force—such a quick fall
there's no safe landing on one's feet.
But I pray the god never will abolish
the rivalry so beneficial to our state.   [880]
That god I will hold on to always,   1050
the one who stands as our protector.[15]

But if a man conducts himself
disdainfully in what he says and does,
and manifests no fear of righteousness,
no reverence for the statues of the gods,
may miserable fate seize such a man
for his disastrous arrogance,
if he does not behave with justice   [890]
when he strives to benefit himself,
appropriates all things impiously,   1060
and, like a fool, profanes the sacred.
What man is there who does such things
who can still claim he will ward off
the arrow of the gods aimed at his heart?
If such actions are considered worthy,
why should we dance to honour god?

No longer will I go in reverence
to the sacred stone, earth's very centre,
or to the temple at Abae or Olympia,   [900]
if these prophecies fail to be fulfilled   1070
and manifest themselves to mortal men.
But you, all-conquering, all-ruling Zeus,
if by right those names belong to you,
let this not evade you and your ageless might.
For ancient oracles which dealt with Laius
are withering—men now set them aside.
Nowhere is Apollo honoured publicly,
and our religious faith is dying away.   [910]

*[JOCASTA enters from the palace and moves to an altar to Apollo which stands outside the
palace doors. She is accompanied by one or two SERVANTS]*

JOCASTA: You leading men of Thebes, I think
    it is appropriate for me to visit   1080
    our god's sacred shrine, bearing in my hands
    this garland and an offering of incense.
    For Oedipus has let excessive pain
    seize on his heart and does not understand
    what's happening now by thinking of the past,
    like a man with sense. Instead he listens to
    whoever speaks to him of dreadful things.
    I can do nothing more for him with my advice,
    and so, Lycean Apollo, I come to you,
    who stand here beside us, a suppliant,   1090   [920]
    with offerings and prayers for you to find
    some way of cleansing what corrupts us.
    For now we are afraid, just like those
    who on a ship see their helmsman terrified.

[JOCASTA sets her offerings on the altar. A MESSENGER enters, an older man]

MESSENGER: Strangers, can you tell me where I find
    the house of Oedipus, your king? Better yet,
    if you know, can you tell me where he is?

CHORUS LEADER: His home is here, stranger, and he's inside.
    This lady is the mother of his children.

MESSENGER: May her happy home always be blessed,   1100
    for she is his queen, true mistress of his house.   [930]

JOCASTA: I wish the same for you, stranger. Your fine words
    make you deserve as much. But tell us now
    why you have come. Do you seek information,
    or do you wish to give us some report?

MESSENGER: Lady, I have good news for your whole house—
    and for your husband, too.

JOCASTA: What news is that?
    Where have you come from?

MESSENGER: I've come from Corinth.
  I'll give you my report at once, and then
  you will, no doubt, be glad, although perhaps   1110
  you will be sad, as well.

JOCASTA: What is your news?
  How can it have two such effects at once?

MESSENGER: The people who live there, in the lands
  beside the Isthmus, will make him their king.[16]
  They have announced it.   [940]

JOCASTA: What are you saying?
  Is old man Polybus no longer king?

MESSENGER: No. He's dead and in his grave.

JOCASTA: What?
  Has Oedipus' father died?

MESSENGER: Yes.
  If what I'm telling you is not the truth,
  then I deserve to die.

JOCASTA: [to a servant]   You there—   1120
  go at once and tell this to your master.

[SERVANT goes into the palace]

  Oh, you oracles of the gods, so much for you.
  Oedipus has for so long been afraid
  that he would murder him. He ran away.
  Now Polybus has died, killed by fate
  and not by Oedipus.

[Enter OEDIPUS from the palace]

OEDIPUS: Ah, Jocasta,
  my dearest wife, why have you summoned me   [950]
  to leave our home and come out here?

JOCASTA: You must hear this man, and as you listen,
    decide for yourself what these prophecies,   1130
    these solemn proclamations from the gods,
    amount to.

OEDIPUS: Who is this man? What report
    does he have for me?

JOCASTA: He comes from Corinth,
    bringing news that Polybus, your father,
    no longer is alive. He's dead.

OEDIPUS: What?
    Stranger, let me hear from you in person.

MESSENGER: If I must first report my news quite plainly,
    then I should let you know that Polybus
    has passed away. He's gone.

OEDIPUS: By treachery,
    or was it the result of some disease?   1140   [960]

MESSENGER: With old bodies a slight weight on the scales
    brings final peace.

OEDIPUS: Apparently his death
    was from an illness?

MESSENGER: Yes, and from old age.

OEDIPUS: Alas! Indeed, lady, why should any man
    pay due reverence to Apollo's shrine,
    where his prophet lives, or to those birds
    which scream out overhead? For they foretold
    that I was going to murder my own father.
    But now he's dead and lies beneath the earth,
    and I am here. I never touched my spear.   1150
    Perhaps he died from a desire to see me—
    so in that sense I brought about his death.   [970]
    But as for those prophetic oracles,

they're worthless. Polybus has taken them
to Hades, where he lies.

JOCASTA: Was I not the one
who predicted this some time ago?

OEDIPUS: You did,
but then I was misguided by my fears.

JOCASTA: You must not keep on filling up your heart
with all these things.

OEDIPUS: But my mother's bed—
I am afraid of that. And surely I should be?   1160

JOCASTA: Why should a man whose life seems ruled by chance
live in fear—a man who never looks ahead,
who has no certain vision of his future?
It's best to live haphazardly, as best one can.
Do not worry you will wed your mother.   [980]
It's true that in their dreams a lot of men
have slept with their own mothers, but someone
who ignores all this bears life more easily.

OEDIPUS: Everything you say would be commendable,
if my mother were not still alive.   1170
But since she is, I must remain afraid,
although what you are saying is right.

JOCASTA: But still,
your father's death is a great comfort to us.

OEDIPUS: Yes, it is good, I know. But I do fear
that lady—she is still alive.

MESSENGER: This one you fear,
what kind of woman is she?

OEDIPUS: Old man,
her name is Merope, wife to Polybus.   [990]

MESSENGER: And what in her makes you so fearful?

OEDIPUS   Stranger,
   a dreadful prophecy sent from the god.

MESSENGER: Is it well known? Or something private,   1180
   which another person has no right to know?

OEDIPUS: No, no. It's public knowledge. Loxias[17]
   once said it was my fate that I would marry
   my own mother and shed my father's blood
   with my own hands. That's why, many years ago,
   I left my home in Corinth. Things turned out well,
   but nonetheless it gives the sweetest joy
   to look into the eyes of one's own parents.

MESSENGER: And because you were afraid of her   [1000]
   you stayed away from Corinth?

OEDIPUS: And because   1190
   I did not want to be my father's killer.

MESSENGER: My lord, since I came to make you happy,
   why don't I relieve you of this fear?

OEDIPUS: You would receive from me a worthy thanks.

MESSENGER: That's really why I came—so your return
   might prove a benefit to me back home.

OEDIPUS: But I will never go back to my parents.

MESSENGER: My son, it is so clear you have no idea
   what you are doing …

OEDIPUS: *[interrupting]*   What do you mean, old man?
   In the name of all the gods, tell me.   1200

MESSENGER: … if that's the reason you're a fugitive   [1010]
   and won't go home.

OEDIPUS: I feared Apollo's prophecy
   might reveal itself in me.

MESSENGER: You were afraid
   you might become corrupted through your parents?

OEDIPUS: That's right, old man. That was my constant fear.

MESSENGER: Are you aware these fears of yours are groundless?

OEDIPUS: And why is that? If I was born their child …

MESSENGER: Because you and Polybus were not related.

OEDIPUS: What do you mean? Was not Polybus my father?

MESSENGER: He was as much your father as this man here,   1210
   no more, no less.

OEDIPUS: But how can any man
   who means nothing to me be the same
   as my own father?

MESSENGER: But Polybus
   was not your father, no more than I am.   [1020]

OEDIPUS: Then why did he call me his son?

MESSENGER: If you must know,
   he received you many years ago as a gift.
   I gave you to him.

OEDIPUS: He really loved me.
   How could he if I came from someone else?

MESSENGER: Well, before you came, he had no children—
   that made him love you.

OEDIPUS: When you gave me to him,   1220
   had you bought me or found me by accident?

MESSENGER: I found you in Cithaeron's forest valleys.

OEDIPUS: What were you doing wandering up there?

MESSENGER: I was looking after flocks of sheep.

OEDIPUS: You were a shepherd, just a hired servant
   roaming here and there?

MESSENGER: Yes, my son, I was.
   But at that time I was the one who saved you.   [1030]

OEDIPUS: When you picked me up and took me off,
   what sort of suffering was I going through?

MESSENGER: The ankles on your feet could tell you that.   1230

OEDIPUS: Ah, my old misfortune. Why mention that?

MESSENGER: Your ankles had been pierced and tied together.
   I set them free.

OEDIPUS: My dreadful mark of shame—
   I've had that scar there since I was a child.

MESSENGER: That's why fortune gave you your very name,
   the one which you still carry.[18]

OEDIPUS: Tell me,
   in the name of heaven, why did my parents,
   my father or my mother, do this to me?

MESSENGER: I don't know. The man who gave you to me
   knows more of that than I do.

OEDIPUS: You mean to say   1240
   you got me from someone else? It wasn't you
   who stumbled on me?

MESSENGER: No, it wasn't me.
   Another shepherd gave you to me.   [1040]

OEDIPUS: Who?
   Who was he? Do you know? Can you tell me
   any details, ones you know for certain?

MESSENGER: Well, I think he was one of Laius' servants—
   that's what people said.

OEDIPUS: You mean king Laius,
   the one who ruled this country years ago?

MESSENGER: That's right. He was one of the king's shepherds.

OEDIPUS: Is he still alive? Can I still see him?   1250

MESSENGER: You people live here. You'd best answer that.

OEDIPUS: [turning to the Chorus] Do any of you here now know the man,
   this shepherd he describes? Have you seen him,
   either in the fields or here in Thebes?
   Answer me. It's critical, time at last
   to find out what this means.   [1050]

CHORUS LEADER: The man he mentioned
   is, I think, the very peasant from the fields
   you wanted to see earlier. But of this
   Jocasta could tell more than anyone.

OEDIPUS: Lady, do you know the man we sent for—   1260
   just minutes ago—the one we summoned here?
   Is he the one this messenger refers to?

JOCASTA: Why ask me what he means? Forget all that.
   There's no point in trying to sort out what he said.

OEDIPUS: With all these indications of the truth
   here in my grasp, I cannot end this now.
   I must reveal the details of my birth.

JOCASTA: In the name of the gods, no! If you have   [1060]
   some concern for your own life, then stop!

Do not keep investigating this.
I will suffer—that will be enough.   1270

OEDIPUS: Be brave. Even if I should turn out to be
born from a shameful mother, whose family
for three generations have been slaves,
you will still have your noble lineage.

JOCASTA: Listen to me, I beg you. Do not do this.

OEDIPUS: I will not be convinced I should not learn
the whole truth of what these facts amount to.

JOCASTA: But I care about your own well being—
what I tell you is for your benefit.   1280

OEDIPUS: What you're telling me for my own good
just brings me more distress.

JOCASTA: Oh, you unhappy man!
May you never find out who you really are!

OEDIPUS: [to Chorus] Go, one of you, and bring that shepherd here.
Leave the lady to enjoy her noble family.   [1070]

JOCASTA: Alas, you poor miserable man!
There's nothing more that I can say to you.
And now I'll never speak again.

[JOCASTA runs into the palace]

CHORUS LEADER: Why has the queen rushed off, Oedipus,
so full of grief? I fear a disastrous storm   1290
will soon break through her silence.

OEDIPUS: Then let it break,
whatever it is. As for myself,
no matter how base born my family,
I wish to know the seed from where I came.
Perhaps my queen is now ashamed of me
and of my insignificant origin—

she likes to play the noble lady.
But I will never feel myself dishonoured.   [1080]
I see myself as a child of fortune—
and she is generous, that mother of mine   1300
from whom I spring, and the months, my siblings,
have seen me by turns both small and great.
That's how I was born. I cannot change
to someone else, nor can I ever cease
from seeking out the facts of my own birth.

CHORUS: If I have any power of prophecy
    or skill in knowing things,
    then, by the Olympian deities,
    you, Cithaeron, at tomorrow's moon   [1090]
    will surely know that Oedipus   1310
    pays tribute to you as his native land
    both as his mother and his nurse,
    and that our choral dance and song
    acknowledge you because you are
    so pleasing to our king.
    O Phoebus, we cry out to you—
    may our song fill you with delight!

    Who gave birth to you, my child?
    Which one of the immortal gods
    bore you to your father Pan,   1320   [1100]
    who roams the mountainsides?
    Was it some daughter of Apollo,
    the god who loves all country fields?
    Perhaps Cyllene's royal king?
    Or was it the Bacchanalian god
    dwelling on the mountain tops
    who took you as a new-born joy
    from maiden nymphs of Helicon
    with whom he often romps and plays?[19]

OEDIPUS: [looking out away from the palace]

    You elders, although I've never seen the man   1330   [1110]
    we've been looking for a long time now,
    if I had to guess, I think I see him.

He's coming here. He looks very old—
as is appropriate, if he's the one.
And I know the people coming with him,
servants of mine. But if you've seen him before,
you'll recognize him better than I will.

CHORUS LEADER: Yes, I recognize the man. There's no doubt.
He worked for Laius—a trusty shepherd.

[Enter SERVANT, an old shepherd]

OEDIPUS: Stranger from Corinth, let me first ask you—   1340
is this the man you mentioned?

MESSENGER: Yes, he is—
he's the man you see in front of you.   [1120]

OEDIPUS: You, old man, over here. Look at me.
Now answer what I ask. Some time ago
did you work for Laius?

SERVANT: Yes, as a slave.
But I was not bought. I grew up in his house.

OEDIPUS: How did you live? What was the work you did?

SERVANT: Most of my life I've spent looking after sheep.

OEDIPUS: Where? In what particular areas?

SERVANT: On Cithaeron or the neighbouring lands.   1350

OEDIPUS: Do you know if you came across this man
anywhere up there?

SERVANT: Doing what?
What man do you mean?

OEDIPUS: The man over here—
this one. Have you ever run into him?   [1130]

SERVANT: Right now I can't say I remember him.

MESSENGER: My lord, that's surely not surprising.
 Let me refresh his failing memory.
 I think he will remember all too well
 the time we spent around Cithaeron.
 He had two flocks of sheep and I had one.   1360
 I was with him there for six months at a stretch,
 from early spring until the autumn season.
 In winter I'd drive my sheep down to my folds,
 and he'd take his to pens that Laius owned.
 Isn't that what happened—what I've just said?   [1140]

SERVANT: You spoke the truth. But it was long ago.

MESSENGER: All right, then. Now, tell me if you recall
 how you gave me a child, an infant boy,
 for me to raise as my own foster son.

SERVANT: What? Why ask about that?

MESSENGER: This man here, my friend,   1370
 was that young child back then.

SERVANT: Damn you!
 Can't you keep quiet about it!

OEDIPUS: Hold on, old man.
 Don't criticize him. What you have said
 is more objectionable than his account.

SERVANT: My noble master, what have I done wrong?

OEDIPUS: You did not tell us of that infant boy,   [1150]
 the one he asked about.

SERVANT: That's what he says,
 but he knows nothing—a useless busybody.

OEDIPUS: If you won't tell us of your own free will,
 once we start to hurt you, you will talk.   1380

SERVANT: By all the gods, don't torture an old man!

OEDIPUS: One of you there, tie up this fellow's hands.

SERVANT: Why are you doing this? It's too much for me!
    What is it you want to know?

OEDIPUS: That child he mentioned—
    did you give it to him?

SERVANT: I did. How I wish
    I'd died that day!

OEDIPUS: Well, you're going to die
    if you don't speak the truth.

SERVANT: And if I do,
    there's an even greater chance that I'll be killed.

OEDIPUS: It seems to me the man is trying to stall.   [1160]

SERVANT: No, no, I'm not. I've already told you—   1390
    I did give him the child.

OEDIPUS: Where did you get it?
    Did it come from your home or somewhere else?

SERVANT: It was not mine—I got it from someone.

OEDIPUS: Which of our citizens? Whose home was it?

SERVANT: In the name of the gods, my lord, don't ask!
    Please, no more questions!

OEDIPUS: If I have to ask again,
    then you will die.

SERVANT: The child was born in Laius' house.

OEDIPUS: From a slave or from some relative of his?

SERVANT: Alas, what I'm about to say now …
   it's horrible.

OEDIPUS: And I'm about to hear it.   1400   [1170]
   But nonetheless I have to know this.

SERVANT: If you must know, they said the child was his.
   But your wife inside the palace is the one
   who could best tell you what was going on.

OEDIPUS: You mean she gave the child to you?

SERVANT: Yes, my lord.

OEDIPUS: Why did she do that?

SERVANT: So I would kill it.

OEDIPUS: That wretched woman was the mother?

SERVANT: Yes.
   She was afraid of dreadful prophecies.

OEDIPUS: What sort of prophecies?

SERVANT: The story went
   that he would kill his father.

OEDIPUS: If that was true,   1410
   why did you give the child to this old man?

SERVANT: I pitied the boy, master, and I thought
   he'd take the child off to a foreign land
   where he was from. But he rescued him,
   only to save him for the greatest grief of all.   [1180]
   For if you're the one this man says you are
   you know your birth carried an awful fate.

OEDIPUS: Ah, so it all came true. It's so clear now.
   O light, let me look at you one final time,
   a man who stands revealed as cursed by birth,   1420

cursed by my own family, and cursed
by murder where I should not kill.

[OEDIPUS moves into the palace]

CHORUS: O generations of mortal men,
    how I count your life as scarcely living.
    What man is there, what human being,
    who attains a greater happiness   [1190]
    than mere appearances, a joy
    which seems to fade away to nothing?
    Poor wretched Oedipus, your fate
    stands here to demonstrate for me   1430
    how no mortal man is ever blessed.

    Here was a man who fired his arrows well—
    his skill was matchless—and he won
    the highest happiness in everything.
    For, Zeus, he slaughtered the hook-taloned Sphinx
    and stilled her cryptic song. For our state,
    he stood there like a tower against death,   [1200]
    and from that moment, Oedipus,
    we have called you our king
    and honoured you above all other men,   1440
    the one who rules in mighty Thebes.

    But now who is there whose story
    is more terrible to hear? Whose life
    has been so changed by trouble,
    by such ferocious agonies?
    Alas, for celebrated Oedipus,
    the same spacious place of refuge
    served you both as child and father,
    the place you entered as a new bridegroom.   [1210]
    How could the furrow where your father planted,   1450
    poor wretched man, have tolerated you
    in such silence for so long?

    Time, which watches everything
    and uncovered you against your will,
    now sits in judgment of that fatal marriage,

where child and parent have been joined so long.
O child of Laius, how I wish
I'd never seen you—now I wail
like one whose mouth pours forth laments.   [1220]
To tell it right, it was through you   1460
I found my life and breathed again,
and then through you my eyesight failed.

[The Second Messenger enters from the palace]

SECOND MESSENGER: O you most honoured citizens of Thebes,
    what actions you will hear about and see,
    what sorrows you will bear, if, as natives here,
    you are still loyal to the house of Labdacus!
    I do not think the Ister or the Phasis rivers
    could cleanse this house. It conceals too much
    and soon will bring to light the vilest things,
    brought on by choice and not by accident.[20]   1470   [1230]
    What we do to ourselves brings us most pain.

CHORUS LEADER: The calamities we knew about before
    were hard enough to bear. What can you say
    to make them worse?

SECOND MESSENGER: I'll waste no words—
    know this—noble Jocasta, our queen, is dead.

CHORUS LEADER: That poor unhappy lady! How did she die?

SECOND MESSENGER: She killed herself. You did not see it,
    so you'll be spared the worst of what went on.
    But from what I recall of what I saw
    you'll learn how that poor woman suffered.   1480   [1240]
    She left here frantic and rushed inside,
    fingers on both hands clenched in her hair.
    She ran through the hall straight to her marriage bed.
    She went in, slamming both doors shut behind her
    and crying out to Laius, who's been a corpse
    a long time now. She was remembering
    that child of theirs born many years ago—
    the one who killed his father, who left her

to conceive cursed children with that son.
She lay moaning by the bed, where she,   1490
poor woman, had given birth twice over—
a husband from a husband, children from a child.   [1250]
How she died after that I don't fully know.
With a scream Oedipus came bursting in.
He would not let us see her suffering,
her final pain. We watched him charge around,
back and forth. As he moved, he kept asking us
to give him a sword, as he tried to find
that wife who was no wife—whose mother's womb
had given birth to him and to his children.   1500
As he raved, some immortal power led him on—
no human in the room came close to him.
With a dreadful howl, as if someone   [1260]
had pushed him, he leapt at the double doors,
bent the bolts by force out of their sockets,
and burst into the room. Then we saw her.
She was hanging there, swaying, with twisted cords
roped round her neck. When Oedipus saw her,
with a dreadful groan he took her body
out of the noose in which she hung, and then,   1510
when the poor woman was lying on the ground—
what happened next was a horrific sight—
from her clothes he ripped the golden brooches
she wore as ornaments, raised them high,
and drove them deep into his eyeballs,   [1270]
crying as he did so: "You will no longer see
all those atrocious things I suffered,
the dreadful things I did! No. You have seen
those you never should have looked upon,
and those I wished to know you did not see.   1520
So now and for all future time be dark!"
With these words he raised his hand and struck,
not once, but many times, right in the sockets.
With every blow blood spurted from his eyes
down on his beard, and not in single drops,
but showers of dark blood spattered like hail.   [1280]
So what these two have done has overwhelmed
not one alone—this disaster swallows up
a man and wife together. That old happiness

they had before in their rich ancestry   1530
was truly joy, but now lament and ruin,
death and shame, and all calamities
which men can name are theirs to keep.

CHORUS LEADER: And has that suffering man found some relief
to ease his pain?

SECOND MESSENGER: He shouts at everyone
to open up the gates and thus reveal
to all Cadmeians his father's killer,
his mother's ... but I must not say those words.
He wants them to cast him out of Thebes,   [1290]
so the curse he laid will not come on this house   1540
if he still lives inside. But he is weak
and needs someone to lead him on his way.
His agony is more than he can bear—
as he will show you—for on the palace doors
the bolts are being pulled back. Soon you will see
a sight which even a man filled with disgust
would have to pity.

[OEDIPUS enters through the palace doors]

CHORUS LEADER: An awful fate for human eyes to witness,
an appalling sight—the worst I've ever seen.
O you poor man, what madness came on you?   1550
What eternal force pounced on your life   [1300]
and, springing further than the longest leap,
brought you this awful doom? Alas! Alas!
You unhappy man! I cannot look at you.
I want to ask you many things—there's much
I wish to learn. You fill me with such horror,
yet there is so much I must see.

OEDIPUS: Aaaiiii, aaaiii ... Alas! Alas!
How miserable I am ... such wretchedness ...
Where do I go? How can the wings of air   1560   [1310]
sweep up my voice? Oh my destiny,
how far you have sprung now!

CHORUS LEADER: To a fearful place from which men turn away,
    a place they hate to look upon.

OEDIPUS: O the dark horror wrapped around me,
    this nameless visitor I can't resist
    swept here by fair and fatal winds.
    Alas for me! And yet again, alas for me!
    The agony of stabbing brooches
    pierces me! The memory of aching shame!   1570

CHORUS LEADER: In your distress it's not astonishing
    you bear a double load of suffering,   [1320]
    a double load of pain.

OEDIPUS: Ah, my friend,
    so you still care for me, as always,
    and with patience nurse me now I'm blind.
    Alas! Alas! You are not hidden from me—
    I recognize you all too clearly.
    Though I am blind, I know that voice so well.

CHORUS LEADER: You have carried out such dreadful things—
    how could you dare to blind yourself this way?   1580
    What god drove you to it?

OEDIPUS: It was Apollo, friends,
    it was Apollo. He brought on these troubles—   [1330]
    the awful things I suffer. But the hand
    which stabbed out my eyes was mine alone.
    In my wretched life, why should I have eyes
    when nothing I could see would bring me joy?

CHORUS LEADER: What you have said is true enough.

OEDIPUS: What is there for me to see, my friends?
    What can I love? Whose greeting can I hear
    and feel delight? Hurry now, my friends,   1590   [1340]
    lead me away from Thebes—take me somewhere,
    a man completely lost, utterly accursed,
    the mortal man the gods despise the most.

CHORUS LEADER: Unhappy in your fate and in your mind
    which now knows all. Would I had never known you!

OEDIPUS: Whoever the man is who freed my feet,
    who released me from that cruel shackle   [1350]
    and rescued me from death, may that man die!
    It was a thankless act. Had I perished then,
    I would not have brought such agony   1600
    to myself or to my friends.

CHORUS LEADER: I agree—
    I would have preferred your death, as well.

OEDIPUS: I would not have come to kill my father,
    and men would not see in me the husband
    of the woman who gave birth to me.
    Now I am abandoned by the gods,   [1360]
    the son of a corrupted mother,
    conceiving children with the woman
    who gave me my own miserable life.
    If there is some suffering more serious   1610
    than all the rest, then it too belongs
    in the fate of Oedipus.

CHORUS LEADER: I do not believe
    what you did to yourself is for the best.
    Better to be dead than alive and blind.

OEDIPUS: Don't tell me what I've done is not the best.
    And from now on spare me your advice.   [1370]
    If I could see, I don't know how my eyes
    could look at my own father when I come
    to Hades or could see my wretched mother.
    Against those two I have committed acts   1620
    so vile that even if I hanged myself
    that would not be sufficient punishment.
    Perhaps you think the sight of my own children
    might give me joy? No! Look how they were born!
    They could never bring delight to eyes of mine.
    Nor could the city or its massive walls,
    or the sacred images of its gods.

I am the most abhorred of men, I,
the finest one of all those bred in Thebes,   [1380]
I have condemned myself, telling everyone   1630
they had to banish for impiety
the man the gods have now exposed
as sacrilegious—a son of Laius, too.
With such polluting stains upon me,
could I set eyes on you and hold your gaze?
No. And if I could somehow block my ears
and kill my hearing, I would not hold back.
I'd make a dungeon of this wretched body,
so I would never see or hear again.
For there is joy in isolated thought,   1640
sealed off from a world of sorrow.   [1390]
O Cithaeron, why did you shelter me?
Why, when I was handed over to you,
did you not do away with me at once,
so I would never then reveal to men
the nature of my birth? Ah Polybus,
and Corinth, the place men called my home,
my father's ancient house, you raised me well—
so fine to look at, so corrupt inside!
Now I've been exposed as something bad,   1650
contaminated in my origins.
Oh you three roads and hidden forest grove,
you thicket and defile where three paths meet,
you who swallowed down my father's blood   [1400]
from my own hands, do you remember me,
what I did there in front of you and then
what else I did when I came here to Thebes?
Ah, you marriage rites—you gave birth to me,
and then when I was born, you gave birth again,
children from the child of that same womb,   1660
creating an incestuous blood family
of fathers, brothers, children, brides,
wives and mothers—the most atrocious act
that human beings commit! But it is wrong
to talk about what it is wrong to do,
so in the name of all the gods, act quickly—
hide me somewhere outside the land of Thebes,   [1410]
or slaughter me, or hurl me in the sea,

where you will never gaze on me again.
Come, allow yourself to touch a wretched man.　　　　　　1670
Listen to me, and do not be afraid—
for this disease infects no one but me.

CHORUS LEADER: Creon is coming. He is just in time
to plan and carry out what you propose.
With you gone he's the only one who's left
to act as guardian of Thebes.

OEDIPUS:　　　　　　　　　　　　Alas,
how will I talk to him? How can I ask him
to put his trust in me? Not long ago　　　　　　　　　　[1420]
I treated him with such contempt.

[Enter Creon]

CREON: Oedipus, I have not come here to mock　　　　　　1680
or blame you for disasters in the past.
But if you can no longer value human beings,
at least respect our lord the sun, whose light
makes all things grow, and do not put on show
pollution of this kind in such a public way,
for neither earth nor light nor sacred rain
can welcome such a sight.

[Creon speaks to the attending servants]

　　　　　　　　　　Take him inside the house
as quickly as you can. The kindest thing
would be for members of his family　　　　　　　　　　[1430]
to be the only ones to see and hear him.　　　　1690

OEDIPUS: By all the gods, since you are acting now
so differently from what I would expect
and have come here to treat me graciously,
the very worst of men, do what I ask.
I will speak for your own benefit, not mine.

CREON: What are you so keen to get from me?

OEDIPUS: Cast me out as quickly as you can,
    away from Thebes, to a place where no one,
    no living human being, will cross my path.

CREON: That is something I could do, of course,   1700
    but first I wish to know what the god says
    about what I should do.

OEDIPUS: But what he said   [1440]
    was all so clear—the man who killed his father
    must be destroyed. And that corrupted man
    is me.

CREON: Yes, that is what was said. But now,
    with things the way they are, the wisest thing
    is to ascertain quite clearly what to do.

OEDIPUS: Will you then be making a request
    on my behalf when I am so depraved?

CREON: I will. For even you must now trust in the gods.   1710

OEDIPUS: Yes, I do. And I have a task for you
    as I make this plea—that woman in the house,
    please bury her as you see fit. You are the one
    to give your own the proper funeral rites.
    But never let my father's city be condemned
    to have me living here while I still live.   [1450]
    Let me make my home up in the mountains
    by Cithaeron, whose fame is now my own.
    When my father and mother were alive,
    they chose it as my special burying place—   1720
    and thus, when I die, I'll be following
    the orders of the ones who tried to kill me.
    And yet I know this much—no disease
    nor any other suffering can kill me—
    for I would never have been saved from death
    unless I was to suffer a strange destiny.
    But wherever my fate leads, just let it go.
    As for my two sons, Creon, there's no need
    for you to care for them on my behalf—

they are men—thus, no matter where they are,   1730   [1460]
they'll always have enough to live on.[21]
But my two poor daughters have never known
my dining table placed away from them
or lacked their father's presence. They shared
everything I touched—that's how it's always been.
So take care of them for me. But first let me
feel them with my hands and then I'll grieve.
Oh my lord, you noble heart, let me do that—
if my hands could touch them it would seem
as if I were with them when I still could see.   1740   [1470]

[Some SERVANTS lead ANTIGONE and ISMENE out of the palace]

What's this? By all the gods I hear something—
is it my two dear children crying … ?
Has Creon taken pity on me
and sent out the children, my dear treasures?
Is that what's happening?

CREON: Yes. I sent for them.
I know the joy they've always given you—
the joy which you feel now.

OEDIPUS: I wish you well.
And for this act, may the god watch over you
and treat you better than he treated me.
Ah, my children, where are you? Come here,   1750   [1480]
come into my arms—you are my sisters now—
feel these hands which turned your father's eyes,
once so bright, into what you see now,
these empty sockets. He was a man, who,
seeing nothing, knowing nothing, fathered you
with the woman who had given birth to him.
I weep for you. Although I cannot see,
I think about your life in days to come,
the bitter life which men will force on you.
What citizens will associate with you?   1760
What feasts will you attend and not come home
in tears, with no share in the rejoicing?   [1490]
When you're mature enough for marriage,

who will be there for you, my children,
what husband ready to assume the shame
tainting my children and their children, too?
What perversion is not manifest in us?
Your father killed his father, and then ploughed
his mother's womb—where he himself was born—
conceiving you where he, too, was conceived.   1770
Those are the insults they will hurl at you.   [1500]
Who, then, will marry you? No one, my children.
You must wither, barren and unmarried.
Son of Menoeceus, with both parents gone,
you alone remain these children's father.
Do not let them live as vagrant paupers,
wandering around unmarried. You are
a relative of theirs—don't let them sink
to lives of desperation like my own.
Have pity. You see them now at their young age   1780
deprived of everything except a share
in what you are. Promise me, you noble soul,
you will extend your hand to them. And you,   [1510]
my children, if your minds were now mature,
there's so much I could say. But I urge you—
pray that you may live as best you can
and lead your destined life more happily
than your own father.

CREON: You have grieved enough.
   Now go into the house.

OEDIPUS: I must obey,
   although that's not what I desire.

CREON: In due time   1790
   all things will work out for the best.

OEDIPUS: I will go.
   But you know there are conditions.

CREON: Tell me.
   Once I hear them, I'll know what they are.

OEDIPUS: Send me away to live outside of Thebes.

CREON: Only the god can give you what you ask.

OEDIPUS: But I've become abhorrent to the gods.

CREON: Then you should quickly get what you desire.

OEDIPUS: So you agree?   [1520]

CREON: I don't like to speak
   thoughtlessly and say what I don't mean.

OEDIPUS: Come then, lead me off.

CREON: All right,   1800
   but let go of the children.

OEDIPUS: No, no!
   Do not take them away from me.

CREON: Don't try to be in charge of everything.
   Your life has lost the power you once had.

[CREON, OEDIPUS, ANTIGONE, ISMENE, and ATTENDANTS all enter the palace][22]

CHORUS: You residents of Thebes, our native land,
   look on this man, this Oedipus, the one
   who understood that celebrated riddle.
   He was the most powerful of men.
   All citizens who witnessed this man's wealth
   were envious. Now what a surging tide   1810
   of terrible disaster sweeps around him.
   So while we wait to see that final day,
   we cannot call a mortal being happy
   before he's passed beyond life free from pain.   [1530]

NOTES

1. *Cadmus*: legendary founder of Thebes. Hence, the citizens of Thebes were often called children of Cadmus or Cadmeians.
2. *Pallas*: Pallas Athena. There were two shrines to her in Thebes. Ismenus: A temple to Apollo Ismenios where burnt offerings were the basis for the priest's divination.
3. *cruel singer*: a reference to the Sphinx, a monster with the body of a lion, wings, and the head and torso of a woman. After the death of king Laius, the Sphinx tyrannized Thebes by not letting anyone into or out of the city, unless the person could answer the following riddle: "What walks on four legs in the morning, on two legs at noon, and three legs in the evening?" Those who could not answer were killed and eaten. Oedipus provided the answer (a human being), and thus saved the city. The Sphinx then committed suicide.
4. *berries*: a suppliant to Apollo's shrine characteristically wore such a garland if he received favourable news.
5. *Ares*, god of war and killing, was often disapproved of by the major Olympian deities. Amphitrite: was a goddess of the sea, married to Poseidon.
6. *lord of Lyceia*: a reference to Apollo, god of light.
7. *... among gods*: Dionysus was also called Bacchus, and Thebes was sometimes called Baccheia (belonging to Bacchus). The Maenads are the followers of Dionysus.
8. *lustral water*: water purified in a communal religious ritual.
9. *Agenor*: founder of the Theban royal family; his son Cadmus moved from Sidon in Asia Minor to Greece and founded Thebes. Polydorus: son of Cadmus, father of Labdacus, and hence grandfather of Laius.
10. *Cithaeron*: the sacred mountain outside Thebes.
11. *Zeus' son*: a reference to Apollo. The Furies are the goddesses of blood revenge. [Back to text]
12. *Parnassus*: a famous mountain some distance from Thebes, but visible from the city.
13. *Polybus*: ruler of Corinth, who raised Oedipus and is thus believed to be his father. The house of Labdacus is the Theban royal family (i.e., Laius, Jocasta, and Creon).
14. There is some argument about who speaks which lines in 622-626 of the Greek text. I follow Jebb's suggestions, ascribing 625 to Creon, to whom it seems clearly to belong (in spite of the manuscripts) and adding a line to indicate Oedipus' response.
15. This part of the choral song makes an important distinction between two forms of self-assertive action: the first breeds self-aggrandizement and greed; the second is necessary for the protection of the state.

16. *Isthmus*: The city of Corinth stood on the narrow stretch of land (the Isthmus) connecting the Peloponnese with mainland Greece, a very strategic position.

17. *Loxias*: a common name for Apollo.

18. *... still carry*: the name Oedipus can be construed to mean either "swollen feet" or "knowledge of one's feet." Both terms evoke a strongly ironic sense of how Oedipus, for all his fame as a man of knowledge, is ignorant about his origin.

19. Cyllene's king is the god Hermes, who was born on Mount Cyllene; the Bacchanalian god is Dionysus.

20. This line refers, not the entire story, but to what Jocasta and Oedipus have just done to themselves.

21. Oedipus' two sons, Eteocles and Polyneices, would probably be fifteen or sixteen years old at this time, not old enough to succeed Oedipus.

22. It is not entirely clear from these final lines whether Oedipus now leaves Thebes or not. According to Jebb's commentary (line 1519), in the traditional story on which Sophocles is relying, Oedipus was involuntarily held at Thebes for some time before the citizens and Creon expelled him from the city. Creon's lines suggest he is going to wait to hear from the oracle before deciding about Oedipus. However, there is a powerful dramatic logic in having Oedipus stumble off away from the palace. In Book 23 of the Iliad, Homer indicates that Oedipus died at Thebes, and there were funeral games held in his honour in that city.

Plato's *Apology*

୮୰୮୰୮୰୮୰୮୰୮୰୮୰୮୰୮୰୮୰

Translated by W. H. D. Rouse

THE DEFENCE OF SOCRATES
Introductory Note

The trial of Socrates took place in 399 B.C., when he was seventy years old. Meletos, Anytos and Lycon (Anytos is one of the characters in the Meno*) accused him of impiety and of corrupting the young men.*

The court which tried Socrates was composed of 501 citizens, and was a subdivision of the larger court of six thousand citizens, chosen by lot, which dealt with such cases. There were no judge and jury in the modern sense; the decision of the court was that of the majority vote.

When the court had pronounced Socrates guilty, the law required him to propose his own penalty, as an alternative to the death penalty proposed by Meletos; no penalty was prescribed by law for his offence. The court then had to choose, by a second vote, between the proposals of the accuser and the accused.

From the mention on page 439 it appears that Plato himself was present at the trial.

How you felt, gentlemen of Athens, when you heard my accusers, I do not know; but I—well, I nearly forgot who I was, they were so persuasive. Yet as for truth—one might almost say they have spoken not one word of truth. But what most astonished me in the many lies they told was when they warned you to take good care not to be deceived by me, because I was a terribly clever speaker." They ought to have been ashamed to say it, because I shall prove them wrong at once by facts when I begin to speak, and you will see that I am not a bit of a clever speaker. That seemed to me the most shameless thing about them, unless of course they call one who speaks the truth a clever speaker. If that is what they mean, I would agree that I am not an orator of their class. Well then, these men, as I said, have spoken hardly one word of truth; but you shall hear from me the whole truth; not eloquence, gentlemen, like their own, decked out in fine words and phrases, not covered with ornaments; not at all—you shall hear things spoken anyhow in the words that first come. For I believe justice is in what I say, and let none of you expect anything else; indeed it would not be proper, gentlemen, for an old man like me to come before you like a boy moulding his words in pretty patterns. One thing, however, gentlemen, I beg and pray you most earnestly; if you hear me using to defend myself here the same words which I speak with generally, in the market or at the banker's counter, where many of you have heard me, and elsewhere, do not be surprised and make a noise on that account. The fact is, this is the first time I ever came up before a court, although I am seventy years old; so I am simply quite strange to the style of this place. If I were really a stranger, a foreigner, I suppose you would not be hard on me if I used the language and manner which I had been brought up to; then I beg you to treat me the same way now, and, as seems fair, to let pass my manner of speaking; perhaps it might be better, and perhaps it might be worse; but please consider only one thing and attend carefully to that—whether my plea is just or not. For that is the merit of the juryman, but the merit of the orator is to speak the truth.

First, then, gentlemen, it is proper for me to answer the first false accusations made against me, and the first accusers; next, to answer the later accusations and accusers. Indeed, I have had many accusers complaining to you, and for a long time, for many years now, and with not a word of truth to say; these I fear, rather than Anytos and his friends, although they, too, are dangerous; but the others are more dangerous, gentlemen, who got hold of most of you while you were boys, and persuaded you, and accused me falsely, and said, "There is a certain Socrates, a highbrow; brainy in skylore, has investigated what is under the earth, makes the weaker argument the stronger." These, gentlemen, who have broadcast this reputation, these are my dangerous accusers; for those who hear believe that anyone who is a student of that sort of lore must be an atheist as well. Yes, these accusers are many, and they have been accusing me for a long time, still saying the same, and moreover saying it to you at an age when you would be most likely to believe, when some of you were children or at least lads, really accusing in a case which goes by default, with no one to defend. The most unreasonable thing is that it is impossible to know their names or to tell who they are unless one of them happens to be a comic poet.[1] But those who have deluded you from envy and malice, or some who are convinced themselves and try to convince others, these are the hardest to deal with. For there is no possibility of having them produced here, or of cross-questioning any one of them, but having to defend oneself against them is just like being compelled to fight with shadows, and cross-question with none answering. Pray remember, then, that my accusers are of two kinds, as I say, one, those who have accused me now, and the other, the old ones I mention; and consider that I must answer the old ones first. You heard them first, you see, and much more than the new ones. Very good; I must answer them, gentlemen, and try to get rid of the prejudice which you have had so long, with only a short time to do it. I hope indeed I may remove it, if it is better so both for you and for me, and I hope my defence may

---

1 Aristophanes was one of them. In *The Clouds* he represented Socrates as an old man hung up in a basket observing the sun, and in other comic situations.

have some success; but I think it is difficult, and I am quite aware what a task it is. All the same, in this let God's will be done; I must obey the law, and make my defence.

Let us go back to the beginnings and see what the accusation is, whence came the prejudice against me, which Meletos believed when he brought this indictment Very well; what did the calumniators say who calumniated me? I will pretend to read a pretended affidavit of my accusers: "Socrates is a criminal and a busybody, prying into things under the earth and up in the heavens, and making the weaker argument the stronger, and teaching these same things to others." It is something like that; for that is what you saw in the comedy² of Aristophanes, a certain Socrates there being carried about, and claiming to be treading on air and talking much other nonsensical nonsense about which I don't understand one jot or tittle. Don't suppose that in saying this I mean to disparage knowledge of that kind, if anyone does know about such things: may I never be prosecuted by Meletos on serious charges such as that! But I have nothing to do with such things, gentlemen. I appeal to most of you to bear me out, and I ask you to inform and tell one another, as many as have ever heard me conversing—and those of you who have heard me are many—tell one another, then, whether any of you has ever heard me conversing about such things, either much or little. Then you will recognise from this that the other things are just the same which people say about me.

But, indeed, as none of these things is true, neither is it true, even if you have heard it from someone, that I undertake to educate people, and take fees. I must say I think it is a grand thing for anyone to be able to educate people as Gorgias of Leontini, and Prodicos of Ceos, and Hippias of Elis do. For each of these, gentlemen, is able to go to any city, and persuade the young men, who can associate for nothing with any one they like of their fellow-citizens, to leave the society of those and to associate with themselves, and to pay for it and thank them besides. Indeed, there is in this place another man, one from Paros, an able man, who I found out was staying here in Athens; for I happened to meet a man, who has paid more money to Sophists³ than all the rest put together, Callias, Hipponicos. son, so I asked him—he has two sons of his own—"Callias," I said, "if your two sons were colts or calves, we should know how to hire and pay a manager for them, to make them well-bred in the virtue proper to those animals; he would be a horse-trainer or a farmer; but now, since they are human beings, whom have you in mind to be their manager? Who is an expert in such virtue, human or political? For I think you have looked for one because you have sons. Is there one," said I, "or not?"

"Certainly there is," said he.

"Who?" said I, "and where does he come from, and what's his fee for teaching?"

---

2   *The Clouds*. See also p. 329, n. 1.
3   See note on *Meno,* p. 49..

"Euenos," he said, "from Paros, my dear Socrates, five minas."[4]

And I said Euenos is a happy man, if really and truly he has this art and teaches it for such a modest fee. I, at least, should give myself fine airs and graces if I had this knowledge. But I have not, gentlemen.

Some one of you then might put in and ask perhaps, "Well, Socrates, what is your business? Where did these calumnies come from? For all this talk about you, and such a reputation, has not arisen, I presume, when you were working at nothing, more unusual than others do; it must be you were doing something different from most people. Then tell us what it is, that we may not be rash and careless about you." That seems to be quite fair, if anyone says it, and I will try to show you what this is which has got me this name[5] and this prejudice. Listen, then. And perhaps some of you will think I am jesting, but be sure I will tell you the whole truth: a sort of wisdom has got me this name, gentlemen, and nothing else. Wisdom! What wisdom? Perhaps the only wisdom that man can have. For the fact is, I really am wise in this wisdom; but it may be that those I just spoke of are wise in a wisdom greater than man's, or I can't think how to describe it—for I don't understand it myself, but whoever says I do, lies, and speaks in calumny of me. And do not protest, gentlemen, even if you should think I am boastful; for what I am going to tell you is not my word, but I will refer it to a speaker of sufficient authority; I will call the god in Delphi as witness of my wisdom, whether indeed it is wisdom at all, and what it is. I suppose you know Chairephon. He has been my friend since I was young, and a friend of your people's party, and he was banished with you lately and with you was restored. And you know, doubtless, what sort of man he was, how impetuous in all he tried to do. Well, once he went to Delphi and dared to ask this question of the oracle—don't make an uproar, gentlemen, at what I say—for he asked if anyone was wiser than I was. The priestess answered, then, that no one was wiser. His brother is here, and he will bear witness to this, as Chairephon is dead. But let me tell you why I say this; I am going to show you where that calumny came from. Well, when I heard that reply I thought: "What in the world does the god mean? What in the world is his riddle? For I know in my con-science that I am not wise in anything, great or small; then what in the world does he mean when he says I am wisest? Surely he is not lying? For he must not lie." I was puzzled for a long time to understand what he meant; then I thought of a way to try to find out, something like this: I approached one of those who had the reputation of being wise, for there, I thought, if anywhere, I should test the revelation and prove that the oracle was wrong: "Here is one wiser than I, but you said I was wiser." When I examined him, then—I need not tell his name, but it was one of our statesmen whom I was examining when I had this strange experience, gentlemen—and when I conversed with him, I thought this man seemed to be wise both to many others and especially to himself, but that he was not; and then I tried to

---

4   About the equivalent of £60, or $180.
5   Of Sophist.

show him that he thought he was wise, but was not. Because of that he disliked me and so did many others who were there, but I went away thinking to myself that I was wiser than this man; the fact is that neither of us knows anything beautiful and good, but he thinks he does know when he doesn't, and I don't know and don't think I do: so I am wiser than he is by only this trifle, that what I do not know I don't think I do. After that I tried another, one of those reputed to be wiser than that man, and I thought just the same; then he and many others took a dislike to me.

So I went to one after another after that, and saw that I was disliked; and I sorrowed and feared; but still it seemed necessary to hold the god's business of the highest importance, so I had to go on trying to find out what the oracle meant, and approaching all those who had the reputation of knowledge. And by the Dog, gentlemen—for I must tell you the truth—this is what happened to me: Those who had the highest reputation seemed to me nearly the most wanting, when I tried to find out in the god's way, but others who were thought inferior seemed to be more capable man as to common sense. You see I must show you my wanderings, as one who had my own Labours[6] to prove that the oracle was unimpeachable. For after the statesmen, I approached the poets, the composers of tragedies and the composers of dithyrambs,[7] and all the rest as well; there I expected to find myself caught in the act as more ignorant than they were. So I took up their poems, those which I thought they had taken most pains to perfect, and questioned them as to what they meant, and I hoped to learn something from them at the same time. Well, gentlemen, I am ashamed to tell you the truth; but I must. Almost all the bystanders, with hardly an exception, one might say, had something better to say than the composers had about their own compositions. I discovered, then, very soon about the poets that no wisdom enabled them to compose as they did, but natural genius and inspiration;[8] like the diviners and those who chant oracles, who say many fine things but do not understand anything of what they say. The poets appeared to me to be in much the same case; and at the same time I perceived that because of their poetry they believed they were the wisest of mankind in other things as well, which they were not. So I left them also, believing that I had the same superiority over them as I had over the statesmen.

At last I approached the craftsmen; for here I was conscious that I knew nothing, one may say, but these I was sure to find knowing much of real value. I was not deceived in that; they knew what I did not, and here they were much wiser than I was. But, gentlemen, they seemed to make the same mistake as the poets, even good workmen; because they could manage their art well, each one claimed to be very wise in other things also, the greatest things, and this fault of theirs appeared to obscure their real wisdom. So I asked myself on behalf of the oracle, whether I should prefer to be as I am, not wise

6 Like Heracles (Hercules).
7 See p. 192 n.
8 See also Ion, p. 18, and generally.

with their wisdom nor ignorant with their ignorance; or to have what they have, both. I answered myself and the oracle, that it was best for me to be as I am.

From this enquiry, gentlemen, many dislikes have arisen against me, and those very dangerous and crushing, so that many calumnies have come out of them, and I got the title of being wise. For the bystanders always believe that I am wise myself in the matters on which I test another; but the truth really is, gentlemen, that the god in fact is wise, and in this oracle he means that human wisdom is worth little or nothing, and it appears that he does not say this of Socrates, but simply adds my name to take me as an example, as if he were to say that this one of you human beings is wisest, who like Socrates knows that he is in truth worth nothing as regards wisdom. This is what I still, even now, go about searching and investigating in the god's way, if ever I think one of our people, or a foreigner, is wise; and whenever I don't find him so, I help the god by proving that the man is not wise. And because of this busy life, I have had no leisure either for pubic business worth mentioning or private, but I remain in infinite poverty through my service of the god.

Besides this, the young men, those who have most leisure, sons of the most wealthy houses, follow me of their own accord, delighted to hear people being cross-examined; and they often imitate me, they try themselves to cross-examine, and then, I think, they find plenty of people who believe they know something, when they know little or nothing. So in consequence those who are cross-examined are angry with me instead of with themselves, and say that Socrates is a blackguard and corrupts the young; and whenever someone asks them, "By doing what and teaching what?" they have nothing to say; they do not know, but, unwilling to own that they are at a loss, they repeat the stock charges against all philosophers, "underground lore and up-in-the-air lore, atheists, making the weaker argument the stronger," For they would not like, I think, to say the truth, that they are shown up as pretending to know when they know nothing. So I think, because they are ambitious, and pushing, and many in number, and they speak in battalions very plausibly about me, they have deafened you long since and now calumniate me vigorously. From among these Meletos has set upon me, and Anytos and Lycon, Meletos being angry on behalf of the poets, and Anytos for the craftsman and statesmen, and Lycon for the orators. The result is, as I began by saying, that I should be surprised if I could erase this prejudice from you in so short a time when it has grown so great. This, gentlemen, is the truth; I have hidden nothing great or small, and dissembled nothing. And I know well enough that these same things make me disliked; which is another proof that I am speaking the truth, and that this is the prejudice against me, and these are the causes. Whether you examine this now or afterwards, you will find the same.

As regards the accusations of my first accusers, let this defence suffice for you; next I will try to answer Meletos, the good patriot, as he calls himself, and the later accusers. Once more, then, let us take their affidavit, as if they were another set of accusers. This is how if runs: It says that Socrates is a criminal, who corrupts the young and does not believe in the gods whom the state believes in, but other new spiritual things instead. Such is the accusation; let us examine each point in this accusation. It says I am a criminal who corrupts the young. But I say, gentlemen, that Meletos is a criminal who is making a jest of serious things by prosecuting people lightly, by pretending to be serious and to care for things which he has ever cared about at all. That this is true, I will try to show you also.

Meletos, stand up here before me, and answer: Don't you think if very important that the younger generation should be as good as possible?

"I do."

Then tell these gentlemen, who is it makes them better? It is clear that you know, since you care about it. You have found the one who corrupts them, as you say, and you bring me before this court here and accuse me; now then, say who makes them better, inform the court who he is. You see, Meletos, you are silent, you cannot say. Yet does it not seem disgraceful to you, and a sufficient proof of what. I am just saying, that you have cared nothing about it? Come, say my good man, who makes them better?

"The laws."

That's not what I ask, dear sir; what *man,* who in the first place knows this very thing, the laws?

"This jury, Socrates."

What do you mean, Meletos? The gentlemen of the jury here are able to educate the young and make them better?

"Yes indeed."

All of them, or only some?

"All."

Excellently said, by Hera, quite an abundance of benefactors, Well. what of the people here listening to us, do they make the young better, or not?

"Yes, they do too."

What about the Councillors?[9]

The Councillors too."

Oh, indeed, Meletos, is it possible that the Commons corrupt the younger generation? Or do they also make them better, all of them?

"They do."

Then the whole nation of the Athenians, it seems, makes them fine gentlemen,[10] except me, and I alone corrupt them? Is that what you say?

"Yes, that is exactly what I do say."

What bad luck for me! You change me with my great bad luck! Answer me now: Are horses in the same case, do you think? All the men in the world are making them better, and only one corrupting them? Isn't the truth quite the opposite of this: There

---

9   The members of the upper house; sat p. 438, n. 1.

10   Literally, "Beautiful and good"

is one, perhaps, able to make them better, or very few—the horse-trainers, but most people, if they have to do with horses and use them, spoil and corrupt them? Isn't that the case, Meletos, both with horses and with all other animals? Most certainly, whether you and Anytos say no or whether you say yes. What a blessing it would be for young people, if only a single one corrupts them, and all the rest do them good! But really, Meletos, that is enough to show that you never were anxious about young people; you show clearly your own carelessness—you have cared nothing, about the things you impeach me for.

I have another question for you; in God's name attend, Meletos. Is it better to live among good citizens or bad ones? Answer me, good sir. There's nothing difficult in my question. Don't the bad ones do some harm to those who are at any time nearest to them, and the good ones some good?

"Certainly."

Then is there anyone who wants to be damaged by his associates rather than to be helped? Answer, my good man; the law commands you to answer. Is there anyone who wants to be damaged?

"No, certainly."

Very well. You bring me here as one who corrupts the young generation and makes them worse: Do you say that I mean to do it, or not?

"You mean to do it is what I say,"

Oh dear me, Meletos! I so old and you so young, and yet you are so much wiser than I am! You know that bad men always do harm to those who are nearest about them, but good men do good; yet look at me—have I indeed come to such a depth of ignorance that I do not know even this—that if I make one of my associates bad I shall risk getting some evil from him—to such a depth as to do so great an evil intentionally, as you say? I don't believe you there, Meletos, nor does anyone else in the world, I think; but either I do not corrupt or if I do, I corrupt without meaning to do it. So you are speaking falsely on both counts. But if I do it without intent, there is no law to bring a man into court for accidental mistakes such as this; on the contrary, the law is that one should take him apart privately and instruct and admonish him: for it is plain that, if I learn better, I shall stop what I do without intent. But you shirked meeting me and instructing me; you would not do that, and you bring me to this court, where it is the law to summon those who need punishment, not instruction.

Well now, gentlemen, thus much is plain by this time, as I said, that Meletos has never cared for these things, not one little bit. All the same, kindly tell us, Meletos how do you say I corrupt the young? It seems plain from the indictment which you made that it is by teaching them not to believe in the gods which the state believes in, but in other new spirits. Don't you say that it is by teaching this that I corrupt them?

"I do say so, and no mistake about it."

In the name of those gods, then, the very ones we speak of, Meletos, make if still clearer to me and these gentlemen. I can't understand whether you say I teach them to believe in some gods—in that ease I do believe myself that there are gods, and I am not a complete atheist, not am I a criminal in that sense—but that I do not believe in the same gods which the state believes in, but others, and this is what you accuse me of, that I believe in others: or, secondly, do you say that I disbelieve in gods altogether and teach this to other people?

"This is what I say, that you believe in no gods at all."

O you amazing creature, Meletos! What makes you say that? Then I don't believe even the sun and the moon are gods, like everyone else in the world?

"No, by Zeus, he does not, gentlemen of the jury, he says the sun is a stone and the moon is earth."

Is Anaxagoras before you, my dear Meletos? Do you think you are accusing him? Do you despise these gentlemen so much, do you think them so illiterate, as not to know that the books of the great Anaxagoras of Clazomenae are full of this lore? And so the young men learn this lore from me, when they might often buy a ticket for one drachma at the most in the orchestra,[11] and have a laugh at Socrates if he says this lore is his, especially when it is so odd! By Zeus, is that what you think of me, that I don't believe in any god?

"No by Zeus, you don't, not one little bit."

Well, Meletos, no one can believe you, and, to my mind, in this matter you don't believe you own words. What I think, gentlemen, is that this man seems to be an impudent bully, and he has made this indictment in the reckless violence of wild youth. He is like one who has made a riddle to test me: Will Socrates the so-called Wise guess that I am jesting and contradicting myself? Or shall I deceive him and the others who hear it? For the man seems to me to be contradicting himself in the indictment, which might be put "Socrates is a criminal for not believing in gods but believing in gods." Truly this is a game he is playing.

Now come with me, gentlemen, while I examine how he seems to me to mean this. You answer us, Meletos, and you gentlemen, remember not to make an uproar, as I asked you before, if I speak in my usual manner.

Is there any man, Meletos, who believes there are human things, but does not believe in human beings?—Let him answer, gentlemen, and let him not go on interrupting again and again. Is there anyone who does not believe in horses, but does believe in horsey things? Or does not believe in pipers, but does believe in things which pipers do? No, there is not, my good friend; I will answer it for you to the court, if you won't answer yourself. But answer what comes next: Is there anyone who believes in spiritual things, but not in spirits?

---

11   The "orchestra" was the space in front of the stage (corresponding roughly to the orchestra's place in a modem theatre) used by the chorus in Greek drama. The reference here is probably to the orchestra of the theatre of Dionysus, where spectators might see plays presenting doctrines of Anaxagoras. The drachma is the ancient drachma—say about 3 shillings or 50 cents now.

"No, there is not."

Many thanks for the answer, wrung from you by the court here. Now then, you say I believe in spiritual things and teach them, whether new or old, at any rate spiritual things; I believe in them according to your words, indeed you even swore to if in the indictment. But if I believe in spiritual things, surely it is 'absolutely necessary that I believe, in spirits. Is not that right? It is then, for I put you down as agreeing since you do not answer. And spirits, do we not believe them to be either gods or the sons of gods? Yes or no?

"Certainly."

I believe in spirits then, as you say; then if spirits are a kind of gods, this would be your riddle or jest which I spoke of, that you said I do not believe in gods and yet again I do, because I believe in spirits; if, again, spirits are sons of gods, a sort of bastards from nymphs or whatnot, as they are said to be, who in the world would believe in sons of gods if they did not believe in gods? It would be just as odd as believing in sons of horses or asses, but not in horses or asses! Well, Meletos, there's no question about it—you were just pulling our legs in making this indictment; perhaps you did not know a true crime to put in; but for you to persuade any man with even a grain of sense that the same man can believe in divine things and in spiritual things, and yet not in gods and spirits and heroes, that is absolutely impossible.

Well, gentlemen, I am no criminal according to Meletos's indictment; that needs no long defence from me to prove, but this is enough. However, when I said some time ago that. I was heartily disliked by many, you may be sure that it is quite true. And this is what will convict me, if anything does, not Meletos or Anytos but the prejudice and dislike of so many people. The same thing has convicted many other good men, and I think will do so again; there is no fear it will stop with me. But perhaps someone may say: Are you not ashamed then, Socrates, at having followed such a practice that you now ran a risk of a sentence of death? I would answer such a one fairly: You are wrong, my friend, if you think a man with a spark of decency in him ought to calculate life or death; the only thing he ought to consider, if he does anything, is whether he does right or wrong, whether it is what a good man does or a bad man. For according to your argument, in the Trojan War those of the demigods who died would have been poor creatures, particularly Thetis' son, Achilles; he so despised danger in comparison with undergoing disgrace that when he wished to kill Hector, and his mother (a goddess herself) said thus to him, if I remember, "My son, if you avenge the slaughter of your friend Patroclos and kill Hector, you will be killed yourself, for right after Hector death is ready for you[12]—when he heard this, he belittled danger and death, and much rather feared to live as a coward who would not avenge his friends, and replied, "Right after this let me die, when I have punished the offender; I don't want to stay here a

---

12   *Iliad* xviii. 96.

laughingstock beside the ships, a burden to the earth."[13] You cannot think he cared about danger and death? And this is true, gentlemen, wherever a man places himself, believing it to be the best place, or wherever he has been placed by his captain, there he must stay, as I think, and run any risk there is, calculating neither death nor anything, before disgrace.

Then, gentlemen, I should have been acting strangely, if at Poteidaia and Amphipolis and Delion[14] I stayed where I was posted by the captains whom you had chosen to command me, like anyone else, and risked death; but where God posted me, as I thought and believed, with the duty to be a philosopher[15] and to test myself and others, there I should fear either death or anything else, and desert my post Strange indeed it would be, and then truly anyone might have brought me to court justly and affirmed that I did not believe in God, because I disbelieved the oracle, and feared death and thought I was wise when I was not. For to fear death, gentlemen, is only to think you are wise when you are not; for it is to think you know what you don't know. No one knows whether death is really the greatest blessing a man can have, but they fear it is the greatest curse, as if they knew well. Surely this is the objectionable kind of ignorance, to think one knows what one does not know? But in this, gentlemen, here also perhaps I am different from the general run of mankind, and if I should claim to be wiser than someone in something it would be in this, that as I do not know well enough about what happens in the house of Hades, so I do not think I know; but to do wrong, and to disobey those who are better than myself, whether god or man, that I know to be bad and disgraceful. Therefore, in comparison with bad things which I know to be bad, rather will I never fear or flee from what may be blessings for all I know. So even if you let me go now and refuse to listen to Anytos—you remember what he said; he said that either I ought not to have been brought into count at all, or if I was, that death was the only possible penalty; and why? He told you that if I escaped, your sons "would at once practise what Socrates teaches, and they would all be utterly corrupted." Then if you were to say to me in answer to this, "We will not this time listen to Anytos, my dear Socrates; we let you go free but on this condition that you will no longer spend your time in this search or in philosophy, and if you are caught doing this again, you shall die"—if should let me go free on these terms which I have mentioned, I should answer you, "Many thanks indeed for your kindness, gentlemen, but I will obey the god rather than you,[16] and as long as I have breath in me, and remain able to do it, I will never cease being a philosopher, and exhorting you, and showing what is in me to any one of you I may meet, by speaking to him in my usual way: My excellent friend, you are an

---

13   *Iliad* xviii. 98,104.

14   In the years 432–429/424, 422 B.C. These places were scenes of battles in the great war between Athens and Sparta.

15   Lover of wisdom.

16   As the apostles said Acts v: 29, "We must obey God rather than men."

Athenian, a citizen of this great city, so famous for wisdom and strength, and you take every care to be as well off as possible in money, reputation and place—then are you not ashamed not to take every care and thought for understanding, for truth, and for the soul, so that it may be perfect? And if any of you argues the point and says he does take every care, I will not at once let him go and depart myself; but I will question and cross-examine and test him, and if I think he does not possess virtue but only says so, I will show that he sets very little value on things most precious, and sets more value on meaner things, and I will put him to shame. This I will do for everyone I meet, young or old, native or foreigner, but more for my fellow-citizens as you are nearer to me in race. For this is what God commands me, make no mistake, and I think there is no greater good for you in the city in any way than my service to God. All I do is to go about and try to persuade you, both young and old, not to care for your bodies or your monies first, and to care more exceedingly for the soul, to make it as good as possible; and I tell you that virtue comes not from money, but from virtue comes both money and all other good things for mankind, both in private and in public. If, then, by saying these things I corrupt the young, these things must be mischievous; but if anyone says I say anything else than these, he talks nonsense. In view of all this, I would say, gentlemen, either obey Anytos or do not obey him, either let me go free or do not let me go free; but I will never do anything else, even if I am to die many deaths.

Don't make an uproar, gentlemen, remain quiet as I begged you, hear me without uproar at what I have to say; for I think it will be to your benefit to hear me. I have something more to say, which perhaps will make you shout, but I pray you, don't do so. Be sure of this, that if you put me to death, being such as I am, you will not hurt me so much as yourselves. I should not be hurt either by Meletos or by Anytos, he could not do it; for I think the eternal law forbids a better man to be hurt by a worse. However, he might put me to deaths or banish me, or make me outcast; perhaps he thinks, perhaps others think, these are great evils, but I do not; I think, rather, that what he is now doing is evil, when he tries unjustly to put a man to death. Now therefore, gentlemen, so far from pleading for my own sake, as one might expect, I plead for your sakes, that you may not offend about God's gift by condemning me. For if you put me to death, you will not easily find such another, really like something stuck on the state by the god, though it is rather laughable to say so; for the state is like a big thoroughbred horse, so big that he is a bit slow and heavy, and wants a gadfly to wake him up. I think the god put me on the state something like that, to wake you up and persuade you and reproach you every one, as I keep settling on you everywhere all day long. Such another will not easily be found by you, gentlemen, and if you will be persuaded, you will spare me. You will be vexed, perhaps, like sleepers being awaked, and if you listen to Anytos and give me a tap, you can easily kill me; then you, can go on sleeping for the rest of your lives, unless God sends you such another in his care for you. That I am really one given to you by God you can easily see from this; for it does not seem human that I have neglected all my own interests, that I have been content with the neglect of my domestic affairs, all these years; while always I was attending to your interests, approaching each of you privately like a father or elder brother and persuading you to care for virtue. And indeed, if I had gained any advantage from this, and taken fees for my advice, there would have been some reason in it; but as if is, you see yourselves that my accusers, although accusing me so shamelessly of everything else, had not the effrontery or ability to produce a single witness to testify that I ever exacted or asked for a fee; and I produce I think, the sufficient witness that I speak the truth, my poverty.

Perhaps, if may seem odd that although I go about and give all this advice privately, quite a busybody, yet I dare not appear before your pubic assembly and advise the state. The reason for this is one which you have often heard me giving in many places, that something divine and spiritual comes to me, which Meletos put into the indictment in caricature. This has been about me since my boyhood, a voice, which when it comes always tarns me away from doing something I am intending to do, but never urges me on.[17] This is what opposes my taking up public business. And quite right too, I think; for you may be sure, gentlemen, that if I had meddled with public business in the past, I should have perished long ago and done no good either to you or to myself. Do not be annoyed at my telling the truth; the fact is that no man in the world will come off safe who honestly opposes either you or any other multitude, and tries to hinder the many unjust and illegal doings in a state. It is necessary that one who really and truly fights for the right, if he is to survive even for a short time, shall act as a private man, not as a public man.

I will bring you strong proof of this, not words but facts, which you respect Just listen to what has happened to me, and you will learn that I would never give way to anyone contrary to right, for fear of death, but rather than give way I would be ready to perish at once. I will tell you a story from the law courts, tiresome perhaps, but true. I have never, gentlemen, held any office in the state but one; I was then a Councillor.[18] It happened that the tribe which was presiding was mine, the Antiochis, when, you wished—illegally, as you all agreed afterwards—to try all the ten generals together for not gathering up the bodies of the dead after the sea fight.[19] Then I alone of the presidents opposed you, and voted against you that nothing should be done contrary to law; and when the orators were ready to denounce me and arrest me on the spot, and you shouted out telling them to do so, I thought it my duty to risk the danger with law and justice on my side, rather than to be on your side for fear of prison

---

17   See also pp. 444–445.

18   There were ten "*φυλδί*," "tribes," who each elected fifty deputies to the "*βουλη*" Council or upper house of five hundred. Each tribe "presided" in turn for thirty-five or thirty-six days, and its committee of fifty selected its managing "Presidency" of ten "presidents."

19   The battle of Arginusai, 406 B.C. The generals ought to have been tried separately.

and death.[20] This happened while the government was still democratic; and when the oligarchy came in, the Thirty again summoned me and four others to the Dome,[21] and ordered us to bring Leon of Salamis from Salamis, whom they meant to put to death. Such things those people used often to do to others, wishing to make as many as possible share their guilt. Then, however, I showed again by acts, not by words, that as for death, if it is not too vulgar to use the expressions I cared not one jot, but all my anxiety was to do nothing unjust or wrong. That government did not terrify me, strong as it was, into doing injustice; but when we came out of the Dome, the other four went to Salamis and brought Leon, but I went away home. And perhaps I should have been put to death for that, if the government had not been overthrown soon. You will find many witnesses of this.

Then do you think I should have survived all these years, if I had engaged in public business, and if then I had acted as a good man should, and defended the just, and made that, as is one's duty, my chief concern? Far from it, gentlemen, nor would anyone else in the world. But through all my life I shall prove to have been just the same, both in public life, if I have done anything there, and in private life; I have never given way to anyone in anything contrary to right, including those whom my slanderers call my pupils. Yet I never was teacher to anyone; but if anyone desires to hear me speaking and doing my business, whether he be young or old, I have never grudged it to any; I do not converse for a fee and refuse without, but I offer myself both to rich and poor for questioning and if a man likes he may hear what I say, and answer. And whether anyone becomes good after this or not, I could not fairly be called the cause of it, when I never promised any learning to anyone and never taught any; and if anyone says he ever learnt or heard anything from me privately which all the others did not, I assure you he does not tell the truth.

But why ever do some people enjoy spending a great deal of time with me? You have heard why, gentlemen; I have told you the whole truth, they enjoy hearing men cross-examined who think they are wise, and are not; indeed that is not unpleasant. And I maintain that I have been commanded by the god to do this through oracles and dreams, and in every way in which some divine influence or other has ever commanded a man to do anything. This, gentlemen, is both true and easy to test For if I really do corrupt any of the young, or if I ever have, then either some of them as they grew older must have understood that I had once given them bad advice in their youths so that they ought to have appeared now in this court and testified and had their revenge; or, if they did not wish to do it themselves, some of their relatives ought to have come instead—fathers and brothers and others of the family, if their own kinsmen had suffered any wrong from me—and they ought to tell it all now and

---

20   He refused to put the motion, according to Xenophon, *Memorabilia,* iv. 4.2.

21   The round chamber where the tribal committee of fifty always met, and where the so-called Thirty Tyrants met in 404 B.C. when they were in power.

have their revenge. At all events there are many of them whom I see here first Criton yonder, my age-mate and fellow-parishioner, father of Critobulos here; then there is Lysanias the Sphettian,[22] father of Aischines here; also Antiphon the Cephisian yonder, father of Epigenes; then others yonder whose brothers have amused themselves in this way, Nicostratos, Theozotides' son and brother of Theodotos—Theodotos himself is dead, so Nicostratos could not beg him to come—and Paralos here, Demodocos' son, whose brother was Theages; here is Adeimantos, Ariston's son, whose brother Plato[23] is there, and Aiantodoros, whose brother is Apollodoros here present. Many others I can mention to you, some of whom Meletos ought certainly to have called as witnesses in his speech, and if he forgot them, let him call them up now; I give place to him; so let him speak if he has any such evidence, But you will find exactly the opposite of this, gentlemen all of them ready to support me, the corrupter, the injurer of their relatives, as Meletos and Anytos call me. The corrupted might have some reason for supporting me; but the uncorrupted, already—elderly men, their kinsmen—what other reason have they for supporting me but the right and just reason, that they know I am telling the truth and Meletos is lying?

Very well, gentlemen; the defence I could offer is this, and more perhaps of the same sort. But perhaps some one among you might be vexed when he remembers what he has done himself; he may have been in a case less important than this, and he may have entreated and prayed the jury with floods of tears, and paraded his children to get all the pity he could, with many relatives and friends besides, but I, as it seems, will not do anything of the sort, and that too although I am probably at the last extremity of danger. Observing this perhaps someone might harden his heart against me because of it, and, being angry, might vote against me in anger. Then if any of you feels like that—I do not in the least expect it, but if he does—I may fairly say to him, My good sir, I too have relatives of my own somewhere, for to quote Homer,[24] no stick or stone is the origin of me, but humanity; so I have relatives and sons too, gentlemen—three of them, one a young man already, two still children—yet I shall parade none of them here and so entreat you to vote for my acquittal. Then why will I do none of these things? Not from obstinacy, gentlemen, not slighting you; whether I can face death confidently or not is another matter; but thinking, of reputation as regards me and you and the whole state, it does not seem to me to be decent that I should do any such thing, at my age and with my fame, whether true or false. At least it is common opinion that Socrates is in some way superior to most people. If, then, those of you who are considered superior, in wisdom or in courage or in any other virtue, are going to behave like these people, it would be a disgrace. I have often seen men of some reputation, when condemned, behaving in the strangest way, as if they thought it

---

22 That is, of the "deme" or parish of Sphettos in Attica.
23 The author.
24 *Odyssey* xix. 163.

would be a cruel fate for them to die, as if indeed they would be immortal if *you* did not put them to death! But these seem to me to be fastening a shame "about the city, so that a foreigner would naturally conceive that those of our Athenian nation who are distinguished for virtue, whom the people choose rather than themselves to place in government and office, are no better than so many women. Things of this kind, gentlemen, we who have any reputation at all should not do, and you should not allow us to do them if we tried; but you ought to show you would prefer to condemn a man who brings these pitiable exhibitions into court, and makes the city ridiculous, rather than one who behaves quietly.

Apart from reputation, gentlemen, it does not seem to me right to entreat the judge,[25] or to be acquitted by entreating; one should instruct and persuade him. For why does the judge sit? Not to make a gracious gift of justice by favour, but to decide what is just; and lie has sworn not to show favour as may please him, but to judge according to law. Then we must not get you into the habit of breaking that oath, nor must you let yourselves fall into that habit; one is as bad as the other in the sight of heaven. Then do not demand, gentlemen, that I should do before you such things as I hold neither honourable nor just nor permissible, most especially, by Zeus, for one who is prosecuted for impiety by Meletos here. For clearly if I should persuade you and compel you by entreaties when you are on oath, I should be teaching you not to believe in gods, and in my own defence I should actually accuse myself of not believing in gods. But I am far from that, gentlemen; I do believe, in a sense in which none of my accusers does; and I trust you, and God himself, to decide about me in the way that shall be best both for me and for you.

(The Court votes and finds him guilty, the voting being 281 for guilty, and 220 for innocent. Socrates then addresses them as to the penalty.)

You have voted for my condemnation, gentlemen of Athens; and if I am not resentful at this which has been done, many things contribute to that, and particularly that I expected this to be done which has been done. Indeed, I am much rather surprised at the actual number of votes on either side. I did not expect the voting to be so close, I thought there would be a large majority; but now, as it seems, if only thirty votes had been changed, I should have been acquitted. Even now to my mind I have been acquitted of Meletos,[26] and not only have I been acquitted, but this indeed is clear to everyone, that if Anytos and Lycon had not joined in accusing me, he would have been liable for the fine of a thousand drachmas as he did not get the fifth part of the votes.

---

25   On p. 444 and elsewhere he addresses the members of the court as his judges.

26   Socrates seems to imply that each of the three accusers should be credited with one-third of the 281 votes. One-third is less than one hundreds that is, less than one-fifth of the whole 501 votes.

Well, the man asks for the penalty of death. Good; and what penalty shall I propose against this, gentlemen? The proper penalty, it is clear surely? But what is that? What is proper for me to suffer or to pay, for not having the sense to be idle in my life, and for neglecting what most people care about, moneymaking and housekeeping and military appointments and oratory, and besides, all the posts and plots and parties which arise in this city—for believing myself to be really too honest to go after these things and survive? I did not go where I thought I should be of no use either to you or to myself, but I went where I hoped I might benefit each man separately with the greatest possible benefit, as I declare; I tried to persuade each one of you to take care for himself first, and how he could become most good and most wise, before he took care for any of his interests, and to take care for the state herself first before he took care of any of her interests: that in other things also, this was the proper order of his care. Then what do I deserve, since I am such as that? Something good, gentlemen, if I am to make the estimate what it ought to be in truth; and further, something good which would be suitable for me. Then what is suitable for a poor benefactor, who craves to have leisure for your encouragement? Nothing gentlemen, is so suitable, as that such a man should be boarded free in the town hall, which he deserves much more than anyone of you who has gained the prize at Olympia, with a pair of horses or a four-in-hand: for this one makes you seem to be happy, but I make you be happy, and he is not in want for food, but I am. Then if I must estimate the just penalty according to my deserts, this is my estimate: free board in the town hall.

Perhaps you think that in saying this, very much as I spoke of appeals for pity, I am just showing off; no such thing, gentlemen; I will tell you what I mean. I am convinced that I never willingly wronged anyone, but I cannot convince you, for we have conversed together only a short time. If we had a law, as other people have, that a trial for life or death is to be spread over many days and not confined to one, I think you would have been convinced; but as it is I cannot disperse great prejudices in a moment. But being convinced that I have wronged no man, I certainly will not wrong myself; I will not give sentence against myself, and say that I am worthy of something bad, I will not estimate anything bad for myself. Why should I? For fear of suffering what Meletos demands as penalty, when I say I do not know whether it is good or bad? Instead of that shall I choose one of the things which I know are bad, and propose that as penalty? Shall if be prison? And why must I live in prison, a slave to those appointed at any time as the officials of the place—the Eleven? Shall it be a fine, and prison until I pay? But that is the same to me, as I told you, for I have no money to pay. Then shall the penalty be banishment? Perhaps you might accept that penalty for me. Indeed, I should be very fond of life to choose that. Could I be so unreasonable! You, my own fellow-countrymen, could not endure my doings and my talkings, they were too burdensome and too detestable for you, so you are now trying to get rid of them; others will easily put up with them, it seems. What a notion! No, Athenians—far from it. A fine life it would be for me if I migrated, at my age, moving from city to city and living on the ran. For I am quite sure that wherever I go young men will listen to my talk as they do here; and if I drive these away, they will drive me out themselves, persuading the older men to let them, but if I don't drive them away, their fathers and families will do it for their sakes.

Perhaps someone might say, Can't you go away from us, Socrates, and keep silent and lead a quiet life? Now here is the most, difficult thing of all to make some of you believe. For if I say that this is to disobey the god, and therefore I cannot keep quiet, you will not believe me but think I am a humbug. If again I say it is the greatest good for a man every day to discuss virtue and the other things, about which you hear me talking and examining myself and everybody else, and that life without enquiry is not worth living for a man, you will believe me still less if I say that. And yet all this is true, gentlemen, as I tell you, but to convince you is not easy And at the same time I have never been accustomed to think I deserve anything bad. If I had money, I would have proposed to pay all I was bound to pay, as a fine, for I should have had no harm by that; but, as it is, I have none, unless, indeed, you are willing to put it at just as much as I am able to pay. Perhaps I could pay you a mina of silver:[27] then I propose that as penalty—Plato here, gentlemen, and Criton and Critobulos and Apollodoros tell me to fix it at thirty minas, and they will be sureties: then I propose so much and these men will be sureties, for the money —ample sureties in your view.

(The Court then votes again, and condemns him to death.)

You would not have had long to wait, gentlemen, but that short time will have given you the name and the blame of killing Socrates, a wise man: so those will say who wish to speak evil of our city, for they will certainly call me wise, even if I am not, when they wish to taunt you. If you had only waited a short time, this would have come to you of itself; look at my age, which is well advanced, and near death already This I say not to you all, but to those who voted for my death; and I have something else to say to those same men. Perhaps you think, gentlemen, it was lack of words which defeated me, such words as might have persuaded you, if I had thought it right to do and say anything and everything so as to be acquitted. Far from it. But it was a lack which defeated me, although not of words; it was, lack of effrontery and shamelessness, and of a willingness to make you the sort of addresses you would have liked best to hear—to hear me wailing and weeping and saying and doing many things, unworthy of me, as I declare—such indeed as you are accustomed to hear from others. But then I did not think I ought to do anything servile because of my danger; and now I do not regret that such was the manner of my defence; I much prefer to die after such a defence than to live by the other sort. Neither in court nor in war ought I or anyone else to do anything and everything to contrive an escape from death. In battle it is often clear that a man

---

27   About £12 or $35.

might escape by throwing away his arms and by begging mercy from his pursuers; and there are many other means in every danger, for escaping death, if a man can bring himself to do and say anything and everything. No, gentlemen, the difficult thing is not to escape death, I think, but to escape wickedness—that is much more difficult, for that runs faster than death. And now I, being slow and old, have been caught by the slower one; but my accusers, being clever and quick, have being caught by the swifter, badness. And now I and they depart I, condemned by you to death, but these, condemned by truth to depravity and injustice. I abide by my penalty, they by theirs. Perhaps this was to be so, and I think it is fair enough.

But as to the future I wish to chant this prophecy to you whose votes have condemned me; for I am now in the place where men chiefly prophesy, in sight of coming death. I foretell, gentlemen, my slayers, that a punishment will come, upon you straight after my death, much harder, I declare, than execution at your hands is to me; for now you have done this, thinking to shake yourselves free from giving account of your life, but if will turn out for you something very different, as I foretell. More than one shall be those who demand from you that account, those whom I have restrained now although you did not perceive it; and they will be harder upon, you inasmuch as they are younger, and you will resent if more. For if you believe that by putting men to death you will stop everyone from reproaching you because your life is wrong,[28] you make a great mistake; for this riddance is neither possible nor honourable; but another is most honourable and most easy, not to cut off lives, but to offer yourselves readily to be made as good as you can be. There is my prophecy for those who condemned me, and there I make an end.

But with those who voted to acquit me I would gladly converse about this event which has taken place here, while the magistrates are busy and I go not yet to the place where I must die. Pray gentlemen, be patient with me so long; for nothing hinders from storytelling a bit together while we may. To you as my friends I wish to show what is the real meaning of what has happened to me. What has happened to me, gentleman of the jury, my judges, for you I could rightly call judges—is a wonderful thing. My familiar prophetic voice of the spirit in all time past has always come to me frequently, opposing me even, in very small things, if I was about to do something not right;[29] but now there has happened to me what you see yourselves, what one might think and what is commonly held to be the extremest of evils, yet for me, as I left home this morning, there was no opposition from the signal of God, nor when I entered this place of the court nor anywhere in my speech when I was about to say anything; although in other speeches of mine it has often checked me while I was stay speaking, yet now in this action it has not opposed me anywhere, either in deed or in word. Then what am I to conceive to be the cause? I will tell you; really this that has happened to

---

28   See Republic, p. 315, n. 2.
29   See also p. 437.

me is good, and it is impossible that any of us conceives it aright who thinks it is an evil thing to die. A strong proof of this has been given to me; for my usual signal would certainly have opposed me, unless I was about to do something good.

Let us consider in another way, how great is the hope that it is good. Death is one of two things; either the dead man is nothing, and has no consciousness of anything at all, or it is, as people say, a change and a migration for the soul from this place here to another place. If there is no consciousness and it is like a sleep, when one sleeping sees nothing, not even in dreams, death would be a wonderful blessing. For I think that if a man should select that night in which he slumbered so deep that he saw not even a dream, and should put beside that night all other nights and days of his life, and were to say, after considering, how many sweeter days and nights than that night he had spent in his whole life, I think that anyone, not only some ordinary man but the Great King of Persia himself, would find few such indeed to compare with it in the other days and nights. If, then, death is like that, I call it a blessing; for so eternity seems no more than one night. But if, again, death is a migration from this world into another place, and if what they say is true, that there all the dead are, what greater good could there be than this, judges of the court? For if one comes to the house of Hades, rid of those who dub themselves judges, and finds those who truly are judges, the same who are said to sit in judgment there, Minos and Rhadamanthys and Aiacos and Triptolemos, and the other demigods who were just in their life, would that migration be a poor thing? On the contrary, to be in company with Orpheus and Musaios and Hesiod and Homer, how much would one of you give for that? For myself, I am willing to die many times, if this is true; since I myself should find staying there a wonderful thing; them I could meet Palamedes, and Aias, Telamon's son, and any other of the ancients who died by an unjust judgment, and to compare my experience with theirs, I think, would be quite agreeable. And best of all, to go on cross-examining the people there, as I did those here, and investigating, which of them is wise, and which thinks lie is, but is not! How much would one give, judges of the court, to cross-examine him who led the great invasion against Troy, or Odysseus, or Sisyphos, or thousands of other men and women? To converse with them there, and to be with, them, and cross-examine them would be an infinity of happiness! There at all events, I don't suppose they put anyone to death for *that*; for in that world they are happier than we are here, particularly because already for the rest of time they are immortal, if what people say is true.

But you also, judges of the court, must have good hopes towards death, and this one thing you must take as true—no evil cam happen to a good man either living or dead, and his business is not neglected by the gods; nor has my business now come about of itself, but it is plain to me that to die now and to be free from trouble was better for me. That is why my signal did not warn me off, and why I am not at all angry with those who condemned me, or with my accusers. Yet this was not their notion when they condemned and accused me; they thought they were hurting me, and that deserves blame in them However, one thing I ask them: Punish my sons, gentlemen, when they grow up; give them this same pain I gave you, if you think they care for money anything else before virtue; and if they have the reputation of being something when they are nothing, reproach them, as I reproach you, that they do not take care for what they should, and think they are something when they are worth nothing. And if you do this, we shall have been justly dealt with by you, both I and my sons.

And now it is time to go, I to die, and you to live; but which of us goes to a better thing is unknown to all but God.

The Clouds

By Aristophanes
Translated by Ian Johnston

TRANSLATOR'S NOTE

In the text below the numbers in square brackets refer to the Greek text.

HISTORICAL NOTE

Clouds was first produced in the drama festival in Athens—the City Dionysia—in 423 BC, where it placed third. Subsequently the play was revised, but the revisions were never completed. The text which survives is the revised version, which was apparently not performed in Aristophanes' time but which circulated in manuscript form. This revised version does contain some anomalies which have not been fully sorted out (e.g., the treatment of Cleon, who died between the original text and the revisions). At the time of the first production, the Athenians had been at war with the Spartans, off and on, for a number of years.

DRAMATIS PERSONAE

STREPSIADES: a middle-aged Athenian
PHEIDIPPIDES: a young Athenian, son of Strepsiades
XANTHIAS: a slave serving Strepsiades
STUDENT: one of Socrates' pupils in the Thinkery
SOCRATES: chief teacher in the Thinkery
CHORUS OF CLOUDS
THE BETTER ARGUMENT: an older man
THE WORSE ARGUMENT: a young man
PASIAS: one of Strepsiades' creditors
WITNESS: a friend of Pasias
AMYNIAS: one of Strepsiades' creditors
STUDENTS OF SOCRATES

[*Scene: In the centre of the stage area is a house with a door to Socrates' educational estab-lishment, the Thinkery.[1] On one side of the stage is Strepsiades' house, in front of which are two beds. Outside the Thinkery there is a small clay statue of a round goblet, and outside Strepsiades' house there is a small clay statue of Hermes. It is just before dawn. Strepsiades and Pheidippides are lying asleep in the two beds. Strepsiades tosses and turns restlessly. Pheidippides lets a very loud fart in his sleep. Strepsiades sits up wide awake*]

STREPSIADES: Damn! Lord Zeus, how this night drags on and on!
   It's endless. Won't daylight ever come?
   I heard a cock crowing a while ago,
   but my slaves kept snoring. In the old days,
   they wouldn't have dared. Oh, damn and blast this war—
   so many problems. Now I'm not allowed
   to punish my own slaves.[2] And then there's him—
   this fine young man, who never once wakes up,
   but farts the night away, all snug in bed,
   wrapped up in five wool coverlets. Ah well,   10   [10]
   I guess I should snuggle down and snore away.

[*Strepsiades lies down again and tries to sleep. Pheidippides farts again. Strepsiades finally gives up trying to sleep*]

STREPSIADES: I can't sleep. I'm just too miserable,
   what with being eaten up by all this debt—
   thanks to this son of mine, his expenses,
   his racing stables. He keeps his hair long
   and rides his horses—he's obsessed with it—
   his chariot and pair. He dreams of horses.[3]
   And I'm dead when I see the month go by—
   with the moon's cycle now at twenty days,
   as interest payments keep on piling up.[4]   20

[*Calling to a slave*]

   Hey, boy! Light the lamp. Bring me my accounts.

[*Enter the slave Xanthias with light and tablets*]

   Let me take these and check my creditors.
   How many are there? And then the interest—   [20]
   I'll have to work that out. Let me see now …

What do I owe? "Twelve minai to Pasias?"
Twelve minai to Pasias! What's that for?
Oh yes, I know—that's when I bought that horse,
the pedigree nag. What a fool I am!
I'd sooner have a stone knock out my eye.[5]

PHEIDIPPIDES: *[talking in his sleep]*
    Philon, that's unfair! Drive your chariot straight.   30

STREPSIADES: That there's my problem—that's what's killing me.
    Even fast asleep he dreams of horses!

PHEIDIPPIDES: *[in his sleep]* In this war-chariot race how many times
    do we drive round the track?

STREPSIADES: You're driving me,
    your father, too far round the bend. Let's see,
    after Pasias, what's the next debt I owe?   [30]
    "Three minai to Amynias." For what?
    A small chariot board and pair of wheels?

PHEIDIPPIDES: *[in his sleep]* Let the horse have a roll. Then take him home.

STREPSIADES: You, my lad, have been rolling in my cash.   40
    Now I've lost in court, and other creditors
    are going to take out liens on all my stuff
    to get their interest.

PHEIDIPPIDES: *[waking up]*   What's the matter, dad?
    You've been grumbling and tossing around there
    all night long.

STREPSIADES: I keep getting bitten—
    some bum bailiff in the bedding.

PHEIDIPPIDES: Ease off, dad.
    Let me get some sleep.

STREPSIADES: All right, keep sleeping.
    Just bear in mind that one fine day these debts   [40]
    will all be your concern.

[Pheidippides rolls over and goes back to sleep]

                                  Damn it, anyway.
I wish that matchmaker had died in pain—   50
the one who hooked me and your mother up.
I'd had a lovely time up to that point,
a crude, uncomplicated, country life,
lying around just as I pleased, with honey bees,
and sheep and olives, too. Then I married—
the niece of Megacles—who was the son
of Megacles. I was a country man,
and she came from the town—a real snob,
extravagant, just like Coesyra.[6]
When I married her and we both went to bed,   60
I stunk of fresh wine, drying figs, sheep's wool—   [50]
an abundance of good things. As for her,
she smelled of perfume, saffron, long kisses,
greed, extravagance, lots and lots of sex.[7]
Now, I'm not saying she was a lazy bones.
She used to weave, but used up too much wool.
To make a point I'd show this cloak to her
and say, "Woman, your weaving's far too thick."[8]

[The lamp goes out]

XANTHIAS: We've got no oil left in the lamp.

STREPSIADES: Damn it!
Why'd you light such a thirsty lamp? Come here.   70
I need to thump you.

XANTHIAS: Why should you hit me?

STREPSIADES: Because you stuck too thick a wick inside.

[The slave ignores Strepsiades and walks off into the house]

After that, when this son was born to us—   [60]
I'm talking about me and my good wife—
we argued over what his name should be.
She was keen to add -hippos to his name,

like Xanthippos, Callipedes, or Chaerippos.[9]
Me, I wanted the name Pheidonides,
his grandpa's name. Well, we fought about it,
and then, after a while, at last agreed.   80
And so we called the boy Pheidippides.
She used to cradle the young lad and say,
"When you're grown up, you'll drive your chariot
to the Acropolis, like Megacles,
in a full-length robe ..." I'd say, "No—   [70]
you'll drive your goat herd back from Phelleus,
like your father, dressed in leather hides ..."
He never listened to a thing I said.
And now he's making my finances sick—
a racing fever. But I've spent all night   90
thinking of a way to deal with this whole mess,
and I've found one route, something really good—
it could work wonders. If I could succeed,
if I could convince him, I'd be all right.
Well, first I'd better wake him up. But how?
What would be the gentlest way to do it?

[Strepsiades leans over and gently nudges Pheidippides]

Pheidippides ... my little Pheidippides ...

PHEIDIPPIDES: *[very sleepily]* What is it, father?   [80]

STREPSIADES: Give me a kiss—
    then give me your right hand.

[Pheidippides sits up, leans over, and does what his father has asked]

PHEIDIPPIDES: All right. There.
    What's going on?

STREPSIADES: Tell me this—do you love me?   100

PHEIDIPPIDES: Yes, I do, by Poseidon, lord of horses.

STREPSIADES: Don't give me that lord of horses stuff—
    he's the god who's causing all my troubles.

But now, my son, if you really love me,
    with your whole heart, then follow what I say.

PHEIDIPPIDES: What do you want to tell me I should do?

STREPSIADES: Change your life style as quickly as you can,
    then go and learn the stuff I recommend.

PHEIDIPPIDES: So tell me—what are you asking me?

STREPSIADES: You'll do just what I say?

PHEIDIPPIDES: Yes, I'll do it—   110   [90]
    I swear by Dionysus.

STREPSIADES: All right then.
    Look over there—you see that little door,
    there on that little house?

PHEIDIPPIDES: Yes, I see it.
    What are you really on about, father?

STREPSIADES: That's the Thinkery—for clever minds.
    In there live men who argue and persuade.
    They say that heaven's an oven damper—
    it's all around us—we're the charcoal.
    If someone gives them cash, they'll teach him
    how to win an argument on any cause,   120
    just or unjust.

PHEIDIPPIDES: Who are these men?

STREPSIADES: I'm not sure   [100]
    just what they call themselves, but they're good men,
    fine, deep-thinking intellectual types.

PHEIDIPPIDES: Nonsense! They're a worthless bunch. I know them—
    you're talking about pale-faced charlatans,
    who haven't any shoes, like those rascals
    Socrates and Chaerephon.[10]

STREPSIADES: Shush, be quiet.
    Don't prattle on such childish rubbish.
    If you care about your father's daily food,
    give up racing horses and, for my sake,   130
    join their company.

PHEIDIPPIDES: By Dionysus, no!
    Not even if you give me as a gift
    pheasants raised by Leogoras.[11]

STREPSIADES: Come on, son—   [110]
    you're the dearest person in the world to me.
    I'm begging you. Go there and learn something.

PHEIDIPPIDES: What is it you want me to learn?

STREPSIADES: They say
    that those men have two kinds of arguments—
    the Better, whatever that may mean,
    and the Worse. Now, of these two arguments,
    the Worse can make an unjust case and win.   140
    So if, for me, you'll learn to speak like this,
    to make an unjust argument, well then,
    all those debts I now owe because of you
    I wouldn't have to pay—no need to give
    an obol's worth to anyone.[12]

PHEIDIPPIDES: No way.
    I can't do that. With no colour in my cheeks
    I wouldn't dare to face those rich young Knights.[13]   [120]

STREPSIADES: Then, by Demeter, you won't be eating
    any of my food—not you, not your yoke horse,
    nor your branded thoroughbred. To hell with you—   150
    I'll toss you right out of this house.[14]

PHEIDIPPIDES: All right—
    but Uncle Megacles won't let me live
    without my horses. I'm going in the house.
    I don't really care what you're going to do.

[Pheidippides stands up and goes inside the house. Strepsiades gets out of bed]

STREPSIADES: Well, I'll not take this set back lying down.
    I'll pray to the gods and then go there myself—
    I'll get myself taught in that Thinkery.
    Still, I'm old and slow—my memory's shot.
    How'm I going to learn hair-splitting arguments,   [130]
    all that fancy stuff? But I have to go.   160
    Why do I keep hanging back like this?
    I should be knocking on the door.

[Strepsiades marches up to the door of the Thinkery and knocks]

                Hey, boy … little boy.

STUDENT *[from inside]* Go to Hell!

[The door opens and the student appears]

            Who's been knocking on the door?

STREPSIADES: I'm Strepsiades, the son of Pheidon,
    from Cicynna.

STUDENT: By god, what a stupid man,
    to kick the door so hard. You just don't think.
    You made a newly found idea miscarry!

STREPSIADES: I'm sorry. But I live in the country,
    far away from here. Tell me what's happened.
    What's miscarried?

STUDENT: It's not right to mention it,   170   [140]
    except to students.

STREPSIADES: You needn't be concerned—
    you can tell me. I've come here as a student,
    to study at the Thinkery.

STUDENT: I'll tell you, then.
    But you have to think of these as secrets,

our holy mysteries. A while ago,
a flea bit Chaerephon right on the eye brow,
and then jumped onto Socrates' head.
So Socrates then questioned Chaerephon
about how many lengths of its own feet
a flea could jump.

STREPSIADES: How'd he measure that?   180

STUDENT: Most ingeniously. He melted down some wax,
then took the flea and dipped two feet in it.   [150]
Once that cooled, the flea had Persian slippers.
He took those off and measured out the space.

STREPSIADES: By Lord Zeus, what intellectual brilliance!

STUDENT: Would you like to hear more of Socrates,
another one of his ideas? What do you say?

STREPSIADES: Which one? Tell me …

[The student pretends to be reluctant

                           I'm begging you.

STUDENT: All right.
Chaerephon of Sphettus once asked Socrates
whether, in his opinion, a gnat buzzed   190
through its mouth or through its anal sphincter.

STREPSIADES: What did Socrates say about the gnat?

STUDENT: He said that the gnat's intestinal tract   [160]
was narrow—therefore air passing through it,
because of the constriction, was pushed with force
towards the rear. So then that orifice,
being a hollow space beside a narrow tube,
transmits the noise caused by the force of air.

STREPSIADES: So a gnat's arse hole is a giant trumpet!
O triply blessed man who could do this,   200

anatomize the anus of a gnat!
A man who knows a gnat's guts inside out
would have no trouble winning law suits.

STUDENT: Just recently he lost a great idea—
　　a lizard stole it!

STREPSIADES:　　　　　　　How'd that happen? Tell me.　　　　　　[170]

STUDENT: He was studying movements of the moon—
　　its trajectory and revolutions.
　　One night, as he was gazing up, open mouthed,
　　staring skyward, a lizard on the roof
　　relieved itself on him.

STREPSIADES:　　　　　　A lizard crapped on Socrates!　　　210
　　That's good!

STUDENT:　　　　　Then, last night we had no dinner.

STREPSIADES: Well, well. What did Socrates come up with,
　　to get you all some food to eat?

STUDENT: He spread some ashes thinly on the table,
　　then seized a spit, went to the wrestling school,
　　picked up a queer, and robbed him of his cloak,
　　then sold the cloak to purchase dinner.[15]

STREPSIADES: And we still admire Thales after that?[16]　　　　[180]
　　Come on, now, open up the Thinkery—
　　let me see Socrates without delay.　　　　　　220
　　I'm dying to learn. So open up the door.

[The doors of the Thinkery slide open to reveal Socrates' students studying on a porch (not inside a room). They are in variously absurd positions and are all very thin and pale]

　　By Hercules, who are all these creatures!
　　What country are they from?

STUDENT:　　　　　　You look surprised.
　　What do they look like to you?

STREPSIADES: Like prisoners—
    those Spartan ones from Pylos.[17] But tell me—
    Why do these ones keep staring at the earth?

STUDENT: They're searching out what lies beneath the ground.

STREPSIADES: Ah, they're looking for some bulbs. Well now,
    you don't need to worry any longer,
    not about that. I know where bulbs are found,   230   [190]
    lovely big ones, too. What about them?
    What are they doing like that, all doubled up?

STUDENT: They're sounding out the depths of Tartarus.

STREPSIADES: Why are their arse holes gazing up to heaven?

STUDENT: *Directed studies in astronomy.*

[The Student addresses the other students in the room]

    Go inside. We don't want Socrates
    to find you all in here.

STREPSIADES: Not yet, not yet.
    Let them stay like this, so I can tell them
    what my little problem is.

STUDENT: It's not allowed.
    They can't spend too much time outside,   240
    not in the open air.

[The students get up from their studying positions and disappear into the interior of the Thinkery. Strepsiades starts inspecting the equipment on the walls and on the tables]

STREPSIADES: My goodness,
    what is this thing? Explain it to me.   [200]

STUDENT: That there's astronomy.

STREPSIADES: And what's this?

STUDENT: That's geometry.

STREPSIADES: What use is that?

STUDENT: It's used to measure land.

STREPSIADES: You mean those lands
    handed out by lottery.[18]

STUDENT: Not just that—
    it's for land in general.

STREPSIADES: A fine idea—
    useful … democratic, too.

STUDENT: Look over here—
    here's a map of the entire world. See?
    Right there, that's Athens.

STREPSIADES: What do you mean?   250
    I don't believe you. There are no jury men—
    I don't see them sitting on their benches.

STUDENT: No, no—this space is really Attica.[19]

STREPSIADES: Where are the citizens of Cicynna,   [210]
    the people in my deme?[20]

STUDENT: They're right here.
    This is Euboea, as you can see,
    beside us, really stretched a long way out.

STREPSIADES: I know—we pulled it apart, with Pericles.[21]
    Where abouts is Sparta?

STUDENT: Where is it? Here.

STREPSIADES: It's close to us. You must rethink the place—   260
    shift it—put it far away from us.

STUDENT: Can't do that.

STREPSIADES: *[threatening]* Do it, by god, or I'll make you cry!

[Strepsiades notices Socrates descending from above in a basket suspended from a rope]

Hey, who's the man in the basket—up there?

STUDENT: The man himself.

STREPSIADES: Who's that?

STUDENT: Socrates.

STREPSIADES: Socrates! Hey, call out to him for me—   [220]
    make it loud.

STUDENT: You'll have to call to him yourself.
    I'm too busy now.

[The Student exits into the interior of the house]

STREPSIADES: Oh, Socrates …
    my dear little Socrates … hello …

SOCRATES: Why call on me, you creature of a day?

STREPSIADES: Well, first of all, tell me what you're doing.   270

SOCRATES: I tread the air, as I contemplate the sun.

STREPSIADES: You're looking down upon the gods up there,
    in that basket? Why not do it from the ground,
    if that's what you're doing?

SOCRATES: Impossible!
    I'd never come up with a single thing
    about celestial phenomena,
    if I did not suspend my mind up high,
    to mix my subtle thoughts with what's like them—   [230]
    the air. If I turned my mind to lofty things,
    but stayed there on the ground, I'd never make   280
    the least discovery. For the earth, you see,

draws moist thoughts down by force into itself—
the same process takes place with water cress.

STREPSIADES: What are you talking about? Does the mind
draw moisture into water cress? Come down,
my dear little Socrates, down here to me,
so you can teach me what I've come to learn.

[Socrates' basket slowly descends]

SOCRATES: Why have you come?

STREPSIADES: I want to learn to argue.
I'm being pillaged—ruined by interest   [240]
and by creditors I can't pay off—   290
they're slapping liens on all my property.

SOCRATES: How come you got in such a pile of debt
without your knowledge?

STREPSIADES: I've been ravaged
by disease—I'm horse sick. It's draining me
in the most dreadful way. But please teach me
one of your two styles of arguing, the one
which never has to discharge any debt.
Whatever payment you want me to make,
I promise you I'll pay—by all the gods.

SOCRATES: What gods do you intend to swear by?   300
To start with, the gods hold no currency with us.

STREPSIADES: Then, what currency do you use to swear?
Is it iron coin, like in Byzantium?

SOCRATES: Do you want to know the truth of things divine,   [250]
the way they really are?

STREPSIADES: Yes, by god, I do,
if that's possible.

SOCRATES: And to commune and talk
    with our own deities the Clouds?

STREPSIADES: Yes, I do.

SOCRATES: Then sit down on the sacred couch.

STREPSIADES: All right.
    I'm sitting down.

SOCRATES: Take this wreath.

STREPSIADES: Why a wreath?
    Oh dear, Socrates, don't offer me up   310
    in sacrifice, like Athamas.[22]

SOCRATES: No, no.
    We go through all this for everyone—
    it's their initiation.

STREPSIADES: What do I get?

SOCRATES: You'll learn to be a clever talker,   [260]
    to rattle off a speech, to strain your words
    like flour. Just keep still.

[Socrates sprinkles flour all over Strepsiades]

STREPSIADES: By god, that's no lie!
    I'll turn into flour if you keep sprinkling me.

SOCRATES: Old man, be quiet. Listen to the prayer.

[Socrates shuts his eyes to recite his prayer]

    O Sovereign Lord, O Boundless Air,
    who keeps the earth suspended here in space,   320
    O Bright Sky, O Sacred Goddesses—
    the Thunder-bearing Clouds—arise,
    you holy ladies, issue forth on high,
    before the man who holds you in his mind.

STREPSIADES: *[lifting his cloak to cover his head]*
    Not yet, not yet. Not 'til I wrap this cloak
    like this so I don't get soaked. What bad luck,
    to leave my home without a cap on.

SOCRATES: [ignoring Strepsiades]
    Come now, you highly honoured Clouds, come—
    manifest yourselves to this man here—
    whether you now sit atop Olympus,   330   [270]
    on those sacred snow-bound mountain peaks,
    or form the holy choruses with nymphs
    in gardens of their father Ocean,
    or gather up the waters of the Nile
    in golden flagons at the river's mouths,
    or dwell beside the marsh of Maeotis
    or snowy rocks of Mimas—hear my call,
    accept my sacrifice, and then rejoice
    in this holy offering I make.

CHORUS [heard offstage]
    Everlasting Clouds—   340
    let us arise, let us reveal
    our moist and natural radiance—
    moving from the roaring deep
    of father Ocean to the tops
    of tree-lined mountain peaks,   [280]
    where we see from far away
    the lofty heights, the sacred earth,
    whose fruits we feed with water,
    the murmuring of sacred rivers,
    the roaring of the deep-resounding sea.   350
    For the unwearied eye of heaven
    blazes forth its glittering beams.
    Shake off this misty shapelessness
    from our immortal form and gaze upon
    the earth with our far-reaching eyes.   [290]

SOCRATES: Oh you magnificent and holy Clouds,
    you've clearly heard my call.

[To Strepsiades]

Did you hear that voice
intermingled with the awesome growl of thunder?

STREPSIADES: Oh you most honoured sacred goddesses,
in answer to your thunder call I'd like to fart—   360
it's made me so afraid—if that's all right …

[Strepsiades pull down his pants and farts loudly in the direction of the offstage Chorus]

Oh, oh, whether right nor not, I need to shit.

SOCRATES: Stop being so idiotic, acting like
a stupid damn comedian. Keep quiet.
A great host of deities is coming here—
they're going to sing.

CHORUS: *[still offstage]*
Oh you maidens bringing rain—
let's move on to that brilliant place,   [300]
to gaze upon the land of Pallas,
where such noble men inhabit   370
Cecrops' lovely native home,[23]
where they hold those sacred rites
no one may speak about,
where the temple of the mysteries
is opened up in holy festivals,[24]
with gifts for deities in heaven,
what lofty temples, holy statues,
most sacred supplication to the gods,
with garlands for each holy sacrifice,
and festivals of every kind   380   [310]
in every season of the year,
including, when the spring arrives,
that joyful Dionysian time,
with rousing choruses of song,
resounding music of the pipes.

STREPSIADES: By god, Socrates, tell me, I beg you,
who these women are who sing so solemnly.
Are they some special kind of heroines?

SOCRATES: No—they're heavenly Clouds, great goddesses
for lazy men—from them we get our thoughts,   390
our powers of speech, our comprehension,
our gift for fantasy and endless talk,
our power to strike responsive chords in speech
and then rebut opponents' arguments.

STREPSIADES: Ah, that must be why, as I heard their voice,
my soul took wing, and now I'm really keen
to babble on of trivialities,
to argue smoke and mirrors, to deflate   [320]
opinions with a small opinion of my own,
to answer someone's reasoned argument   400
with my own counter-argument. So now,
I'd love to see them here in front of me,
if that's possible.

SOCRATES: Just look over there—
towards Mount Parnes. I see them coming,
slowly moving over here.[25]

STREPSIADES: Where? Point them out.

SOCRATES: They're coming down here through the valleys—
a whole crowd of them—there in the thickets,
right beside you.

STREPSIADES: This is weird. I don't see them.

SOCRATES: [pointing into the wings of the theatre]
There—in the entrance way.

STREPSIADES: Ah, now I see—
but I can barely make them out.

[The Clouds enter from the wings]

SOCRATES: There—   410
    surely you can see them now, unless your eyes
    are swollen up like pumpkins.

STREPSIADES: I see them.
    My god, what worthy noble presences!
    They're taking over the entire space.

SOCRATES: You weren't aware that they are goddesses?
    You had no faith in them?

STREPSIADES: I'd no idea.
    I thought clouds were mist and dew and vapour.   [330]

SOCRATES: You didn't realize these goddesses
    support a multitude of charlatans—
    prophetic seers from Thurium, quacks   420
    who specialize in books on medicine,
    lazy long-haired types with onyx signet rings,
    poets who produce the twisted choral music
    for dithyrambic songs, those with airy minds—
    all such men so active doing nothing
    the Clouds support, since in their poetry
    these people celebrate the Clouds.

STREPSIADES: Ah ha, so that's why they poeticize
    "the whirling radiance of watery clouds
    as they advance so ominously,"   430
    "waving hairs of hundred-headed Typho,"26
    with "roaring tempests," and then "liquid breeze,"
    or "crook-taloned, sky-floating birds of prey,"
    "showers of rain from dewy clouds"—and then,
    as a reward for this, they stuff themselves
    on slices carved from some huge tasty fish
    or from a thrush.27

SOCRATES: Yes, thanks to these Clouds.   [340]
    Is that not truly just?

STREPSIADES: All right, tell me this—
    if they're really clouds, what's happened to them?

They look just like mortal human women.   440
   The clouds up there are not the least like that.

SOCRATES: What are they like?

STREPSIADES: I don't know exactly.
   They look like wool once it's been pulled apart—
   not like women, by god, not in the least.
   These ones here have noses.

SOCRATES: Let me ask you something.
   Will you answer me?

STREPSIADES: Ask me what you want.
   Fire away.

SOCRATES: Have you ever gazed up there
   and seen a cloud shaped like a centaur,
   or a leopard, wolf, or bull?

STREPSIADES: Yes, I have.
   So what?

SOCRATES: They become anything they want.   450
   So if they see some hairy savage type,
   one of those really wild and wooly men,
   like Xenophantes' son, they mock his moods,
   transforming their appearance into centaurs.[28]   [350]

   STREPSIADES: What if they glimpse a thief of public funds,
   like Simon? What do they do then?[29]

SOCRATES: They expose
   just what he's truly like—they change at once,
   transform themselves to wolves.

STREPSIADES: Ah ha, I see.
   So that's why yesterday they changed to deer.
   They must have caught sight of Cleonymos—   460
   the man who threw away his battle shield—
   they knew he was fearful coward.[30]

SOCRATES: And now it's clear they've seen Cleisthenes—
    that's why, as you can see, they've changed to women.[31]

STREPSIADES: *[to the Chorus of Clouds]*
    All hail to you, lady goddesses.
    And now, if you have ever spoken out
    to other men, let me hear your voice,
    you queenly powers.

CHORUS LEADER: Greetings to you, old man born long ago,
    hunter in love with arts of argument—   470
    you, too, high priest of subtlest nonsense,
    tell us what you want. Of all the experts   [360]
    in celestial matters at the present time,
    we take note of no one else but you—
    and Prodicus[32]—because he's sharp and wise,
    while you go swaggering along the street,
    in bare feet, shifting both eyes back and forth.
    You keep moving on through many troubles,
    looking proud of your relationship with us.

STREPSIADES: By the Earth, what voices these Clouds have—   480
    so holy, reverent, and marvelous!

SOCRATES: Well, they're the only deities we have—
    the rest are just so much hocus pocus.

STREPSIADES: Hang on—by the Earth, isn't Zeus a god,
    the one up there on Mount Olympus?

SOCRATES: What sort of god is Zeus? Why spout such rubbish?
    There's no such being as Zeus.

STREPSIADES: What do you mean?
    Then who brings on the rain? First answer that.

SOCRATES: Why, these women do. I'll prove that to you
    with persuasive evidence. Just tell me—   490   [370]
    where have you ever seen the rain come down
    without the Clouds being there? If Zeus brings rain,

then he should do so when the sky is clear,
when there are no Clouds in view.

STREPSIADES: By Apollo, you've made a good point there—
it helps your argument. I used to think
rain was really Zeus pissing through a sieve.
Tell me who causes thunder? That scares me.

SOCRATES: These Clouds do, as they roll around.

STREPSIADES: But how?   500
Explain that, you who dares to know it all.

SOCRATES: When they are filled with water to the brim
and then, suspended there with all that rain,
are forced to move, they bump into each other.
They're so big, they burst with a great boom.

STREPSIADES: But what's forcing them to move at all?
Doesn't Zeus do that?

SOCRATES: No—that's the aerial Vortex.[33]

STREPSIADES: Vortex? Well, that's something I didn't know.   [380]
So Zeus is now no more, and Vortex rules
instead of him. But you still have not explained
a thing about those claps of thunder.   510

SOCRATES: Weren't you listening to me? I tell you,
when the Clouds are full of water and collide,
they're so thickly packed they make a noise.

STREPSIADES: Come on now—who'd ever believe that stuff?

SOCRATES: I'll explain, using you as a test case.
Have you ever gorged yourself on stew
at the Panathenaea and later
had an upset stomach—then suddenly
some violent movement made it rumble?[34]

STREPSIADES: Yes, by Apollo! It does weird things—   520
    I feel unsettled. That small bit of stew
    rumbles around and makes strange noises,
    just like thunder. At first it's quite quiet—   [390]
    "pappax pappax"—then it starts getting louder—
    "papapappax"—and when I take a shit,
    it really thunders "papapappax"—
    just like these Clouds.

SOCRATES: So think about it—
    if your small gut can make a fart like that,
    why can't the air, which goes on for ever,
    produce tremendous thunder. Then there's this—   530
    consider how alike these phrases sound,
    "thunder clap" and "fart and crap."

STREPSIADES: All right, but then explain this to me—
    Where does lightning come from, that fiery blaze,
    which, when it hits, sometimes burns us up,
    sometimes just singes us and lets us live?
    Clearly Zeus is hurling that at perjurers.

SOCRATES: You stupid driveling idiot, you stink
    of olden times, the age of Cronos![35] If Zeus
    is really striking at the perjurers,   540
    how come he's not burned Simon down to ash,
    or else Cleonymos or Theorus?
    They perjure themselves more than anyone.   [400]
    No. Instead he strikes at his own temple
    at Sunium, our Athenian headland,
    and at his massive oak trees there. Why?
    What's his plan? Oak trees can't be perjured.

STREPSIADES: I don't know. But that argument of yours
    seems good. All right, then, what's a lightning bolt?

SOCRATES: When a dry wind blows up into the Clouds   550
    and gets caught in there, it makes them inflate,
    like the inside of a bladder. And then
    it has to burst them all apart and vent,
    rushing out with violence brought on

by dense compression—its force and friction
cause it to consume itself in fire.

STREPSIADES: By god, I went through that very thing myself—
    at the feast for Zeus. I was cooking food,
    a pig's belly, for my family. I forgot
    to slit it open. It began to swell—   560   [410]
    then suddenly blew up, splattering blood
    in both my eyes and burning my whole face.

CHORUS LEADER: Oh you who seeks from us great wisdom,
    how happy you will be among Athenians,
    among the Greeks, if you have memory,
    if you can think, if in that soul of yours
    you've got the power to persevere,
    and don't get tired standing still or walking,
    nor suffer too much from the freezing cold,
    with no desire for breakfast, if you abstain   570
    from wine, from exercise, and other foolishness,
    if you believe, as all clever people should,
    the highest good is victory in action,
    in deliberation and in verbal wars.

STREPSIADES: Well, as for a stubborn soul and a mind   [420]
    thinking in a restless bed, while my stomach,
    lean and mean, feeds on bitter herbs, don't worry.
    I'm confident about all that—I'm ready
    to be hammered on your anvil into shape.

SOCRATES: So now you won't acknowledge any gods   580
    except the ones we do—Chaos, the Clouds,
    the Tongue—just these three?

STREPSIADES: Absolutely—
    I'd refuse to talk to any other gods,
    if I ran into them—and I decline
    to sacrifice or pour libations to them.
    I'll not provide them any incense.

CHORUS LEADER: Tell us then what we can do for you.
    Be brave—for if you treat us with respect,

if you admire us, and if you're keen
to be a clever man, you won't go wrong.   590

STREPSIADES: Oh you sovereign queens,
    from you I ask one really tiny favour—
    to be the finest speaker in all Greece,   [430]
    within a hundred miles.

CHORUS LEADER: You'll get that from us.
    From now on, in time to come, no one will win
    more votes among the populace than you.

STREPSIADES: No speaking on important votes for me!
    That's not what I'm after. No, no. I want
    to twist all legal verdicts in my favour,
    to evade my creditors.

CHORUS LEADER: You'll get that,   600
    just what you desire. For what you want
    is nothing special. So be confident—
    give yourself over to our agents here.

STREPSIADES: I'll do that—I'll place my trust in you.
    Necessity is weighing me down—the horses,
    those thoroughbreds, my marriage—all that
    has worn me out. So now, this body of mine   [440]
    I'll give to them, with no strings attached,
    to do with as they like—to suffer blows,
    go without food and drink, live like a pig,   610
    to freeze or have my skin flayed for a pouch—
    if I can just get out of all my debt
    and make men think of me as bold and glib,
    as fearless, impudent, detestable,
    one who cobbles lies together, makes up words,
    a practised legal rogue, a statute book,
    a chattering fox, sly and needle sharp,
    a slippery fraud, a sticky rascal,
    foul whipping boy or twisted villain,   [450]
    troublemaker, or idly prattling fool.   620
    If they can make those who run into me
    call me these names, they can do what they want—

no questions asked. If, by Demeter, they're keen,
they can convert me into sausages
and serve me up to men who think deep thoughts.

CHORUS: Here's a man whose mind's now smart,
no holding back—prepared to start
When you have learned all this from me   [460]
you know your glory will arise
among all men to heaven's skies.   630

STREPSIADES: What must I undergo?

CHORUS: For all time, you'll live with me
a life most people truly envy.

STREPSIADES: You mean I'll really see that one day?

CHORUS: Hordes will sit outside your door
wanting your advice and more—   [470]
to talk, to place their trust in you
for their affairs and lawsuits, too,
things which merit your great mind.
They'll leave you lots of cash behind.   640

CHORUS LEADER: *[to Socrates]*
So get started with this old man's lessons,
what you intend to teach him first of all—
rouse his mind, test his intellectual powers.

SOCRATES: Come on then, tell me the sort of man you are—
once I know that, I can bring to bear on you
my latest batteries with full effect.   [480]

STREPSIADES: What's that? By god, are you assaulting me?

SOCRATES: No—I want to learn some things from you.
What about your memory?

STREPSIADES: To tell the truth
   it works two ways. If someone owes me something,   650
   I remember really well. But if it's poor me
   that owes the money, I forget a lot.

SOCRATES: Do you have any natural gift for speech?

STREPSIADES: Not for speaking—only for evading debt.

SOCRATES: So how will you be capable of learning?

STREPSIADES: Easily—that shouldn't be your worry.

SOCRATES: All right. When I throw out something wise
   about celestial matters, you make sure
   you snatch it right away.   [490]

STREPSIADES: What's that about?
   Am I to eat up wisdom like a dog?   660

SOCRATES: *[aside]* This man's an ignorant barbarian!
   Old man, I fear you may need a beating.
   [to Strepsiades] Now, what do you do if someone hits you?

STREPSIADES: If I get hit, I wait around a while,
   then find witnesses, hang around some more,
   then go to court.

SOCRATES: All right, take off your cloak.

STREPSIADES: Have I done something wrong?

SOCRATES: No. It's our custom
   to go inside without a cloak.

STREPSIADES: But I don't want
   to search your house for stolen stuff.[36]

SOCRATES: What are you going on about? Take it off.   670

STREPSIADES: *[removing his cloak and his shoes]*
    So tell me this—if I pay attention   [500]
    and put some effort into learning,
    which of your students will I look like?

SOCRATES: In appearance there'll be no difference
    between yourself and Chaerephon.

STREPSIADES: Oh, that's bad.
    You mean I'll be only half alive?

SOCRATES: Don't talk such rubbish! Get a move on
    and follow me inside. Hurry up!

STREPSIADES: First, put a honey cake here in my hands.   680
    I'm scared of going down in there. It's like
    going in Trophonios' cave.[37]

SOCRATES: Go inside.
    Why keep hanging round this doorway?

[Socrates picks up Strepsiades' cloak and shoes. Then Strepsiades and Socrates exit into the interior of the Thinkery]

CHORUS LEADER: Go. And may you enjoy good fortune,   [510]
    a fit reward for all your bravery.

CHORUS: We hope this man
                thrives in his plan.
                For at his stage
                of great old age   690
                he'll take a dip
                in new affairs
                to act the sage.

CHORUS LEADER *[stepping forward to address the audience directly]*
    You spectators, I'll talk frankly to you now,
    and speak the truth, in the name of Dionysus,
    who has cared for me ever since I was a child.
    So may I win and be considered a wise man.[38]   [520]
    For I thought you were a discerning audience

and this comedy the most intelligent
of all my plays. Thus, I believed it worth my while   700
to produce it first for you, a work which cost me
a great deal of effort. But I left defeated,
beaten out by vulgar men—which I did not deserve.
I place the blame for this on you intellectuals,
on whose behalf I went to all that trouble.
But still I won't ever willingly abandon
the discriminating ones among you all,
not since that time when my play about two men—
one was virtuous, the other one depraved—
was really well received by certain people here,   710
whom it pleases me to mention now. As for me,
I was still unmarried, not yet fully qualified   [530]
to produce that child. But I exposed my offspring,
and another woman carried it away.
In your generosity you raised and trained it.[39]
Since then I've had sworn testimony from you
that you have faith in me. So now, like old Electra,
this comedy has come, hoping she can find,
somewhere in here, spectators as intelligent.
If she sees her brother's hair, she'll recognize it.[40]   720
Consider how my play shows natural restraint.
First, she doesn't have stitched leather dangling down,
with a thick red knob, to make the children giggle.[41]
She hasn't mocked bald men or danced some drunken reel.   [540]
There's no old man who talks and beats those present
with a stick to hide bad jokes. She doesn't rush on stage
with torches or raise the cry "Alas!" or "Woe is me!"
No—she's come trusting in herself and in the script.
And I'm a poet like that. I don't preen myself.
I don't seek to cheat you by re-presenting here   730
the same material two or three times over.
Instead I base my art on framing new ideas,
all different from the rest, and each one very deft.
When Cleon was all-powerful, I went for him.
I hit him in the gut. But once he was destroyed,
I didn't have the heart to kick at him again.   [550]
Yet once Hyperbolos let others seize on him,
they've not ceased stomping on the miserable man—
and on his mother, too.[42] The first was Eupolis—

he dredged up his *Maricas*, a wretched rehash   740
of my play *The Knights*—he's such a worthless poet—
adding an aging female drunk in that stupid dance,
a woman Phrynichos invented years ago,
the one that ocean monster tried to gobble up.[43]
Then Hermippos wrote again about Hyperbolos,
Now all the rest are savaging the man once more,
copying my images of eels. If anyone
laughs at those plays, I hope mine don't amuse him.   [560]
But if you enjoy me and my inventiveness,
then future ages will commend your worthy taste.   750

CHORUS: For my dance I first here call
             on Zeus, high-ruling king of all
             among the gods—and on Poseidon,
             so great and powerful—the one
             who with his trident wildly heaves
             the earth and all the brine-filled seas,
             and on our famous father Sky,
             the most revered, who can supply   [570]
             all things with life. And I invite
             the Charioteer whose dazzling light   760
             fills this wide world so mightily
             for every man and deity.

CHORUS LEADER: The wisest in this audience should here take note—
       you've done us wrong, and we confront you with the blame.
       We confer more benefits than any other god
       upon your city, yet we're the only ones
       to whom you do not sacrifice or pour libations,
       though we're the gods who keep protecting you.
       If there's some senseless army expedition,   [580]
       then we respond by thundering or bringing rain.   770
       And when you were selecting as your general
       that Paphlagonian tanner hated by the gods,[44]
       we frowned and then complained aloud—our thunder pealed
       among the lightning bursts, the moon moved off her course,
       the sun at once pulled his wick back inside himself,
       and said if Cleon was to be your general
       then he'd give you no light. Nonetheless, you chose him.
       They say this city likes to make disastrous choices,

but that the gods, no matter what mistakes you make,
convert them into something better. If you want   780
your recent choice to turn into a benefit,
I can tell you how—it's easy. Condemn the man—   [590]
that seagull Cleon—for bribery and theft.[45]
Set him in the stocks, a wooden yoke around his neck.
Then, even if you've made a really big mistake,
for you things will be as they were before your vote,
and for the city this affair will turn out well.

CHORUS: Phoebus Apollo, stay close by,
               lord of Delos, who sits on high,
               by lofty Cynthos mountain sides;   790
               and holy lady, who resides
               in Ephesus, in your gold shrine,
               where Lydian girls pray all the time;   600]
               Athena, too, who guards our home,
               her aegis raised above her own,
               and he who holds Parnassus peaks
               and shakes his torches as he leaps,
               lord Dionysus, whose shouts call
               amid the Delphic bacchanal.[46]

CHORUS LEADER: When we were getting ready to   800
   move over here,
   Moon met us and told us, first of all, to greet,
   on her behalf, the Athenians and their allies.
   Then she said she was upset—the way you treat her   [610]
   is disgraceful, though she brings you all benefits—
   not just in words but in her deeds. To start with,
   she saves you at least one drachma every month
   for torchlight— in the evening, when you go outside,
   you all can say, "No need to buy a torch, my boy,
   Moon's light will do just fine." She claims she helps you all
   in other ways, as well, but you don't calculate   810
   your calendar the way you should—no, instead
   you make it all confused, and that's why, she says,
   the gods are always making threats against her,
   when they are cheated of a meal and go back home
   because their celebration has not taken place
   according to a proper count of all the days.[47]

And then, when you should be making sacrifice,   [620]
you're torturing someone or have a man on trial.
And many times, when we gods undertake a fast,
because we're mourning Memnon or Sarpedon,[48]   820
you're pouring out libations, having a good laugh.
That's the reason, after his choice by lot this year
to sit on the religious council, Hyperbolos
had his wreath of office snatched off by the gods.
That should make him better understand the need
to count the days of life according to the moon.[49]

[Enter Socrates from the interior of the Thinkery]

SOCRATES: By Respiration, Chaos, and the Air,
    I've never seen a man so crude, stupid,
    clumsy, and forgetful. He tries to learn
    the tiny trifles, but then he forgets   830   [630]
    before he's even learned them. Nonetheless,
    I'll call him outside here into the light.

[Socrates calls back into the interior of the Thinkery]

    Strepsiades, where are you? Come on out—
    and bring your bed.

STREPSIADES: *[from inside]*   I can't carry it out—
    the bugs won't let me.

SOCRATES: Get a move on. Now!

[Strepsiades enters carrying his bedding]

SOCRATES: Put it there. And pay attention.

STREPSIADES: *[putting the bed down]*   There!

SOCRATES: Come now, of all the things you never learned
    what to you want to study first? Tell me.

[Strepsiades is very puzzled by the question]

SOCRATES: Poetic measures? Diction? Rhythmic verse?

STREPSIADES: I'll take measures. Just the other day   840
    the man who deals in barley cheated me—   [640]
    about two quarts.

SOCRATES: That's not what I mean.
    Which music measure is most beautiful—
    the triple measure or quadruple measure?

STREPSIADES: As a measure nothing beats a gallon.

SOCRATES: My dear man, you're just talking nonsense.

STREPSIADES: Then make me a bet—I say a gallon
    is made up of quadruple measures.

SOCRATES: Oh damn you—you're such a country bumpkin—
    so slow! Maybe you can learn more quickly   850
    if we deal with rhythm.

STREPSIADES: Will these rhythms
    help to get me food?

SOCRATES: Well, to begin with,
    they'll make you elegant in company—
    and you'll recognize the different rhythms,   [650]
    the enoplian and the dactylic,
    which is like a digit.[50]

STREPSIADES: Like a digit!
    By god, that's something I do know!

SOCRATES: Then tell me.

STREPSIADES: When I was a lad a digit meant this!

[Strepsiades sticks his middle finger straight up under Socrates' nose]

SOCRATES: You're just a crude buffoon!

STREPSIADES: No, you're a fool—
    I don't want to learn any of that stuff.   860

SOCRATES: Well then, what?

STREPSIADES: You know, that other thing—
    how to argue the most unjust cause.

SOCRATES: But you need to learn these other matters
    before all that. Now, of the quadrupeds
    which one can we correctly label male?

STREPSIADES: Well, I know the males, if I'm not witless—   [660]
    the ram, billy goat, bull, dog, and fowl.

SOCRATES: And the females?

STREPSIADES: The ewe, nanny goat,
    cow, bitch and fowl.[51]

SOCRATES: You see what you're doing?
    You're using that word "fowl" for both of them,   870
    Calling males what people use for females.

STREPSIADES: What's that? I don't get it.

SOCRATES: What's not to get?
    "Fowl" and "Fowl" …

STREPSIADES: By Poseidon, I see your point.
    All right, what should I call them?

SOCRATES: Call the male a "fowl"—
    and call the other one "fowlette."

STREPSIADES: "Fowlette?"
    By the Air, that's good! Just for teaching that
    I'll fill your kneading basin up with flour,
    right to the brim.[52]

SOCRATES: Once again, another error!   [670]
  You called it basin—a masculine word—
  when it's feminine.

STREPSIADES: How so? Do I call   880
  the basin masculine?

SOCRATES: Indeed you do.
  It's just like Cleonymos.[53]

STREPSIADES: How's that?
  Tell me.

SOCRATES: You treated the word basin
  just as you would treat Cleonymos.

STREPSIADES: [totally bewildered by the conversation]
  But my dear man, he didn't have a basin—
  not Cleonymos—not for kneading flour.
  His round mortar was his prick—the wanker—
  he kneaded that to masturbate.[54]
  But what should I call a basin from now on?

SOCRATES: Call it a basinette, just as you'd say   890
  the word Sostratette.

STREPSIADES: Basinette—it's feminine?

SOCRATES: It is indeed.

STREPSIADES: All right, then, I should say
  Cleonymette and basinette.[55]   [680]

SOCRATES: You've still got to learn about people's names—
  which ones are male and which are female.

STREPSIADES: I know which ones are feminine.

SOCRATES: Go on.

STREPSIADES: Lysilla, Philinna, Cleitagora,
    Demetria …

SOCRATES: Which names are masculine?

STREPSIADES: There are thousands of them—Philoxenos,
    Melesias, Amynias …

SOCRATES: You fool,   900
    those names are not all masculine.[56]

STREPSIADES: What?
    You don't think of them as men?

SOCRATES: Indeed I don't.
    If you met Amynias, how would you greet him?

STREPSIADES: How? Like this, "Here, Amynia, come here."[57]   [690]

SOCRATES: You see? You said "Amynia," a woman's name.

STREPSIADES: And that's fair enough, since she's unwilling
    to do army service. But what's the point?
    Why do I need to learn what we all know?

SOCRATES: That's irrelevant, by god. Now lie down—
    [indicating the bed] right here.

STREPSIADES: And do what?

SOCRATES: You should contemplate—   910
    think one of your own problems through.

STREPSIADES: Not here,
    I beg you—no. If I have to do it,
    let me do my contemplating on the ground.

SOCRATES: No—you've got no choice.

STREPSIADES: [crawling very reluctantly into the bedding]
                                   Now I'm done for—
    these bugs are going to punish me today.

[Socrates exits back into the Thinkery]

CHORUS: Now ponder and think,   [700]
            focus this way and that.
            Your mind turn and toss.
            And if you're at a loss,
            then quickly go find   920
            a new thought in your mind.
            From your eyes you must keep
            all soul-soothing sleep.

STREPSIADES: Oh, god … ahhhhh …

CHORUS: What's wrong with you? Why so distressed?

STREPSIADES: I'm dying a miserable death in here!
    These Corinthian crawlers keep biting me.[58]   [710]
    gnawing on my ribs,
    slurping up my blood,
    yanking off my balls,   930
    tunneling up my arse hole—
    they're killing me!

CHORUS: Don't complain so much.

STREPSIADES: Why not? When I've lost my goods,
    lost the colour in my cheeks, lost my blood,
    lost my shoes, and, on top of all these troubles,   [720]
    I'm here like some night watchman singing out—
    it won't be long before I'm done for.

[Enter Socrates from inside the Thinkery]

SOCRATES: What are you doing? Aren't you thinking something?

STREPSIADES: Me? Yes I am, by Poseidon.

SOCRATES: What about?   940

STREPSIADES: Whether there's going to be any of me left
    once these bugs have finished.

SOCRATES: You imbecile,
    why don't you drop dead!

[Socrates exits back into the Thinkery]

    STREPSIADES: But my dear man,
    I'm dying right now.

CHORUS LEADER: Don't get soft. Cover up—
    get your whole body underneath the blanket.
    You need to find a good idea for fraud,
    a sexy way to cheat.

STREPSIADES: Damn it all—
    instead of these lambskins here, why won't someone
    throw over me a lovely larcenous scheme?   [730]

[Strepsiades covers his head with the wool blankets. Enter Socrates from the Thinkery and
looks around thinking what to do]

SOCRATES: First, I'd better check on what he's doing.   950
    You in there, are you asleep?

STREPSIADES: [uncovering his head]   No, I'm not.

SOCRATES: Have you grasped anything?

STREPSIADES: No, by god, I haven't.

SOCRATES: Nothing at all?

STREPSIADES: I haven't grasped a thing—
    except my right hand's wrapped around my cock.

SOCRATES: Then cover your head and think up something—
    get a move on!

STREPSIADES: What should I think about?
Tell me that, Socrates.

SOCRATES: First you must formulate
what it is you want. Then tell me.

STREPSIADES: You've heard
what I want a thousand times—I want to know
about interest, so I'll not have to pay   960
a single creditor.

SOCRATES: Come along now,
cover up.

[Strepsiades covers his head again, and Socrates speaks to him through the blanket]

          Now, carve your slender thinking   [740]
into tiny bits, and think the matter through,
with proper probing and analysis.

STREPSIADES: Ahhh… bloody hell!

SOCRATES: Don't shift around.
If one of your ideas is going nowhere,
let it go, leave it alone. Later on,
start it again and weigh it one more time.

STREPSIADES: My dear little Socrates …

SOCRATES: Yes, old man,
what is it?

STREPSIADES: I've got a lovely scheme   970
to avoid paying interest.

SOCRATES: Lay it out.

STREPSIADES: All right. Tell me now…

SOCRATES: What is it?

STREPSIADES: What if I purchased a Thessalian witch
   and in the night had her haul down the moon—   [750]
   then shut it up in a circular box,
   just like a mirror, and kept watch on it.

SOCRATES: How would that provide you any help?

STREPSIADES: Well, if no moon ever rose up anywhere,
   I'd pay no interest.

SOCRATES: And why is that?

STREPSIADES: Because they lend out money by the month.   980

SOCRATES: That's good. I'll give you another problem—
   it's tricky. If in court someone sued you
   to pay five talents, what would you do
   to get the case discharged.

STREPSIADES: How? I don't know.
   I'll have to think.   [760]

SOCRATES: These ideas of yours—
   don't keep them wound up all the time inside you.
   Let your thinking loose—out into the air—
   with thread around its foot, just like a bug.[59]

STREPSIADES: Hey, I've devised a really clever way
   to make that lawsuit disappear—it's so good,   990
   you'll agree with me.

SOCRATES: What's your way?

STREPSIADES: At the drug seller's shop have you seen
   that beautiful stone you can see right through,
   the one they use to start a fire?

SOCRATES: You mean glass?

STREPSIADES: Yes.

SOCRATES: So what?

STREPSIADES: What if I took that glass,
and when the scribe was writing out the charge,   [770]
I stood between him and the sun—like this—
some distance off, and made his writing melt,
just the part about my case?[60]

SOCRATES: By the Graces,
that's a smart idea!

STREPSIADES: Hey, I'm happy—   1000
I've erased my law suit for five talents.

SOCRATES: So hurry up and tackle this next problem.

STREPSIADES: What is it?

SOCRATES: How would you evade a charge
and launch a counter-suit in a hearing
you're about to lose without a witness?

STREPSIADES: No problem there—it's easy.

SOCRATES: So tell me.

STREPSIADES: I will. If there was a case still pending,
another one before my case was called,
I'd run off and hang myself.   [780]

SOCRATES: That's nonsense.

STREPSIADES: No, by the gods, it's not. If I were dead,   1010
no one could bring a suit against me.

SOCRATES: That's rubbish. Just get away from here.
I'll not instruct you any more.

STREPSIADES: Why not?
Come on, Socrates, in god's name.

SOCRATES: There's no point—
     as soon as you learn anything, it's gone,
     you forget it right away. Look, just now,
     what was the very first thing you were taught?

STREPSIADES: Well, let's see … The first thing—what was it?
     What was that thing we knead the flour in?
     Damn it all, what was it?

SOCRATES: To hell with you!   1020
     You're the most forgetful, stupidest old man …   [790]
     Get lost!

STREPSIADES: Oh dear! Now I'm in for it.
     What going to happen to me? I'm done for,
     if I don't learn to twist my words around.
     Come on, Clouds, give me some good advice.

CHORUS LEADER: Old man, here's our advice: if you've a son
     and he's full grown, send him in there to learn—
     he'll take your place.

STREPSIADES: Well, I do have a son—
     a really good and fine one, too—trouble is
     he doesn't want to learn. What should I do?   1030

CHORUS LEADER: You just let him do that?

STREPSIADES: He's a big lad—
     and strong and proud—his mother's family
     are all high-flying women like Coesyra.   [800]
     But I'll take him in hand. If he says no,
     then I'll evict him from my house for sure.
     [to Socrates] Go inside and wait for me a while.

[Strepsiades moves back across the stage to his own house]

CHORUS: *[to Socrates]*
     Don't you see you'll quickly get
     from us all sorts of lovely things
     since we're your only god?

This man here is now all set   1040
to follow you in anything,
you simply have to prod.

You know the man is in a daze.
He's clearly keen his son should learn.
So lap it up—make haste—
get everything that you can raise.   [810]
Such chances tend to change and turn
into a different case.

[Socrates exits into the Thinkery. Strepsiades and Pheidippides come out of their house. Strepsiades is pushing his son in front of him]

STREPSIADES: By the foggy air, you can't stay here—
    not one moment longer! Off with you—   1050
    go eat Megacles out of house and home!

PHEIDIPPIDES: Hey, father—you poor man, what's wrong with you?
    By Olympian Zeus, you're not thinking straight.

STREPSIADES: See that—"Olympian Zeus"! Ridiculous—
    to believe in Zeus—and at your age!

PHEIDIPPIDES: Why laugh at that?

STREPSIADES: To think you're such a child—
    and your views so out of date. Still, come here,
    so you can learn a bit. I'll tell you things.
    When you understand all this, you'll be a man.
    But you mustn't mention this to anyone.   1060

PHEIDIPPIDES: All right, what is it?

STREPSIADES: You just swore by Zeus.

PHEIDIPPIDES: That's right. I did.

STREPSIADES: You see how useful learning is?
    Pheidippides, there's no such thing as Zeus.

PHEIDIPPIDES: Then what is there?

STREPSIADES: Vortex now is king—
he's pushed out Zeus.

PHEIDIPPIDES: Bah, that's nonsense!

STREPSIADES: You should know that's how things are right now.

PHEIDIPPIDES: Who says that?

STREPSIADES: Socrates of Melos[61]   [830]
and Chaerephon—they know about fleas' footprints.

PHEIDIPPIDES: Have you become so crazy you believe
these fellows? They're disgusting!

STREPSIADES: Watch your tongue.   1070
Don't say nasty things about such clever men—
men with brains, who like to save their money.
That's why not one of them has ever shaved,
or oiled his skin, or visited the baths
to wash himself. You, on the other hand,
keep on bathing in my livelihood,
as if I'd died.[62] So now get over there,
as quickly as you can. Take my place and learn.

PHEIDIPPIDES: But what could anyone learn from those men
that's any use at all?   [840]

STREPSIADES: You have to ask?   1080
Why, wise things—the full extent of human thought.
You'll see how thick you are, how stupid.
Just wait a moment here for me.

[Strepsiades goes into his house]

PHEIDIPPIDES: Oh dear,
    What will I do? My father's lost his wits.
    Do I haul him off to get committed,
    on the ground that he's a lunatic,
    or tell the coffin-makers he's gone nuts.

[Strepsiades returns with two birds, one in each hand. He holds out one of them]

STREPSIADES: Come on now, what do you call this? Tell me.

PHEIDIPPIDES: It's a fowl.

STREPSIADES: That's good. What's this?

PHEIDIPPIDES: That's a fowl.

STREPSIADES: They're both the same? You're being ridiculous.   1090
    From now on, don't do that. Call this one "fowl,"   [850]
    and this one here "fowlette."

PHEIDIPPIDES:"   Fowlette"? That's it?
    That's the sort of clever stuff you learned in there,
    by going in with these Sons of Earth?[63]

STREPSIADES: Yes, it is—
    and lots more, too. But everything I learned,
    I right away forgot, because I'm old.

PHEIDIPPIDES: That why you lost your cloak?

STREPSIADES: I didn't lose it—
    I gave it to knowledge—a donation.

PHEIDIPPIDES: And your sandals—what you do with them,
    you deluded man?

STREPSIADES: Just like Pericles,   1100
    I lost them as a "necessary expense."[64]
    But come on, let's go. Move it. If your dad   [860]
    asks you to do wrong, you must obey him.
    I know I did just what you wanted long ago,

when you were six years old and had a lisp—
with the first obol I got for jury work,
at the feast of Zeus I got you a toy cart.

PHEIDIPPIDES: You're going to regret this one fine day.

STREPSIADES: Good—you're doing what I ask.

[Strepsiades calls inside the Thinkery]

                                                Socrates,
come out here …

[Enter Socrates from inside the Thinkery]

                 Here—I've brought my son to you.   1110
He wasn't keen, but I persuaded him.

SOCRATES: He's still a child—he doesn't know the ropes.

PHEIDIPPIDES: Go hang yourself up on some rope,   [870]
and get beaten like a worn-out cloak.

STREPSIADES: Damn you! Why insult your teacher?

SOCRATES: Look how he says "hang yourself"—it sounds
like baby talk. No crispness in his speech.[65]
With such a feeble tone how will he learn
to answer to a charge or summons
or speak persuasively? And yet it's true   1120
Hyperbolos could learn to master that—
it cost him one talent.[66]

STREPSIADES: Don't be concerned.
Teach him. He's naturally intelligent.
When he was a little boy—just that tall—
even then at home he built small houses,
carved out ships, made chariots from leather,   [880]
and fashioned frogs from pomegranate peel.
You can't imagine! Get him to learn
those two forms of argument—the Better,

whatever that may be, and the Worse.   1130
    If not both, then at least the unjust one—
    every trick you've got.

SOCRATES: He'll learn on his own
    from the two styles of reasoning. I'll be gone.

STREPSIADES: But remember this—he must be able
    to speak against all just arguments.

[Enter the Better Argument from inside the Thinkery, talking to the Worse Argument who is still inside]

BETTER ARGUMENT: Come on. Show yourself to the people here—
    I guess you're bold enough for that.   [890]

[The Worse Argument emerges from the Thinkery]

WORSE ARGUMENT: Go where you please.
    The odds are greater I can wipe you out
    with lots of people there to watch us argue.

BETTER ARGUMENT: You'll wipe me out? Who'd you think you are? 1140

WORSE ARGUMENT: An argument.

BETTER ARGUMENT: Yes, but second rate.

WORSE ARGUMENT: You claim that you're more powerful than me,
but I'll still conquer you.

BETTER ARGUMENT: What clever tricks
    do you intend to use?

WORSE ARGUMENT: I'll formulate
    new principles.

BETTER ARGUMENT: *[indicating the audience]* Yes, that's in fashion now,
    thanks to these idiots.

WORSE ARGUMENT: No, no. They're smart.

BETTER ARGUMENT: I'll destroy you utterly.

WORSE ARGUMENT: And how?
    Tell me that.

BETTER ARGUMENT: By arguing what's just.   [900]

WORSE ARGUMENT: That I can overturn in my response,
    by arguing there's no such thing as Justice.   1150

BETTER ARGUMENT: It doesn't exist? That's what you maintain?

WORSE ARGUMENT: Well, if it does, where is it?

BETTER ARGUMENT: With the gods.

WORSE ARGUMENT: Well, if Justice does exist, how come Zeus
    hasn't been destroyed for chaining up his dad.[67]

BETTER ARGUMENT: This is going from bad to worse. I feel sick.
    Fetch me a basin.

WORSE ARGUMENT: You silly old man—
    you're so ridiculous.

BETTER ARGUMENT: And you're quite shameless,
    you bum fucker.

WORSE ARGUMENT: Those words you speak—like roses!

BETTER ARGUMENT: Buffoon!   [910]

WORSE ARGUMENT: You adorn my head with lilies.

BETTER ARGUMENT: You destroyed your father!

WORSE ARGUMENT: You don't mean to,   1160
    but you're showering me with gold.

BETTER ARGUMENT: No, not gold—
    before this age, those names were lead.

WORSE ARGUMENT: But now,
    your insults are a credit to me.

BETTER ARGUMENT: You're too obstreperous.

WORSE ARGUMENT: You're archaic.

BETTER ARGUMENT: It's thanks to you that none of our young men
    is keen to go to school. The day will come
    when the Athenians will all realize
    how you teach these silly fools.

WORSE ARGUMENT: You're dirty—
    it's disgusting.

BETTER ARGUMENT: But you're doing very well—   [920]
    although in earlier days you were a beggar,   1170
    claiming to be Telephos from Mysia,
    eating off some views of Pandeletos,
    which you kept in your wallet.[68]

WORSE ARGUMENT: That was brilliant—
    you just reminded me ...

BETTER ARGUMENT: It was lunacy!
    Your own craziness—the city's, too.
    It fosters you while you corrupt the young.

WORSE ARGUMENT: You can't teach this boy—you're old as Cronos.

BETTER ARGUMENT: Yes, I must—if he's going to be redeemed   [930]
    and not just prattle empty verbiage.

WORSE ARGUMENT: *[to Pheidippides]*
    Come over here—leave him to his foolishness.   1180

BETTER ARGUMENT: You'll regret it, if you lay a hand on him.

CHORUS LEADER: Stop this fighting, all these abusive words.

[addressing first the Better Argument and then the Worse Argument]

Instead, explain the things you used to teach
to young men long ago—then you lay out
what's new in training now. He can listen
as you present opposing arguments
and then decide which school he should attend.

BETTER ARGUMENT: I'm willing to do that.

WORSE ARGUMENT: All right with me.

CHORUS LEADER: Come on then, which one of you goes first?   [940]

WORSE ARGUMENT: I'll grant him that right. Once he's said his piece, 1190
    I'll shoot it down with brand-new expressions
    and some fresh ideas. By the time I'm done,
    if he so much as mutters, he'll get stung
    by my opinions on his face and eyes—
    like so many hornets—he'll be destroyed.

CHORUS: Trusting their skill in argument,
                  their phrase-making propensity,   [950]
             these two men here are now intent
                  to show which one will prove to be
                  the better man in oratory.   1200
             For wisdom now is being hard pressed—
             my friends, this is the crucial test.

CHORUS LEADER: *[addressing the Better Argument]*
    First, you who crowned our men in days gone by
    with so much virtue in their characters,
    let's hear that voice which brings you such delight—
    explain to us what makes you what you are.   [960]

BETTER ARGUMENT: All right, I'll set out how we organized
    our education in the olden days,
    when I talked about what's just and prospered,
    when people wished to practise self-restraint.   1210
    First, there was a rule—children made no noise,
    no muttering. Then, when they went outside,

walking the streets to the music master's house,
groups of youngsters from the same part of town
went in straight lines and never wore a cloak,
not even when the snow fell thick as flour.
There he taught them to sing with thighs apart.[69]
They had memorize their songs—such as,
"Dreadful Pallas Who Destroys Whole Cities,"
and "A Cry From Far Away." These they sang   1220
in the same style their fathers had passed down.
If any young lad fooled around or tried
to innovate with some new flourishes,
like the contorted sounds we have today
from those who carry on the Phrynis style,[70]   [970]
he was beaten, soundly thrashed, his punishment
for tarnishing the Muse. At the trainer's house,
when the boys sat down, they had to keep
their thighs stretched out, so they would not expose
a thing which might excite erotic torments   1230
in those looking on. And when they stood up,
they smoothed the sand, being careful not to leave
imprints of their manhood there for lovers.
Using oil, no young lad rubbed his body
underneath his navel—thus on his sexual parts
there was a dewy fuzz, like on a peach.
He didn't make his voice all soft and sweet
to talk to lovers as he walked along,
or with his glances coyly act the pimp.   [980]
When he was eating, he would not just grab   1240
a radish head, or take from older men
some dill or parsley, or eat dainty food.
He wasn't allowed to giggle, or sit there
with his legs crossed.

WORSE ARGUMENT: Antiquated rubbish!
    Filled with festivals for Zeus Polieus,
    cicadas, slaughtered bulls, and Cedeides.[71]

BETTER ARGUMENT: But the point is this—these very features
    in my education brought up those men
    who fought at Marathon. But look at you—
    you teach these young men now right from the start   1250

to wrap themselves in cloaks. It enrages me
when the time comes for them to do their dance
at the Panathenaea festival
and one of them holds his shield low down,
over his balls, insulting Tritogeneia.[72]
And so, young man, that's why you should choose me,   [990]
the Better Argument. Be resolute.
You'll find out how to hate the market place,
to shun the public baths, to feel ashamed
of shameful things, to fire up your heart   1260
when someone mocks you, to give up your chair
when older men come near, not to insult
your parents, nor act in any other way
which brings disgrace or which could mutilate
your image as an honourable man.
You'll learn not to run off to dancing girls,
in case, while gaping at them, you get hit
with an apple thrown by some little slut,
and your fine reputation's done for,
and not to contradict your father,   1270
or remind him of his age by calling him
Iapetus—not when he spent his years
in raising you from infancy.[73]

WORSE ARGUMENT: My boy, if you're persuaded by this man,   [1000]
   then by Dionysus, you'll finish up
   just like Hippocrates' sons—and then
   they'll all call you a sucker of the tit.[74]

BETTER ARGUMENT: You'll spend your time in the gymnasium—
   your body will be sleek, in fine condition.
   You won't be hanging round the market place,   1280
   chattering filth, as boys do nowadays.
   You won't keep on being hauled away to court
   over some damned sticky fierce dispute
   about some triviality. No, no.
   Instead you'll go to the Academy,[75]
   to race under the sacred olive trees,
   with a decent friend the same age as you,
   wearing a white reed garland, with no cares.
   You'll smell yew trees, quivering poplar leaves,

as plane trees whisper softly to the elms,   1290
rejoicing in the spring. I tell you this—
if you carry out these things I mention,
if you concentrate your mind on them,   [1010]
you'll always have a gleaming chest, bright skin,
broad shoulders, tiny tongue, strong buttocks,
and a little prick. But if you take up
what's in fashion nowadays, you'll have,
for starters, feeble shoulders, a pale skin,
a narrow chest, huge tongue, a tiny bum,
and a large skill in framing long decrees.⁷⁶   1300
And that man there will have you believing
what's bad is good and what's good is bad.   [1020]
Then he'll give you Antimachos' disease—
you'll be infected with his buggery. ⁷⁷

CHORUS: O you whose wisdom stands so tall,
the most illustrious of all.
The odour of your words is sweet,
the flowering bloom of modest ways—
happy who lived in olden days!

[to the Worse Argument]

Your rival's made his case extremely well,   1310
so you who have such nice artistic skill.
must in reply give some new frill.   [1030]

CHORUS LEADER: If you want to overcome this man
it looks as if you'll need to bring at him
some clever stratagems—unless you want
to look ridiculous.

WORSE ARGUMENT: It's about time!
My guts have long been churning with desire
to rip in fragments all those things he said,
with counter-arguments. That's why I'm called
Worse Argument among all thinking men,   1320
because I was the very first of them
to think of coming up with reasoning
against our normal ways and just decrees.   [1040]

And it's worth lots of money—more, in fact,
than drachmas in six figures[78]—to select
the weaker argument and yet still win.
Now just see how I'll pull his system down,
that style of education which he trusts.
First, he says he won't let you have hot water
when you take a bath. What's the idea here?   1330
Why object to having a warm bath?

BETTER ARGUMENT: The effect they have is very harmful—
they turn men into cowards.

WORSE ARGUMENT: Wait a minute!
The first thing you say I've caught you out.
I've got you round the waist. You can't escape.
Tell me this—of all of Zeus' children
which man, in your view, had the greatest heart
and carried out the hardest tasks? Tell me.

BETTER ARGUMENT: In my view, no one was a better man   [1050]
than Hercules.

WORSE ARGUMENT: And where'd you ever see   1340
cold water in a bath of Hercules? But who
was a more manly man than him?[79]

BETTER ARGUMENT: That's it, the very things which our young men
are always babbling on about these days—
crowding in the bath house, leaving empty
all the wrestling schools.

WORSE ARGUMENT: Next, you're not happy
when they hang around the market place—
but I think that's good. If it were shameful,
Homer would not have labelled Nestor—
and all his clever men—great public speakers.[80]   1350
Now, I'll move on to their tongues, which this man
says the young lads should not train. I say they should.
He also claims they should be self-restrained.
These two things injure them in major ways.   [1060]
Where have you ever witnessed self-restraint

bring any benefit to anyone?
Tell me. Speak up. Refute my reasoning.

BETTER ARGUMENT: There are lots of people. For example,
    Peleus won a sword for his restraint.[81]

WORSE ARGUMENT: A sword! What a magnificent reward   1360
    the poor wretch received! While Hyperbolos,
    who sells lamps in the market, is corrupt
    and brings in lots of money, but, god knows,
    he's never won a sword.

BETTER ARGUMENT: But his virtue
    enabled Peleus to marry Thetis.[82]

WORSE ARGUMENT: Then she ran off, abandoning the man,
    because he didn't want to spend all night
    having hard sweet sex between the sheets—
    that rough-and-tumble love that women like.
    You're just a crude old-fashioned Cronos.   1370   [1070]
    Now, my boy, just think off all those things
    that self-restraint requires—you'll go without
    all sorts of pleasures—boys and women,
    drunken games and tasty delicacies,
    drink and riotous laughter. What's life worth
    if you're deprived of these? So much for that.
    I'll now move on to physical desires.
    You've strayed and fallen in love—had an affair
    with someone else's wife. And then you're caught.
    You're dead, because you don't know how to speak.   1380
    But if you hang around with those like me,
    you can follow what your nature urges.
    You can leap and laugh and never think
    of anything as shameful. If, by chance,
    you're discovered screwing a man's wife,
    just tell the husband you've done nothing wrong.
    Blame Zeus—alleging even he's someone   [1080]
    who can't resist his urge for sex and women.
    And how can you be stronger than a god?
    You're just a mortal man.

BETTER ARGUMENT: All right—but suppose   1390
  he trusts in your advice and gets a radish
  rammed right up his arse, and his pubic hairs
  are burned with red-hot cinders. Will he have
  some reasoned argument to demonstrate
  he's not a loose-arsed bugger?[83]

WORSE ARGUMENT: So his asshole's large—
  why should that in any way upset him?

BETTER ARGUMENT: Can one suffer any greater harm
  than having a loose asshole?

WORSE ARGUMENT: What will you say
  if I defeat you on this point?

BETTER ARGUMENT: I'll shut up.
  What more could a man say?

WORSE ARGUMENT: Come on, then—   1400
  Tell me about our legal advocates.
  Where are they from?

BETTER ARGUMENT: They come from loose-arsed buggers.

WORSE ARGUMENT: I grant you that. What's next? Our tragic poets,   [1090]
  where they from?

BETTER ARGUMENT: They come from major assholes.

WORSE ARGUMENT: That's right. What about our politicians—
  where do they come from?

BETTER ARGUMENT: From gigantic assholes!

WORSE ARGUMENT: All right then—surely you can recognize
  how you've been spouting rubbish? Look out there—
  at this audience—what sort of people
  are most of them?

BETTER ARGUMENT: All right, I'm looking at them.   1410

WORSE ARGUMENT: Well, what do you see?

BETTER ARGUMENT: By all the gods,
    almost all of them are men who spread their cheeks.
    It's true of that one there, I know for sure …
    and that one … and the one there with long hair.   [1100]

WORSE ARGUMENT: So what do you say now?

BETTER ARGUMENT: We've been defeated.
    Oh you fuckers, for gods' sake take my cloak—
    I'm defecting to your ranks.

[The Better Argument takes off his cloak and exits into the Thinkery]

WORSE ARGUMENT: *[to Strepsiades]*
                                         What now?

    Do you want to take your son away?
    Or, to help you out, am I to teach him
    how to argue?

STREPSIADES: Teach him—whip him into shape.   1420
    Don't forget to sharpen him for me,
    one side ready to tackle legal quibbles.
    On the other side, give his jaw an edge
    for more important matters.   [1110]

WORSE ARGUMENT: Don't worry.
    You'll get back a person skilled in sophistry.

PHEIDIPPIDES: Someone miserably pale, I figure.

CHORUS LEADER: All right. Go in.
    I think you may regret this later on.

[Worse Argument and Pheidippides go into the Thinkery, while Strepsiades returns into his own house]

CHORUS LEADER: We'd like to tell the judges here the benefits
    they'll get, if they help this chorus, as by right they should.
    First, if you want to plough your lands in season,   1430

we'll rain first on you and on the others later.
Then we'll protect your fruit, your growing vines,
so neither drought nor too much rain will damage them.   [1120]
But any mortal who dishonours us as gods
should bear in mind the evils we will bring him.
From his land he'll get no wine or other harvest.
When his olive trees and fresh young vines are budding,
we'll let fire with our sling shots, to smash and break them.
If we see him making bricks, we'll send down rain,
we'll shatter roofing tiles with our round hailstones.   1440
If ever there's a wedding for his relatives,
or friends, or for himself, we'll rain all through the night,
so he'd rather live in Egypt than judge this wrong.   [1130]

[Strepsiades comes out of his house, with a small sack in his hand]

STREPSIADES: Five more days, then four, three, two—and then
    the day comes I dread more than all the rest.
    It makes me shake with fear—the day that stands
    between the Old Moon and the New—the day
    when any man I happen to owe money to
    swears on oath he'll put down his deposit,
    take me to court.[84] He says he'll finish me,   1450
    do me in. When I make a modest plea
    for something fair, "My dear man, don't demand
    this payment now, postpone this one for me,
    discharge that one," they say the way things are
    they'll never be repaid—then they go at me,   [1140]
    abuse me as unfair and say they'll sue.
    Well, let them go to court. I just don't care,
    not if Pheidippides has learned to argue.
    I'll find out soon enough. Let's knock here,
    at the thinking school.

[Strepsiades knocks on the door of the Thinkery]

                                    Boy ... Hey, boy ... boy!   1460

[Socrates comes to the door]

SOCRATES: Hello there, Strepsiades.

STREPSIADES: Hello to you.
    First of all, you must accept this present.

[Strepsiades hands Socrates the small sack]

    It's proper for a man show respect
    to his son's teacher in some way. Tell me—
    has the boy learned that style of argument
    you brought out here just now?

SOCRATES: Yes, he has.

STREPSIADES: In the name of Fraud, queen of everything,
    that's splendid news!

SOCRATES: You can defend yourself
    in any suit you like—and win.

STREPSIADES: I can?
    Even if there were witnesses around   1470
    when I took out the loan?

SOCRATES: The more the better—
    even if they number in the thousands.

STREPSIADES: *[in a parody of tragic style]*
    Then I will roar aloud a mighty shout—
    Ah ha, weep now you petty money men,
    wail for yourselves, wail for your principal,
    wail for your compound interest. No more
    will you afflict me with your evil ways.
    On my behalf there's growing in these halls
    a son who's got a gleaming two-edged tongue—   [1160]
    he's my protector, saviour of my home,   1480
    a menace to my foes. He will remove
    the mighty tribulations of his sire.
    Run off inside and summon him to me.

[Socrates goes back into the Thinkery]

My son, my boy, now issue from the house—
and hearken to your father's words.

[Socrates and Pheidippides come out of the Thinkery. Pheidippides has been transformed in appearance, so that he now looks, moves, and talks like the other students in the Thinkery]

SOCRATES: Here's your young man.

STREPSIADES: Ah, my dear, dear boy.

SOCRATES: Take him and go away.

[Socrates exits back into the Thinkery]

STREPSIADES: Ah ha, my lad—
    what joy. What sheer delight for me to gaze,   [1170]
    first, upon your colourless complexion,
    to see how right away you're well prepared   1490
    to deny and contradict—with that look
    which indicates our national character
    so clearly planted on your countenance—
    the look which says, "What do you mean?"—the look
    which makes you seem a victim, even though
    you're the one at fault, the criminal.
    I know that Attic stare stamped on your face.
    Now you must rescue me—since you're the one
    who's done me in.

PHEIDIPPIDES: What are you scared about?

STREPSIADES: The day of the Old Moon and the New.   1500

PHEIDIPPIDES: You mean there's a day that's old and new?

STREPSIADES: The day they say they'll make deposits
    to charge me in the courts!   [1180]

PHEIDIPPIDES: Then those who do that
    will lose their cash. There's simply no way
    one day can be two days.

STREPSIADES: It can't?

PHEIDIPPIDES: How?
    Unless it's possible a single woman
    can at the same time be both old and young.

STREPSIADES: Yet that seems to be what our laws dictate.

PHEIDIPPIDES: In my view they just don't know the law—
    not what it really means.

STREPSIADES: What does it mean?   1510

PHEIDIPPIDES: Old Solon by his nature loved the people.[85]

STREPSIADES: But that's got no bearing on the Old Day—
    or the New.

PHEIDIPPIDES: Well, Solon set up two days   [1190]
    for summonses—the Old Day and the New,
    so deposits could be made with the New Moon.[86]

STREPSIADES: Then why did he include Old Day as well?

PHEIDIPPIDES: So the defendants, my dear fellow,
    could show up one day early, to settle
    by mutual agreement, and, if not,
    they should be very worried the next day   1520
    was the start of a New Moon.

STREPSIADES: In that case,
    why do judges not accept deposits
    once the New Moon comes but only on the day
    between the Old and New?

PHEIDIPPIDES: It seems to me
    they have to act like those who check the food—   [1200]

they want to grab as fast as possible
at those deposits, so they can nibble them
a day ahead of time.

STREPSIADES: That's wonderful!
    [to the audience] You helpless fools! Why do you sit there—   1530
    so idiotically, for us wise types
    to take advantage of? Are you just stones,
    ciphers, merely sheep or stacked-up pots?
    This calls for a song to me and my son here,
    to celebrate good luck and victory.

[He sings]

    O Strepsiades is truly blessed
    for cleverness the very best,
    what a brainy son he's raised.
    So friends and townsfolk sing his praise.
    Each time you win they'll envy me—   1540   [1210]
    you'll plead my case to victory.
    So let's go in—I want to treat,
    and first give you something to eat.

[Strepsiades and Pheidippides go together into their house. Enter one of Strepsiades' creditors,
Pasias, with a friend as his witness]

PASIAS: Should a man throw away his money?
    Never! But it would have been much better,
    back then at the start, to forget the loan
    and the embarrassment than go through this—
    to drag you as a witness here today
    in this matter of my money. I'll make
    this man from my own deme my enemy.[87]   1550
    But I'll not let my country down—never—   [1220]
    not as long as I'm alive. And so …
    [raising his voice] I'm summoning Strepsiades …

STREPSIADES: Who is it?

PASIAS: … on this Old Day and the New.

STREPSIADES: I ask you here
    to witness that he's called me for two days.
    What's the matter?

PASIAS: The loan you got, twelve minai,
    when you bought that horse—the dapple grey.

STREPSIADES: A horse? Don't listen to him. You all know
    how I hate horses.

PASIAS: What's more, by Zeus,
    you swore on all the gods you'd pay me back.   1560

STREPSIADES: Yes, by god, but Pheidippides back then
    did not yet know the iron-clad argument
    on my behalf.

PASIAS: So now, because of that,
    you're intending to deny the debt?   [1230]

STREPSIADES: If I don't, what advantage do I gain
    from everything he's learned?

PASIAS: Are you prepared
    to swear you owe me nothing—by the gods—
    in any place I tell you?

STREPSIADES: Which gods?

PASIAS: By Zeus, by Hermes, by Poseidon.

STREPSIADES: Yes, indeed, by Zeus—and to take that oath   1570
    I'd even pay three extra obols.[88]

PASIAS: You're shameless—may that ruin you some day!

STREPSIADES: [patting Pasias on the belly]
    This wine skin here would much better off
    if you rubbed it down with salt.[89]

PASIAS: Damn you—
   you're ridiculing me!

STREPSIADES: *[still patting Pasias' paunch]* About four gallons,
   that's what it should hold.

PASIAS: By mighty Zeus,
   by all the gods, you'll not make fun of me
   and get away with it!

STREPSIADES: Ah, you and your gods—   [1240]
   that's so incredibly funny. And Zeus—
   to swear on him is quite ridiculous   1580
   to those who understand.

PASIAS: Some day, I swear,
   you're going to have to pay for all of this.
   Will you or will you not pay me my money?
   Give me an answer, and I'll leave.

STREPSIADES: Calm down—
   I'll give you a clear answer right away.

[Strepsiades goes into his house, leaving Pasias and the Witness by themselves]

PASIAS: Well, what do you think he's going to do?
   Does it strike you he's going to pay?

[Enter Strepsiades carrying a kneading basin]

STREPSIADES: Where's the man who's asking me for money?
   Tell me—what's this?

PASIAS: What's that? A kneading basin.

STREPSIADES: You're demanding money when you're such a fool?   1590
   I wouldn't pay an obol back to anyone   [1250]
   who called a basinette a basin.

PASIAS: So you won't repay me?

STREPSIADES: As far as I know,
    I won't. So why don't you just hurry up
    and quickly scuttle from my door.

PASIAS: I'm off.
    Let me tell you—I'll be making my deposit.
    If not, may I not live another day!

[Pasias exits with the Witness]

STREPSIADES: *[calling after them]*
    That'll be more money thrown away—
    on top of the twelve minai. I don't want
    you going thorough that just because you're foolish   1600
    and talk about a kneading basin.

[Enter Amynias, another creditor, limping He has obviously been hurt in some way]

AMYNIAS: Oh, it's bad. Poor me!

STREPSIADES: Hold on. Who's this
    who's chanting a lament? Is that the cry   [1260]
    of some god perhaps—one from Carcinus?[90]

AMYNIAS: What's that? You wish to know who I am?
    I'm a man with a miserable fate!

STREPSIADES: Then go off on your own.

AMYNIAS: *[in a grand tragic manner]*   "O cruel god,
    O fortune fracturing my chariot wheels,
    O Pallas, how you've annihilated me!"[91]

STREPSIADES: How's Tlepolemos done nasty things to you?[92]   1610

AMYNIAS: Don't laugh at me, my man—but tell your son
    to pay me back the money he received,
    especially when I'm going through all this pain.

STREPSIADES: What money are you talking about?

AMYNIAS: The loan he got from me.   [1270]

STREPSIADES: It seems to me
    you're having a bad time.

AMYNIAS: By god, that's true—
    I was driving in my chariot and fell out.

STREPSIADES: Why then babble on such utter nonsense,
    as if you'd just fallen off a donkey?

AMYNIAS: If I want him to pay back my money   1620
    am I talking nonsense?

STREPSIADES: I think it's clear
    your mind's not thinking straight.

AMYNIAS: Why's that?

STREPSIADES: From your behaviour here, it looks to me
    as if your brain's been shaken up.

AMYNIAS: Well, as for you,
    by Hermes, I'll be suing you in court,
    if you don't pay the money.

STREPSIADES: Tell me this—
    do you think Zeus always sends fresh water
    each time the rain comes down, or does the sun   [1280]
    suck the same water up from down below
    for when it rains again?

AMYNIAS: I don't know which—   1630
    and I don't care.

STREPSIADES: Then how can it be just
    for you to get your money reimbursed,
    when you know nothing of celestial things?

AMYNIAS: Look, if you haven't got the money now,
    at least repay the interest.

STREPSIADES: This "interest"—
    What sort of creature is it?

AMYNIAS: Don't you know?
    It's nothing but the way that money grows,
    always getting larger day by day
    month by month, as time goes by.

STREPSIADES: That's right.
    What about the sea? In your opinion,   1640   [1290]
    is it more full of water than before?

AMYNIAS: No, by Zeus—it's still the same. If it grew,
    that would violate all natural order.

STREPSIADES: In that case then, you miserable rascal,
    if the sea shows no increase in volume
    with so many rivers flowing into it,
    why are you so keen to have your money grow?
    Now, why not chase yourself away from here?
    [calling inside the house] Bring me the cattle prod!

AMYNIAS: I have witnesses!

[The slave comes out of the house and gives Strepsiades a cattle prod. Strepsiades starts poking Amynias with it]

STREPSIADES: Come on! What you waiting for? Move it,   1650
    you pedigree nag!

AMYNIAS: This is outrageous!

STREPSIADES: *[continuing to poke Amynias away]*
    Get a move on—or I'll shove this prod   [1300]
    all the way up your horse-racing rectum!

[Amynias runs off stage]

    You running off? That's what I meant to do,
    get the wheels on that chariot of yours
    really moving fast.

[Strepsiades goes back into his house]

CHORUS: Oh, it's so nice
to worship vice.
This old man here
adores it so   1660
he will not clear
the debts he owes.
But there's no way
he will not fall
some time today,
done in by all
his trickeries,
he'll quickly fear
depravities
he's started here.   1670

It seems to me
he'll soon will see
his clever son
put on the show
he wanted done
so long ago—
present a case
against what's true
and beat all those
he runs into   1680
with sophistry.
He'll want his son
(it may well be)
to be struck dumb.   [1320]

[Enter Strepsiades running out of his house with Pheidippides close behind him hitting him over the head]

STREPSIADES: Help! Help! You neighbours, relatives,
    fellow citizens, help me—I'm begging you!
    I'm being beaten up! Owww, I'm in such pain—
    my head … my jaw. *[To Pheidippides]* You good for nothing,
    are you hitting your own father?

PHEIDIPPIDES: Yes, dad, I am.

STREPSIADES: See that! He admits he's beating me.   1690

PHEIDIPPIDES: I do indeed.

STREPSIADES: You scoundrel, criminal—
    a man who abuses his own father!

PHEIDIPPIDES: Go on—keep calling me those very names—
    the same ones many times. Don't you realize
    I just love hearing streams of such abuse?

STREPSIADES: You perverted asshole!

PHEIDIPPIDES: Ah, some roses!   [1330]
    Keep pelting me with roses!!

STREPSIADES: You'd hit your father?

PHEIDIPPIDES: Yes, and by the gods I'll now demonstrate
    how I was right to hit you.

STREPSIADES: You total wretch,
    how can it be right to strike one's father?   1700

PHEIDIPPIDES: I'll prove that to you—and win the argument.

STREPSIADES: You'll beat me on this point?

PHEIDIPPIDES: Indeed, I will.
    It's easy. So of the two arguments
    choose which one you want.

STREPSIADES: What two arguments?

PHEIDIPPIDES: The Better or the Worse.

STREPSIADES: By god, my lad,
    I really did have you taught to argue
    against what's just, if you succeed in this—

and make the case it's fine and justified
for a father to be beaten by his son.

PHEIDIPPIDES: Well, I think I'll manage to convince you,   1710
    so that once you've heard my arguments,
    you won't say a word.

STREPSIADES: Well, to tell the truth,
    I do want to hear what you have to say.

CHORUS: You've some work to do, old man.
    Think how to get the upper hand.
    He's got something he thinks will work,
    or he'd not act like such a jerk.
    There's something makes him confident—
    his arrogance is evident.   [1350]

CHORUS LEADER: *[addressing Strepsiades]*
    But first you need to tell the Chorus here   1720
    how your fight originally started.
    That's something you should do in any case.

STREPSIADES: Yes, I'll tell you how our quarrel first began.
    As you know, we were having a fine meal.
    I first asked him to take up his lyre
    and sing a lyric by Simonides[93]—
    the one about the ram being shorn.
    But he immediately refused—saying
    that playing the lyre while we were drinking
    was out of date, like some woman singing   1730
    while grinding barley.

PHEIDIPPIDES: Well, at that point,
    you should have been ground up and trampled on—
    asking for a song, as if you were feasting   [1360]
    with cicadas.

STREPSIADES: The way he's talking now—
    that's just how he was talking there before.
    He said Simonides was a bad poet.
    I could hardly stand it, but at first I did.

Then I asked him to pick up a myrtle branch
and at least recite some Aeschylus for me.[94]
He replied at once, "In my opinion,   1740
Aeschylus is first among the poets
for lots of noise, unevenness, and bombast—
he piles up words like mountains." Do you know
how hard my heart was pounding after that?
But I clenched my teeth and kept my rage inside,
and said, "Then recite me something recent,
from the newer poets, some witty verse."   [1370]
So he then right off started to declaim
some passage from Euripides in which,
spare me this, a brother was enjoying sex   1750
with his own sister— from a common mother.
I couldn't keep my temper any more—
so on the spot I verbally attacked
with all sorts of nasty, shameful language.
Then, as one might predict, we went at it—
hurling insults at each other back and forth.
But then he jumped up, pushed me, thumped me,
choked me, and started killing me.

PHEIDIPPIDES: Surely I was entitled to do that
   to a man who will not praise Euripides,   1760
   the cleverest of all.

STREPSIADES: Him? The cleverest? Ha!
   What do I call you? No, I won't say—
   I'd just get beaten one more time.

PHEIDIPPIDES: Yes, by Zeus,
   you would—and with justice, too.

STREPSIADES: How would that be just? You shameless man,
   I brought you up. When you lisped your words,
   I listened 'til I recognized each one.
   If you said "waa," I understood the word
   and brought a drink; if you asked for "foo foo,"
   I'd bring you bread. And if you said "poo poo"   1770
   I'd pick you up and carry you outside,
   and hold you up. But when you strangled me

just now, I screamed and yelled I had to shit—
but you didn't dare to carry me outside,
you nasty brute, you kept on throttling me,
until I crapped myself right where I was.   [1390]

CHORUS: I think the hearts of younger spry
    are pounding now for his reply—
    for if he acts in just this way
    and yet his logic wins the day   1780
    I'll not value at a pin
    any older person's skin.

CHORUS LEADER: Now down to work, you spinner of words,
    you explorer of brand new expressions.
    Seek some way to persuade us, so it will appear
    that what you've been saying is right.

PHEIDIPPIDES: How sweet it is to be conversant with
    things which are new and clever, capable   [1400]
    of treating with contempt established ways.
    When I was only focused on my horses,   1790
    I couldn't say three words without going wrong.
    But now this man has made me stop all that,
    I'm well acquainted with the subtlest views,
    and arguments and frames of mind. And so,
    I do believe I'll show how just it is
    to punish one's own father.

STREPSIADES: By the gods,
    keep on with your horses then—for me
    caring for a four-horse team is better
    than being beaten to a pulp.

PHEIDIPPIDES: I'll go back
    to where I was in my argument,   1800
    when you interrupted me. First, tell me this—
    Did you hit me when I was a child?

STREPSIADES: Yes.
    But I was doing it out of care for you.

PHEIDIPPIDES: Then tell me this: Is it not right for me
    to care for you in the same way—to beat you—
    since that's what caring means—a beating?
    Why must your body be except from blows,
    while mine is not? I was born a free man, too.
    "The children howl—you think the father
    should not howl as well?" You're going to claim   1810
    the laws permit this practice on our children.
    To that I would reply that older men
    are in their second childhood. More than that—
    it makes sense that older men should howl
    before the young, because there's far less chance
    their natures lead them into errors.

STREPSIADES: There's no law that fathers have to suffer this.   [1420]

PHEIDIPPIDES: But surely some man first brought in the law,
    someone like you and me? And way back then
    people found his arguments convincing.   1820
    Why should I have less right to make new laws
    for future sons, so they can take their turn
    and beat their fathers? All the blows we got
    before the law was brought in we'll erase,
    and we'll demand no payback for our beatings.
    Consider cocks and other animals—
    they avenge themselves against their fathers.
    And yet how are we different from them,
    except they don't propose decrees?

STREPSIADES: Well then,   [1430]
    since you want to be like cocks in all you do,   1830
    why not sleep on a perch and feed on shit?

PHEIDIPPIDES: My dear man, that's not the same at all—
    not according to what Socrates would think.

STREPSIADES: Even so, don't beat me. For if you do,
    you'll have yourself to blame.

PHEIDIPPIDES: Why's that?

STREPSIADES: Because I have the right to chastise you,
    if you have a son, you'll have that right with him.

PHEIDIPPIDES: If I don't have one, I'll have cried for nothing,
    and you'll be laughing in your grave.

STREPSIADES: *[addressing the audience]*
    All you men out there my age, it seems to me   1840
    he's arguing what's right. And in my view,
    we should concede to these young sons what's fair.
    It's only right that we should cry in pain
    when we do something wrong.

PHEIDIPPIDES: Consider now another point.

STREPSIADES: No, no.
    It'll finish me!   [1440]

PHEIDIPPIDES: But then again
    perhaps you won't feel so miserable
    at going through what you've suffered.

STREPSIADES: What's that?
    Explain to me how I benefit from this.

PHEIDIPPIDES: I'll thump my mother, just as I hit you.   1850

STREPSIADES: What's did you just say? What are you claiming?
    This second point is even more disgraceful.

PHEIDIPPIDES: But what if, using the Worse Argument,
    I beat you arguing this proposition—
    that it's only right to hit one's mother?

STREPSIADES: What else but this—if you do a thing like that,
    then why stop there? Why not throw yourself
    and Socrates and the Worse Argument   [1450]
    into the execution pit?

[Strepsiades turns towards the Chorus]

It's your fault,
you Clouds, that I have to endure all this.   1860
I entrusted my affairs to you.

CHORUS LEADER: No.
You're the one responsible for this.
You turned yourself toward these felonies.

STREPSIADES: Why didn't you inform me at the time,
instead of luring on an old country man?

CHORUS: That's what we do each time we see someone
who falls in love with evil strategies,
until we hurl him into misery,   [1460]
so he may learn to fear the gods.

STREPSIADES: Oh dear. That's harsh, you Clouds, but fair enough. 1870
I shouldn't have kept trying not to pay
that cash I borrowed. Now, my dearest lad,
come with me—let's exterminate those men,
the scoundrel Chaerephon and Socrates,
the ones who played their tricks on you and me.

PHEIDIPPIDES: But I couldn't harm the ones who taught me.

STREPSIADES: Yes, you must. Revere Paternal Zeus.[95]

PHEIDIPPIDES: Just listen to that—Paternal Zeus.
How out of date you are! Does Zeus exist?

STREPSIADES: He does.

PHEIDIPPIDES: No, no, he doesn't—there's no way,   1880   [1470]
for Vortex has now done away with Zeus
and rules in everything.

STREPSIADES: He hasn't killed him.

[He points to a small statue of a round goblet which stands outside Thinkery]

> I thought he had because that statue there,
> the cup, is called a vortex.[96] What a fool
> to think this piece of clay could be a god!

PHEIDIPPIDES: Stay here and babble nonsense to yourself.

[Pheidippides exits][97]

STREPSIADES: My god, what lunacy. I was insane
>   to cast aside the gods for Socrates.

[Strepsiades goes up and talks to the small statue of Hermes outside his house]

> But, dear Hermes, don't vent your rage on me,
> don't grind me down. Be merciful to me.   1890
> Their empty babbling made me lose my mind.   [1480]
> Give me your advice. Shall I lay a charge,
> go after them in court. What seems right to you?

[He looks for a moment at the statue]

> You counsel well. I won't launch a law suit.
> I'll burn their house as quickly as I can,
> these babbling fools.

[Strepsiades calls into his house]

>   Xanthias, come here.
> Come outside—bring a ladder—a mattock, too.
> then climb up on top of that Thinkery
> and, if you love your master, smash the roof,
> until the house collapses in on them.   1900

[Xanthias comes out with ladder and mattock, climbs up onto the Thinkery and starts demolishing the roof]

Someone fetch me a flaming torch out here.
They may brag all they like, but here today   [1490]
I'll make somebody pay the penalty
for what they did to me.

[Another slave comes out and hands Strepsiades a torch. He joins Xanthias on the roof and tries to burn down the inside of the Thinkery]

STUDENT: *[from inside the Thinkery]*   Help! Help!

STREPSIADES: Come on, Torch, put your flames to work.

[Strepsiades sets fire to the roof of the Thinkery. A student rushes outside and looks at Strepsiades and Xanthias on the roof]

STUDENT: You there, what are you doing?

STREPSIADES: What am I doing?
    What else but picking a good argument
    with the roof beams of your house?

[A second student appears at a window as smoke starts coming out of the house]

STUDENT: Help! Who's setting fire to the house?

STREPSIADES: It's the man
    whose cloak you stole.

STUDENT: We'll die. You'll kill us all!   1910

STREPSIADES: That's what I want—unless this mattock
    disappoints my hopes or I fall through somehow   [1500]
    and break my neck.

[Socrates comes out of the house in a cloud of smoke. He is coughing badly]

SOCRATES: What are you doing up on the roof?

STREPSIADES: I walk on air and contemplate the sun.

SOCRATES: *[coughing]* This is bad—I'm going to suffocate.

STUDENT: *[still at the window]* What about poor me? I'll be burned up.

[Strepsiades and Xanthias come down from the roof]

STREPSIADES: *[to Socrates]* Why were you so insolent with gods
    in what you studied and when you explored
    the moon's abode? Chase them off, hit them,
    throw things at them—for all sorts of reasons,
    but most of all for their impiety.   1920

[Strepsiades and Xanthias chase Socrates and the students off the stage and exit after them]

CHORUS LEADER: Lead us on out of here. Away!
    We've had enough of song and dance today.

[The Chorus exits]

NOTES ON THE CLOUDS

1.   *Thinkery:* The Greek word phrontisterion (meaning school or academy) is translated here as Thinkery, a term borrowed from William Arrowsmith's translation of *The Clouds*.
2.   During the war it was easy for slaves to run away into enemy territory, so their owners had to treat them with much more care.
3.   wearing one's hair long and keeping race horses were characteristics of the sons of very rich families.
4.   the interest on Strepsiades' loans would increase once the lunar month came to an end.
5.   *twelve minai* is 100 drachmas, a considerable sum. The Greek reads "the horse branded with a *koppa* mark." That brand was a guarantee of its breeding.
6.   *Megacle*s was a common name in a very prominent aristocratic family in Athens. *Coesyra* was the mother of a Megacles from this family, a woman well known for her wasteful expenditures and pride.
7.   The Greek has "of Colias and Genetyllis" names associated with festivals celebrating women's sexual and procreative powers.
8.   Packing the wool tight in weaving uses up more wool and therefore costs more. Strepsiades holds up his cloak which is by now full of holes.
9.   *-hippos* means "horse." The mother presumably wanted her son to have the marks of the aristocratic classes. Xanthippos was the name of Pericles' father and his son. The other names are less obviously aristocratic or uncommon.
10.   *Chaerephon*: a well-known associate of Socrates.

11. *pheasants* were a rich rarity in Athens. Leogoras was a very wealthy Athenian.
12. *an obol* was a relatively small amount, about a third of a day's pay for a jury member.
13. *Knights* is a term used to describe the affluent young men who made up the cavalry. Pheidippides has been mixing with people far beyond his father's means.
14. A *yoke horse* was part of the four-horse team which was harnessed to a yoke on the inside.
15. I adopt Sommerstein's useful reading of this very elliptical passage, which interprets the Greek word *diabetes* as meaning a passive homosexual (rather than its usual meaning, "a pair of compasses"—both senses deriving from the idea of spreading legs apart). The line about selling the cloak is added to clarify the sense.
16. *Thales* was a very famous thinker from the sixth century BC.
17. The Athenians had captured a number of Spartans at Pylos in 425 and brought them to Athens where they remained in captivity.
18. Athenians sometimes apportioned land by lot outside the state which they had appropriated from other people.
19. Attica is the territory surrounded by and belonging to Athens.
20. A deme was a political unit in Athens. Membership in a particular deme was a matter of inheritance from one's father.
21. In 446 BC the Athenians under Pericles put down a revolt in Euboea, a large island just off the coast of Attica.
22. *Athamas*, a character in one of Sophocles' lost plays who was prepared for sacrifice. He was rescued by Hercules.
23. *Cecrops*: a legendary king of Athens. Pallas is Pallas Athena, patron goddess of Athens.
24. *holy festivals*: the Eleusinian mysteries, a traditionally secret and sacred festival for those initiated into the band of cult worshippers.
25. *Mount Parnes*: a mountain range to the north of Athens.
26. *Typho*: a monster with a hundred heads, father of the storm winds (hence, our word *typhoon*).
27. *thrush*: meat from a thrush was considered a delicacy, something that might be given to the winner of a public competition. These lines are mocking the dithyrambic poets (perhaps in comparison with the writers of comic drama).
28. *Xenophantes' son*: a reference to Hieronymos, a dithyrambic and tragic poet. A centaur was known for its savage temper and wild appearance.
29. Simon: an allegedly corrupt Athenian public official.
30. *Cleonymos*: an Athenian accused of dropping his shield and running away from a battle.
31. *Cleisthenes*: a notorious homosexual whom Aristophanes never tires of holding up to ridicule.

32. *Prodicus*: a well-known Athenian intellectual, who wrote on a wide variety of subjects. Linking Socrates and Prodicus as intellectual equals would strike many Athenians as quite absurd.

33. *Vortex*: the Greek word is *dinos* meaning a *whirl* or *eddy*. I adopt Sommerstein's suggestion for this word here.

34. *Panathenaea*: a major annual festival in Athens.

35. *Cronos*: the divine father of Zeus, the age of Cronos is part of the mythic past.

36. Legally an Athenian who believed someone had stolen his property could enter the suspect's house to search. But he first had to remove any garments in which he might conceal something which he might plant in the house.

37. *Trophonios' cave* was a place people went to get prophecies. A suppliant carried a honey cake as an offering to the snakes in the cave.

38. *win*: this is a reference to the fact that the play is part of a competition. The speech obviously is part of the revisions made after the play failed to win first prize in its initial production. The speaker may have been Aristophanes himself or the Chorus Leader speaking on his behalf.

39. *trained it*: This passage is a reference to Aristophanes' first play, *The Banqueters*, and to those who helped him get the work produced. The child mentioned is a metaphorical reference to that work or to his artistic talent generally. The other woman is a metaphorical reference to Callistratos, who produced *The Banqueters*.

40. *Electra* was the sister of Orestes and spent a long time waiting to be reunited with him. That hope kept her going. When she saw her brother's lock of hair on their father's tomb, she was overjoyed that he had come back. The adjective "old" refers to the story, which was very well known to the audience.

41. These lines may indicate that in *The Clouds* the male characters did not wear the traditional phalluses or that the phalluses they did wear were not of a particular kind.

42. *Cleon* was a very powerful Athenian politician after Pericles. Aristophanes savagely attacked him in *Knights*. Cleon was killed in battle (in 422). Hyperbolos became a very influential politician after Cleon's death.

43. Eupolis, Phrynichos, and Hermippos were comic playwrights, rivals of Aristophanes.

44. *Paphlagonian tanner* is a reference to Cleon, who earned his money from tanneries. Paphlagonia is an area in Asia Minor. The word here implies that Cleon was not a true Athenian.

45. *seagull* was a bird symbolic of thievery and greed. The contradiction in these speeches in the attitude to Cleon (who died the year following the original production) may be accounted for by the incomplete revision of the script.

46. *holy lady* is a reference to the goddess Artemis. The *aegis* is a divine cloak which has invincible powers to strike fear into the god's enemies. Here it is invoked as

a protection for Athens, Athena's city. *Dionysus* lived in Delphi when Apollo was absent from the shrine during the winter.

47. *Athenians* followed a lunar calendar, but there were important discrepancies due to a very careless control over inserting extra days.

48. *Memnon or Sarpedon*: Memnon, the son of Dawn, was killed at Troy, as was Sarpedon, a son of Zeus, and leader of the Lycian allies of the Trojans.

49. *religious council*: the Amphictyonic Council, which controlled some important religious shrines, was made up of delegates from different city states. In Athens the delegate was chosen by lot. It's not clear how the gods could have removed the wreath in question.

50. the *dactyl* is named from the Greek word for finger because it consists of one long stress followed by two short stresses, like the structure of bones in a finger. The phrase "which is like a digit" has been added to make the point clearer.

51. I adopt Sommerstein's suggested insertion of this line and a half in order to clarify what now follows in the conversation, which hinges on the gender of words (masculine, feminine, or neuter) and the proper ascription of a specific gender to words which describe male and female objects. The word "fowl" applies to both male and females and therefore is not, strictly speaking masculine. This whole section is a satire on the "nitpicking" attention to language attributed to the sophists.

52. *kneading basin*: a trough for making bread.

53. *Cleonymos* was an Athenian politician who allegedly ran away from the battle field, leaving his shield behind.

54. *to masturbate*: the Greek here says literally "Cleonymos didn't have a kneading basin but kneaded himself with a round mortar [i.e., masturbated]."

55. The point of this very laboured joke seems to be making Cleonymos feminine, presumably because of his cowardice (running away in battle).

56. The three names mentioned belong to well known Athenians, who may have all been famous for their dissolute life style. Socrates is taking issue with the spelling of the last two names which (in some forms) look like feminine names. Strepsiades, of course, thinks Socrates is talking about the sexuality of the people.

57. *Amynia*: in Greek (as in Latin) the name changes when it is used as a direct form of address-in this case the last letter is dropped, leaving a name ending in -a, normally a feminine ending.

58. *Corinthian* is obviously a reference to bed bugs, but the link with Corinth is unclear (perhaps it was a slang expression).

59. *bug*: children sometimes tied a thread around the foot of a large flying bug and played with it.

60. the scribe would be writing on a wax tablet which the heat would melt.

61. *Melos*: Strepsiades presumably is confusing Socrates with Diagoras, a well known materialistic atheist, who came from Melos (whereas Socrates did not).

62. *died*: part of the funeral rituals in a family required each member to bathe thoroughly.

63. *Sons of Earth*: a phrase usually referring to the Titans who warred against the Olympian gods. Here it also evokes a sense of the materialism of Socrates' doctrine in the play and, of course, ironically ridicules the Thinkery.

64. *"necessary expense"*: refers to the well-known story of Pericles who in 445 BC used this phrase in official state accounts to refer to an expensive but secret bribe he paid to a Spartan general to withdraw his armies from Athenian territories around Athens. No one asked any embarrassing questions about the entry.

65. *speech*: the Greek says "with his lips sagging [or loosely apart]." Socrates is criticizing Pheidippides' untrained voice.

66. *talent*: an enormous fee to pay for lessons in rhetoric. Socrates is, of course, getting Strepsiades ready to pay a lot for his son's education.

67. Zeus overthrew his father, Cronos, and the Titans and imprisoned them deep inside the earth.

68. *Telephos from Mysia* was a hero in a play by Euripides in which a king was portrayed as a beggar. Pandeletos was an Athenian politician. The imputation here is that the Worse Argument once did very badly, barely surviving on his wits and borrowed ideas.

69. *thighs apart*: keeping the thighs together was supposed to enable boys to stimulate themselves sexually.

70. *Phrynis style*: Phrynis was a musician who introduced certain innovations in music around 450 BC.

71. *Cedeides*: a dithyrambic poet well known for his old-fashioned style. The other references are all too ancient customs and rituals (like the old tradition of wearing a cicada broach or the ritual killing of oxen).

72. *Marathon*: a battle in 490 BC in which a small band of Greeks, mainly Athenians, defeated the Persian armies which had landed near Athens. The Panathenaea was a major religious festival in Athens. Tritogeneia was one of Athena's titles.

73. *Iapetus* was a Titan, a brother of Cronos, and hence very ancient.

74. Hippocrates was an Athenian, a relative of Pericles. He had three sons who had a reputation for childishness.

75. *Academy*: this word refers, not to Plato's school (which was not in existence yet) but to a public park and gymnasium in Athens.

76. *long decrees*: The Greek says "and a long decree," which makes little sense in English. The point of the joke is to set the audience up to expect "and a long prick" (which was considered a characteristic of barbarians).

77. Antimachos was satirized in comedy as a particularly effeminate man.

78. *drachmas*: the Greek has "more than ten thousand staters." A stater was a general term for non-Athenian coins, usually of high value. The idea, of course, is equivalent to "a ton of money."

79. *bath of Hercules* was a term commonly applied to thermal hot springs.

80. This part of the argument is impossible to render quickly in English. Homer's word is *agoretes*, meaning "speaking in the assembly." The Worse Argument is implying that, since the word *agora* means market place, Homer is commending these men for "talking the market place."

81. *Peleus* once refused the sexual advances of the wife of his host. She accused him of immoral activity, and her husband set Peleus unarmed on a mountain. The gods admired Peleus' chastity and provided him a sword so he could defend himself against the wild animals.

82. *Peleus*, a mortal king, married Thetis, a sea goddess, with the blessing of the gods. Their child was the hero Achilles. She later left him to return to her father (but not for the reason given in the lines following).

83. *asshole*: Someone caught in the act of adultery was punished by having a radish shoved up his anus and his pubic hair singed with hot ash. The various insults here ("loose-arsed bugger," "gigantic asshole," and so on) stand for the Greek perjorative phrase "wide arsed," which, in addition to meaning "lewd" or "disgusting," also carries the connotation of passive homosexuality, something considered ridiculous in mature men. Terms like "bum fucker" are too active to capture this sense of the insult.

84. The person making the charge in court had to make a cash deposit which was forfeit if he lost the case.

85. *Solon*: was a very famous Athenian law maker. In the early sixth century he laid down the basis for Athenian laws.

86. Pheidippides' hair-splitting argument which follows supposedly establishes that the law suits against Strepsiades are illegal and should be tossed out because (in brief) the court had taken the deposit, which the creditor had to make to launch the suit, on the wrong day (the last day of the month instead of the first day of the new month). The case rests on a misinterpretation of the meaning of the term Old and New Day—which was single day between the old and the new moon. The passage is, of course, a satire on sophistic reasoning and legal quibbling for self-interest.

87. *my own deme*: the deme was the basic political unit in Athens. Membership in it passed down from one's father.

88. *three extra obols*: Strepsiades means here that swearing the oath will be such fun he's prepared to pay for the pleasure—an obvious insult to Pasias.

89. *salt*: leather was rubbed down as part of the tanning process. The phrase "wine skin" has been added to clarify the sense.

90. *Carcinus*: an Athenian writer of tragic drama.

91. Amynias is here quoting from a tragedy written by Carcinus' son Xenocles.

92. *Tlepolemos* is a character in the tragedy mentioned in the previous note.

93. *Simonides*: was a well-known lyric poet of the previous century.

94. *myrtle branch*: traditionally a person singing at a drinking party held a myrtle branch unless he was playing a musical instrument.

95. *Paternal Zeus*: This seems to be an appeal to Zeus as the guardian of the father's rights and thus a way or urging Pheidippides to go along with what his father wants. The line may be a quote from a lost tragedy.

96. *Vortex*: the Greek word dinos, meaning "whirl," "eddy," or "vortex," also means a round goblet. The statue of such a goblet outside the Thinkery represents the presiding deity of the house.

97. It's not clear whether Pheidippides goes back into his house or back into the school. If he does the latter, then the comic violence at the end of the play takes on a much darker tone, since Strepsiades' murderous anger includes his son. In fact, the loss of his son might be the key event which triggers the intensity of the final destruction.

Virgil's *Aeneid* (Book 2)

Translated by Stanley Lombardo

The room fell silent, all eyes on Aeneas,
Who from his high couch now began to speak:

"My Queen, you are asking me to relive
Unspeakable sorrow, to recall how the Greeks
Pulled down Troy, that tragic realm   5
With all its riches. I saw those horrors myself
And played no small part in them. What Myrmidon
Or Dolopian, what brutal soldier of Ulysses
Could tell such a tale and refrain from tears?
And now dewy night is rushing from the sky,   10
And the setting stars make sleep seem sweet.
But if you are so passionate to learn
Of our misfortunes, to hear a brief account
Of Troy's last struggle—although my mind
Shudders to remember and recoils in pain,   15
I will begin.

Broken by war and rebuffed by the Fates
For so many years, the Greek warlords
Built a horse, aided by the divine art
Of Pallas, a horse the size of a mountain,   20
Weaving its ribs out of beams of fir.
They pretended it was a votive offering
For their safe return home. So the story went.
But deep within the Horse's cavernous dark
They concealed an elite band, all their best,   25
Stuffing its huge womb with men at arms.

Within sight of Troy lies a famous island,
Tenedos, prosperous while Priam's kingdom stood,
Now just a bay with poor anchorage for ships.
The Greeks sailed there and hid on the desolate shore;   *30*
They were gone, we thought, sailed off to Mycenae.

And so all of Troy shook off its long sorrow.
The gates were opened. It was a joy to visit
The Doric camp, the abandoned beachhead,
The deserted sites. Here the Dolopians   *35*
Pitched their tents, here fierce Achilles,
Here lay the ships, here were the battle-lines.
Some of us gaped at the virgin Minerva's
Fatal gift, amazed at the massive Horse.
Thymoetes wanted it dragged inside the walls   *40*
And installed in the citadel. Treason perhaps.
Or Troy's doom was already in motion.
But Capys, and other wiser heads, urged us
To either pitch this insidious Greek gift
Into the sea, or burn it on the spot, or else   *45*
Pierce and probe the belly's hidden hollows.
The crowd took sides, uncertain what to do.

And now Laocoön comes running down
From the citadel at the head of a great throng
And in his burning haste he cries from afar: *50*
'Are you out of your minds, you poor fools?
Are you so easily convinced that the enemy
Has sailed away? Do you honestly think
That any Greek gift comes without treachery?
What is Ulysses known for? Either this lumber   *55*
Is hiding Achaeans inside, or it has been built
As an engine of war to attack our walls.
To spy on our homes and come down on the city
From above. Or some other evil lurks inside.
Do not trust the Horse, Trojans! Whatever it is,   *60*
I fear the Greeks, even when they bring gifts.'

With that, he hurled his spear with enormous force
Into the vaulting belly of the beast. The shaft
Stood quivering, and the hollow insides

Reverberated with a cavernous moan.   *65*
If we had not been on the gods' wrong side,
If we had been thinking right, Laocoön
Would have driven us to hack our way into
The Greek lair, and Troy would still stand,
And you, high rock of Priam, would remain.   *70*

But at that moment a band of Dardan shepherds
Came up with loud shouts, dragging to the king
A prisoner with his hands bound behind his back.
This man had deliberately gotten himself captured
With one purpose in mind, to open Troy to the Greeks,   *75*
Ready to either work his deceits or face certain death.
The Trojan youths streamed in from all sides
To see the captive and jeer at him.
                                          Hear now
The treachery of the Greeks, and from one offense
Learn all their evil.
                              The man stood in full sight   *80*
Of the crowd, dismayed, unarmed, and glancing
Around at the ranks of men he cried out:

'Ah, what land, what sea, can receive me now,
What will be my final wretched fate?
I have no place among the Greeks,   *85*
And the Trojans are clamoring for my blood.'

At this our mood changed, and we prodded him
To tell us what he meant. Who were his people,
And what was he counting on to save him
Now that he was our prisoner? Finally,   *90*
He stopped trembling and began to speak:

'Come what may, King, I will tell you all
And not deny, first, that I am a Danaan.
Fortune may have damned Sinon to misery,
But she will not make him a liar as well.   *95*
You may have heard the name Palamedes,
Belus' glorious son, whom the Greeks
Condemned to death, under false charges,
Because he opposed the war. He was innocent.

Now they mourn him, now that he is dead.   *100*
He was my kinsman, and my father,
A poor man, sent me here in his company
When I was just a boy. While Palamedes
Was still in good standing, still thrived in council,
I too had somewhat of a name, some honor.   *105*
But when through the malice of cunning Ulysses
(Everyone knows this) he passed from this world,
I was a ruined man and dragged on my life
In darkness and grief, eating my heart out
Over the fate of my innocent friend.   *110*
Nor was I silent, but I raved
That if I ever had the chance, ever returned
As victor to Argos, I would have my vengeance.
My words aroused resentment, and my life
Was now infected. Ulysses made it his mission   *115*
To terrorize me with countless new charges.
Sowing rumors in everyone's ears, searching
In his guilt for weapons against me. In the end
He found Fortune's tool, Calchas the soothsayer—
But you don't want to hear all this. And why   *120*
Should I stall? If you paint all Greeks
With the same stripe, if "he's Achaean"
Is all you need to hear, take your vengeance
At once. This is what the Ithacan would want.
And what Atreus' sons would, pay dearly for.'   *125*

Now indeed we burned to know more,
Strangers as we were to infamy so great
And to Greek guile. Trembling, he went on:

'Weary with the long war, the Greeks
Often wanted to quit Troy and sail home.   *130*
If only they had! But stormy weather
And rough seas would scare them from leaving.
And when they'd hammered together
The maple horse, the sky rumbled even more.
Anxious, we sent Eurypylus to consult   *135*
The oracle of Phoebus Apollo,
And he brought back these dismal words:

You placated the winds with a virgin's blood
To come, O Danaans, to the shores of Troy.
Your return must be won with an Argive life.   *140*

When the god's words reached the army's ears
Everyone was dazed, and an icy fear
Seeped into their bones. Which man was doomed,
Whom would Apollo claim? The Ithacan.
Dragged Calchas out into the roaring crowd   *145*
And demanded to know what heaven portended.
Many divined that this despicable ploy
Was aimed at me and saw what was coming.
Five days and five more the seer sat in his hut,
Silent, refusing to sentence anyone to death.   *150*
Finally, forced by the Ithacan's cries,
Calchas broke his silence and, as agreed.
Doomed me to the altar. Everyone approved,
And the ruin each had feared for himself
They bore well when it devolved upon one.   *155*

'And now the dark day dawned. The salted grain.
The sacral headbands were being prepared
For my ritual slaughter, when, I confess,
I broke my bonds and snatched myself from death.
I skulked all night in a muddy swamp,   *160*
Hidden in the sedge, holding my breath
Until they sailed. Now I have no hope
Of seeing my homeland, my sweet children.
The father I long for. And the Greeks
May make them pay for my escape, poor things,   *165*
And by their death expiate my sin.
And so I pray, by whatever powers above
Still witness Truth, and by any Faith we men
Still have uncorrupted, show mercy
To a suffering soul, guiltless and wronged.'   *170*

We spared him for his tears and pitied him
Of our own accord. Priam himself ordered
His shackles removed and spoke to him kindly:

'Whoever you are, take no further thought
Of the Greeks. You are one of us now.   175
But tell me, and speak the whole truth:
Why did they erect this monstrous horse?
Who devised it, and to what purpose?
Is it a religious offering or an. engine of war?'

Thus Priam. And Sinon, the consummate liar,   180
Lifting his unchained hands to the stars:

'Eternal fires of heaven, I summon you
And your inviolable Power to witness,
And you altars and nefarious blades
Which I escaped, and you consecrated fillets   185
Which as victim I wore: it is just for me
To break the sacred oaths of the Greeks,
Just to abhor those men, and to lay bare to the sky
Every secret they would conceal. I am bound
By no law of my country. But you, Troy,   190
Stand by your word and keep your faith,
If what I say proves to be your salvation.

'From the war's beginning, Pallas Athena
Was the Greeks' entire hope. But when
Wicked Diomedes and Ulysses,   195
With his criminal mind, entered
Her high temple, murdered the guards,
And stole the fateful Palladium,
Daring to handle her virgin fillets
With bloodstained fingers—then   200
The Danaans' fortunes began to falter,
Their strength was broken, and the goddess
Turned her back on them. Tritonia
Gave us clear portents of her displeasure.
As soon as her statue was set up in camp,   205
Flames glittered from her upturned eyes,
Sweat poured down her limbs, and three times
She flashed up from the ground, miraculous,
Holding her shield and quivering spear.
Calchas at once began to prophesy: 210

"The Greeks must attempt a retreat by sea.
Troy cannot be taken by Argive weapons
Until they seek new omens in Argos
And return the godhead carried away
In curved keels over open water."   215

'They are sailing over to Mycenae now.
And when they have recruited soldiers and gods
They will recross the water all unforeseen.
So Calchas sifted the omens and counseled the Greeks
To erect this Horse, in expiation   220
Of the Palladium's theft and the godhead wronged.
And he ordered them to build its oaken bulk
Up to the sky, so it could not be brought
Through the city's gates or walls and there protect
The Trojan people under the old religion.   225
For if you lay violent hands
Upon this offering to Minerva,
Destruction will fall—may the gods turn this omen
Against the Greeks—upon Priam's realm.
But if your hands bring it into the city,   230
Asia will wage war upon Pelops' walls,
And this fate awaits our children's children.'

And so through Sinon's treacherous art
His story was believed, and we were taken
With cunning, captured with forced tears,   235
We whom neither great Diomedes
Nor Achilles of Larissa could subdue.
Nor ten years of war, nor a thousand ships.

What happened next was more horrible still
And threw us into deepening chaos.   240
Laocoön, serving by lot as Neptune's priest,
Was sacrificing a great bull at the god's altar,
When we saw, coming from Tenedos
Over the calm water, a pair of serpents—
I shudder to recall them—making for shore.   245
Trailing huge coils they sheared through the sea,
And their bloody crests arched over the waves
As they writhed and twisted in the seething surf.

They were almost ashore. Their eyes
Were shot with blood and fire, and their tongues   *250*
Hissed and flickered in their open mouths.
We scattered, pale with fear, as the sea-snakes
Glided through the sand straight for Laocoön.
First, they entwined the priest's two sons
In great looping spirals, and then they sank their fangs   *255*
Into the boys' wretched bodies and began to feed.
Then they seized Laocoön as he ran to their aid,
Weapon in hand, and lashed their scaly bodies
Twice around his waist and twice around his neck,
Their heads reared high. As the priest struggled   *260*
To wrench himself free from the knotted coils,
His headbands were soaked with venom, and gore,
And his horrible cries reached up to the stars.

    Wounded by an ill-aimed blow, a bull will bellow
    As it flees the altar and shakes the axe from his neck.   *265*

So too Laocoön. But the twin serpents
Slithered off to the high temple of Pallas
And took refuge at the grim goddess's feet,
Vanished behind the disk of her shield.

An inhuman terror coiled through our hearts.   *270*
Shuddering with horror, everyone said Laocoön
Had received the punishment he deserved
For wounding the sacred wood of the Horse
With his accursed spear. All proclaimed
The Horse should be drawn to Minerva's temple   *275*
And her godhead appeased. We breached the walls,
Everyone girding themselves for the work.
And set wheels beneath the feet of the Horse.
A noose was made taut around its neck
And the fateful contraption inched up the battlements,   *280*
Pregnant with arms. Boys and unwed girls
Circled around it, singing hymns
And touching the rope with glee. On it moved.
Gliding like a threat into the city.
O my country! O Ilium, home of the gods!   *285*
O walls of Troy famed in war! Four times

At the very threshold of the city gate
The Horse halted, and four times
Weapons clattered in its belly. Yet we pressed on
Mindlessly, blind with passion, and installed   *290*
The ill-starred monster on our high holy rock.
Even then Cassandra opened her lips
Against the coming doom, lips cursed by a god
Never to be believed by the Teucrians,
And we pitiful Trojans, on our last day,   *295*
Wreathed the shrines of the gods with flowers.

The sky turned, and night swept up from Ocean,
Enfolding in its great shadow earth and heaven—
And the Myrmidons' treachery. The Trojans
Spread out along the wall were dead silent now,   *300*
Slumber entwining their weary limbs,
And the Argive fleet started to sail from Tenedos
Through the silent, complicit moonlight,
Making for the shore they knew all too well.
The flagship raised a beacon, and at this signal *305*
Sinon, cloaked by the gods' unjust decrees,
Stealthily unlocked the pine trapdoor,
And the Horse released from its open womb
The enclosed Danaans, glad to push themselves out
Of the hollow oak into the cool night air,   *310*
Thessandrus and Sthenelus and grim Ulysses—
Sliding down the rope—Acamas and Thoas,
Achilles' son, Neoptolemus, great Machaon,
Menelaus, and Epeos himself,
The fabricator of the insidious horse.   *315*
They fanned out through a city drowned in sleep,
Slit the guards' throats, opened all the gates,
And joined as planned the invading Greeks.

At that late hour, when sleep begins to drift
Upon fretful humanity as grace from the gods,   *320*
Hector appeared to me in my dreams,
Pitiful spirit, weeping, black with blood
And dust from the ruts of Achilles' chariot,
Thongs piercing his swollen ankles. Ah,
How he looked, how different from that Hector   *325*

Who returned to Troy wearing Achilles' armor,
The Hector who threw fire on the Danaan ships!
His beard was matted, his hair clotted with gore,
And he bore all the wounds he had received
Fighting before his country's walls. In my dream   *330*
I blurted out to him these tearful words:

'Light of Dardania, Troy's finest hope,
What has delayed you? From what shores have you come
To answer our prayers? We have suffered
Many losses since you left us, Hector.   *335*
Yet, we have labored on, and now we see you
At the end of our strength. Why has your face
Been defiled, and what are these wounds I see?'

My empty questions meant nothing to him.
With a heavy sigh from deep within, he said: *340*

'Run, child of the goddess, save yourself
From these flames! The enemy holds the walls.
Great Troy is falling. Enough has been given
To Priam and his country. If Pergamum's height
Could be defended by a hero's hand,   *345*
Its defense would have been this hand of mine.
Troy commends to you the gods of the city.
Accept them as companions of your destiny
And seek for them the great walls you will found
After you have wandered across the sea.'   *350*

He spoke, and brought out from the sanctuary
Great Vesta, her chaplets, and her eternal, fire.

By now the lamentation in the city
Had grown to such proportions that it reached
My father Anchises' house, secluded though it was   *355*
Among the pines. The sickening sound of battle
Startled me from sleep, and I climbed to the roof
And stood at the very top, upright and listening.

> *It was as if the South Wind were fanning fire*
> *Through the fields, or a mountain torrent had leveled*   *360*

The farmlands and swept away the oxen's tillage,
Flattening the hedgerows, and I was a shepherd
Listening in the dark from some towering rock.

Then the truth was revealed. The Danaans' treachery
Lay open before me. Deiphobus' great house 365
Was collapsing in flames, as was Ucalegon's
Next door. The Sigean straits burned
With the inferno's reflected light.
Men's shouts rose with the shrill sound of horns.
Out of my mind, I took up arms—no battle plan, 370
But my soul burned to gather a war party
And storm the citadel. Rage and fury
Sent my mind reeling, and my only thought
Was how glorious it is to die in combat.

At that moment Panthus, priest of Apollo, 375
Ran up to my door, dragging his grandson
Away from Greek swords, the sacred images
Of our vanquished gods clutched in his arms.
'Where is the fighting thickest, Panthus?
What position should we try to hold?'

                      My words 380
Were scarcely out when he answered, groaning:

'Troy's last day and final hour have come.
We are Trojans no more. Ilium is no more.
The great glory of the Teucrians is gone.
Jupiter in his rage has given all to Argos, 385
And Greeks are lords of our burning city.
High stands the Horse, pouring forth armed men,
And Sinon, insolent in victory,
Sets fires everywhere. Thousands of troops.
As many as ever came from Mycenae, 390
Are at the wide-open gates. Others patrol the streets.
A line of unsheathed, glistening steel
Stands ready for slaughter. Our night guard
Is barely resisting and fighting blind.'

Panthus' words and will of the gods   395
Drove me through the inferno of battle
Wherever the grim Fury called, wherever
The roars and shouts rose to the sky.
Falling in with me in the moonlight
Were Rhipeus and Epytus, one of Troy's best,   400
Hypanis and Dymas, a little throng now,
And young Coroebus, son of Mygdon.
He had come to Troy in those last days,
Madly in love with Cassandra, and brought
Aid to Priam, a sturdy son-in-law. Poor boy,   405
If only he had listened to the warnings
Of his raving bride.
When I saw them close ranks, eager for battle,
I began:

            'Brave hearts—brave in vain
If you are committed to follow me to the end—   410
You see how we stand. All the gods
Who sustained this realm are gone, leaving
Altar and shrine. You are fighting to save
A city in flames. All that is left for us
Is to rush onto swords and die. The only chance   415
For the conquered is to hope for none.'

This added fury to the young men's courage.
Like wolves in a black mist, blind with hunger.
Their whelps waiting with dry throats, we passed
Through the enemy's swords to certain death   420
And held our course to the city's center.
Ebony night swirled around us. Who could tell
That night's carnage, or match it with tears?
The ancient city fell, that had for many years
Been queen. Corpses lay piled everywhere,   425
In the streets, the houses, the hallowed thresholds
Of the temples. And it was not only Trojans
Who paid in blood. At times the vanquished
Felt their valor pulse through their hearts,
And the conquering Greeks fell. Raw fear   430
Was everywhere, grief was everywhere,
Everywhere the many masks of death.

Androgeos offered himself to us first.
Heading up a large company of Greeks,
He mistook us for an allied band and called: *435*

'On the double, men! What took you so long?
We're burning and looting Pergamum here,
And you're just arriving from, the ships?'

He realized at once from our tentative reply
That we were the enemy. He froze, choked   *440*
On his own words, and then tried to backpedal,

>   *Like a man who has stepped on a snake*
>   *Hidden in briars and in sudden terror cringes*
>   *When it rears and puffs out its purple hood.*

Androgeos was shaking and backing away   *445*
When we charged and hedged them in.
Unfamiliar with the terrain, they panicked.
And we cut them down, Fortune smiling
On our first effort. Flushed with success,
Coroebus cried:

>   'Let's follow Fortune's lead   *450*
And exchange our armor for Danaan gear.
Who cares if this is deceit or valor?
The enemy will supply us with weapons.'

With that he put on Androgeos' plumed helmet.
Hefted his emblazoned shield, and hung   *455*
An Argive sword by his side. So too Rhipeus,
Dymas, and my other boys, their spirits high
As they armed themselves in new-won spoils.
We moved out, mingling with the Greeks
And with gods not ours. In the blind night   *460*
We engaged in many skirmishes, and sent
Many a Greek into the jaws of Orcus.
Some scattered to the safety of the shore
And the ships. Others, like terrified children,
Climbed back up into the belly of the Horse.   *465*

Never rely on the gods for anything
Against their will. The next thing we saw
Was Cassandra, Priam's daughter,
Being dragged, hair streaming, from the shrine
Of Minerva's temple, lifting to heaven   *470*
Her burning eyes—her eyes only,
For her tender hands were bound. Coroebus
Could not endure this. He threw himself
Into the midst of the band, determined to die.
We closed ranks and charged, but were overwhelmed.   *475*
First, our countrymen targeted our uniforms.
The misleading crests on our Greek helmets.
hen the Greeks themselves, grunting with anger
APicking us off from the roof, a piteous slaughter.
Tt the attempted rescue of Cassandra,   *480*
Came at us from all sides, Ajax most viciously.
Then the two sons of Atreus and Ulysses' men.

    It was like a hurricane when winds clash
    Front every direction, Winds West and South
    And the East proud with his colts of Dawn.   *485*
    The forests groan, and Nereus foams with rage
    As he stirs with his trident the lowest depths.

The men we had routed with our stratagem
In the dim of night rematerialized, the first
To recognize our mendacious shields   *490*
And discordant accents. We were outnumbered.
Coroebus fell first, killed by Peneleos
At the war goddess's altar. Then Rhipeus,
Of all Teucrians the most righteous (but the gods
Saw otherwise) went down. Hypanis   *495*
And Dymas were run through by friends;
And you, Panthus, neither your piety
Nor Apollo's fillet protected you
When you fell. O ashes of Ilium!
O last flames of my people! Be witness   *500*
That in your fall I shunned neither fight nor chance,
And had my fate been to die by Greek hands
I had earned that fate. We were torn from there,
Iphitus, Pelias, and myself, we three,

Iphitus heavy with years, Pelias slowed   505
By a wound from Ulysses. Without pause
We were called by the clamor to Priam's house.

Here was an enormous battle, so intense
It was as if there was no one fought anywhere else,
And men were not dying throughout the city.   510
Here we saw the War God unchained. Greeks
Scrambled to the roof, and the threshold
Was besieged by a bulge of shields. Ladders
Hugged the walls, and men inched their way
Upward on the rungs, left hands holding up shields   515
Against projectiles, right hands clutching
Posts and battlements. Above, the Trojans
Tore down the towers and all the rooftop
To use as missiles—they saw the end was near—
Defending themselves to the death, rolling down   520
Gilded rafters, their fathers' splendors of old.
Other troops, swords drawn, massed around the doors,
Blocking the entrances. Our pulses quickened
With new energy to protect the palace
And come to the aid of our vanquished men.   525

There was a secret entry in the rear,
A passageway through Priam's palace
By which Andromache, poor soul,
Would come unattended to her husband's parents
While Troy still stood and lead her boy,   530
Astyanax, to see his grandfather.
I scaled the roof, where the Teucrians
Were lobbing their useless missiles to little effect.
Rising to the sky from the roof's sheer edge
Stood a tower from which all Troy   535
Could once be seen, and in the distance
A thousand Greek ships and their beachhead camp.
We pried at its upper stories with our swords
Until the joints gave way, wrenched it loose,
And sent it crashing down like rolling thunder   540
Onto the ranks of the Greeks. But more Greeks
Kept coming, and more stones kept falling.

Framed by the portal to the entrance court
Pyrrhus stood in his glory, haloed in bronze,

As a snake raised on poison basks in the light   *545*
After a cold winter has kept him underground,
Venomous and swollen. Now, having sloughed
His old skin, glistening with youth, he puffs out
His breast and slides his lubricious coils
Toward, the sun, flicking his three-forked tongue.   *550*

At his side loomed Periphas, and Automedon,
Once Achilles' charioteer, now the armor-bearer
Of Achilles' son. Massed around them
Were all the tough troops from Scyros,
Hurling torches onto the roof as they closed in   *555*
On Priam's palace. Pyrrhus led the charge,
Cleaving through the solid threshold
With a battle-axe, tearing the brass-bound doors
From their hinges, and hatcheting a hole
The size of a window in a huge oaken panel,   *560*
Revealing all the house in a grim tableau.
Open to view were the long halls; laid bare
Was the inner sanctum of Priam
And the kings of old, who now saw
Armed men standing on their very threshold.   *565*

A tumultuous roar tore through the house;
Its vaulted halls echoed with women's wails,
And the din reverberated to the golden stars.
Trembling matrons roamed lost through the rooms.
Clinging to the doors, lips pressed against them.   *570*
Pyrrhus moved on with all his father's might.
And nothing could stop him. The gate gave way
Before the battering ram, and the doors,
Wrenched from their sockets, fell to the floor.
The Greeks forced their way in, butchered   *575*
The Trojans who stood up against them,
And filled the whole space with their soldiery,

Worse than a river bursting through its banks,
The water churning in overwhelming fury,

Flooding the fields and. sweeping herds and folds   580
Over the plain.

                    I saw with my own eyes
Neoptolemus, lusting for slaughter,
And Atreus' two sons, there on the threshold.
I saw Hecuba, with her hundred daughters,
And Priam, polluting with his blood   585
The very altars he had consecrated himself.
Those fifty bedchambers, that promise of offspring,
The doorposts proud with barbarian gold—
All lost. The Greeks held what the fire spared.

And what, you may ask, was Priam's fate?   590
When he saw that his city had fallen,
The doors of his palace shattered,
And the enemy at his very hearth,
The old man slung his long-unused armor
Over his trembling shoulders, strapped on   595
His useless sword, and, bound to die,
Charged the enemy.
                    In the middle of the palace,
Under heaven's naked wheel, an enormous altar
Lay beneath the branches of an ancient laurel
Whose shade embraced the household gods.   600
In this sacred place Hecuba and her daughters
Huddled like doves driven by a black storm,
Clutching the gods' images. But when she saw
Priam, himself clad in the armor of his youth.
She cried out:

                    'My poor husband,   605
What insanity has driven you
To take up these weapons? Where
Are you rushing to? The hour is past
For defense like this, even if my Hector
Were still here. Come to this altar, please,   610
It will protect us all, or you will die with us.'

Hecuba said these things, took the aged man
In her arms, and placed him on the holy seat.

And now Polites, one of Priam's sons,
Pursued by Pyrrhus, came running   615
Through the colonnades, wounded.
When he reached the vast atrium
Pyrrhus was breathing down his neck.
And yet he slipped away to face his parents' eyes.

There he fell, Pyrrhus' spear in his back,   620
And poured out his life in a pool of blood.
Then Priam, in death's grip as he was,
Did not hold back his anger or spare his voice.

'For this heinous crime,' he cried, 'this outrage,
May the gods in heaven—if there is in heaven   625
Any spirit that cares for what is just and good—
May the gods treat you as you deserve
For making me watch my own son's murder
And defiling with death a father's face.
Not so was Achilles, whom you falsely claim   630
To be your father, in the face of Priam his foe,
But honored a suppliant's rights and trust,
And allowed the bloodless corpse of Hector
Burial, and sent me back to my own realm.'

And the old man threw his feeble spear. Its tip   635
Clanged against the bronze of Pyrrhus' shield
And dangled uselessly from its boss. And Pyrrhus:

'Then you can take this news to my father,
The son of Peleus. Be sure to tell him
About my sad behavior and how degenerate   640
His son has become. Now die.'

                    So saying,
He dragged Priam, trembling and slipping
In his son's blood, up to the altar. Winding
His left hand in the old man's hair, with his right
He lifted his flashing sword and buried it   645
Up to its hilt in his side. So ended Priam,
Such was his fated doom, as Troy burned

Before his eyes and Pergamum fell.
Once the lord of so many peoples,
The sovereign of Asia, he lies now   650
A huge trunk upon the shore, head severed
From his neck, a corpse without a name.

Then an awful sense of dread enveloped me.
I stood in a daze, and there rose before me
The image of my dear father, the same age   655
As the wounded king whom. I was watching
Gasp out his life. Before me rose Creüsa,
Abandoned, the pillaged house, and the plight
Of little Iülus. I looked around
For my troops. They had all deserted me.   660
Too fatigued to fight, they had either jumped
To a welcome death or dropped limply into the flames.

Now I alone was left, when I saw,
Hiding in the shadows of Vesta's shrine,
Helen, daughter of Tyndareus. The bright fires   665
Gave me light as I wandered here and there
Casting my eyes over everything.
Fearing the Trojans' anger for Troy's fall,
The vengeance of the Greeks, and the wrath
Of her deserted husband, Helen, destroyer   670
Alike of her own country and ours,
This detestable woman, crouched by the altars.
My soul flared with a burning desire
To avenge Troy and make her pay for her sins.

'So she will look upon Sparta unscathed   675
And enter Mycenae as a triumphant queen?
She will get to see her husband and home,
Her parents and children, attended
By Trojan women and Phrygian slaves?
Was it for this that Priam was slaughtered,   680
Ilium burned, and our shore soaked with blood?
Never! Although there is no heroic name
In killing a woman, no victory,
I will be praised for snuffing out evil

And meting out justice. And it will be sweet   *685*
To quench my soul with vengeful fire
And satisfy my people's ashes.'

I was carried away by this frenzy, when,
Shining through the dark in a halo of light.
My mother appeared before my eyes, more clearly   *690*
Than ever before, revealing herself
As a radiant goddess, just as the great ones
In heaven see her, so beautiful, so tall.
She caught me by the hand and, in grace,
Spoke these words from her pale-rose lips: *695*

'What anguish is behind this uncontrollable rage?
Why so angry, my son? And where has your love
For our family gone? Will you not first see
Where you left your father, Anchises,
Feeble with age, or whether Creüsa   *700*
And your child, Ascanius, are still alive?
They are surrounded by Greek soldiers
And but for my loving care would have died
In the flames by now, or the swords of the enemy
Would have tasted their blood. It is not   *705*
The detestable beauty of Tyndarean Helen
Or sinful Paris that is to blame. No, it is the gods,
The remorseless gods, who have ruined Troy
And burnt the topless towers of Ilium.
See for yourself. I will dispel the mist   *710*
That enshrouds you and dulls your mortal vision.
You might not trust your mother otherwise,
And disregard her kind instructions.

                               Here,
Where you see piles of rubble, stones
Wrenched from stones, and plumes of smoke and dust,   *715*
Is Neptune, shaking the walls he has pried up
With his great trident and uprooting the city
From its foundations. Over here, Juno,
Ferocious in her iron vest, first to hold
The Western Gates, summons with her usual   *720*
Fury reinforcements from the ships.

And now look up. Tritonian Pallas
Is already seated on the highest towers,
Glowing from a thunderhead, grim
With her Gorgon. The Father himself   725
Gives the Greeks courage and strength
And incites the gods to oppose the Trojans.
Hurry away, my son, and end your struggle.
I will bring you safely to your father's door.'

And she plunged into night's shadows.
                                         Dire faces,   730
Numinous presences hostile to Troy, now loomed
In the darkness visible.

To my eyes it seemed that all Ilium
Was sinking in flames, and Neptune's Troy
Was being overturned from its base.   735

> *It was just like an ancient mountain ash*
> *That woodsmen are straining to fell Iron axes*
> *Ring thick and fast on its trunk, hacking it through,*
> *And it threatens to fall, nodding front its crest,*
> *Its foliage trembling, until, bit by bit,*   740
> *Overcome with wounds, it gives one last groan*
> *And torn from the hillside comes crashing down.*

I descended and, guided by a god,
Somehow got through fire and foe.
Weapons gave way; the flames receded.   745

When I reached the doors of my father's house,
My old home, I sought him first and wanted
More than anything to lift him up
Into the mountains—but he refused
To draw out his life and suffer exile   750
With Troy in ashes.

                   'You are young,'
He cried, 'and still strong; you must take flight.
If the gods wanted to prolong ray life
They would have preserved this home of mine.

It is enough and more that I have seen   755
Such destruction once before and have survived
One capture of my city. Say farewell
To my body lying just as it is
And depart. I shall die by my own hand.
The Greeks will pick over my spoils and pity me.   760
Loss of burial is light. Despised by heaven
And useless, I have lived too many years
Since the Lord of Gods and Men breathed winds
Of lightning upon me and touched me with fire.'

He kept repeating words such as these   765
And would not move. We were all in tears,
My wife, Creüsa, Ascanius, all our household,
Pleading with my father not to compound
Our desperate plight and destroy us with him.
He refused, and remained just as he was.   770
I reached for my gear, wanting only to die.
What hope was there for deliverance now?

'Did you think I could leave without you, Father?
How could such a thing come out of your mouth?
If it pleases the gods that nothing be left   775
Of this great city, and if you are determined,
If it is your pleasure, to throw yourself
And all of us into Troy's holocaust—
The door to that fate is wide open. Pyrrhus,
Grimed with Priam's gore, will be here soon;   780
Pyrrhus, who mutilates the son
Before the father's eyes, butchers the father
Like a beast at the altar. O my merciful mother,
Was it for this you saved me from the enemy,
So I could see the enemy in my own home785
And Ascanius, and my father, and Creüsa
Slaughtered In each other's blood?
                                        To arms, men!
The last light calls the vanquished. Take me back
To the Greeks. Let me start the battle again.
Never this day shall we all die unavenged!'   790

Once more I strapped on my sword, gripped my shield
In my left hand, and was hurrying out of the door,
When Creüsa embraced my feet at the threshold
And held up little Iülus to his father, saying:

'If you go to die, take us with you,   795
To whatever fate. But if experience has taught you
 To rely on your weapons, guard first this house.
To whom do you leave us, little Iülus,
Your father, and me, once called your wife?'

Her voice filled the house with moaning,   800
And then, without warning, a strange portent
Flickered between the faces and hands
Of Iülus' anxious parents: a light tongue of flame
Gleaming above his head. Harmless to the touch,
It licked his soft locks and grazed his temples.   805
Trembling with fear, we shook the fire from his hair
Quickly and doused the holy flames with water.
But my father, Anchises, enraptured,
Raised his eyes to the stars above
And lifted his hands and his voice to heaven: 810

'Almighty Jupiter, if you are moved
By any prayers, only look upon us,
And if by our piety we have earned it,
Give us your aid and confirm this omen.'

His aged words had just finished, when suddenly   815
Thunder crashed on our left, and a star
Shot down from the sky, sliding through the dark
And trailing a luminous flood of sparks.
We watched it glide over the palace roof
And bury its splendor in Ida's forest,   820
Leaving a shining furrow in its wake.
The air reeked with sulfur all around.

Overwhelmed, my father lifted himself up
In adoration of the star and spoke to heaven:

'No more delay. I follow, and where yon lead,   *825*
There I am. Gods of our fathers, save this house,
Save my grandson. Yours is this omen,
In your power is Troy. And now, my son,
I am ready to go as your companion.'

He spoke, and now the sound of the fire   *830*
Could be heard more clearly, and the inferno
Rolled its seething heat ever closer.

'Come, dear Father, onto my shoulders now.
You will not weigh me down, and come what may
We will face it together, peril or salvation.   *835*
Little Iulus will walk beside me, and my wife
Will walk in my footsteps some distance behind.
Now listen to me, all of my household:
Just outside the city there is a mound,
And a temple of Ceres, long deserted.   *840*
Beside these stands an ancient cypress
Worshiped by my ancestors for many years.
There, by our separate ways, we will meet.
Take into your hands, Father, the sacred gods
Of our country. It would be a sacrilege   *845*
If I touched them before I washed away
The bloody filth of battle in a living river.'

This said, I spread upon my shoulders
A golden lionskin and bent to my burden.
Little Iulus held my hand and kept up,   *850*
Although his stride could not match his father's,
And my wife followed behind.
                                    We kept
To the shadows and I undisturbed before
By any number of weapons thrust my way
And whole platoons of Greeks, now was frightened   *855*
By every breeze and startled by every sound,
Afraid for my companion and my burden.

We were nearing the gates, and it looked like
We had made it through, when suddenly

The sound of marching feet drifted on the wind.   *860*
Squinting through the gloom, my father cried:

'Run for it, Son! They're getting close.
I can see the bronze glitter of their shields.'

I panicked. Some malignant spirit
Robbed me of my wits, for while I ran   *865*
Down back alleys, leaving the familiar streets,
My wife, Creüsa, was taken from me
By some evil fortune. Had she stopped,
Or got lost and sat down exhausted?
I never saw her again, didn't even look back   *870*
Or think of her behind me until we arrived
At the mound by Ceres' ancient temple.
When finally we were all gathered there,
She alone was missing. No one had seen her,
Not her husband, not her son, no one.   *875*
What man or god did I not accuse
In my delirium? What cruder thing
Had I seen in our overturned city?
I entrusted Ascanius, Anchises,
And the gods of Troy to my companions   *880*
And hid them in a bend of the valley.
Myself, I strapped on my glittering armor
And went back to the city, hell-bent
On running every risk again,
Combing through all of Troy,   *885*
And putting my life on the line once more.

I started at the walls and the dark gate
Where I had escaped and retraced my steps
Through the night, looking everywhere by torchlight.
Everywhere there was fear. The very silence   *890*
Was terrifying. Then I turned homeward,
In case, just in case, she had gone there.
The Greeks were there in force, and the house
Consumed with fire. Fanned by the wind,
It spiraled up past the eaves and gnawed at the roof,   *895*
Blasting the sky with its heat. I moved on
And saw once more the palace of Priam

On the citadel. There, in the empty court
Of Juno's sanctuary, stood Phoenix
And dire Ulysses, chosen to guard the spoils, 900
Treasures from, every part of Troy, ripped
Out of burning temples—tables of the gods,
Solid gold bowls, and plundered robes—
All in a heap. Boys and trembling matrons
Stood around in long rows. 905

I even risked casting my voice into the night
And filled the streets with shouts, calling
'Creüsa' over and over again
In my misery, all in vain.
                                But as I rushed
Through the empty shells of buildings, frantic 910
To find her, there rose before my eyes
The sad ghost of Creüsa herself, an image
Larger than life. I was transfixed,
My hair stood on end, and my voice choked.
Then she spoke to me and calmed my fears: 915

'What good does it do, my sweet husband,
To indulge in such mad grief? These things
Do not happen without the will of the gods.
You may not take your Creüsa with you;
The Lord of Olympus does not allow it. 920
Long exile is yours, plowing a vast stretch
Of sea. Then you will come to Hesperia,
Where the Lydian Tiber runs gently
Through fertile fields. There, happy times.
Kingship, and a royal wife shall be yours. 925
Dry your tears for your beloved Creüsa.
I shall not look upon the proud domains
Of the Myrmidons or Dolopians,
Nor go to be a slave for Greek matrons,
I, a Trojan woman, and wife of the son 930
Of the goddess Venus. No,
The Great Mother keeps me on these shores.
Farewell, and keep well your love for our child.'

Creüsa spoke, and then left me there,
Weeping, with many things yet to say.   *935*

She vanished into thin air. Three times
I tried to put my arms around her; three times
Her wraith slipped through my hands,
Soft as a breeze, like a vanishing dream.

The long night was spent, and at last   *940*
I went back to rejoin my people.

I was surprised by the great number
Of new arrivals I found, women and men,
Youth gathered for exile, a wretched band
Of refugees who had poured in from all over,   *945*
Prepared to journey across the sea
To whatever lands I might lead them.
The brilliant morning star was rising
Over Ida's ridges, ushering in the day.
The Greeks held all the city gates.   *950*
There was no hope of help. I yielded
And, lifting up my father, sought the mountains."

*Book 3 is omitted. Aeneas continues his story. Having built a fleet, Aeneas sails from Troy
with his band of refugees. They stop in Thrace, but are warned off by the ghost of Polydorus,
Priam's youngest son, who was killed by the king of Thrace. Sailing on they arrive at Delos,
where Aeneas consults the oracle of Apollo, who tells him to seek his ancient homeland.
Anchises thinks the oracle means Crete, but after attempting to settle there the Trojans
realize that Italy is their true homeland and they sail on. They are attacked by the Harpies
in the Strophades and finally arrive in Buthrotum, in northwest Greece, where they are
welcomed by Priam's son Helenus and his wife, Andromache, the widow of the Trojan hero
Hector. Following Helenas' advice the Trojans sail to Italy and then to Sicily, where they
encounter the Cyclops Polyphemus. Acestes gives them hospitality in Drepanum, and there
Anchises dies. When the fleet sails from Sicily they are caught in the storm that takes them
to Carthage. Aeneas finishes his story.*

Nero

By Suetonius

1

Of the Domitian family two branches have acquired distinction, the Calvini and the Ahenobarbi. The latter have as the founder of their race and the origin of their surname Lucius Domitius, to whom, as he was returning from the country, there once appeared twin youths of more than mortal majesty, so it is said, and bade him carry to the senate and people the news of a victory, which was as yet unknown. And as a token of their divinity it is said that they stroked his cheeks and turned his black beard to a ruddy hue, like that of bronze. This sign was perpetuated in his descendants, a great part of whom had red beards. After they had attained seven consulships, a triumph, and two censorships, and were enrolled among the patricians, they all continued to use the same surname. They confined their forenames to Gnaeus and Lucius, and used even these with a noteworthy variation, now conferring each one on three members of the family in succession, and now giving them to individual members in turn. Thus the first, second, and third of the Ahenobarbi, we are told, were called Lucius, the next three in order Gnaeus, while all those that followed were called in turn first Lucius and then Gnaeus. It seems to me worth while to give an account of several members of this family, to show more clearly that though Nero degenerated from the good qualities of his ancestors, he yet reproduced the vices of each of them, as if transmitted to him by natural inheritance.

2

To begin then somewhat far back, his great-grandfather's grandfather, Gnaeus Domitius, when tribune of the commons, was enraged at the pontiffs for choosing another than himself in his father's place among them, and transferred the right of filling vacancies in the priesthoods from the colleges themselves to the people. Then having vanquished the Allobroges and the Arverni in his consulship, he rode through the province on an elephant, attended by a throng of soldiers, in a kind of triumphal procession. He it was of whom the orator Licinius Crassus said that it was not surprising that he had a brazen beard, since he had a face of iron and a heart of lead. His son, who was praetor at the time, summoned Gaius Caesar to an investigation before the senate at the close of his consulship, because it was thought that his administration had been in violation of the auspices and the laws. Afterwards in his own consulship he tried to deprive Caesar of the command of the armies in Gaul, and being named Caesar's successor by his party, was taken prisoner at Corfinium at the beginning of the civil war. Granted his freedom, he at first gave courage by his presence to the people of Massilia, who were hard pressed by their besiegers, but suddenly abandoned them and at last fell in the battle at Pharsalus. He was a man of no great resolution, though he had a violent temper, and when he once attempted to kill himself in a fit of despair and terror, he so shrank from the thought of death that he changed his mind and vomited up the poison, conferring freedom on his physician, since, knowing his master, he had purposely given him what was not a fatal dose. When Gnaeus Pompeius brought forward the question of the treatment of those who were neutral and sided with neither party, he alone was for regarding them as hostile.

3

He left a son, who was beyond all question better than the rest of the family. He was condemned to death by the Pedian law among those implicated in Caesar's death, though he was guiltless, and accordingly joined Brutus and Cassius, who were his near relatives. After the death of both leaders he retained the fleet of which he had previously been made commander, and even added to it, and it was not until his party had been everywhere routed that he surrendered it to Mark Antony, of his own free will and as if it were a great favour. He too was the only one of those who were condemned by that same law who was allowed to return to his native land, where he successively held all the highest offices. When the civil strife was subsequently renewed, and he was appointed one of Antony's lieutenants, he did not venture, owing to a sudden attack of illness, to accept the chief command when it was offered by those who were ashamed of Cleopatra, nor yet positively to decline it; but he went over to Augustus and a few days later died. Even he did not escape with an unblemished reputation, for Antony openly declared that he had changed sides from desire for the company of his mistress, Servilia Nais.

4

He was the father of the Domitius who was later well known from being named in Augustus' will as the purchaser of his goods and chattels, a man no less famous in his youth for his skill in driving than he was later for winning the insignia of a triumph in the war in Germany. But he was haughty, extravagant, and cruel, and when he was only an aedile, forced the censor Lucius Plancus to make way for him on the street. While holding the offices of praetor and consul, he brought Roman knights and matrons on the stage to act a farce. He gave beast-baitings both in the Circus and in all the regions of the city; also a gladiatorial show, but with such inhuman cruelty that Augustus, after his private warning was disregarded, was forced to restrain him by an edict.

5

He had by the elder Antonia a son Domitius who became the father of Nero, a man hateful in every walk of life; for when he had gone to the East on the staff of the young Gaius Caesar, he slew one of his own freedmen for refusing to drink as much as he ordered, and when he was in consequence dismissed from the number of Gaius' friends, he lived not a whit less lawlessly. On the contrary, in a village on the Appian Way, suddenly whipping up his team, he purposely ran over and killed a boy; and right in the Roman Forum he gouged out the eye of a Roman knight for being too outspoken in chiding him. He was moreover so dishonest that he not only cheated some bankers of the prices of wares which he had bought, but in his praetorship he even defrauded the victors in the chariot races of the amount of their prizes. When for this reason he was held up to scorn by the jests of his own sister, and the managers of the troupes made complaint, he issued an edict that the prizes should thereafter be paid on the spot. Just before the death of Tiberius he was also charged with treason, as well as with acts of adultery and incest with his sister Lepida, but escaped owing to the change of rulers and died of dropsy at Pyrgi, after acknowledging Nero son of Agrippina, the daughter of Germanicus.

6

Nero was born at Antium nine months after the death of Tiberius, on the eighteenth day before the Kalends of January, just as the sun rose, so that he was touched by its rays almost before he could be laid upon the ground. Many people at once made many direful predictions from his horoscope, and a remark of his father Domitius was also regarded as an omen; for while receiving the congratulations of his friends, he said that "nothing that was not abominable and a public bane could be born of Agrippina and himself." Another manifest indication of Nero's future unhappiness occurred on the day of his purification; for when Gaius Caesar was asked by his sister to give the child whatever name he liked, he looked at his uncle Claudius, who later became emperor and adopted Nero, and said that he gave him his name. This he did, not seriously, but in jest, and Agrippina scorned the proposal, because at that time Claudius was one of the laughing-stocks of the court.

At the age of three he lost his father, being left heir to a third of his estate; but even this he did not receive in full, since his fellow heir Gaius seized all the property. Then his mother was banished too, and he was brought up at the house of his aunt Lepida almost in actual want, under two tutors, a dancer and a barber. But when Claudius became emperor, Nero not only recovered his father's property, but was also enriched by an inheritance from his stepfather, Passienus Crispus. When his mother was recalled from banishment and reinstated, he became so prominent through her influence that it leaked out that Messalina, wife of Claudius, had sent emissaries to strangle him as he was taking his noonday nap, regarding him as a rival of Britannicus. An addition to this bit of gossip is, that the would-be assassins were frightened away by a snake which darted out from under his pillow. The only foundation for this tale was, that there was found in his bed near the pillow the slough of a serpent; but nevertheless at his mother's desire he had the skin enclosed in a golden bracelet, and wore it for a long time on his right arm. But when at last the memory of his mother grew hateful to him, he threw it away, and afterwards in the time of his extremity sought it again in vain.

7

While he was still a young, half-grown boy he took part in the game of Troy at a performance in the Circus with great self-possession and success. In the eleventh year of his age he was adopted by Claudius and consigned to the training of Annaeus Seneca, who was then already a senator. They say that on the following night Seneca dreamed that he was teaching Gaius Caesar, and Nero soon proved the dream prophetic by revealing the cruelty of his disposition at the earliest possible opportunity. For merely because his brother Britannicus had, after his adoption, greeted him as usual as Ahenobarbus, he tried to convince his father that Britannicus was a changeling. Also when his aunt Lepida was accused, he publicly gave testimony against her, to gratify his mother, who was using every effort to ruin Lepida.

At his formal introduction into public life he announced a largess to the people and a gift of money to the soldiers, ordered a drill of the praetorians and headed them shield in hand; and thereafter returned thanks to his father in the senate. In the latter's consulship he pleaded the cause of the people of Bononia before him in Latin, and of those of Rhodes and Ilium in Greek. His first appearance as judge was when he was prefect of the city during the Latin Festival, when the most celebrated pleaders vied with one another in bringing before him, not trifling and brief cases according to the usual custom, but many of the highest importance, though this had been forbidden by Claudius. Shortly afterwards he took Octavia to wife and gave games and a beast-baiting in the Circus, that health might be vouchsafed Claudius.

8

When the death of Claudius was made public, Nero, who was seventeen years old, went forth to the watch between the sixth and the seventh hour, since no earlier time for the formal beginning of his reign seemed suitable because of bad omens throughout the day. Hailed emperor on the steps of the Palace, he was carried in a litter to the praetorian camp, and after a brief address to the soldiers was taken from there to the House, which he did not leave until evening, of the unbounded honours that were heaped upon him refusing but one, the title of father of his country, and that because of his youth.

9

Then beginning with a display of filial piety, he gave Claudius a magnificent funeral, spoke his eulogy, and deified him. He paid the highest honours to the memory of his father Domitius. He left to his mother the management of all public and private business. Indeed, on the first day of his rule he gave to the tribune on guard the watchword "The Best of Mothers," and afterwards he often rode with her through the streets in her litter. He established a colony at Antium, enrolling the veterans of the praetorian guard and joining with them the wealthiest of the chief centurions, whom he compelled to change their residence; and he also made a harbour there at great expense.

10

To make his good intentions still more evident, he declared that he would rule according to the principles of Augustus, and he let slip no opportunity for acts of generosity and mercy, or even for displaying his affability. The more oppressive sources of revenue he either abolished or moderated. He reduced the rewards paid to informers against violators of the Papian law to one fourth of the former amount. He distributed four hundred sesterces to each man of the people, and granted to the most distinguished of the senators who were without means an annual salary, to some as much as five hundred thousand sesterces; and to the praetorian cohorts he gave a monthly allowance of grain free of cost. When he was asked according to custom to sign the warrant for the execution of a man who had been condemned to death, he said: "How I wish I had never learned to write!" He greeted men of all orders off-hand and from memory. When the senate returned thanks to him, he replied, "When I shall have deserved them." He admitted even the commons to witness his exercises in the Campus, and often declaimed in public. He read his poems too, not only at home but in the theatre as well, so greatly to the delight of all that a thanksgiving was voted because of his recital, while that part of his poems was inscribed in letters of gold and dedicated to Jupiter of the Capitol.

11

He gave many entertainments of different kinds: the Juvenales, chariot races in the Circus, stage-plays, and a gladiatorial show. At the first mentioned he had even old men of consular rank and aged matrons take part. For the games in the Circus he assigned places to the knights apart from the rest, and even matched chariots drawn by four camels. At the plays which he gave for the "Eternity of the Empire," which by his order were called the Ludi Maximi, parts were taken by several men and women of both the orders; a well known Roman knight mounted an elephant and rode down a rope; a Roman play of Afranius, too, was staged, entitled "The Fire," and the actors were allowed to carry off the furniture of the burning house and keep it. Every day all kinds of presents were thrown to the people; these included a thousand birds of every kind each day, various kinds of food, tickets for grain, clothing, gold, silver, precious stones, pearls, paintings, slaves, beasts of burden, and even trained wild animals; finally, ships, blocks of houses, and farms.

12

These plays he viewed from the top of the proscenium. At the gladiatorial show, which he gave in a wooden amphitheatre, erected in the district of the Campus Martius within the space of a single year, he had no one put to death, not even criminals. But he compelled four hundred senators and six hundred Roman knights, some of whom were well to do and of unblemished reputation, to fight in the arena. Even those who fought with the wild beasts and performed the various services in the arena were of the same orders. He also exhibited a naval battle in salt water with sea monsters swimming about in it; besides pyrrhic dances by some Greek youths, handing each of them certificates of Roman citizenship at the close of his performance. The pyrrhic dances represented various scenes. In one a bull mounted Pasiphae, who was concealed in a wooden image of a heifer; at least many of the spectators thought so. Icarus at his very first attempt fell close by the imperial couch and bespattered the emperor with his blood; for Nero very seldom presided at the games, but used to view them while reclining on a couch, at first through small openings, and then with the entire balcony uncovered.

He was likewise the first to establish at Rome a quinquennial contest in three parts, after the Greek fashion, that is in music, gymnastics, and riding, which he called the Neronia; at the same time he dedicated his baths and gymnasium, supplying every member of the senatorial and equestrian orders with oil. To preside over the whole contest he appointed ex-consuls, chosen by lot, who occupied the seats of the praetors. Then he went down into the orchestra among the senators and accepted the prize for Latin oratory and verse, for which all the most eminent men had contended but which was given to him with their unanimous consent; but when that for lyre-playing was also offered him by the judges, he knelt before it and ordered that it be laid at the feet of Augustus' statue. At the gymnastic contest, which he gave in the Saepta, he shaved his first beard to the accompaniment of a splendid sacrifice of bullocks, put it in a golden box adorned with pearls of great price, and dedicated it in the Capitol. He invited the Vestal virgins also to witness the contests of the athletes, because at Olympia the priestesses of Ceres were allowed the same privilege.

13

I may fairly include among his shows the entrance of Tiridates into the city. He was a king of Armenia, whom Nero induced by great promises to come to Rome; and since he was prevented by bad weather from exhibiting him to the people on the day appointed by proclamation, he produced him at the first favourable opportunity, with the praetorian cohorts drawn up in full armour about the temples in the Forum, while he himself sat in a curule chair on the rostra in the attire of a triumphing general, surrounded by military ensigns and standards. As the king approached along a sloping platform, the emperor at first let him fall at his feet, but raised him with his right hand and kissed him. Then, while the king made supplication, Nero took the turban from his head and replaced it with a diadem, while a man of praetorian rank translated the words of the suppliant and proclaimed them to the throng. From there the king was taken to the theatre, and when he had again done obeisance, Nero gave him a seat at his right hand. Because of all this Nero was hailed as Imperator, and after depositing a laurel wreath in the Capitol, he closed the two doors of the temple of Janus, as a sign that no war was left anywhere.

14

He held four consulships, the first for two months, the second and the last for six months each, the third for four months. The second and third were in successive years, while a year intervened between these and each of the others.

15

In the administration of justice he was reluctant to render a decision to those who presented cases, except on the following day and in writing. The procedure was, instead of continuous pleadings, to have each point presented separately by the parties in turn. Furthermore, whenever he withdrew for consultation, he did not discuss any matter with all his advisers in a body, but had each of them give his opinion in written form; these he read silently and in private and then gave a verdict according to his own inclination, as if it were the view of the majority.

For a long time he would not admit the sons of freedmen to the senate and he refused office to those who had been admitted by his predecessors. Candidates who were in excess of the number of vacancies received the command of a legion as compensation for the postponement and delay. He commonly appointed consuls for a period of six months. When one of them died just before the Kalends of January, he appointed no one in his place, expressing his disapproval of the old-time case of Caninius Rebilus, the twenty-four hour consul. He conferred the triumphal regalia even on men of the rank of quaestor, as well as on some of the knights, and sometimes for other than military services. As regards the speeches which he sent to the senate on various matters, he passed over the quaestors, whose duty it was to read them, and usually had them presented by one of the consuls.

16

He devised a new form for the buildings of the city and in front of the houses and apartments he erected porches, from the flat roofs of which fires could be fought; and these he put up at his own cost. He had also planned to extend the walls as far as Ostia and to bring the sea from there to Rome by a canal.

During his reign many abuses were severely punished and put down, and no fewer new laws were made: a limit was set to expenditures; the public banquets were confined to a distribution of food; the sale of any kind of cooked viands in the taverns was forbidden, with the exception of pulse and vegetables, whereas before every sort of dainty was exposed for sale. Punishment was inflicted on the Christians, a class of men given to a new and mischievous superstition. He put an end to the diversions of the chariot drivers, who from immunity of long standing claimed the right of ranging at large and amusing themselves by cheating and robbing the people. The pantomimic actors and their partisans were banished from the city.

17

It was in his reign that a protection against forgers was first devised, by having no tablets signed that were not bored with holes through which a cord was thrice passed. In the case of wills it was provided that the first two leaves should be presented to the signatories with only the name of the testator written upon them, and that no one who wrote a will for another should put down a legacy for himself; further, that clients should pay a fixed and reasonable fee for the services of their advocates, but nothing at all for benches, which were to be furnished free of charge by the public treasury; finally as regarded the pleading of cases, that those connected with the treasury should be transferred to the Forum and a board of arbiters, and that any appeal from the juries should be made to the senate.

18

So far from being actuated by any wish or hope of increasing or extending the empire, he even thought of withdrawing the army from Britain and changed his purpose only because he was ashamed to seem to belittle the glory of his father. He increased the provinces only by the realm of Pontus, when it was given up by Polemon, and that of Cottius in the Alps on the latter's death.

19

He planned but two foreign tours, to Alexandria and Achaia; and he gave up the former on the very day when he was to have started, disturbed by a threatening portent. For as he was making the round of the temples and had sat down in the shrine of Vesta, first the fringe of his garment caught when he attempted to get up, and then such darkness overspread his eyes that he could see nothing. In Achaia he attempted to cut through the Isthmus and called together the praetorians and urged them to begin the work; then at a signal given on a trumpet he was first to break ground with a mattock and to carry off a basketful of earth upon his shoulders. He also prepared for an expedition to the Caspian Gates, after enrolling a new legion of raw recruits of Italian birth, each six feet tall, which he called the "phalanx of Alexander the Great."

I have brought together these acts of his, some of which are beyond criticism, while others are even deserving of no slight praise, to separate them from his shameful and criminal deeds, of which I shall proceed now to give an account.

20

Having gained some knowledge of music in addition to the rest of his early education, as soon as he became emperor he sent for Terpnus, the greatest master of the lyre in those days, and after listening to him sing after dinner for many successive days until late at night, he little by little began to practise himself, neglecting none of the exercises which artists of that kind are in the habit of following, to preserve or strengthen their voices. For he used to lie upon his back and hold a leaden plate on his chest, purge himself by the syringe and by vomiting, and deny himself fruits and all foods injurious to the voice. Finally encouraged by his progress, although his voice was weak and husky, he began to long to appear on the stage, and every now and then in the presence of his intimate friends he would quote a Greek proverb meaning "Hidden music counts for nothing." And he made his début at Naples, where he did not cease singing until he had finished the number which he had begun, even though the theatre was shaken by a sudden earthquake shock. In the same city he sang frequently and for several days. Even when he took a short time to rest his voice, he could not keep out of sight but went to the theatre after bathing and dined in the orchestra with the people all about him, promising them in Greek, that when he had wetted his whistle a bit, he would ring out something good and loud. He was greatly taken too with the rhythmic applause of some Alexandrians, who had flocked to Naples from a fleet that had lately arrived, and summoned more men from Alexandria. Not content with that, he selected some young men of the order of knights and more than five thousand sturdy young commoners, to be divided into groups and learn the Alexandrian styles of applause (they called them "the bees," "the roof-tiles," and "the bricks"), and to ply them vigorously whenever he sang. These men were noticeable for their thick hair and fine apparel; their left hands were bare and without rings, and the leaders were paid four hundred thousand sesterces each.

21

Considering it of great importance to appear in Rome as well, he repeated the contest of the Neronia before the appointed time, and when there was a general call for his "divine voice," he replied that if any wished to hear him, he would favour them in the gardens; but when the guard of soldiers which was then on duty seconded the entreaties of the people, he gladly agreed to appear at once. So without delay he had his name added to the list of the lyre-players who entered the contest, and casting his own lot into the urn with the rest, he came forward in his turn, attended by the prefects of the Guard carrying his lyre, and followed by the tribunes of the soldiers and his intimate friends. Having taken his place and finished his preliminary speech, he announced through the ex-consul Cluvius Rufus that "he would sing Niobe"; and he kept at it until late in the afternoon, putting off the award of the prize for that event and postponing the rest of the contest to the next year, to have an excuse for singing oftener. But since even that seemed too long to wait, he did not cease to appear in public from time to time. He even thought of taking part in private performances among the professional actors, when one of the praetors offered him a million sesterces. He also put on the mask and sang tragedies representing gods and heroes and even heroines and goddesses, having the masks fashioned in the likeness of his own features or those of the women of whom he chanced to be enamoured. Among other themes he sang "Canace in Labor," "Orestes the Matricide," "The Blinding of Oedipus" and the "Frenzy of Hercules." At the last named performance they say that a young recruit, seeing the emperor in mean attire and bound with chains, as the subject required, rushed forward to lend him aid.

22

From his earliest years he had a special passion for horses and talked constantly about the games in the Circus, though he was forbidden to do so. Once when he was lamenting with his fellow pupils the fate of a charioteer of the "Greens," who was dragged by his horses, and his preceptor scolded him, he told a lie and pretended that he was talking of Hector. At the beginning of his reign he used to play every day with ivory chariots on a board, and he came from the country to all the games, even the most insignificant, at first secretly, and then so openly that no one doubted that he would be in Rome on that particular day. He made no secret of his wish to have the number of prizes increased, and in consequence more races were added and the performance was continued to a late hour, while the managers of the troupes no longer thought it worth while to produce their drivers at all except for a full day's racing. He soon longed to drive a chariot himself and even to show himself frequently to the public; so after a trial exhibition in his gardens before his slaves and the dregs of the populace, he gave all an opportunity of seeing him in the Circus Maximus, one of his freedmen dropping the napkin from the place usually occupied by the magistrates.

Not content with showing his proficiency in these arts at Rome, he went to Achaia, as I have said, influenced especially by the following consideration. The cities in which it was the custom to hold contests in music had adopted the rule of sending all the lyric prizes to him. These he received with the greatest delight, not only giving audience before all others to the envoys who brought them, but even inviting them to his private table. When some of them begged him to sing after dinner and greeted his performance with extravagant applause, he declared that "the Greeks were the only ones who had an ear for music and that they alone were worthy of his efforts." So he took ship without delay and immediately on arriving at Cassiope made a preliminary appearance as a singer at the altar of Jupiter Cassius, and then went the round of all the contests.

23

To make this possible, he gave orders that even those which were widely separated in time should be brought together in a single year, so that some had even to be given twice, and he introduced a musical competition at Olympia also, contrary to custom. To avoid being distracted or hindered in any way while busy with these contests, he replied to his freedman Helius, who reminded him that the affairs of the city required his presence, in these words: "However much it may be your advice and your wish that I should return speedily, yet you ought rather to counsel me and to hope that I may return worthy of Nero."

While he was singing no one was allowed to leave the theatre even for the most urgent reasons. And so it is said that some women gave birth to children there, while many who were worn out with listening and applauding, secretly leaped from the wall, since the gates at the entrance were closed, or feigned death and were carried out as if for burial. The trepidation and anxiety with which he took part in the contests, his keen rivalry of his opponents and his awe of the judges, can hardly be credited. As if his rivals were of quite the same station as himself, he used to show respect to them and try to gain their favour, while he slandered them behind their backs, sometimes assailed them with abuse when he met them, and even bribed those who were especially proficient.

Before beginning, he would address the judges in the most deferential terms, saying that he had done all that could be done, but the issue was in the hands of Fortune; they however, being men of wisdom and experience, ought to exclude what was fortuitous. When they bade him take heart, he withdrew with greater confidence, but not even then without anxiety, interpreting the silence and modesty of some as sullenness and ill-nature, and declaring that he had his suspicions of them.

24

In competition he observed the rules most scrupulously, never daring to clear his throat and even wiping the sweat from his bow with his arm. Once indeed, during the performance of a tragedy, when he had dropped his sceptre but quickly recovered it, he was terribly afraid that he might be excluded from the competition because of his slip, and his confidence was restored only when his accompanist swore that it had passed unnoticed amid the delight and applause of the people. When the victory was won, he made the announcement himself; and for that reason he always took part in the contests of the heralds. To obliterate the memory of all other victors in games and leave no trace of them, their statues and busts were all thrown down by his order, dragged off with hooks, and cast into privies.

He also drove a chariot in many places, at Olympia even a ten-horse team, although in one of his own poems he had criticised Mithridates for just that thing. But after he had been thrown from the car and put back in it, he was unable to hold out and gave up before the end of the course; but he received the crown just the same. On his departure he presented the entire province with freedom and at the same time gave the judges Roman citizenship and a large sum of money. These favours he announced in person on the day of the Isthmian Games, standing in the middle of the stadium.

25

Returning from Greece, since it was at Naples that he had made his first appearance, he entered that city with white horses through a part of the wall which had been thrown down, as is customary with victors in the sacred games. In like manner he entered Antium, then Albanum, and finally Rome; but at Rome he rode in the chariot which Augustus had used in his triumphs in days gone by, and wore a purple robe and a Greek cloak adorned with stars of gold, bearing on his head the Olympic crown and in his right hand the Pythian, while the rest were carried before him with inscriptions telling where he had won them and against what competitors, and giving the titles of the songs or of the subject of the plays. His car was followed by his claque as by the escort of a triumphal procession, who shouted that they were the attendants of Augustus and the soldiers of his triumph. Then through the arch of the Circus Maximus, which was thrown down, he made his way across the Velabrum and the Forum to the Palatine and the temple of Apollo. All along the route victims were slain, the streets were sprinkled from time to time with perfume, while birds, ribbons, and sweetmeats were showered upon him. He placed the sacred crowns in his bed-chambers around the couches, as well as statues representing him in the guise of a lyre-player; and he had a coin too struck with the same device. So far from neglecting or relaxing his practice of the art after this, he never addressed the soldiers except by letter or in a speech delivered by another, to save his voice; and he never did anything for amusement or in earnest without an elocutionist by his side, to warn him to spare his vocal organs and hold a handkerchief to his mouth. To many men he offered his friendship or announced his hostility, according as they had applauded him lavishly or grudgingly.

26

Although at first his acts of wantonness, lust, extravagance, avarice and cruelty were gradual and secret, and might be condoned as follies of youth, yet even then their nature was such that no one doubted that they were defects of his character and not due to his time of life. No sooner was twilight over than he would catch up a cap or a wig and go to the taverns or range about the streets playing pranks, which however were very far from harmless; for he used to beat men as they came home from dinner, stabbing any who resisted him and throwing them into the sewers. He would even break into shops and rob them, setting up a market in the Palace, where he divided the booty which he took, sold it at auction, and then squandered the proceeds. In the strife which resulted he often ran the risk of losing his eyes or even his life, for he was beaten almost to death by a man of the senatorial order, whose wife he had maltreated. Warned by this, he never afterwards ventured to appear in public at that hour without having tribunes follow him at a distance and unobserved. Even in the daytime he would be carried privately to the theatre in a sedan, and from the upper part of the proscenium would watch the brawls of the pantomimic actors and egg them on; and when they came to blows and fought with stones and broken benches, he himself threw many missiles at the people and even broke a praetor's head.

27

Little by little, however, as his vices grew stronger, he dropped jesting and secrecy and with no attempt at disguise openly broke out into worse crime. He prolonged his revels from midday to midnight, often livening himself by a warm plunge, or, if it were summer, into water cooled with snow. Sometimes too he closed the inlets and banqueted in public in the great tank, in the Campus Martius, or in the Circus Maximus, waited on by harlots and dancing girls from all over the city. Whenever he drifted down the Tiber to Ostia, or sailed about the Gulf of Baiae, booths were set up at intervals along the banks and shores, fitted out for debauchery, while bartering matrons played the part of inn-keepers and from every hand solicited him to come ashore. He also levied dinners on his friends, one of whom spent four million sesterces for a banquet at which turbans were distributed, and another a considerably larger sum for a rose dinner.

28

Besides abusing freeborn boys and seducing married women, he debauched the vestal virgin Rubria. The freedwoman Acte he all but made his lawful wife, after bribing some ex-consuls to perjure themselves by swearing that she was of royal birth. He castrated the boy Sporus and actually tried to make a woman of him; and he married him with all the usual ceremonies, including a dowry and a bridal veil, took him to his house attended by a great throng, and treated him as his wife. And the witty jest that someone made is still current, that it would have been well for the world if Nero's father Domitius had had that kind of wife. This Sporus, decked out with the finery of the empresses and riding in a litter, he took with him to the assizes and marts of Greece, and later at Rome through the Street of the Images, fondly kissing him from time to time. That he even desired illicit relations with his own mother, and was kept from it by her enemies, who feared that such a help might give the reckless and insolent woman too great influence, was notorious, especially after he added to his concubines a courtesan who was said to look very like Agrippina. Even before that, so they say, whenever he rode in a litter with his mother, he had incestuous relations with her, which were betrayed by the stains on his clothing.

29

He so prostituted his own chastity that after defiling almost every part of his body, he at last devised a kind of game, in which, covered with the skin of some wild animal, he was let loose from a cage and attacked the private parts of men and women, who were bound to stakes, and when he had sated his mad lust, was dispatched by his freedman Doryphorus; for he was even married to this man in the same way that he himself had married Sporus, going so far as to imitate the cries and lamentations of a maiden being deflowered. I have heard from some men that it was his unshaken conviction that no man was chaste or pure in any part of his body, but that most of them concealed their vices and cleverly drew a veil over them; and that therefore he pardoned all other faults in those who confessed to him their lewdness.

30

He thought that there was no other way of enjoying riches and money than by riotous extravagance, declaring that only stingy and niggardly fellows kept a correct account of what they spent, while fine and genuinely magnificent gentlemen wasted and squandered. Nothing in his uncle Gaius so excited his envy and admiration as the fact that he had in so short a time run through the vast wealth which Tiberius had left him. Accordingly he made presents and wasted money without stint. On Tiridates, though it would seem hardly within belief, he spent eight hundred thousand sesterces a day, and on his departure presented him with more than a hundred millions. He gave the lyre-player Menecrates and the gladiator Spiculus properties and residences equal to those of men who had celebrated triumphs. He enriched the monkey-faced usurer Paneros with estates in the country and in the city and had him buried with almost regal splendour. He never wore the same garment twice. He played at dice for four hundred thousand sesterces a point. He fished with a golden net drawn by cords woven of purple and scarlet threads. It is said that he never made a journey with less than a thousand carriages, his mules shod with silver and their drivers clad in wool of Canusium, attended by a train of Mazaces and couriers with bracelets and trappings.

31

There was nothing however in which he was more ruinously prodigal than in building. He made a palace extending all the way from the Palatine to the Esquiline, which at first he called the House of Passage, but when it was burned shortly after its completion and rebuilt, the Golden House. Its size and splendour will be sufficiently indicated by the following details. Its vestibule was large enough to contain a colossal statue of the emperor a hundred and twenty feet high; and it was so extensive that it had a triple colonnade a mile long. There was a pond too, like a sea, surrounded with buildings to represent cities, besides tracts of country, varied by tilled fields, vineyards, pastures and woods, with great numbers of wild and domestic animals. In the rest of the house all parts were overlaid with gold and adorned with gems and mother-of-pearl. There were dining-rooms with fretted ceils of ivory, whose panels could turn and shower down flowers and were fitted with pipes for sprinkling the guests with perfumes. The main banquet hall was circular and constantly revolved day and night, like the heavens. He had baths supplied with sea water and sulphur water. When the edifice was finished in this style and he dedicated it, he deigned to say nothing more in the way of approval than that he was at last beginning to be housed like a human being.

He also began a pool, extending from Misenum to the lake of Avernus, roofed over and enclosed in colonnades, into which he planned to turn all the hot springs in every part of Baiae; a canal from Avernus all the way to Ostia, to enable the journey to be made by ship yet not by sea; its length was to be a hundred and sixty miles and its breadth sufficient to allows ships with five banks of oars to pass each other. For the execution of these projects he had given orders that the prisoners all over the empire should be transported to Italy, and that those who were convicted even of capital crimes should be punished in no other way than by sentence to this work.

He was led to such mad extravagance, in addition to his confidence in the resources of the empire, by the hope of a vast hidden treasure, suddenly inspired by the assurance of a Roman knight, who declared positively that the enormous wealth which queen

Dido had taken with her of old in her flight from Tyre was hidden away in huge caves in Africa and could be recovered with but trifling labour.

32

When this hope proved false, he resorted to false accusations and robbery, being at the end of his resources and so utterly impoverished that he was obliged to postpone and defer even the pay of the soldiers and the rewards due to the veterans.

First of all he made a law, that instead of one-half, five-sixths of the property of deceased freedmen should be made over to him, if without good and sufficient reason they bore the name of any family with which he himself was connected; further, that the estates of those who were ungrateful to their emperor should belong to the privy purse, and that the advocates who had written or dictated such wills should not go unpunished. Finally, that any word or deed on which an informer could base an action should be liable to the law against lese-majesty. He demanded the return of the rewards which he had given in recognition of the prizes conferred on him by any city in competition. Having forbidden the use of amethystine or Tyrian purple dyes, he secretly sent a man to sell a few ounces on a market day and then closed the shops of all the dealers. It is even said that when he saw a matron in the audience at one of his recitals clad in the forbidden colour he pointed her out to his agents, who dragged her out and stripped her on the spot, not only of her garment, but also of her property. He never appointed anyone to an office without adding: "You know what my needs are," and "Let us see to it that no one possess anything." At last he stripped many temples of their gifts and melted down the images of gold and silver, including those of the Penates, which however Galba soon afterwards restored.

33

He began his career of parricide and murder with Claudius, for even if he was not the instigator of the emperor's death, he was at least privy to it, as he openly admitted; for he used afterwards to laud mushrooms, the vehicle in which the poison was adminis-tered to Claudius, as "the food of the gods," as the Greek proverb has it. At any rate, after Claudius's death he vented on him every kind of insult, in act and word, charging him now with folly and now with cruelty; for it was a favourite joke of his to say that Claudius had ceased "to play the fool" among mortals, lengthening the first syllable of the word morari, and he disregarded many of his decrees and acts as the work of a madman and a dotard. Finally, he neglected to enclose the place where his body was burned except with a low and mean wall.

He attempted the life of Britannicus by poison, not less from jealousy of his voice (for it was more agreeable than his own) than from fear that he might sometime win a higher place than himself in the people's regard because of the memory of his father. He procured the potion from an archpoisoner, one Locusta, and when the effect was slower than he anticipated, merely physicing Britannicus, he called the woman to him and flogged her with his own hand, charging that she had administered a medicine instead of a poison; and when she said in excuse that she had given a smaller dose to shield him from the odium of the crime, he replied: "It's likely that I am afraid of the Julian law;" and he forced her to mix as swift and instant a potion as she knew how in his own room before his very eyes. Then he tried it on a kid, and as the animal lingered for five hours, had the mixture steeped again and again and threw some of it before a pig. The beast instantly fell dead, whereupon he ordered that the poison be taken to the dining-room and given to Britannicus. The boy dropped dead at the very first taste, but Nero lied to his guests and declared that he was seized with the falling sickness, to which he was subject, and the next day had him hastily and unceremoniously buried in a pouring rain. He rewarded Locusta for her eminent services with a full pardon and large estates in the country, and actually sent her pupils.

34

His mother offended him by too strict surveillance and criticism of his words and acts, but at first he confined his resentment to frequent endeavours to bring upon her a burden of unpopularity by pretending that he would abdicate the throne and go off to Rhodes. Then depriving her of all her honours and of her guard of Roman and German soldiers, he even forbade her to live with him and drove her from the Palace. After that he passed all bounds in harrying her, bribing men to annoy her with lawsuits while she remained in the city, and after she had retired to the country, to pass her house by land and sea and break her rest with abuse and mockery. At last terrified by her violence and threats, he determined to have her life, and after thrice attempting it by poison and finding that she had made herself immune by antidotes, he tampered with the ceiling of her bedroom, contriving a mechanical device for loosening its panels and dropping them upon her while she slept. When this leaked out through some of those connected with the plot, he devised a collapsible boat, to destroy her by shipwreck or by the falling in of its cabin. Then he pretended a reconciliation and invited her in a most cordial letter to come to Baiae and celebrate the feast of Minerva with him. On her arrival, instructing his captains to wreck the galley in which she had come, by running into it as if by accident, he detained her at a banquet, and when she would return to Bauli, offered her his contrivance in place of the craft which had been damaged, escorting her to it in high spirits and even kissing her breasts as they parted. The rest of the night he passed sleepless in intense anxiety, awaiting the outcome of his design. On learning that everything had gone wrong and that she had escaped by swimming, driven to desperation he secretly had a dagger thrown down beside her freedman Lucius Agermus, when he joyfully brought word that she was safe and sound, and then ordered that the freedman be seized and bound, on the charge of being hired to kill the emperor; that his mother be put to death, and the pretence made that she had escaped the consequences of her detected guilt by suicide. Trustworthy authorities add still more gruesome details: that he hurried off to view the corpse, handled her limbs, criticising some and commending others, and that becoming thirsty meanwhile, he took a drink. Yet he could not either then or ever afterwards endure the stings of conscience, though soldiers, senate and people tried to hearten him with their congratulations; for he often owned that he was hounded by his mother's ghost and by the whips and blazing torches of the Furies. He even had rites performed by the Magi, in the effort to summon her shade and entreat it for forgiveness. Moreover, in his journey through Greece he did not venture to take part in the Eleusinian mysteries, since at the beginning the godless and wicked are warned by the herald's proclamation to go hence.

To matricide he added the murder of his aunt. When he once visited her as she was confined to her bed from costiveness, and she, as old ladies will, stroking his downy beard (for he was already well grown) happened to say fondly: "As soon as I receive this, I shall gladly die," he turned to those with him and said as if in jest: "I'll take it off at once." Then he bade the doctors give the sick woman an overdose of physic and seized her property before she was cold, suppressing her will, that nothing might escape him.

35

Besides Octavia he later took two wives, Poppaea Sabina, daughter of an ex-quaestor and previously married to a Roman knight, and then Statilia Messalina, daughter of the great-granddaughter of Taurus, who had been twice consul and awarded a triumph. To possess the latter he slew her husband Atticus Vestinus while he held the office of consul. He soon grew tired of living with Octavia, and when his friends took him to task, replied that "she ought to be content with the insignia of wifehood." Presently after several vain attempts to strangle her, he divorced her on the ground of barrenness, and when the people took it ill and openly reproached him, he banished her besides; and finally he had her put to death on a charge of adultery that was so shameless and unfounded, that when all who were put to the torture maintained her innocence, he bribed his former preceptor Anicetus to make a pretended confession that he had violated her chastity by a stratagem. He dearly loved Poppaea, whom he married twelve days after his divorce from Octavia, yet he caused her death too by kicking her when she was pregnant and ill, because she had scolded him for coming home late from the races. By her he had a daughter, Claudia Augusta, but lost her when she was still an infant.

Indeed there is no kind of relationship that he did not violate in his career of crime. He put to death Antonia, daughter of Claudius, for refusing to marry him after Poppaea's death, charging her with an attempt at revolution; and he treated in the same way all others who were in any way connected with him by blood or by marriage. Among these was the young Aulus Plautius, whom he forcibly defiled before his death, saying "Let my mother come now and kiss my successor," openly charging that Agrippina had loved Plautius and that this had roused him to hopes of the throne. Rufrius Crispinus, a mere boy, his stepson and the child of Poppaea, he ordered to be drowned by the child's own slaves while he was fishing, but it was said that he used to play at being a general and an emperor. He banished his nurse's son Tuscus, because when procurator in Egypt, he had bathed in some baths which were built for a visit of Nero's. He drove his tutor Seneca to suicide, although when the old man often pleaded to be allowed to retire and offered to give up his estates, he had sworn most solemnly that he did wrong to suspect him and that he would rather die than harm him. He sent poison to Burrus, prefect of the Guard, in place of a throat medicine which he had promised him. The old and wealthy freedmen who had helped him first to his adoption and later to the throne, and aided him by their advice, he killed by poison, administered partly in their food and partly in their drink.

36

Those outside his family he assailed with no less cruelty. It chanced that a comet had begun to appear on several successive nights, a thing which is commonly believed to portend the death of great rulers. Worried by this, and learning from the astrologer Balbillus that kings usually averted such omens by the death of some distinguished man, thus turning them from themselves upon the heads of the nobles, he resolved on the death of all the eminent men of the State; but the more firmly, and with some semblance of justice, after the discovery of two conspiracies. The earlier and more dangerous of these was that of Piso at Rome; the other was set on foot by Vinicius at Beneventum and detected there. The conspirators made their defence in triple sets of fetters, some voluntarily admitting their guilt, some even making a favour of it, saying that there was no way except by death that they could help a man disgraced by every kind of wickedness. The children of those who were condemned were banished or put to death by poison or starvation; a number are known to have been slain all together at a single meal along with their preceptors and attendants, while others were prevented from earning their daily bread.

37

After this he showed neither discrimination nor moderation in putting to death whomsoever he pleased on any pretext whatever. To mention but a few instances, Salvidienus Orfitus was charged with having let to certain states as headquarters three shops which formed part of his house near the Forum; Cassius Longinus, a blind jurist, with retaining in the old family tree of his house the mask of Gaius Cassius, the assassin of Julius Caesar; Paetus Thrasea with having a sullen mien, like that of a preceptor. To those who were bidden to die he never granted more than an hour's respite, and to avoid any delay, he brought physicians who were at once to "attend to" such as lingered; for that was the term he used for killing them by opening their veins. It is even believed that it was his wish to throw living men to be torn to pieces and devoured by a monster of Egyptian birth, who would crunch raw flesh and anything else that was given him. Transported and puffed up by such successes, as he considered them, he boasted that no prince had ever known what power he really had, and he often threw out unmistakable hints that he would not spare even those of the senate who survived, but would one day blot out the whole order from the State and hand over the rule of the provinces and the command of the armies to the Roman knights and to his freedmen. Certain it is that neither on beginning a journey nor on returning did he kiss any member or even return his greeting; and at the formal opening of the work at the Isthmus the prayer which he uttered in a loud voice before a great throng was, that the event might result favourably "for himself and the people of Rome," thus suppressing any mention of the senate.

38

But he showed no greater mercy to the people or the walls of his capital. When someone in a general conversation said:

> "When I am dead, be earth consumed by fire,"

he rejoined "Nay, rather while I live," and his action was wholly in accord. For under cover of displeasure at the ugliness of the old buildings and the narrow, crooked streets, he set fire to the city so openly that several ex-consuls did not venture to lay hands on his chamberlains although they caught them on their estates with tow and fire-brands, while some granaries near the Golden House, whose room he particularly desired, were demolished by engines of war and then set on fire, because their walls were of stone. For six days and seven nights destruction raged, while the people were driven for shelter to monuments and tombs. At that time, besides an immense number of dwellings, the houses of leaders of old were burned, still adorned with trophies of victory, and the temples of the gods vowed and dedicated by the kings and later in the Punic and Gallic wars, and whatever else interesting and noteworthy had survived from antiquity. Viewing the conflagration from the tower of Maecenas and exulting, as he said, in "the beauty of the flames," he sang the whole of the "Sack of Ilium," in his regular stage costume. Furthermore, to gain from this calamity too all the spoil and booty possible, while promising the removal of the debris and dead bodies free of cost he allowed no one to approach the ruins of his own property; and from the contributions which he not only received, but even demanded, he nearly bankrupted the provinces and exhausted the resources of individuals.

39

To all the disasters and abuses thus caused by the prince there were added certain accidents of fortune; a plague which in a single autumn entered thirty thousand deaths in the accounts of Libitina; a disaster in Britain, where two important towns were sacked and great numbers of citizens and allies were butchered; a shameful defeat in the Orient, in consequence of which the legions in Armenia were sent under the yoke and Syria was all but lost. It is surprising and of special note that all this time he bore nothing with more patience than the curses and abuse of the people, and was particularly lenient towards those who assailed him with gibes and lampoons. Of these many were posted or circulated both in Greek and Latin, for example the following:

"Nero, Orestes, Alcmeon their mothers slew."

"A calculation new. Nero his mother slew."

"Who can deny the descent from Aeneas' great line of our Nero?
One his mother took off, the other one took off his sire."

"While our ruler his lyre doth twang and the Parthian his bowstring,
Paean-singer our prince shall be, and Far-darter our foe."

"Rome is becoming one house; off with you to Veii, Quirites!
If that house does not soon seize upon Veii as well."

He made no effort, however, to find the authors; in fact, when some of them were reported to the senate by an informer, he forbade their being very severely punished. 3 As he was passing along a public street, the Cynic Isidorus loudly taunted him, "because he was a good singer of the ills of Nauplius, but made ill use of his own goods." Datus also, an actor of Atellan farces, in a song beginning:

"Farewell to thee, father; farewell to thee, mother,"

represented drinking and swimming in pantomime, referring of course to the death of Claudius and Agrippina; and in the final tag,

"Orcus guides your steps,"

he indicated the senate by a gesture. Nero contented himself with banishing the actor and the philosopher from the city, either because he was impervious to all insults, or to avoid sharpening men's wits by showing his vexation.

40

After the world had put up with such a ruler for nearly fourteen years, it at last cast him off, and the Gauls took the first step under the lead of Julius Vindex, who at that time governed their province as propraetor.

Astrologers had predicted to Nero that he would one day be repudiated, which was the occasion of that well known saying of his: "A humble art affords us daily bread," doubtless uttered to justify him in practising the art of lyre-playing, as an amusement while emperor, but a necessity for a private citizen. Some of them, however, had promised him the rule of the East, when he was cast off, a few expressly naming the sovereignty of Jerusalem, and several the restitution of all his former fortunes. Inclining rather to this last hope, after losing Armenia and Britain and recovering both, he began to think that he had suffered the misfortunes which fate had in store. And after consulting the oracle at Delphi and being told that he must look out for the seventy-third year, assuming that he would die only at that period, and taking no account of Galba's years, he felt so confident not only of old age, but also of unbroken and unusual good fortune, that when he had lost some articles of great value by shipwreck, he did not hesitate to say among his intimate friends that the fish would bring them back to him.

He was at Naples when he learned of the uprising of the Gallic provinces, on the anniversary of his mother's murder, and received the news with such calmness and indifference that he incurred the suspicion of actually rejoicing in it, because it gave him an excuse for pillaging those wealthy provinces according to the laws of war. And he at once proceeded to the gymnasium, where he watched the contests of the athletes with rapt interest. At dinner too when interrupted by a more disturbing letter, he fired up only so far as to threaten vengeance on the rebels. In short for eight whole days making no attempt to write a reply to anyone, nor even to give any commission or command, he blotted out the affair with silence.

41

At last he was driven by numerous insulting edicts of Vindex, to urge the senate in a letter to avenge him and the state, alleging a throat trouble as his excuse for not appearing in person. Yet there was nothing which he so much resented as the taunt that he was a wretched lyre-player and that he was addressed as Ahenobarbus instead of Nero. With regard to his family name, which was cast in his teeth as an insult, he declared that he would resume it and give up that of his adoption. He used no other arguments to show the falsity of the rest of the reproaches than that he was actually taunted with being unskilled in an art to which he had devoted so much attention and in which he had so perfected himself, and he asked various individuals from time to time whether they knew of any artist who was his superior. Finally, beset by message after message, he returned to Rome in a panic; but on the way, when but slightly encouraged by an insignificant omen, for he noticed a monument on which was sculptured the overthrow of a Gallic soldier by a Roman horseman, who was dragging him along by the hair, he leaped for joy at the sight and lifted up his hands to heaven. Not even on his arrival did he personally address the senate or people, but called some of the leading men to his house and after a hasty consultation spent the rest of the day in exhibiting some water-organs of a new and hitherto unknown form, explaining their several features and lecturing on the theory and complexity of each of them; and he even declared that he would presently produce them all in the theatre "with the kind permission of Vindex."

42

Thereafter, having learned that Galba also and the Spanish provinces had revolted, he fainted and lay for a long time insensible, without a word and all but dead. When he came to himself, he rent his robe and beat his brow, declaring that it was all over with him; and when his old nurse tried to comfort him by reminding him that similar evils had befallen other princes before him, he declared that unlike all others he was suffering the unheard of and unparalleled fate of losing the supreme power while he still lived. Nevertheless he did not abandon or amend his slothful and luxurious habits; on the contrary, whenever any good news came from the provinces, he not only gave lavish feasts, but even ridiculed the leaders of the revolt in verses set to wanton music, which have since become public, and accompanied them with gestures; then secretly entering the audience room of the theatre, he sent word to an actor who was making a hit that he was taking advantage of the emperor's busy days.

43

At the very beginning of the revolt it is believed that he formed many plans of monstrous wickedness, but in no way inconsistent with his character: to depose and assassinate the commanders of the armies and the governors of the provinces, on the ground that they were all united in a conspiracy against him; to massacre all the exiles everywhere and all men of Gallic birth in the city: the former, to prevent them from joining the rebels; the latter, as sharing and abetting the designs of their countrymen; to turn over the Gallic provinces to his armies to ravage; to poison the entire senate at banquets; to set fire to the city, first letting the wild beasts loose, that it might be harder for the people to protect themselves. But he was deterred from these designs, not so much by any compunction, as because he despaired of being able to carry them out, and feeling obliged to take the field, he deposed the consuls before the end of their term and assumed the office alone in place of both of them, alleging that it was fated that Gallic provinces could not be subdued except by a consul. Having assumed the fasces, he declared as he was leaving the dining-room after a banquet, leaning on the shoulders of his comrades, that immediately on setting foot in the province he would go before the soldiers unarmed and do nothing but weep; and having thus led the rebels to change their purpose, he would next days rejoice among his rejoicing subjects and sing paeans of victory, which he ought at that very moment to be composing.

44

In preparing for his campaign his first care was to select wagons to carry his theatrical instruments, to have the hair of his concubines, whom he planned to take with him, trimmed man-fashion, and to equip them with Amazonian axes and shields. Next he summoned the city tribes to enlist, and when no eligible person responded, he levied on their masters a stated number of slaves, accepting only the choicest from each household and not even exempting paymasters and secretaries. He also required all classes to contribute a part of their incomes, and all tenants of private houses and apartments to pay a year's rent at once to the privy purse. With great fastidiousness and rigour he demanded newly minted coin, refined silver, and pure gold, so that many openly refused to make any contribution at all, unanimously demanding that he should rather compel the informers to give up whatever rewards had been paid them.

45

The bitter feeling against him was increased because he also turned the high cost of grain to his profit; for indeed, it so fell out that while the people were suffering from hunger it was reported that a ship had arrived from Alexandria, bringing sand for the court wrestlers.

When he had thus aroused the hatred of all, there was no form of insult to which he was not subjected. A curl was placed on the head of his statue with the inscription in Greek: "Now there is a real contest and you must at last surrender." To the neck of another statue a sack was tied and with it the words: "I have done what I could, but you have earned the sack." People wrote on the columns that he had stirred up even the Gauls by his singing. When night came on, many men pretended to be wrangling with their slaves and kept calling out for a defender.

46

In addition he was frightened by manifest portents from dreams, auspices and omens, both old and new. Although he had never before been in the habit of dreaming, after he had killed his mother it seemed to him that he was steering a ship in his sleep and that the helm was wrenched from his hands; that he was dragged by his wife Octavia into thickest darkness, and that he was now covered with a swarm of winged ants, and now was surrounded by the statues of the nations which had been dedicated in Pompey's theatre and stopped in his tracks. A Spanish steed of which he was very fond was changed into the form of an ape in the hinder parts of its body, and its head, which alone remained unaltered, gave forth tuneful neighs. The doors of the Mausoleum flew open of their own accord, and a voice was heard from within summoning him by name. After the Lares had been adorned on the Kalends of January, they fell to the ground in the midst of the preparations for the sacrifice. As he was taking the auspices, Sporus made him a present of a ring with a stone on which was engraved the rape of Proserpina. When the vows were to be taken and a great throng of all classes had assembled, the keys of the Capitol could not be found for a long time. When a speech of his in which he assailed Vindex was being read in the senate, at the words "the wretches will suffer punishment and will shortly meet the end which they deserve," all who were present cried out with one voice: "You will do it, Augustus." It also had not failed of notice that the last piece which he sang in public was "Oedipus in Exile," and that he ended with the line:

> "Wife, father, mother drive me to my death."

47

When meanwhile word came that the other armies had revolted, he tore to pieces the dispatches which were handed to him as he was dining, tipped over the table, and dashed to the ground two favourite drinking cups, which he called "Homeric," because they were carved with scenes from Homer's poems. Then taking some poison from Locusta and putting it into a golden box, he crossed over into the Servilian gardens, where he tried to induce the tribunes and centurions of the Guard to accompany him in his flight, first sending his most trustworthy freedmen to Ostia, to get a fleet ready. But when some gave evasive answers and some openly refused, one even cried:

"Is it so dreadful a thing then to die?"

Whereupon he turned over various plans in his mind, whether to go as a suppliant to the Parthians or Galba, or to appear to the people on the rostra, dressed in black, and beg as pathetically as he could for pardon for his past offences; and if he could not soften their hearts, to entreat them at least to allow him the prefecture of Egypt. Afterwards a speech composed for this purpose was found in his writing desk; but it is thought that he did not dare to deliver it for fear of being torn to pieces before he could reach the Forum.

Having therefore put off further consideration to the following day, he awoke about midnight and finding that the guard of soldiers had left, he sprang from his bed and sent for all his friends. Since no reply came back from anyone, he went himself to their rooms with a few followers. But finding that all the doors were closed and that no one replied to him, he returned to his own chamber, from which now the very caretakers had fled, taking with them even the bed-clothing and the box of poison. Then he at once called for the gladiator Spiculus or any other adept at whose hand he might find death, and when no one appeared, he cried "Have I then neither friend nor foe?" and ran out as if to throw himself into the Tiber.

48

Changing his purpose again, he sought for some retired place, where he could hide and collect his thoughts; and when his freedman Phaon offered his villa in the suburbs between the Via Nomentana and the Via Salaria near the fourth milestone, just as he was, barefooted and in his tunic, he put on a faded cloak, covered his head, and holding a handkerchief before his eyes, mounted a horse with only four attendants, one of whom was Sporus. At once he was startled by a shock of earthquake and a flash of lightning full in his face, and he heard the shouts of the soldiers from the camp hard by, as they prophesied destruction for him and success for Galba. He also heard one of the wayfarers whom he met say: "These men are after Nero," and another ask: "Is there anything new in the city about Nero?" Then his horse took fright at the smell of a corpse which had been thrown out into the road, his face was exposed, and a retired soldier of the Guard recognised him and saluted him. When they came to a by-path leading to the villa, they turned the horses loose and he made his way amid bushes and brambles and along a path through a thicket of reeds to the back wall of the house, with great difficulty and only when a robe was thrown down for him to walk on. Here the aforesaid Phaon urged him to hide for a time in a pit, from which sand had been dug, but he declared that he would not go under ground while still alive, and after waiting for a while until a secret entrance into the villa could be made, he scooped up in his hand some water to drink from a pool close by, saying: "This is Nero's distilled water." Then, as his cloak had been torn by the thorns, he pulled out the twigs which had pierced it, and crawling on all fours through a narrow passage that had been dug, he entered the villa and lay down in the first room he came to, on a couch with a common mattress, over which an old cloak had been thrown. Though suffering from hunger and renewed thirst, he refused some coarse bread which was offered him, but drank a little lukewarm water.

49

At last, while his companions one and all urged him to save himself as soon as possible from the indignities that threatened him, he bade them dig a grave in his presence, proportioned to the size of his own person, and at the same time bring water and wood for presently disposing of his body. As each of these things was done, he wept and said again and again: "What an artist the world is losing!"

While he hesitated, a letter was brought to Phaon by one of his couriers. Nero snatching it from his hand read that he had been pronounced a public enemy by the senate, and that they were seeking him to punish in the ancient fashion; and he asked what manner of punishment that was. When he learned that the criminal was stripped, fastened by the neck in a fork and then beaten to death with rods, in mortal terror he seized two daggers which he had brought with him, and then, after trying the point of each, put them up again, pleading that the fatal hour had not yet come. Now he would beg Sporus to begin to lament and wail, and now entreat someone to help him take his life by setting him the example; anon he reproached himself for his cowardice in such words as these: "To live is a scandal and a shame—this does not become Nero, does not become him—one should be resolute at such times—come, rouse thyself!" And now the horsemen were at hand who had orders to take him off alive. When he heard them, he quavered:

"Hark, now strikes on my ear the trampling of swift-footed coursers!"

and drove a dagger into his throat, aided by Epaphroditus, his private secretary. He was all but dead when a centurion rushed in, and as he placed a cloak to the wound, pretending that he had come to aid him, Nero merely gasped: "Too late!" and "This is fidelity!" With these words he was gone, with eyes so set and starting from their sockets that all who saw him shuddered with horror. First and beyond all else he had forced from his companions a promise to let no one have his head, but to contrive in some way that he be buried unmutilated. And this was granted by Icelus, Galba's freedman, who had shortly before been released from the bondage to which he was consigned at the beginning of the revolt.

50

He was buried at a cost of two hundred thousand sesterces and laid out in white robes embroidered with gold, which he had worn on the Kalends of January. His ashes were deposited by his nurses, Egloge and Alexandria, accompanied by his mistress Acte, in the family tomb of the Domitii on the summit of the Hill of Gardens, which is visible from the Campus Martius. In that monument his sarcophagus of porphyry, with an altar of Luna marble standing above it, is enclosed by a balustrade of Thasian stone.

51

He was about the average height, his body marked with spots and malodorous, his hair light blond, his features regular rather than attractive, his eyes blue and somewhat weak, his neck over thick, his belly prominent, and his legs very slender. His health was good, for though indulging in every kind of riotous excess, he was ill but three times in all during the fourteen years of his reign, and even then not enough to give up wine or any of his usual habits. He was utterly shameless in the care of his person and in his dress, always having his hair arranged in tiers of curls, and during the trip to Greece also letting it grow long and hang down behind; and he often appeared in public in a dining-robe, with a handkerchief bound about his neck, ungirt and unshod.

52

When a boy he took up almost all the liberal arts; but his mother turned him from philosophy, warning him that it was a drawback to one who was going to rule, while Seneca kept him from reading the early orators, to make his admiration for his teacher endure the longer. Turning therefore to poetry, he wrote verses with eagerness and without labour, and did not, as some think, publish the work of others as his own. I have had in my possession note-books and papers with some well-known verses of his, written with his own hand and in such wise that it was perfectly evident that they were not copied or taken down from dictation, but worked out exactly as one writes when thinking and creating; so many instances were there of words erased or struck through and written above the lines. He likewise had no slight interest in painting and sculpture.

53

But above all he was carried away by a craze for popularity and he was jealous of all who in any way stirred the feeling of the mob. It was the general belief that after his victories on the stage he would at the next lustrum have competed with the athletes at Olympia; for he practised wrestling constantly, and all over Greece he had always viewed the gymnastic contests after the fashion of the judges, sitting on the ground in the stadium; and if any pairs of contestants withdrew too far from their positions, he would force them forward with his own hand. Since he was acclaimed as the equal of Apollo in music and of the Sun in driving a chariot, he had planned to emulate the exploits of Hercules as well; and they say that a lion had been specially trained for him to kill naked in the arena of the amphitheatre before all the people, with a club or by the clasp of his arms.

54

Towards the end of his life, in fact, he had publicly vowed that if he retained his power, he would at the games in celebration of his victory give a performance on the water-organ, the flute, and the bagpipes, and that on the last day he would appear as an actor and dance "Vergil's Turnus." Some even assert that he put the actor Paris to death as a dangerous rival.

55

He had a longing for immortality and undying fame, though it was ill-regulated. With this in view he took their former appellations from many things and numerous places and gave them new ones from his own name. He also called the month of April Neroneus and was minded to name Rome Neropolis.

56

He utterly despised all cults, with the sole exception of that of the Syrian God, and even acquired such a contempt for her that he made water on her image, after he was enamoured of another superstition, which was the only one to which he constantly clung. For he had received as a gift from some unknown man of the commons, as a protection against plots, a little image of a girl; and since a conspiracy at once came to light, he continued to venerate it as a powerful divinity and to offer three sacrifices to it every day, encouraging the belief that through its communication he had knowledge of the future. A few months before his death he did attend an inspection of victims, but could not get a favourable omen.

57

He met his death in the thirty-second year of his age, on the anniversary of the murder of Octavia, and such was the public rejoicing that the people put on liberty-caps and ran about all over the city. Yet there were some who for a long time decorated his tomb with spring and summer flowers, and now produced his statues on the rostra in the fringed toga, and now his edicts, as if he were still alive and would shortly return and deal destruction to his enemies. Nay more, Vologaesus, king of the Parthians, when he sent envoys to the senate to renew his alliance, earnestly begged this too, that honour be paid to the memory of Nero. In fact, twenty years later, when I was a young man, a person of obscure origin appeared, who gave out that he was Nero, and the name was still in such favour with the Parthians that they supported him vigorously and surrendered him with great reluctance.

Catullus: Selections

Translated by Frederic Raphael and Kenneth McLeish

I

Who's to be offered my brand-new slim volume
Slickly polished with dry-as-dust pumice-stone?
Cornelius, it's yours! After all, you always said
My little pieces had 'a modicum of merit'.
That to one side, you alone of Italy's sons has dared
To epitomise mankind in three installments—
What style! What wit! What a performance!
Now take this offering of mine, for what it's worth,
And may my virgin mistress
Make it last, if only an aeon or two.

2

Well, little sparrow, who's my darling's darling, then?
Does she like to play with it and hold it in her lap?
Does she? Does she get it to stretch its beak
To tip her fingertip—provoke the little pecker's peck?
My shining love, my own glittering passion—
Does she sometimes have a little game? Does she?
I'm told she does. I'm told she has no time
For serious feelings, lets them all go hang.
And a sparrow helps a bit. Tell me little sparrow,
When can I play with you as she does
And have you unload my heart? Tell me—
I'll look as sharp as that sharp girl (they say)
When a little golden apple came along
And undid her, undid her belt, her girdle,
And pushed her over, at last, into love's free zone.

3

Come, join the mourners; come, Gods of Love,
Gods of desire; come, whoever loves Venus first
And join the dirge. Death has struck my love.
Her sparrow's dead. My darling's darling,
Dead, who knew his mistress better than a girl
Her mother. He was never out of her lap,
Jumping here, jumping there, jumping back again!
As soon as he saw her, up he piped and piped
For no one else. Now it's over forever.
Down that dark tunnel he's gone, from where, they
say,
Once vanished, you never rise again.
The hell with you, you shades of Hell.
You get us all down in the end,
Even the most beautiful. Beautiful sparrows
You won't even spare us; It's cruel.
It's murder; that poor little bird!
In passing, sparrow, do you know
That you went and made Lesbia cry?
Her eyes are red-rimmed and puffy.
You've actually made them look *small*.

4

That far-sailing craft you see, my friends,
Silly at anchor was once, if you believe it,
The slickest thing afloat. Aye, it insists:
No log in all the world can claim
It was ever overtaken: oar or canvas
Makes no odds. She goes further
Dares the pouting Adriatic say otherwise,
Or the Cyclades, island by island;

Rhodes—*noblesse oblige*—will bear her out,
And the bristling Propontis (Thracian branch);
Even surly Pontus ought to own it's true.
After all, she hails from there:
What became a streamlined clipper
Used to bear a full head of leaves

On a high Cytorean ridge.
Where do you think she learned
To hiss at the passing wind?

Amastris on the Pontus—Cytorus, boxed with trees—
Come back: you're called as referees.
She says you know her, intimately too—
In fact, she claims descent from the highest
In the land, this crafty character,
And swears she dipped virgin oars
Into your very waters.

The rest was easy: she bore her owner
Through seas never high enough
To touch him, forget how the wind was blowing—
From the left, the right, even (by Jove!) in the centre.
Never an S.O.S. to the Gods on shore,
Not from the day she first wet her keel
Till she limped to a last anchorage,
In the lake, right here. Or that's her story.
Now she's a quiet old lady,
With only the sky to sail,
And she gives way at last to you, twin Castor—
And equally to Castor's twin.

5

We can live, my Lesbia, and love.
What do you mean, people are talking?
Asinine rumours, old husbands' tales;
You could mount their wits on a farthing.
The sun rises (they tell us); the sun sets,
Rises and sets again. But not for you and me:
For us it happens once. Our day dies;
Night comes, and in that night we sleep
Forever. So, for ever, kiss me now.
A thousand, so … a hundred, good …
Another thousand, and a hundred more …
Another thousand … hundred … thousand …
We *must* do it over and over—

It's obvious—surely you see?
If even we lose track of the figures,
No one can tax us for loving at all.

6

Flavius, this little dish of yours—
Out with it, tell me the truth:
When am I going to meet her?
She's on the plain side of dumb,
Am I right? If I'm wrong,
What's keeping you so quiet?
All right, she's a hot-cunted whore, then—
She must be, I tell you, or else
You'd have let it out by now.
You're not spending your nights alone,
Now are you?
There's too much noise in your room
(And a strong smell of Syrian musk).

Just take a look at your bolster:
It's shagged out, even if you aren't,
Your bed's got the shakes as well—
Presumably overwork.
So you might as well spill it now:
Give us your side of the story.
Why! You're clapped out, that's why—
Or have you some other limp excuse?
What's she like, man? Come on!
What? What business of mine? Poetic, of course:
I'm poised to sing praises of passion
That can ride up to heaven on high.
Or I could just send you up instead.

7

Your questions, Lesbia, are these:
(a) How many kisses to sate
(b) How many to surfeit my passion?

Answer: go to Cyrene
And count the grains of Libya's sand
Yes, the whole lasarpiciferous[1] desert.
Begin where Jupiter breathes hot tips
For his .oracle's Ammonian branch
And count on going to old Battus' tomb
(He founded the place, you'll recall).

Or: go number the numberless stars
That look down in the wordless night
On men that are out to steal kisses.
To kiss you as often as that
Would suffice any normal madman
And possibly one called Catullus.

As many as not the peepingest Tom
Could keep up with—a number too fat
To get any envious tongue around.

8

Catullus, Catullus, Catullus,
You're being a fool. So stop.
What's dead is dead. Now face it.
Once the sun shone full upon you, once.
Her wish was your desire. We know.
Wish? Desire? I loved her
As no woman will ever be loved.
If she was happy, you were happy—
What you wanted, she came to want it too.
We know. The sun shone full upon you.
Now she wants no more to do with you
And there's nothing more you can do.
Why run after what's already run out?
Or live with your face in your hands?
Put her out of your mind. Don't weaken. Forget.
I tell you, tell her *Goodbye,* That's it.
Catullus seen doing the obvious thing.
Mouth shut; ears shut. Finished. All right?

---

1   It means: bearing an alliaceous fruit.

Oh but oh she'll be sorry
When no one comes wanting her love.
Bitch, bitch, for the rest of your life
Who's going to bother, quite frankly,
To tell you how lovely you are?

Whom will you love? Who'll have you then?
And then what about kisses?
Whose lips will you bite in the end?
Catullus, Catullus, remember: forget.

9

Veranius, I'm not short of friends:
I've got exactly three hundred thousand;
It just so happens you're number one.
Is it true you're back home again
With your old mother and those brothers
Who love you one hundred per cent?
It's true? You're safe? That's great.
And when do I get to see you,
And to hear all your usual nonsense—
Who's who and what's what in Spain?
I'm coming over, yes, right now,
To fall on your neck like a lover
And kiss you hullo on the mouth, on the eyes.
I mean it; I couldn't be happier;
I'm the happiest man in the world.

10

Friend Varus nabs me down in the Forum
(Where I'm busily hanging about):
I must come and meet her, he says.
Meet who? His latest tart, of course-
It didn't take long to see that.
Not bad either: nice taste, nice tits:
So far so good. But then we talk.
We talk about this, we talk about that.
Bithynia comes up. How did I do there?
What was it like? How were the pickings?

'Not a soul made a penny I heard of,
Not in the heavy or the light brigade.
No palms were greased, no heads patted—
How could they be, with H.E. on top?'
(That bugger was always on top.)
'Rubbish!' they said. 'Bithynian
Bearers—surely you picked up a set
Of those?' Well, what could I say?
I had to give her the works.
'All right, so I did have some luck—
I'm not quite as green as I look.
Eight of them came back with me—eight
Upstanding lads with good hard backs'
That was my story. But you know me,
I haven't one, not even to carry
A chairleg across the room, or back.
It took her in, of course
(I said she was easily had).
'O Catullus, do be a love,
Let me give them a canter—say
Up to the East End and back?'
What can you do with girls like that?
'Hold it,' I said, 'Let me finish.
They're Cinna's, not mine—and you know Gaius,
His, mine, what's the difference?
I use them as if they were mine.
Must you be so literal minded?
You made me stick my neck right out,
And now I've tripped over my tongue.'

11

Aurelius and Furius, dear friends,
Let's take a trip together—all the way
To India, perhaps, where all land ends
    In fretting, foaming sea;
To far Hyrcania, Arabia gay;
To arrow-darting Parthia; to see
The Sagans, or that wide Egyptian bay
    The seven-mouthed Nile stains brown;
We'll struggle up the Alps (you follow me?)

And on the topmost tips stand looking down
On mighty Caesar's monuments; we'll free-
      wheel down the Rhine, and then
We'll cross the bristling sea to Britain—town
By ghastly town, my friends, like gallant men
Well sample every one. But first, don't frown
      When asked to see that bitch
I used to love; go seek her out again
And tell her this from me: that itch
Of hers, good luck to it! Good scratching, when
      She mounts three hundred pricks
At once, and fills that ever-gaping niche
That once was mine, and cracks their balls for kicks.

I drooped and fell for her, like an evening flower
Cut by a heedless plough, dead in an hour.

12

Asinius Marrucinus! Yes, you:
I saw what your left hand was doing.
When everyone's laughing and drinking,
You whip your hosts' napkins for fun.
I presume it's supposed to be funny;
In fact it's just crummy and cheap.
Exaggerating am I? Ask Pollio.
He'd give a fortune to have you change.
Since your brother has charm and wit,
He doesn't stoop to stealing his laughs.
Look, do you want another instalment,
300 memory-jogging lines? No?
Then send back my napkin, express.
It's nothing to do with the money:
It reminds me of absent friends,
Being part of some Spanish linen
Fabullus and Veranius sent.
And as they are people I do love,
I feel keenly about that napkin as well.

13

You're going to eat like a king, Fabullus,
At my house in a couple of days—
Assuming the Gods send you well,
And assuming you bring the supplies.
(Quality and quantify, please):
First, a delicious girl—
And wine and wit and a fresh catch of laughs.
Pick them up on your way, lover boy
And you'll not go short of a feast.
Am I out of funds, did you ask?
My dear chap, my wallet is bulging:
Bulging with cobwebs.
Will you accept a draught of love?
Or—no pro quo could be quidder than this—
A dab of my mistress's secret scent
(Exclusive, from Venus, Cupid and co.).
One sniff and you're down on your knees,
Praying to the Gods, Fabullus,
To make all your faculties nose.

14 A

Calvus, you charming young bastard,
I'm, in receipt of your gift.
If didn't love you more than my eyes,
I'd hate you for it, my dear:
Same hatred you keep for Vatlnius.
What did I do, what can I have said
To merit such measures against me?
The Gods should punish the toady
Who sent you such ungodly junk.
But If—and I have my suspicions –
They came from a well-known source –
Sulla, anthologist, pundit and critic,
All right, I'll do my good deed for the day,
If It saves you wasting your time.
Gods, what unspeakable rubbish!
A token of friendship, you say?
I've wasted my whole Saturnalia,
My favourite day of the year.

No, smarty, you shan't get away with it:
I'll be up as soon as it's light
And down to the second-hand stalls.
Any Caeslus? Any Aquinus? Suffenus?
I'll make up a poisonous package
And pay you back for your pains.
As for you lot, be off, false quantities all,
Limp home on your wretched club-feet.
'Signs of the critical times!'
Bloody awful poets, that's what.

14 B (I)

Readers, do you plan to be readers of mine?
If my little efforts amuse you,
Might I suggest? Don't ever flinch
From applause.

14 B (II)

So readers, you think you'll get a rise
From what I have to offer? Fine:
Stretch out your hands, take hold …

15

Myself and the one I love, Aurelius,
I put under your protection.
So grant me this modest favour:
If ever you have wanted
To keep just one thing chaste
(Or even roughly pollution-free),
Keep this young man so for me.
I don't mean just from the plebs—
They don't bother me much,
A virgin's safe in the rush-hour:
No room to mix business with pleasure.
Quite frankly, it's you that I fear:
You prick, you've a hard reputation—
You've got it in for all the boys.
As far as I'm concerned, keep it up,

Wherever, whoever you like,
As long as it's not around here.
Look, one simple exception:
In my view, it isn't a lot.
So: if you get any nasty ideas,
You sod, and dare to get cracking
(Tempting that soft head into your noose),
I give you a solemn warning:
You'll wish you'd had a different end.
I'll lash you up with the door open
And stuff your back passage with fish
(Mullet garnished with radishes),
Prescribed suppository.

16

Bugger you and likewise sucks,
Aurelius who stoops and Furius who stabs.
So you deduce from my little verses—
Which I concede to be pretty indecent'—
That I am pretty and indecent too?
A true poet must be pure and devoted;
His work is another thing.
It gives a poem wit and attack
To be a little bit juicy
And not invariably nice.
I like a line that gives one a lift.
Youth hardly needs such a service,
But why not a leavening prod
For hairy old sods with ponderous cocks
Who don't find it easy to rise?
So you've read of my thousands of kisses
(Bestowed on a girl, as you know),
And now you call me less than a man?
Well, bugger you, as I hinted above,
And when that's over, sucks.

17

Wanted by the town of Colonia:
A reliable span for a great, long bridge.

The old worlde one is arthritic,
Rickety, lurching on second-hand crutches:
Who's going dancing on *that!*
'We don't want our fete's name to be mud!'
Right: build whatever bridge you fancy—
Go to whatever lengths you need—
Test it with jackboots, morris-men, can-cans.
But prior to building permission'
Give me the nod for one final laugh.
There's one particular Colonial
I'd love to see in it, right up to his neck,
Right there where the stuff is thickest
And has a characteristic nose.
They don't come much thicker than chummy:
He hasn't the brains of a baby
Nodding on Dadda's arm. He's married
A very young girl, green as a bud
At its greenest, frisky as a kid
(But you know how goats can develop).
Kid-glove treatment is just what she needs,
Handling you'd give a quality grape.
He lets her do as she likes, and guess
What she likes to do! He must have piles:
He never gets off his arse.
He might as well be a log, sawn off
At the root in some Ligurian ditch.
He knows as much about what she's at
As if he'd never had her. Sans eyes,
Sans ears, doesn't know if he's coming
Or going, or even if he can.
That's my candidate to go flying.
I thought the shock of walking the plank
Might do wonders for stick-in-the-muds.
I'm hoping he'll shed his narcosis:
Cf. mules shedding shoes in a bog.

21

Aurelius, you king of eaters out,
Today, yesterday, tomorrow too,
The one I love, you fancy. There's no doubt:
You don't exactly hide it, do you?
You're both one big laugh, and in public.
(So *that's* what's meant by sticking to it!)
You greedy sod, you don't miss a trick.
But all in vain, if you did but know it.
So you've scored first, you've got a head start—
Well, I shall come from behind, my dear.
If you'd acted from fullness of heart,
I'd be silent. As it is, I fear
Your appetites in meat and drink
Infect my lover. Here appended
My advice: stop sensibly and think,
Or be literally upended.

22

Your old friend Suffenus is at it again,
Varus. Agreed, he's nobody's fool,
Has charm, talks well, knows his way around,
And writes by far the longest verses in the world,
Ten thousand lines—revised, what's more—
Unless I counted wrong. Unabridged texts:
He's not heard of the paper shortage.
Crown octavo, quality parchment;
Stiff endpapers, flashy bindings,
Tailor-made linen jackets, the lot
Hand-ruled and polished to perfection.
Then comes the reading. And *then* where's
The charm, the sophistication?
He bleats; he hacks. You'd reckon his line
Was milking goats or digging ditches.
Talk about bad! What a change was there!
I mean, can you explain why smartyboots—
Or whatever is smarter than that—
Becomes rustier than a rustic
The moment he fingers a dactyl?
Yet he's never so happy as then:

He's in heaven: Narcissus the poet!
Oh, I daresay we're all much the same.
Who isn't some kind of Suffenus
Somewhere along the line? Everyone's
Blind to what's there, on his own spine.

23

From Furius: 'I haven't a penny,
Not a servant to my name, nothing'
Well, you haven't got fleas either.
'Not a spider, not a spark in the grate'
Then be grateful: you live with Daddy;
And dear old Daddy's second wife.
You sit and split rocks with your teeth.
What with your pater and his lady
(Your step-mother's the original
Chip off the old block) you've got it
Made: the cushiest *ménage-à-trois*.
If you're skint, what can be the problem?
No call for the fire brigade,
No wear and tear, no burglars
After the family portraits, no danger
From poisonous heirs: you're covered
By nature's All Risks Policy!
Your bodies (God knows) are dry as bones;
And if you want a dustier image,
What is there drier than dry?
The sun? Ten degrees of frost?
Or might I venture—deliberate greed?
Oh do go and count your blessings:
No sweat; nose never blocked;
No saliva; no sinusitis.
In fact, your refinement's finer still:
Salt would run smooth from your arse-hole.
You don't crap ten times in a year;
And when you do, it's baked beans
And issues in pebble form.
Rub it between the fingers
And they come up smelling of roses.
You've got the perfect set-up,

And you need 'ten thousand, cash'?
My dear, don't push your luck.

24

Flosculus I call you, little flower, floweret,
(Later: the part of the fruit where the blossom was).
Pride and ornament of the Juventii,
Of this and past and future generations;
I'd sooner you gave him the touch that Midas had
Than let him touch you, the one I'm thinking of.
He's never a servant, nowhere *(area)* to put his
  treasure.
Don't let him be your lover, will you, ever?
'Why? Isn't he a handsome fellow?' Yes indeed.
A handsome fellow with never a servant and nowhere
To put his treasure *(arca)*. Yes indeed.
If that's your pleasure, chuck me over
And hoist him up. Give him a servant
And somewhere to put his treasure.

25

Thallus, you very bad fairy,
Softer than a rabbit's furry,
Softer than *pâté de foie gras,*
Softer than an ear-lobe you are;
Boneless as a spider's skein is
Or an old man's mingy penis;
Thallus, you're a grabbing whirlwind
When Sloth, your Goddess, has a mind
To lull the witnesses to sleep
And lets you play the thief, you drip.
Send back that cloak you filched of mine
And my, Saetaban napkins from Spain,
And my Bithynian primitives
(You claim those wogs as *relatives!*).
42Give, sticky fingers; send 'em back—
Or do limp wrist and downy flank
Fancy the scoring of the lash?
(Yes, nether cheeks can also blush.)

You'll leap about like a baby boat
Caught out at sea by a wind distraught.

26 (I)

The South Wind never lashes it,
The North Wind never bashes it,
Nor dust from East, nor rain from West:
Furius has a cosy nest.
Meets no draught, safe from every quarter—
Save every quarter when he ought to
Cover his banker's draft again.
Furius gets the wind up then.

26 (II)

The South Wind never lashes it,
The North Wind never bashes it,
Nor dust from East, nor rain from West:
Furius, mine's a cosy nest.
Meets no draught, safe from every quarter—
Save every quarter when I ought to
Cover my banker's draft again.
I really get the wind up then.

27

Waiter, you with the keys
To the little old Falernian!
Bring in a case of the hard stuff,
As Postumia's law lays down,
(She's judiciously more juiced
Than the very juiciest grape.)
All mineral waters—out!
You only blight the wine.
Go piss on the Catos' doorsteps.
This here (hic) is Domaine de Bacchus.
I propose to drink it neat

28

Well well, so now you're Piso's men?
You flabby pair: you always travel light.
There's no snugger-fitting, no emptier bag
Than yours, Veranius dear, or yours,
Fabullus. How goes every little thing?
Hungry business, soldiering, is it?
Chilblains making you complain?
What? Piso's a pisser, you say?
So: write your memoirs and flog 'em,
Like I did with my C. O.
Baby, I was screwed into the ground
By Memmius, and took it lying down.
I felt every inch of that yard of his:
He took his pleasures slowly, that one.
And now *you're* getting shafted
By a prick of much the same bore.
Well, you asked for it: you wanted classy friends!
Every possible bad luck to you both,
You spotted dicks, end of the Roman line.

29

Who can stand and look at it?
Who car; look and stand it?
A rooting pig, I suppose,
And a dicey one at that.
Unspoiled Gaul despoiled,
Distant Britain poached!
Rome, you're fucked, but can you stand it?
Look: he's always on the rise;
He's coming up—first storey high.
Or do you fancy him cock-of-the-walk?
Are you ready to call him Adonis?
O Romulus, even in drag
Can you really fancy that?
A rooting pig, I call him,
And a dicey one at that.

Was it for this, O generalissimo,
That you marched

To the westest isle of them all?
Was it your strategic plan
That .a clapped-out prick like this
Should piss away your millions?
An unusual use of funds!
Hasn't he got through enough
One way and another?
Have you ever watched him at table?
First course: his old man's goodies.
Second: the meat of the Pontic wars.
Third: fresh from the Spanish campaign,
The golden fruits of the Tagus.
No wonder Britain and Gaul
Are shaking like table jellies.

Why in hell do you stand it?
He'd never have downed it all
Without help. You two
Supplied the softening sauce,
Caesar and Pompey, well-known double-act.
Was Mamurra's the name on your scutcheons
When you pulled the plug on the world?

30

What *can* you remember, Alfenus,
When you forget your own best friends?
One must be realistic, you say,
You've got no time for regrets,
I was 'the sweetest thing in your life',
But you're letting me go regardless;
You haven't a qualm, you say.
Liars don't get away with lying:
The Gods come down heavily on it.
Had you forgotten that, in your haste
To be shot of my miserable moaning'?
Tell me, what ought one to do next?
Where can I put my trust?
You weren't short of words, I must say,
When you wanted me next to your heart'!
Everything was going to be fine.

Weren't those roughly your words?
Bastard. Now you take it all back.
What you said, what you did: all kaput.
Gone with the wind. I'm given the air.
My dear, *you* may have forgotten;
But the gods still remember,
And honour remembers too.
You'll be damned sorry one day
For what you did, and what you do.

31

Of every place that's ail-but Island, Sirmio,
Of all islands too, the peach,
As many as Neptune-bitter/Neptune-sweet
Holds out on brimming lake or flowing sea,
How I've lusted for you—and how! Glad to see you?
A pause: for believing my eyes.
Goodbye to jolly old 'thynia
And those B- thynian marches. Me. You. Here. Safe.
Oh what's more heaven than this,
To be done with doing one's duty?
Wit sheds its uniform: we're through
With diplomatic bags, and home, my God, we're home.
Oh my lucky stars, to nod off in a bed that fits: beat
    that!
Down payment for services rendered.
How goes it with you, my pretty little Sirmio?
Where's a smile for a smiling master?
And what can you do, lake of Lydian wave
(My Etruscan compliments to you?)
Cackle out loud, as much as you like:
Waves of laughter for lovers caught in the act.
Catullus and Sirmio at it. He he he he he.

32

Intention: love.
My dear sweet Ipsitilla,
My pet, you're the very girl:
Have me report to you this pip emma.

If the answer's Roger, be sure
(a) No one bolts your door before I do
(b) You don't get an itch to go roaming.

I want you indoors,
With nine complete plans of campaign.
The exercise? Fucking by numbers.
So: if you're on, send a runner,
I've had my hot meal and I'm in the picture:
Lying here stiff at attention
Bashing holes in my Number One Dress.

33

Bracketed top of the league,
Changing-room thieves' division,
Vibennius father and sod of a son
(The old man's a right shit,
The boy's arse-hole pinches things too),
Why not take a one-way ticket
To some far from salubrious shore?
It is, as of now, time to scarper:
Dad, you're facing serious charges—
Everybody in town knows that—
And as for you, sonny boy,
The market's fallen out of your bottom.

34

To Diana are we pledged,
We boys and girls unfledged;
May she our song inspire,
Pure boys and girls in choir.

Leto's great child we love,
Daughter of greatest Jove;
Propped 'gainst an olive tree,
In Delos she bore thee,

To be of hills the queen
And woodlands turning green;

In magic groves you hide
And booming rivers ride.

Mothers call you midwife:
'Juno, from pain bring life!'
Trivia, warlock, your names,
And moon with sun-filched flames.

Goddess, your monthly course
Gives years their driving force:
The farmer's crude abode
With healthy fruits you load.

Be called whatever you please,
We pray you without cease
To keep a smiling face
For Romulus' good race.

The Art of Love (Book 1)

By Ovid
Translated by J. H. Mozley

I f anyone among this people knows not the art of loving, let him read my poem, and having read be skilled in love. By skill swift ships are sailed and rowed, by skill nimble chariots are driven: by skill most Love be guided. Well fitted for chariots and pliant reins was Automedon, and Tiphys was the helmsman of the Haemonian ship: me hath Venus set over tender Love as master in the art; I shall be called the Tiphys and Automedon of Love. Wild indeed is he, and apt often to fight against me; but he is a boy, tender his age and easily controlled. The son of Philyra made the boy Achilles accomplished on the lyre, and by his peaceful art subdued those savage passions. He who terrified his friends so often and so often his foes, cowered, we are told, before an aged man. Those hands that Hector was to feel, he held out to the lash obediently, when his master bade, Chiron taught Aeacides, I am Love's teacher: a fierce lad each, and each born of a goddess. Yet even the bull's neck is burdened by the plough, and the high-mettled steed champs the bridle with his teeth; and to me Love shall yield, though he wound my breast with his bow, and whirl aloft his brandished torch. The more violently Love has pierced and branded me, the better shall I avenge the wound that he has made: I will not falsely claim that my art is thy gift, O Phoebus, nor am I prompted by the voice of a bird of the air, neither did Clio and Clio's sisters appear to me while I kept flocks in thy vale, O Ascra: experience inspires this work: give ear to an experienced bard ; true will be my song: favour my enterprise, O mother of Love. Keep far away, ye slender fillets, emblems of modesty, and the long skirt that hides the feet in its folds. Of safe love-making do I sing, and permitted secrecy, and in my verse shall be no wrong-doing.

First, strive to find an object for your love, you who now for the first time come to fight in warfare new. The next task is, to win the girl that takes your fancy; the third, to make love long endure. This is my limit, this the field whose bound my chariot shall mark, this the goal my flying wheel shall graze.

While yet you are at liberty and can go at large with loosened rein, choose to whom you will say, "You alone please me." She will not come floating down to you through the tenuous air, she must be sought, the girl whom your glance approves. Well knows the hunter where to spread his nets for the stag, well knows he in what glen the boar

Ovid, "Book One" of *The Art of Love*. Translation by J. H. Mozley, *Ovid in Six Volumes II: The Art of Love, and Other Poems*, pp. 13–65. Copyright © 1979 Harvard University Press. Permission to reprint granted by the publisher.

with gnashing teeth abides; familiar are the copses to fowlers, and he who holds the hook is aware in what waters many fish are swimming; you too, who seek the object of a lasting passion, learn first what places the maidens haunt I will not bid you in your search set sails before the wind, nor, that you may find, need a long road be travelled. Though Perseus brought Andromeda from the dusky Indians though the Phrygian lover carried off a Grecian girl, yet Rome will give you so many maidens and so fair that, "Here" you will say, "is all the beauty of the world." As numerous as the crops upon Gargara, as the grape-bunches of Methymna, as the fishes that lurk within the sea, or the birds among the leaves, as many as are the stars of heaven, so many maidens doth thine own Rome contain : the mother of Aeneas has settled in the city of her son. Are you attracted by early and still ripening years? a real maid will come before your eyes. Would you have a full-grown beauty? a thousand such will please you, and you will be at a loss which one to desire. Or do you perchance prefer a later and staider age? still more numerous, believe me, will be their array.

Only walk leisurely beneath the Pompeian shade, when the sun draws nigh to Hercules' shaggy lion, or where the mother has added her own gifts to her son's, a work rich with marble coating. Nor should you avoid the Livian colonnade which, scattered o'er with ancient paintings keeps its founder's name, or where the daughters of Belus dare to plot death for their wretched cousins, and their fierce sire stands with drawn sword. Nor let Adonis bewailed of Venus escape you, nor the seventh day that the Syrian Jew holds sacred. Avoid not the Memphian shrine of the linen-clothed heifer: many a maid does she make what she was herself to Jove. Even the law-courts (who could believe it?) are suitable to love, often has its flame been found in the shrill-tongued court: where set beneath the marble shrine of Venus, the Appian nymph strikes the air with her upspringing waters, there often is the lawyer surprised by Love, and he who was careful for others is not careful for himself: often there does the glib speaker fail for words: a new case comes on and his own cause must be pleaded. Venus laughs at him from her neighbouring shrine: he who was of late an advocate would fain be a client now,

But specially do your hunting in the round theatres: more bountifully do these repay your vows. There will you find an object for passion or for deception, something to taste but once, or to keep, if so you wish. As crowded ants pass and repass in a long train, bearing in grain-burdened mouth their wonted food, or as bees, having gained their dells and fragrant pastures; flit o'er the blossoms and hover o'er the thyme: so hasten the smartest women to the crowded games; many a time have their numbers made my judgment falter. They come to see, they come that they may be seen: to chastity that place is fatal. Thou first, Romulus, didst disturb the games, when the rape of Sabine women consoled the wifeless men. No awnings then hung o'er a marble theatre, nor was the platform ruddy with crocus-spray; there, artlessly arranged, were garlands which the leafy Palatine had borne; the stage was unadorned; the people sat on steps of turf, any chance leaves covering their unkempt hair. They look about them, and each notes with his glance the woman he desires, and they brood much in their secret hearts. And while to the Tuscan flute-player's rude strains the dancer struck thrice with his foot the levelled floor, in the midst of the applause (the applause then was rough and rude) the king gave to the people the expected sign of rape. Straightway they leap forth, by their shouts betraying their eagerness, and lay lustful hand upon the maidens. As doves, most timorous of birds, flee from the eagles, as the weanling lamb from the hated wolf, so feared they the men rushing wildly on them in none remained her former colour. For their fear was one, but not one was the appearance of their fear: some tear their hair, some sit crazed; one is silent in dismay, one calls in vain upon her mother; this one bewails, that one is struck dumb; this one remains, that one flees. The captured women are led off, spoil for the marriage-couch, and to many their very fear had power to lend grace. If any struggled overmuch and resisted her mate, upborne on his eager breast he carried her off himself, saying: "Why do you spoil those tender eyes with tears? What your sire was to your mother that will I be to you" Ah, Romulus, thou only didst know how to bestow bounty on thy warriors; so thou but bestow such bounty upon me, I will be a warrior. And, mark you, by hallowed custom from that time our theatres even now are fraught with danger to the fair.

Nor let the contest of noble steeds escape you; the spacious Circes holds many opportunities. No need is there of fingers for secret speech nor need you receive a signal by means of nods. Sit next to your lady, none will prevent you; sit side by side as close as you can; and it is good that the rows compel closeness, like it or not, and that by the conditions of space your girl must be touched. Here seek an opening for friendly talk, and begin with words that all may hear. Mind you are zealous in asking whose horses are entering, and quick! whomsoever she favours be sure to favour too. But when the long procession of ivory statues of the gods passes by applaud Queen Venus with favouring hand. And if perchance, as will happen, a speck of dust falls on your lady's lap, flick it off with your fingers; even if none fall, then flick off—none; let any pretext serve to show your attentiveness. If her cloak hangs low and trails upon the ground, gather it up and lift it carefully from the defiling earth; straightway, a reward for your service, with the girl's permission your eyes will catch a glimpse of her ankles. Then again look round to see that whoever is sitting behind you is not pressing his knee against her tender back. Frivolous minds are won by trifles: many have found useful the deft arranging of a cushion. It has helped too to stir the air with a light fan, or to set a stool beneath a dainty foot.

Such openings will the Circus afford to a new courtship, and the melancholy sand scattered on the busy Forum. Often has Venus Boy fought upon that sand, and he who watched the wounds has himself been wounded. While he is speaking and touching her hand and asking for the book, and inquiring which is winning as he lays his stake, he feels the winged barb and groans with the wound, and is himself part of the show which he is watching.

What when Caesar of late brought on Persian and Athenian vessels under the fashion of a naval fight? Why, youths and maidens came from either sea: the mighty world was in our city. Who found not in that crowd some object for his passion? alas! how many did a foreign love o'erthrow!

Lo! Caesar is preparing to add what was lacking to the conquered world: now, farthest East, shalt thou be ours. Parthian, thou shalt pay penalty; rejoice, ye buried Crassi, and ye standards that shamefully endured barbarian violence. Your avenger is at hand, and, though his years be few, proclaims his captaincy, and, though a boy, handles wars that no boy should handle. Cease, timid ones, to count the birthdays of the gods; valour falls early to the lot of Caesars. Heavenly power grows more swiftly than its years, and ill brooks the penalties of slow delay. Small was the Tirynthian when in his hands he strangled two snakes, and already in his cradle he was worthy of Jove. And thou who even now art a youth, how big then wert thou, O Bacchus, when conquered India feared thy wands? With the authority and experience of thy sire shalt thou, O youth, make war, and with the experience and authority of thy sire shalt thou conquer: such, bearing so great a name, should by thy earliest exploit, prince now of the youth, but one day of the elders; since thou hast brothers, avenge wrongs done to brothers, and since thou hast a sire, guard the rights of a sire. Thy father and the father of thy country hath girded thee with arms: thy enemy seized the throne from his unwilling sire; rightful weapons shalt thou bear, dastardly arrows, he; right and duty shall stand to defend thy cause. The Parthians are defeated in their cause: let them be defeated in battle also; let my prince add to Latium the riches of the East. Father Mars and father Caesar, vouchsafe him your presence as he goes; for one of you is, and one will be, a god. Lo! I prophesy: victory shall be thine, and I shall duly pay my votive song, and owe thee loud utterance of praise. Thou wilt stand and in my own words exhort thy warriors; O let not my words fall short of thy valour. I shall tell of Parthian backs and Roman breasts, and of the weapons which the foe shoots from his retreating steed. Thou who dost flee to conquer, what, O Parthian, dost thou leave the conquered? Already, O Parthian, hath thy warfare an evil omen. Therefore that day shall dawn whereon thou, fairest of beings, shalt ride all golden behind four snow-white steeds. Chieftains shall go before thee, their necks laden with chains, lest they be able to save themselves by the flight they used before. Joyous youths shall look on and maidens with them, and that day shall make all hearts overflow. And when some girl among them asks the names of the monarchy or what places, what mountains, what rivers are borne along, do you answer everything, nor only if she ask you; ay, even if you know not, tell her as if you knew it well. That is Euphrates, his forehead fringed with reeds; he with the dark blue locks down-hanging must be Tigris. These, say, are Armenians, here is Persia, sprung from Danae;¹ that was a city in the Achaemenian valleys. That one, or that, are chieftains; and you will have names to give them, correct, if you can, but if not, yet names that are fitting.

Banquets too give openings, when the tables are set; somewhat beside wine may you find there. Often has bright-hued Love with soft arms drawn to him and held down the horns of Bacchus as he there reclined: and when wine has sprinkled Cupid's thirsty wings, he abides and stands overburdened, where he has taken his place. He indeed quickly shakes out his dripping plumes, yet does it hurt even to be sprinkled on the breast with love. Wine gives courage and makes men apt for passion; care flees and is drowned in much wine. Then laughter comes, then even the poor find vigour, then sorrow and care and the wrinkles of the brow depart. Then simplicity, most rare in our age, lays bare the mind, when the god dispels all craftiness. At such time often have women bewitched the minds of men, and Venus in the wine has been fire in fire. Trust not at such a time o'ermuch to the treacherous lamp; darkness and drink impair your judgment of beauty. It was in heaven's light unveiled that Paris beheld the goddesses, when he said to Venus, "Venus, thou dost surpass the other two." By night are blemishes hid, and every fault is forgiven: that hour makes any woman fair. Consult the daylight for jewels, for wool dyed in purple, consult it too for the face and bodily form.

Why should I recount to you all the gatherings of women, fit occasions for hunting? the sand would yield to my counting. Why tell of Baiae, a shore fringed with boats, and the water that smokes with hot sulphur? Someone came hence with a wound in his heart, and said: "Those waters were not, as fame reports them, healthy." Lo! hard by the city is Dian's woodland shrine, and the realm won by the sword and guilty hand: because she is a maid and hates the darts of Cupid, she has given and will give to our people many a wound.

So far my muse, borne upon unequal wheels, teaches you where to select an object for your love, and where to spread your nets. Now do I essay a task of preeminent skill, to tell you by what arts to catch her whom you have chosen. Ye men, whoever, wherever ye may be, attend with docile minds; and, common folk, lend favouring presence to my enterprise.

First let assurance come to your minds, that all women can be caught; spread but your nets and you will catch them. Sooner would birds be silent in spring, or grasshoppers in summer, or the hound of Maenalus flee before the hare than a woman persuasively wooed resist a lover: nay, even she, whom you will think cruel, will be kind. And as stolen love is pleasant to a man, so is it also to a woman; the man dissembles badly: she conceals desire better. Did it suit us males' not to ask any woman first, the woman, already won, would play the asker. In soft meads the heifer lows to the bull, the mare always whinnies to the horn-footed steed. In us desire is weaker and not so frantic: the manly flame knows a lawful bound. Why should I speak of Byblis, who burnt with a forbidden passion for her brother, and with a rope's noose bravely atoned her sin? Myrrha loved her father, but not as a daughter should, and now lies imprisoned in the confining bark: with her tears, poured forth from the fragrant tree, are we anointed: the drops preserve their mistress' name. Once in the shady vales of woody Ida there was a white bull, the glory of the herd; marked was he by a spot of black between his horns; that was the only blemish, the rest was white as milk. Him would the Cretan and Cy-donian heifers fain have borne upon their backs: Pasiphaë rejoiced to become the leman of a bull, and regarded with envious hate the comely cows. Well known is that I sing of: Crete, that holds a hundred cities, cannot deny this, liar though she be. Herself she is said to have plucked new leaves and tenderest meadow-grass for the bull with unaccustomed hand. She goes in company with the herds, nor does thought of her lord delay her going, and a bull triumphed over Minos. What gain to thee, Pasiphaë, to wear thy purple gowns? that lover of thine recks not of any splendour. What dost thou with a mirror, seeking the herds upon the mountains? Why so oft, foolish one, dost thou dress thy braided hair? Nay, believe thy mirror when it tells thee thou art no heifer. How hadst thou wished that horns grew on thy brow! If 'tis Minos pleases thee, seek no adulterer; or if thou wilt deceive thy man, with a man deceive him! Leaving her bower the queen hies her to the woods and glens, like a Bacchanal sped by the Aonian god. Ah, how oft did she look askance upon a cow, and say, "Why does she find favour with my lord? See how she sports before, him on the tender grass: nor doubt I but the foolish thing imagines she is comely." She spoke, and straightway ordered her to be taken from the mighty herd, and undeserving to be dragged beneath the curving yoke, or forced her to fall before the altar in a feigned sacrifice, and held in exultant hands her rival's entrails. How oft with her rivals' bodies did she appease the gods, and say, as she held their entrails, "Now go and find favour with my lord!" And now she craves to be Europa and now to be Io, for the one was a cow, and the other was borne by a cow's mate. Her none the less did the leader of the herd make pregnant, deceived by a cow of maple-wood, and by her offspring was the sire betrayed. Had the Cretan woman abstained from love for Thyestes (and is it such a feat to be able to do without a particular man?), Phoebus had not broken off in mid-career, and wresting his car about turned round his steeds to face the dawn. From Nisus his daughter stole the purple hairs, and now holds raving hounds within her womb and loins. The son of Atreus, who escaped Mars on land and Neptune on the deep, was the dire victim of his wife. Who has not bewailed the flames of Creusa of Ephyre, and the mother stained with her children's blood? Phoenix, son of Amyntor, shed tears from empty eyes; ye frightened horses, ye tore Hippolytus in pieces. Why piercest thou, O Phineus, the eyes of thine innocent sons? upon thine own head will the punishment fall. All those crimes were prompted by women's lust; keener is it than ours, and has more of madness. Come then, doubt not that you may win all women; scarce one out of many will there be to say you nay. And, grant they or deny, yet are they pleased to have been asked: suppose, say, yon are mistaken, your rejection brings no danger. But why should you be mistaken, since 'tis new delights that win welcome, and what is not ours charms more than our own? In fields not ours the crops are ever more bounteous, and the neighbouring herd has richer udders.

But take care first to know the handmaid of the woman you would win; she will make your approach easy. See that she be nearest the counsels of her mistress, and one who may be trusted with the secret of your stolen sport. Corrupt her with promises, corrupt her with prayers; if she be willing, you will gain your end with ease. She will choose a time (physicians also observe times) when her mistress is in an easy mood and apt for winning. Then will her mind be apt for winning when in the fulness of joy she grows wanton like the corn crop in a rich soil. When hearts are glad, and not fast bound by grief, then do they lie open, and Venus steals in with persuasive art Ilios, when sad, was defended by its hosts; rejoicing, it received the warrior-burdened horse. Then too may she be tried, when she grieves beneath a rival's smart; see then that by your efforts she lack not vengeance. Let her maid incite her, as she combs her tresses in the morning, and add the help of an oarsman to the sail, and let her say, sighing softly to herself, "But, I suppose you could not yourself pay him back in kind. Then let her speak of you, then add persuasive words, and swear that you are dying of frantic love. But be speedy, lest the sails sink and the breezes fail: like brittle ice, so perishes anger by delaying. You will ask, whether it profits to seduce the maid herself; such an enterprise involves much hazard. An intrigue makes one more eager another more sluggish; this one wins you for her mistress, that one for herself. It may turn out well or ill; though the issue favour the hazard, yet my counsel is, abstain. I am not the man to go by precipitous paths and rocky heights; no youth under my leadership will be captured. Yet while she gives and takes your letters, should her figure and not her services alone find favour, see that you gain the mistress first, and let the servant follow: do not begin your wooing with the maid. This only do I urge (if you but trust my art, and the rapacious breeze blows not my words across the sea): either make no venture or be successful; the informer vanishes when once she shares the guilt. The bird cannot make good its escape when once its wings are limed; the boar issues not easily from the entangling nets. Let the fish be held that is wounded from seizing the hook; once you assail her, press the attack, nor depart unless victorious. Then, sharing a common guilt, she will not betray you, you will know her mistress' words and deeds. But keep her secret well; if the informer's secret be well kept, she will always gladly foster your intimacy.

He errs who thinks that seasons are to be marked by sailors only, and by those who till the toilsome fields; not always must the corn be entrusted to the treacherous fields, nor always the hollow bark to the green main, nor always is it safe to angle for young girls; the same thing often goes better at the appointed season. Whether it is her birthday, or the Kalends which delight to join Venus to Mars, or whether the Circus is adorned not, as before, by images, but holds the wealth of kings displayed, put off your attempt: the storm is lowering then, and the Pleiads threaten, the tender Kid is merged in the watery waves: then it is wise to stop; then, if any entrusts him to the deep, scarce can he cling to a broken spar of his wrecked ship. You may begin on the day on which woeful Allia flows stained with the blood of Latian wounds, or on that day, less fit for business, whereon returns the seventh-day feast that the Syrian of Palestine observes.

But hold in awful dread your lady's birthday; let that be a black day whereon a present must be given. Shun it as you may, yet she will carry off the spoil; a woman knows the way to fleece an eager lover of his wealth. A lewd pedlar will come to your mistress when in buying mood, and will spread his wares before her, while you sit by in misery; and she, that you may fancy yourself a judge, will ask you to inspect them; then she will kiss you; then she will ask you to buy. She will swear that this will satisfy her for many a long year, that she needs it now, that now is a good time to buy it. If you make excuse that you have not the cash at home she will ask for a note of hand—lest you should be glad you ever learned to write. What, when she claims a gift to buy, as she says, a birthday cake, and has a birthday as often as she requires? What when she weeps for a feigned loss in deepest sorrow, and pretends a jewel has slipped from the pierced lobe of her ear? Many things do they beg to borrow, but, once borrowed, they will not give them back: you have lost them, but gain no credit for your loss. Ten months and as many tongues would not suffice me to tell the unholy ruses of the fair.

Let wax, spread on smooth tablets, attempt the crossing; let wax go first to show your mind. Let that carry your flatteries and words that play the lover; and, whoever you are, add earnest entreaties. Entreaty moved Achilles to give Hector back to Priam; a god when angry is moved by the voice of prayer. See that you promise: what harm is there in promises? In promises anyone can be rich. Hope, once conceived, endures for long; a treacherous goddess is she, but a timely one. Once you have given, you may be abandoned with good reason: your gift is gone, she will have taken it and lost nothing her-self. But what you have not given you may seem always on the point of giving: thus many a time has a barren field deceived its owner; thus, lest he shall have lost, the gambler ceases not to lose, and often do the dice recall his greedy hands. "Herein the task, herein the toil"—to win her favour with no preceding gift; lest what she has given be given for nothing, she will give yet more. Therefore let a letter speed, traced with persuasive words, and explore her feelings, and be the first to try the path. A letter carried in an apple betrayed Cydippe, and the maid was deceived unawares by her own words.

Learn noble arts, I counsel you, young men of Rome, not only that you may defend trembling clients: a woman, no less than populace, grave judge or chosen senate, will surrender, defeated, to eloquence. But hide your powers, nor put on a learned brow; let your pleading avoid troublesome words. Who, save an idiot, would declaim to his tender sweetheart? often has a letter been a potent cause of hate. Your language should inspire trust and your words be familiar, yet coaxing too, so that you seem to be speaking in her presence. If she does not receive your message and sends it back unread, hope that one day she will read, and hold to your purpose. In time refractory oxen come to the plough, in time horses are taught to bear the pliant reins; an iron ring is worn by constant use, a curved share wastes by constant ploughing of the ground. What is harder than rock, what softer than water? yet soft water hollows out hard rock. Only persevere; you will overcome Penelope herself; late, as you see, did Pergamus fall, yet fall it did. Suppose she has read, but will not write back: compel her not; only see that she is ever reading your flatteries. She who has consented to read will consent to answer what she has read ; that will come by its own stages and degrees. Perhaps even an angry letter will first come to you asking you to be pleased not to vex her. What she asks, she fears; what she does not ask, she desires—that you will continue; press on, then, and soon you will have gained your wish.

Meanwhile, whether she be borne reclining on her cushions, approach your mistress' litter in dissembling fashion, and lest someone intrude hateful ears to your words, hide them, so far as you may, in cunning ambiguities; or whether the spacious colonnade be trodden by her leisurely feet, do you also make friendly dalliance there; and contrive now to go before her, now to follow behind, now hurry, now go slowly. Neither hesitate to slip past some of the columns that part you, nor to join your side to hers; nor let her sit in the round theatre, her fair looks by you unheeded: something worth looking at she will bring on her shoulders. On her you may turn your looks, her you may admire: much let your eyebrows, much let your gestures say. Applaud when an actor portrays some woman in his dance, and favour whoever be the lover that is played. When she rises you will rise; while she sits you will sit too; waste time at your mistress' will.

But take no pleasure in curling your hair with the iron, or in scraping your legs with biting pumice-stone. Bid them do that by whom mother Cybele is sung in howling chorus of Phrygian measures. An uncared-for beauty is becoming to men; Theseus carried off Minos' daughter, though no clasp decked his temples. Phaedra loved Hippolytus, nor yet was he a dandy; Adonis, born to the woodland, was a goddess' care. Let your person please by cleanliness, and be made swarthy by the Campus; let your toga fit, and be spotless; let your shoe-strap not be too tight, let its buckle be free from rust, and let your feet not float about in shoes too loose; nor let your stubborn locks be spoilt by bad cutting; let hair and beard be dressed by a practised hand. Do not let your nails project, and let them be free of dirt; nor let any hair be in the hollow of your nostrils. Let not the breath of your mouth be sour and unpleasing, nor let the lord and master of the herd offend the nose. All else let wanton women practise, and such men of doubtful sex as wish to have a man.

Lo! Liber summons his bard; he too helps lovers, and favours the flame wherewith he burns himself. The Cretan maid wandered distractedly on the unknown sand, where little Dia is lashed by the sea waves. Just as she came from sleep, clad in an ungirt tunic, barefoot, with yellow hair unbound, she cried upon Theseus over the deaf waters, while an innocent shower bedewed her tender cheeks. She clamoured and wept together, but both became her; nor was she made less comely by her tears. Again she beats her soft bosom with her hands, and cries, "He is gone, the faithless one; what will become of me?" "What will become of me?" she cries: then o'er all the shore cymbals resounded and drums beaten by frenzied hands. She fainted for fear, and broke off her latest words; no blood was there in her lifeless frame. Lo! Bacchanals with tresses streaming behind them, lo! wanton Satyrs, the god's forerunning band; lo! drunken old Silenus scarce sits his crookbacked ass, and leaning clings to the mane before him. While he pursues the Bacchanals, and the Bacchanals flee and again attack, and while the unskilful horseman urges his beast with a rod, he falls off the long-eared ass and topples head-foremost and the Satyrs cry, "Come, get up, father, get up!" And now on his car, that he had covered with grape-clusters, the god was giving the golden reins to his yoked tigers: voice, colour—and Theseus, all were gone from the girl; thrice she tried flight, thrice fear stayed her. She shuddered, as slender stalks that are shaken by the wind, or as the light rush that trembles in the watery marsh. "Lo, here am I," said the god to her, "a more faithful lover; have no fear, Cretan maid, thou shalt be the spouse of Bacchus. For thy gift take the sky; as a star in the sky thou shalt be gazed at; as the Cretan Crown shalt thou oft guide the doubtful bark." He spoke, and lest she should fear the tigers leapt down from the chariot; the sand gave place to his alighting foot; and clasping her to his bosom (for she had no strength to fight) he bore her away; easy is it for a god to be all-powerful. Some chant "Hail, Hymenaeus!" some shout Euhoe, Euhlan!" So do the bride and the god meet on the sacred couch.

Therefore when the bounty of Bacchus set before you falls to your lot, and a woman shares your convivial couch, beseech the Nyctelian sire and the spirits of the night that they bid not the wines to hurt your head. Here may you say many things lurking in covered speech, so that she may feel they are said to her, and you may trace light flatteries in thin characters of wine, that on the table she may read herself your mistress; you may gaze at her eyes with eyes that confess their flame: there are often voice and words in a silent look See that you are the first to seize the cup her lips have touched, and drink at that part where she has drank; and whatever, food she has touched with her fingers see that you ask for, and while you ask contrive to touch her hand. Let it also be your aim to please your lady's husband; he will be more useful to you, if made a friend. To him, if you drink by lot, concede the first turn; give him the garland which has dropped from your head. Be he below you or hold an equal place, let him take of all before you; nor hesitate to yield him place in talk. 'Tis a safe and oft-trodden path, to deceive under the name of friend; safe and oft-trodden though it be, 'tis the path of guilt. Thus too an agent pursues his agency too far and looks after more than was committed to his charge.

I will give you a sure measure of drinking: let mind and feet perform their duty. Especially beware of quarrels caused by wine, and of hands too quick to brutal fight. Eurytion fell by stupidly drinking the liquor set before him; the table and the wine-cup are fitter for mirthful jests. Sing, if you have a voice; If your arms are lithe, dance; please by whatever gifts you can. As real drunkenness does harm, so will feigned bring profit: make your crafty tongue stumble in stammering talk, so that, whatever you do or say more freely than you should, may be put down to too much wine. And "Here's luck," say, "to the lady," and "Luck to him who sleeps with her!": but in your silent soul let the prayer be "Deuce take the husband." But when the tables are removed and the company depart, and the crowd itself gives you chance of access, join the crowd, and gently drawing nigh to her as she goes pull her sleeve with your fingers, and let your foot touch hers. Now is the time for talk with her; away with you, rustic shame! Chance and Venus help the brave. Let not your eloquence submit to our poets' laws; see but that you wish to succeed: your eloquence will come of itself. You must play the lover, and counterfeit heartache with words: her belief in that you must win by any device. Nor is it hard to be believed: each woman thinks herself lovable; hideous though she be, there is none her own looks do not please. Yet often the pretender begins to love truly after all, and often becomes what he has feigned to be. Wherefore, you women, be more compliant to pretenders; one day will the love be true which but now was false. Now be the time to ensnare the mind with crafty flatteries, as the water eats away an overhanging bank. Nor be weary of praising her looks, her hair, her shapely fingers, her small foot: even honest maids love to hear their charms extolled; even to the chaste their beauty is a care and a delight. For why even now are Juno and Pallas ashamed that they won not the judgment in the Phrygian woods? When you praise her the bird of Juno displays her plumes: should you gaze in silence she hides away her wealth. Even steeds, amid the contests of the rapid course, delight to have their manes combed and their necks patted.

Nor be timid in your promises; by promises women are betrayed; call as witnesses what gods you please. Jupiter from on high smiles at the perjuries of lovers, and bids the winds of Aeolus carry them unfulfilled away. Jupiter was wont to swear falsely by Styx to Juno; now he favours his own example. It is expedient there should be gods, and as it is expedient let us deem that gods exist; let incense and wine be poured on the ancient hearths; nor does careless quiet like unto slumber hold them; live innocently, gods are nigh; return what is given to your keeping; let duty keep her covenant; let fraud be absent; keep your hands clean of blood. If you are wise, cheat women only; and avoid trouble; keep faith save for this one deceitfulness. Deceive the deceivers; they are mostly an unrighteous sort; let them fall into the snare which they have laid. Egypt is said to have lacked the rains that bless its fields, and to have been parched for nine years, when Thrasius approached Busiris, and showed that Jove could be propitiated by the outpoured blood of a stranger. To him said Busiris, "Thou shalt be Jove's first victim, and as a stranger give water unto Egypt." Phalaris too roasted in his fierce bull the limbs of Perillus; its maker first made trial of his ill-omened work. Both were just; for there is no juster law than that contrivers of death should perish by their own contrivances. Therefore, that perjuries may rightly cheat the perjured, let the woman feel the smart of a wound she first inflicted.

Tears too are useful; with tears you can move iron; let her see, if possible, your moistened cheeks. If tears fail (for they do not always come at need), touch your eyes with a wet hand. Who that is wise would not mingle kisses with coaxing words? Though she give them not, yet take the kisses she does not give. Perhaps she will struggle at first, and cry "You villain!" yet she will wish to be beaten in the struggle. Only beware lest snatching them rudely you hurt her tender lips, and she be able to complain of your roughness. He who has taken kisses, if he take not the rest beside, will deserve to lose even what was granted. After kisses how much was lacking to your vow's fulfilment? ah! that was awkwardness, not modesty. You may use force; women like you to use it; they often wish to give unwillingly what they like to give. She whom a sudden assault has taken by storm is pleased, and counts the audacity as a compliment. But she who, when she might have been compelled, departs untouched, though her looks feign joy, will yet be sad. Phoebe suffered violence, violence was used against her sister:[1] each ravisher found favour with the ravished. Well-known, yet not undeserving of mention, is the tale of the Scyrian maid and her Thessalian lover. Already had the goddess given the ill-fated reward for her beauty's praising, she who triumphed o'er the twain 'neath Ida's mount; already from distant lands his daughter-in-law had come to Priam, and a Grecian wife was within the walls of Troy; all were swearing allegiance to the injured spouse, for the grief of one became the people's cause. Basely, had he not so far yielded to his mother's prayers, Achilles had disguised his manhood in a woman's robe. What dost thou, Aeacides? wools are not thy business; by another art of Pallas do thou seek fame. What hast thou to do with baskets? thy arm is fitted to bear a shield. Why boldest thou a skein in the hand by which Hector shall die? Cast away the spindle girt about with toilsome windings! That hand must shake the Pelian spear. It chanced that in the same chamber was the royal maid; by her rape she found him to be a man. By force indeed was she vanquished, so one must believe; yet by force did she wish to be vanquished all the same. Often cried she, "Stay" when already Achilles was hasting from her; for, the distaff put away, he had taken valiant arms. Where is that violence now? Why with coaxing words, Deidamia, dost thou make to tarry the author of thy rape? In truth, just as there is shame sometimes in beginning first, so when another begins it is pleasant to submit. Ah, too confident in his own charms is a lover, if he wait until she ask him first. Let the man take the first step, let the man speak entreating words; she will listen kindly to coaxing entreaties. That you may gain her, ask: she only wishes to be asked; provide the cause and starting-point, of your desire. Jupiter went a suppliant to the heroines of old: no woman seduced the mighty Jove. Yet if you find that your prayers cause swollen pride, stop what you have begun, draw back a pace. Many women desire what flees them; they hate what is too forward; moderate your advance, and save them from getting tired of you. Nor must the hope of possession be always proclaimed in your entreaties; let love find entrance veiled in friendship's name. I have seen an unwilling mistress deluded by this approach; he who had been an admirer became a lover.

White is a shameful colour in a sailor; swarthy should he be, both from the sea-waves and from heaven's beams; shameful too in a husbandman, who ever beneath the sky turns up the ground with curved ploughshare and heavy harrows. Thou too who seekest the prize of Pallas' garland art shamed if thy body be white. But let every lover be pale; this is the lover's hue. Such looks become him; only fools think that such looks avail not. Pale over Side did Orion wander in the woods, pale was Daphnis when the naiad proved unkind. Let leanness also prove your feelings; nor deem it base to set a hood on your bright locks. Nights of vigil make thin the bodies of lovers, and anxiety and the distress that a great passion brings. That you may gain your desire be pitiable, so that whoso sees you may say, "You are in love." Shall I complain, or warn you, that right and wrong are all confounded? Friendship is but a name, faith is an empty name. Alas, it is not safe to praise to a friend the object of your love; so soon as he believes your praises, he slips into your place. But, you will say, the son of Actor stained not Achilles' couch, and as concerned Pirithous, Phaedra was chaste. Pylades loved Hermione as Phoebus Pallas, and as twin Castor was to thee, O Tyndaris. If anyone has this hope, let him hope that tamarisks will bear apples, let him seek honey in the middle of a river. Naught pleases but what is shameful, none cares but for his own pleasure, and sweet is that when it springs from another's pain. Ah, the reproach of it! no foe need a lover fear; fly those whom you deem faithful, and you will be safe. Kinsman, brother—beware of them and of thy boon companion; they will cause you real fears.

I was about to end, but various are the hearts of women; use a thousand means to waylay as many hearts. The same earth bears not everything; this soil suits vines, that olives; in that, wheat thrives. Hearts have as many fashions as the face has features; the wise man will suit himself to countless fashions, and like Proteus will now resolve himself into light waves, and now will be a lion, now a tree, now a shaggy boar. These fish are caught with spears, those with hooks; these ones are dragged with taut ropes in bulging nets. Nor let one method suit all ages; a grown hind will regard the snare from further away. Should you seem learned to the simple, or wanton to the prude, she will straightway feel a pitiful self-distrust. And so comes it that she who has feared to commit herself to an honourable lover degrades herself to the embraces of a mean one.

Part of my enterprise remains, part is now finished. Here let the anchor be thrown, and hold my bark secure.

On the Spectacles

By Martial

Translated by D. R. Shackleton Bailey

1

Let barbarous Memphis speak no more of the wonder of her pyramids, nor Assyrian toil boast of Babylon; nor let the soft Ionians be extolled for Trivia's temple; let the altar of many horns say naught of Delos; nor let the Carians exalt to the skies with extravagant praises the Mausoleum poised in empty air. All labor yields to Caesar's Amphitheater. Fame shall tell of one work in lieu of all.

2

Where the starry colossus sees the constellations at close range and lofty scaffolding rises in the middle of the road, once gleamed the odious halls of a cruel monarch, and in all Rome there stood a single housed. Where rises before our eyes the august pile of the Amphitheater, was once Nero's lake. Where we admire the warm baths, a speedy gift, a haughty tract of land had robbed the poor of their dwellings. Where the Claudian colonnade unfolds its wide-spread shade, was the outermost part of the palace's end. Rome has been restored to herself, and under your rule, Caesar, the pleasances that belonged to a master now belong to the people.

3

What race is so remote, so barbarous, Caesar, that no spectator from it is in your city? The farmer of Rhodope has come from Orphic Haemus, the Sarmatian fed on draughts of horses' blood has come, and he who drinks discovered Nile's first stream, and he on whom beats the wave of farthest Tethys! The Arab has sped hither, the Sabaeans too, and the Cilicians have here been sprayed with their own showers. Sygambrians have come with hair curled in a knot and Ethiopians with hair curled otherwise. Diverse sounds the speech of the peoples, and yet it is one, when you are called true father of the fatherland.

4 (4.1–4)

A company dangerous to peace and inimical to placid tranquility, ever harrying hapless wealth, was led in parade, and the vast arena did not have room enough for the guilty. The informer has the exile he used to give.

5 (4.5–6)

The informer is a fugitive in exile from the Ausonian city. This you may reckon among our prince's expenses.

6 (5)

Believe that Pasiphae was mated to the Dictaean bull; we have seen it, the old legend has won credence. And let not hoary antiquity plume itself, Caesar: whatever Fame sings of, the arena affords you.

7 (6)

It is not enough that warrior Mars serves you in unconquered arms, Caesar. Venus herself serves you too.

8 (6B)

Illustrious Fame used to sing of the lion laid low in Nemea's spacious vale, Hercules' work. Let ancient testimony be silent, for after your shows, Caesar we have now seen such things done by women's valor.

9 (7)

As Prometheus, bound on Scythian crag, fed the tireless bird with his too abundant breast, so did Laureolus, hanging on no sham cross, give his naked flesh to a Caledonian boar. His lacerated limbs lived on, dripping gore, and in all his body, body there was none. Finally he met with the punishment he deserved; the guilty wretch had plunged a sword into his father's throat or his master's or his madness had robbed a temple of its secret gold, or laid a cruel torch to Rome. The criminal had out done the misdeeds of ancient story in him, what had been a play became an execution.

10 (8)

Daedalus, when you are being thus torn by a Lucanian bear, how you wish you now had your wings!

11 (9)

The rhinoceros, displayed all over the arena, performed for you, Caesar, battles that he did not promise. How he lowered his head and flamed into fearful rage! How mighty a bull was he, to whom a bull was as a dummy!

12 (10)

A treacherous lion had harmed his master with his ingrate mouth, daring to violate the hands he knew so well; but he paid a fitting penalty for such a crime, and suffered weapons who had not suffered stripes. What should be the manners of men under such a prince, who commands wild beasts to be of milder nature?

13 (11)

A bear, whirling headlong in the bloody arena, got entangled in birdlime and lost his escape. Now let shining spears lie idle with covered points, and let not the lance fly, launched by extended arm. Let the hunter catch his quarry in the empty air, if it pleases us to hunt wild beasts with the fowler's art.

14 (12)

Amid the cruel perils of Caesar's hunt a light spear had pierced a pregnant sow. One of her litter lept out of the hapless mother's wound. Savage Lucina was *this* a delivery? She would have wished to die wounded by further weapons, so that the sad path might open for all her brood. Who denies that Bacchus sprang from his mother's death? Believe that a deity was so given birth: so born was a beast.

15 (13)

A mother sow, struck by a heavy weapon and laid open by the wound, lost life and gave it at one and the same time. How sure was the hand that poised the steel! I believe this hand was Lucina's. Dying the creature sampled the divine power of either Diana. By one the parent was delivered, by the other the beast was slain.

16 (14)

A wild sow, now pregnant, sent forth her progeny, pledge of her ripe womb, made parent by a wound. Nor did the offspring lie on the ground, but ran as the mother fell. How ingenious are sudden chances!

17 (15)

That which was the topmost glory of your renown, Meleager, how small a portion is it of Carpophorus's, a felled boar! He plunged his spear in a charging bear, once prime in the peak of the Arctic pole; he laid low a lion of unprecedented size, a sight to see, who might have done honor to Hercules' hands; he stretched dead a fleet leopard with a wound dealt from afar * * * since one bore off glory as his reward, the other a dish.

18 (16)

The bull was snatched up in the midst of the arena and departed for the sky. This was the work, not of art, but of devotion.

19 (16B)

A bull had carried Europa through his brother's sea; but now a bull has borne Alcides to the stars. Compare now, Fame, the steers of Caesar and of Jove; even though they bore an equal load, this one bore his load higher.

20 (17)

Devoted and suppliant the elephant adores you, Caesar, he who but lately was so formidable to the bull. He does it unbidden, no master teaches him. Believe me, he too feels our god.

21 (18)

A tigress, wont to lick the hand of the fearless trainer, rare glory from Hyrcanian mountains, fiercely tore a wild lion with rabid tooth; a novelty, unknown in any times. She dared do no such thing while she lived in the high forests, but since she has been among us she has gained ferocity.

22 (19)

The bull, that goaded with fire through the whole arena had just snatched up dummies and tossed them to the stars, at length met his death, trampled by a horned mouth. He thought it would be easy to toss an elephant so.

23 (20)

One party wanted Myrinus, the other Triumphus. Caesar with either hand promised both alike. There was no better way for him to end the merry dispute. Oh pleasant device of our unconquered prince!

24 (21)

Whatever Rhodope is said to have watched on Orpheus' stage, the arena, Caesar, displayed to you. Rocks crept and a wondrous forest ran, such as the grove of the Hesperides is believed to have been. Every kind of wild beast was present, mingling with the tame, and many a bird hovered above the bard. But himself lay torn by an ungrateful bear. This thing alone was done contrary to the legend.

25 (21B)

Earth through a sudden opening sent a bear to attack Orpheus. She came from Eurydice.

26 (22)

While the trembling trainers were goading the rhinoceros and the great beast's anger was long a-gathering, men were giving up hope of the combats of promised warfare; but at length the fury we earlier knew returned. For with his double horn he tossed a heavy bear as a bull tosses dummies from his head to the stars. [With how sure a stroke does the strong hand of Carpophorus, still a youth, aim Norican spears!] He lifted two steers with his mobile neck, to him yielded the fierce buffalo and the bison. A lion fleeing before him ran headlong upon the spears. Go now, you crowd, complain of tedious delays!

27 (24)

If you are here from distant land, a late spectator for whom this was the first day of the sacred show, let not the naval warfare deceive you with its ships, and the water like to a sea: here but lately was land. You don't believe it? Watch while the waters weary Mars. But a short while hence you will be saying: "Here but lately was sea."

28 (25)

Cease to wonder, Leander, that the night wave spared you. 'Twas Caesar's wave.

29 (25B)

When bold Leander was seeking his sweetheart and the swollen waters were already overwhelming his weary body, he is said, poor fellow, to have addressed the surging waves in these words: "Spare me as I hasten, drown me as I return."

30 (26)

The well-trained bevy of Nereids sported all over the surface and in various conformations decorated the yielding waters. The trident menaced with upright tooth, the anchor with curved. We thought we saw an oar, we thought we saw a boat, and the Laconians' star shining, welcome to seamen, and broad sails bellying in conspicuous folds. Who invented such devices in the clear water? Thetis either taught these games or learned them.

31 (27; 29)

As Priscus and Verus each drew out the contest and the struggle between the pair long stood equal, shouts loud and often sought discharge for the combatants. But Caesar obeyed his own law (the law was that the bout go on without shield until a finger be raised). What he could do, he did, often giving dishes and presents. But an end to the even strife was found: equal they fought, equal they yielded. To both Caesar sent wooden swords and to both palms. Thus valor and skill had their reward. This has happened under no prince but you, Caesar: two fought and both won.

32 (28; 27)

If the ages of old, Caesar, in which a barbarous earth brought forth wild monsters, had produced Carpophorus, Marathon would not have feared her bull, nor leafy Nemea her lion, nor Arcadians the boar of Maenalus. When he armed his hands, the Hydra would have met a single death, one stroke of his would have sufficed for the entire Chimaera. He could yoke the fire-bearing bulls without the Coleman, he could conquer both the beasts of Pasiphae. If the ancient tale of the sea monster were recalled, he would release Hesione and Andromeda single-handed. Let the glory of Hercules' achievement be numbered: it is more to have subdued twice ten wild beasts at one time.

33 (29; 30)

As the startled hind fled the swift Molossians and with various cunning spun lingering delays, suppliant and like to one begging she halted at Caesar's feet; and the hounds did not touch their prey. * * * Such was the boon she won from knowing her prince. Caesar has divine power; sacred, sacred is this potency, believe it. Wild beasts never learned to lie.

34 (30; 28)

It had been Augustus' labor to pit fleets against each other here and rouse the waters with naval clarion. How small a part is this of our Caesar! Thetis and Galatea saw in the waves beasts they never knew. Triton saw chariots in hot career in the sea's dust and thought his master's horses had passed by. As Nereus prepared fierce battle for ferocious ships, he was startled to find himself walking on foot in the liquid expanse. Whatever is viewed in the Circus and the Amphitheater, that, Caesar, the wealth of your water has afforded you. So no more of Fucinus and the lake of direful Nero; let this be the only sea fight known to posterity.

35 (31)

Pardon the hasty work. He deserves not to displease you, Caesar, who hurries to please you.

36 (32)

To yield to a superior is valor's second glory; but grievous is the palm that a lesser enemy holds.

37 (33)

Flavian race, how much the third inheritor took away from you! It would almost have been worth while not to have had the other two.

Pliny's *Letters* (Book 10)

佪佪佪佪佪佪佪佪佪佪佪佪佪佪佪佪

Translated by Wynne Williams

EPISTLES X
15. C. Plinius to Traianus Imperator

Because I feel sure, sir, that you are interested, I am reporting to you that, together with all my people, I have reached Ephesus by sea, after "rounding Malea", despite being held up by opposing winds. Now I intend to set out for the province, by coastal vessels for part of the way, by carriages for the rest. For, just as oppressive heat is an obstacle to travel by land, so are the Etesian winds to an unbroken voyage by sea.

16. Traianus to Plinius

You were right to report to me, my dearest Secundus. For I do feel concern about what kind of journey you are having on the way to the province. It is a wise decision of yours to use ships for part of the time, and carriages for part of the time, according to what local conditions require.

17A. C. Plinius to Traianus Imperator

(1) Although I had a very healthy voyage, as far as Ephesus, sir, yet thereafter, when I had begun to pursue my journey by carriage, I was troubled by the most oppressive heat and also by slight attacks of fever, and I halted at Pergamum. (2) Subsequently, when I had shifted to coastal vessels, I was held back by opposing winds, and I entered Bithynia rather later than I had hoped, that is on September 17th. I cannot, however, complain about this delay, since it was my good fortune to celebrate your birthday in the province, which was a very good omen. (3) At the moment I am examining the expenditures, revenues and debtors of the state of Prusa; from the very process of investigation I am learning more and more that this is necessary. For many sums of money are being kept in their possession by private persons under different pretexts; moreover some sums are being paid out on wholly unlawful outlays. (4) I have written to you about this, sir, at the very moment of my arrival.

17B. C. Plinius to Traianus Imperator

(1) On September 17th, sir, I entered the province, which I found in that state of reverence and of loyalty to yourself which you deserve from the human race. (2) Consider, sir, whether you think it necessary to send a surveyor here. For it appears that considerable sums of money could be recovered from the administrators of public works if measurements were carried out honestly. Such at any rate is my estimate on the basis of the balance-sheet of Prusa with which I am dealing at this very moment.

18. Traianus to Plinius

(1) I could wish that you had been able to reach Bithynia without any complaint about your own physical condition or that of your people, and that your journey from Ephesus had been similar to your experience of the voyage as far as there. (2) The date of your arrival in Bithynia I learnt from your letter, my dearest Secundus. The provincials, I believe, will understand that I have taken thought for their interests. For you in your turn will see to it that it is evident to them that you have been picked out to be sent to them in my place. (3) Moreover, you must above all examine the accounts of the communities: for it is an established fact that they have been in confusion. I have scarcely enough surveyors for those works which are in progress at Rome or nearby; but men who can be trusted are to be found in every province, and therefore you will have no lack of them, if only you are willing to search for them diligently.

19. C. Plinius to Traianus Imperator

(1) I ask you, sir, to guide me with your advice in my doubts about whether I ought to have prisoners guarded by public slaves owned by the cities, which has hitherto been the practice, or by soldiers. For I fear both that an insufficiently reliable watch will be kept by the public slaves and also that this responsibility will call a considerable number of soldiers away from their duties. (2) For the time being I have included a few soldiers among the public slaves. However, I see that there is a risk that this may itself be a reason for neglect of duty by both groups, as the former feel certain that they can throw the burden of their shared guilt upon the latter, and the latter upon the former.

20. Traianus to Plinius

(1) There should be no necessity, my dearest Secundus, for more of my fellow-soldiers to be transferred to guarding prisoners. Let us persist with what is the custom in that province, to have prisoners guarded by public slaves. (2) And in fact it is up to you by your strictness and thoroughness to see that they do it conscientiously. For, as you say in your letter, what is to be feared above all is that, if soldiers were to be mixed in with public slaves, they would become more negligent as a result of either group relying

upon the other; but let us also stick to this rule, that as few of them as possible should be called away from their units.

21. C. Plinius to Traianus Imperator

Gavius Basses, the Prefect of the Poetic shore, has come to me, sir, showing me the greatest respect and attention, and has been with me for several days, a worthy man, so far as I have been able to judge, and one deserving of your generosity, I informed him that you had given instructions that he should be satisfied with 10 privileged men, two cavalrymen and one centurion, drawn from the cohorts which you wanted me to have under my command. (2) He replied that this number was not enough for him, and that he would write to you to this effect. It was for this reason that I decided that the soldiers he has in excess of the total should not be recalled at once.

22. Traianus to Plinius

Gavius Bassus has also written to me that the number of soldiers which I laid down in my instructions should be given to him was not large enough for him. I have ordered a copy of what I wrote back to him to be appended to this letter, for your information. It makes a great difference whether the situation requires it or whether he wants to make wider use of them on this pretext. (2) But we should consider only what is useful, and, as far as possible, ensure that soldiers are not absent from their units.

23. C. Plinius to Traianus Imperator

(1) The people of Prusa, sir, have a bath-house: it is squalid and old. They therefore regard it as of great importance to have a new one built; it seems to me that you can grant their request in this matter. (2) For there will be the money for it to be built in the first place that which I have already begun to recover and to exact from private persons; in the second place they are ready to transfer to the building of the bath-house the money which they have themselves been in the practice of spending on olive-oil; besides it is something which both the standing of the city and the splendour of your age requires.

24. Traianus to Plinius

If the building of a bath-house is not going to put a burden on the resources of the people of Prusa, we can grant their request, provided that no special tax is imposed for that purpose and that they do not have less available for necessary expenditures in the future.

25. C. Plinius to Traianus Imperator

Servilius Pudens, my deputy, came to me at Nicomedia on November 24th, sir, and freed me from the anxiety caused by a long period of waiting.

26. C. Plinius to Traianus Imperator

(1) Your kindnesses to me have bound Rosianus Geminus to me by the closest of links, sir: for I had him as quaestor in my consulship. I have found him to be most attentive to me: so great is the respect he shows me since my consulship, and he heaps personal services on top of the tokens of our official relationship. (2) So I ask that you yourself in response to my prayers show him on your side the favour appropriate to his rank. You will also, if you have any trust in my judgment, show him your generosity; he himself will devote his efforts in those tasks which you will have entrusted to him to show he deserves greater honours. What makes me more sparing in my praise is the fact that I hope his integrity and honesty and diligence are very well known to you, as a result not only of the offices which he has filled in the city under your own eyes, but also from his military service with you. (3) This one request I keep making again and again, something which, because of my affection for him, I cannot convince myself that I have yet done in full measure, and I beg you, sir, to allow me as soon as possible to rejoice in the enhanced standing of my quaestor, and so, through him, in my own.

27. C. Plinius to Traianus Imperator

Your freedman and procurator Maximus, sir, asserts that he too needs six soldiers apart from the ten privileged soldiers whom you ordered to be allocated by me to that excellent man Gemellinus. For the time being I have decided that these men should be left in attendance upon him, just as I had found them, especially since he was setting off for Paphlagonia to collect grain. In fact I even added two cavalrymen to guard him, since he requested it. I ask you to write back about the rule you wish to have followed in future.

28. Traianus to Plinius

Since he was in fact at that moment setting off to collect grain you were right to supply my freedman Maximus with soldiers. For he too was undertaking a special duty. When he has returned to his old post, two soldiers supplied by you and the same number by my procurator Virdius Gemellinus, whose assistant he is, will be enough for him.

29. C. Plinius to Traianus Imperator

(1) Sempronius Caelianus, an excellent young man, has sent two slaves who had been discovered among the recruits to me. I postponed their sentence until I could ask your

advice as the founder and upholder of military discipline about the manner of their punishment. (2) For I am myself in doubt principally because of the fact that, while they had already sworn the oath, they had not yet been enrolled in the ranks. So I ask you, sir, to write to me about what course I should follow, especially since this would set a precedent.

30. Traianus to Plinius

(1) Sempronius Caelianus acted in obedience to my instructions in sending to you those persons who will need to be the subject of a hearing to decide whether they should be held to have deserved the capital penalty. Now it makes a difference whether they put themselves forward as volunteers or were conscripted or even offered as substitutes. (2) If they are conscripts, it is the examination which was at fault; if they were offered as substitutes, blame lies at the door of those who offered them; if they came forward on their own initiative, when they had full knowledge of their status, they will deserve execution. For the fact that they have not yet been enrolled in the ranks is of no great importance. For that day on which they were first approved demanded that they tell the truth about their origin.

31. C. Plinius to Traianus Imperator

(1) You can condescend to attend to my worries, sir, without injury to your dignity, since you have given me the privilege of placing before you matters about which I am in doubt. (2) In very many of the cities, and at Nicomedia and Nicaea in particular, individuals who were sentenced to forced labour or to appearing at the games and similar kinds of penalties to these are carrying out the functions and duties of public slaves, and even receiving a yearly allowance as public slaves. When I had learned of this, I was for a long time in great uncertainty about what I ought to do. (3) For I both considered it excessively harsh to send back to finish their sentences after a long interval a considerable number of men who are now old and who, so it is claimed, lead a simple and respectable life, and I also thought it quite improper to continue to use convicts in official posts; again I reflected that it was inexpedient to have these same men supported in idleness at public expense, but also dangerous not to have them supported at all. (4) Of necessity, therefore, I left the whole matter undecided, until I could take your advice. You will perhaps enquire how it came about that they were released from the penalties to which they had been sentenced: I too enquired, but I found out nothing which I could tell you for certain. Although the judgments in which they had been sentenced were produced, yet there were no documents in which they could be shown to have been set free. (5) There were, however, some who claimed that, upon appealing for mercy, they had been released at the orders of proconsuls or legates. What made this more convincing was the fact that it was unbelievable that anyone should have ventured to do this without authority.

32. Traianus to Plinius

(1) Let us remember that it was for this reason that you were sent to that province, because many things in it evidently stood in need of correction. Now this will especially need to be put right, that men sentenced to punishment have not only been released from it without authority, as you say in your letter, but are also restored to the position of respectable officials. (2) So it will be necessary for those who were sentenced within these last ten years, and were released without any proper authorisation to be sent back to their punishment; if any shall be found to be convicts of longer standing and old men sentenced more than ten years ago, we should assign them to those functions which would not be very different from a punishment. They are usually allocated to the public baths, to cleaning sewers, likewise to the repair of roads and streets.

33. C. Plinius to Traianus Imperator

(1) While I was travelling through a distant part of the province, a very extensive fire in Nicomedia destroyed many houses belonging to private persons and two public buildings, the Gerusia and the temple of Isis, even though there was a road separating them. (2) It spread quite widely, in the first place because there was a strong wind, in the second place because of the inactivity of the people: it is generally agreed that they stood around, idle and motionless spectators of so great a disaster; besides, nowhere was there publicly available any pump, any bucket, indeed any apparatus at all for fighting fires. These things too will in fact be supplied in accordance with instructions I have already given; (3) pray consider, sir, whether you think an association of firemen should be set up, provided that it has only 150 members. I shall myself see to it that no one except a fireman is admitted and that they do not use the permission they have been granted for any other purpose; and it will not be hard to keep watch over so few.

34. Traianus to Plinius

You are in fact following the example set by very many people in conceiving a plan that an association of firemen could be established at Nicomedia. But let us recall that province and especially those cities have been troubled by cliques of that kind. Whatever name we may give, for whatever reason, to those who gather together for a common purpose, they will turn into political clubs, and that in a short time. (2) It is therefore more appropriate to have those things which can be of use in checking fires made available, and to urge the owners of properties both themselves to make use of them, and, if the situation requires it, to use for this purpose the crowd which gathers.

35. C. Plinius to Traianus Imperator

The customary vows for your preservation, upon which the safety of the state depends, we have both undertaken, sir, and at the same time fulfilled, praying to the gods that they be willing for these vows to be perpetually fulfilled and perpetually sealed.

36. Traianus to Plinius

I learnt with pleasure from your letter, my dearest Secundus, that you along with the provincials had both fulfilled and pronounced vows to the immortal gods for my safety and preservation.

37. C. Plinius to Traianus Imperator

(1) The people of Nicomedia, sir, have spent 3,318,000 sesterces on an aqueduct, which was abandoned while still unfinished, and was also demolished; subsequently 200,000 were laid out on another aqueduct. Since this too was abandoned, fresh expenditure is required in order that those who have wasted so much money may get their water. (2) I have myself visited a very pure spring, from which it appears that the water must be brought, as was attempted on the first occasion, on an arched structure, so that it may not reach just the flat and low-lying parts of the city. A very few arches are still standing: some can also be built up from the dressed stone which was pulled down from the earlier structure; some part of it, in my judgment, should be made of brickwork, for this would be both easier and cheaper. (3) But what is needed above all is for you to send out a water engineer or an architect in order that what has happened may not occur again. This one thing I assert, that both the usefulness and the beauty of the work are fully worthy of your age.

38. Traianus to Plinius

The effort must be made to bring water to the city of Nicomedia. I am truly confident that you will approach this task with the diligence which you ought to show. But, by heaven, it is also your duty diligently to investigate whose fault it is that the people of Nicomedia have until now wasted so much money, in case it was in the course of doing each other favours that they began and abandoned aqueducts. What you thus discover, bring to my attention.

39. C. Plinius to Traianus Imperator

A theatre at Nicaea, sir, most of which has already been built, though it is still in-complete, has swallowed up more than ten million sesterces (so I am informed; for the balance-sheet for the project has not been examined); I fear it may have been in vain. (2) For it is sinking and it gapes with huge cracks, either because the soil is wet and spongy, or because the stone itself is soft and crumbling; at all events it is worth considering whether it should be finished or abandoned or even demolished. For the supports and substructures, on which it is held up from below, appear to me not to be as strong as they are expensive. (3) Many embellishments for this theatre were promised by private persons and are still owed, for example halls around it, and a colonnade above the auditorium. All these are postponed now that the building which needs to be finished first is at a stop. (4) These same people of Nicaea began, before my arrival, to restore a gymnasium which had been destroyed in a fire, on a much more lavish and extensive scale than before, and they have already spent a considerable sum; the danger is that it will have been to little practical purpose; for it is ill-planned and rambling. Moreover, an architect, admittedly a rival of the one by whom the building was started, claims that the walls, despite being twenty-two feet thick, cannot support the load put upon them, because they are made up of a core of rabble and are not encased in brickwork.

(5) The people of Claudiopolis too are excavating rather than building a huge bath-house on a low-lying site which also has a mountain hanging over it, and indeed they are using that money which those members who were added to their council through your act of favour either have already paid upon their admission, or will contribute when we extract it from them. (6) Therefore, since I fear that in the former case the city's money, in the latter your gift, which is more valuable than any money, is being ill-spent, I am forced to ask you to send out an architect, not only on account of the theatre, but also of this bath-house, to consider whether it will be more expedient, after the expenditure which has already been made, to finish by some means or other the buildings in the form in which they have been started, or to put right what it appears can be corrected, and to change the sites where it appears they can be changed, in case we waste additional expenditure in our anxiety to save what has been spent.

40. Traianus to Plinius

(1) As the man on the spot you will be the best person to consider and decide what ought to be done with the theatre which has been begun at Nicaea. It will be enough for me to be informed of the decision you arrive at. After that make the private individuals add the embellishments, when the theatre in connection with which those embellishments were promised has been finished. (2) The Greeklings do enjoy their gymnasia; perhaps it was for that reason that the people of Nicaea set about building one in an over-ambitious spirit: but they must be content with the kind which can meet their needs. (3) You shall decide what advice should be given to the people of Claudiopolis about the bath-house they have begun to build on a site which, as you say in your letter, is quite unsuitable. You cannot be short of architects. There is no province which does not have men who are both expert and skilful; only do not suppose that it is quicker

to have them sent from the capital, when they are actually accustomed to come from Greece to us.

41. C. Plinius to Traianus Imperator

When I reflect on the greatness of both your station and your character, it seems to me most appropriate that projects should be brought to your notice which are as worthy of your eternal fame as of your glory and will have as much utility as beauty. (2) There is a very large lake in the territory of the people of Nicomedia. Across it marble, grain, firewood and timber are carried by boat as far as the road with little expense and effort, but by cart from there to the sea with great effort and at even greater cost ... [Probable lacuna in the text]. This project calls for many hands. But those are readily available. For there is both a plentiful supply of men in the countryside and a very plentiful one in the town, and the sure prospect that they will all most gladly take part in a project which is of advantage to all. (3) It remains for you, if you see fit, to send a surveyor or an architect, to make a thorough investigation to see whether the lake is at a higher level than the sea; the experts in this district claim that it is forty cubits higher. (4) I myself learn that a ditch was cut through the same area by one of the kings, but it is uncertain whether it was done to drain off water from the surrounding fields or to link the lake to the river; for it is incomplete. It is also a matter of doubt whether the king was cut off by sudden death or whether the success of the enterprise was despaired of. (5) But what spurs me on and inspires me (you will bear with my aspirations to advance your glory) is my desire to see what the kings had merely begun completed by your agency.

42. Traianus to Plinius

That lake of yours can incite us to wish to link it to the sea; but clearly there must be a thorough investigation to find out how much water it collects and from what sources, in case, if let out into the sea, it would drain away entirely. You will be able to apply to Calpurnius Macer for a surveyor, and I shall send from here someone skilled in projects of this kind.

43. C. Plinius to Traianus Imperator

(1) When I was examining the very heavy expenditures which the state of the Byzantines has been making, it was pointed out to me, sir, that an envoy is sent every year with a resolution to bring you greetings, and that he is given twelve thousand sesterces. (2) Mindful, therefore, of your policy, I have decided that the envoy should be kept at home, but that the resolution should be sent on, in order that the expense may be lightened and the city's act of loyalty may at the same time be carried out. (3) Sums of

three thousand sesterces have been charged to the account of the same city, which were being paid every year under the heading of travelling expenses to an envoy who went to bring the city's greetings to the person who is governor of Moesia. I thought this should be cut back for the future. (4) I ask you, sir, to write back what you think and to deign either to confirm my decision or to correct my mistake.

44. Traianus to Plinius

You acted quite correctly, dearest Secundus, in remitting to the Byzantines those twelve thousand sesterces which were being spent on an envoy to bring me greetings. They will be carrying out this duty even if the resolution on its own is sent on through you. The governor of Moesia also will excuse them if they pay their respects to him in a less expensive way.

45. C. Plinius to Traianus Imperator

I ask you to write, sir, and free me from my uncertainty about whether you would want passes which have reached their expiry date to be respected at all, and for how long. For I am concerned not to err in either direction through ignorance or to sanction what is unlawful or to stand in the way of essential business.

46. Traianus to Plinius

Passes which have reached their expiry date ought not to be in use. It is for that reason that I lay it upon myself as one of my first duties to send new passes out through all the provinces before they can be required.

41. C. Plinius to Traianus Imperator

(1) When I wanted, sir, to investigate the public debtors and revenue and expenditures at Apamea, the answer given to me was that the whole citizen-body was in fact anxious to have the colony's accounts examined by me, but that they had never been examined by any of the proconsuls; that they had had the privilege and long-established custom of running their community according to their own judgment. (2) I required them to include the statements they were making and the precedents they were quoting in a memorandum; this I have sent to you in the form in which I had received it, although I was aware that a great deal in it was not relevant to the issue which is in dispute. (3) I ask you to deign to guide me about the principle which you think I ought to follow. For I am concerned not to be thought either to have exceeded the bounds of my duty or not to have fulfilled it.

48. Traianus to Plinius

(1) The memorandum of the people of Apamea, which you had attached to your letter, has relieved me of the need to weigh the kind of reasons they had for wishing it to be seen that the proconsuls who ruled this province had refrained from an examination of their accounts, since they have not refused to let you examine them. (2) Their honesty should therefore be rewarded, so that they should now know that by my wish you will be carrying out this inspection which you are going to make without prejudice to the privileges which they now possess.

49. C. Plinius to Traianus Imperator

Before my arrival, sir, the people of Nicomedia began to add a new forum to their old one; to a corner of it there is a very ancient temple of the Great Mother which needs either to be rebuilt or moved to another site, principally for the reason that it is at a considerably lower level than the buildings which are going up at this very moment.

(2) When I enquired whether the temple had any foundation charter, I discovered that the practice of consecration here is different from ours. Consider therefore, sir, whether you think that a temple without any foundation charter can be moved to another site without any breach of religious law: apart from that, if religious law is not an obstacle, this is the most suitable course.

50. Traianus to Plinius

You can, my dearest Secundus, without anxiety about religious law, move the temple of the Mother of the Gods, if the situation of its site seems to require it, to that site which is more convenient; and do not let the fact that no foundation charter is to be found trouble you, since land in a foreign state is incapable of undergoing the consecration which takes place under our law.

51. C. Plinius to Traianus Imperator

(1) It is hard, sir, to put into words how much joy I felt because you granted both myself and my mother-in-law the favour of transferring her kinsman Caelius Clemens to this province. (2) For, from this, I also comprehend profoundly the scope of your kindness, when, along with my whole family, I experience generosity so full that I do not even venture to respond with equal gratitude, however much it may be in my power to do so. Accordingly I resort to prayers and I beg the gods that I may not be considered unworthy of those favours which you are constantly bestowing upon me.

52. C. Plinius to Traianus Imperator

The day, sir, upon which you saved the empire by taking it over, we have celebrated with as great a joy as you deserve, praying to the gods to bestow upon the human race, whose protection and safety have depended upon your well-being, the favour of keeping you unharmed and prosperous. We have also administered the oath to our fellow-soldiers in the customary manner, while the provincials vied with them in swearing the oath with the same loyalty.

53. Traianus to Plinius

With how much devotion and joy my fellow-soldiers, along with the provincials, celebrated the day of my accession under your guidance, I learnt with pleasure from your letter, my dearest Secundus.

54. C. Plinius to Traianus Imperator

(1) The moneys of the cities, sir, by your foresight and my efforts have already been and are still being recovered; I am concerned that they do not lie idle. For there is no opportunity, or only a very rare one, of buying estates, and men who would be willing to become debtors to the community are not to be found, especially at a rate of twelve asses, the rate at which they borrow from private persons. (2) Consider, therefore, sir, whether you think the rate of interest should be lowered and suitable borrowers should be attracted by this means, and whether, if they are not forthcoming even on these terms, the money should be allocated among the decurions, on condition that they provide their community with adequate security; although they may be unwilling and refuse, this step will be less harsh if a lighter rate of interest is fixed.

55. Traianus to Plinius

I myself also see no other remedy, my dearest Secundus, than to reduce the amount of interest in order that the moneys of the cities may the more easily be put out on loan. Its level you shall determine in accordance with the numbers of those who will take up loans. To force men to accept against their will that which may perhaps lie idle on their hands is not in accordance with the justice of our age.

56. C. Plinius to Traianus Imperator

(1) I offer you my most profound thanks, sir, because in the midst of your most pressing duties you have deigned to guide me also on those points on which I have consulted you: which is what I ask you to do on this occasion as well. (2) For a man has come to me and informed me that his opponents, who had been banished for three years by

that most distinguished man Servilius Calvus, were still residing in the province; they asserted in rebuttal that they had their status restored by the same governor and they read out his edict. For this reason I believed it necessary to refer the case to you as it stands. (3) For, while it is laid down in your instructions that I should not restore the status of men banished by another person or by myself, yet no provision is made for those whom another person has both banished and restored to their former status. So you had to be consulted, sir, about what rule you wish me to follow, as well, of course, as about those who, having been banished in perpetuity and not having had their status restored, are apprehended in the province. (4) For this category also has come before me for judgment. For a man who had been banished in perpetuity by the proconsul Iulius Bassus was brought before me. Because I was aware that Bassus' decisions had been revoked and that the right had been granted by the Senate to all those who had been involved in cases decided by him to plead their cases afresh, provided that they applied within two years, I asked this man whom he (Bassus) had banished whether he had approached a proconsul and informed him. He said he had not. (5) It was this which led me to consult you about whether you think he should be sent back to serve out his sentence or whether a heavier sentence should be imposed, and which sentence in particular, both on this man and on any others who may by chance be found to be in a similar position. I have appended to this letter Calvus' judgment and edict, and likewise Bassus' judgment.

57. Traianus to Plinius

I shall write back to you presently about what decision should be taken about the status of those who had been banished for three years by the proconsul Publius Servilius Calvus and afterwards had their status restored by an edict of the same person, and have stayed on in the province, after I have ascertained from Calvus the reasons for this action. (2) The man who was banished in perpetuity by Iulius Bassus, since he had for two years the opportunity of going to law if he thought he had been banished wrongfully, and since he did not do this and persisted in staying on in the province, ought to be sent in chains to the Prefects of my Praetorian Guard. For it is not enough for him to be sent back to serve out his sentence which he insolently evaded.

58. C. Plinius to Traianus Imperator

(1) While I was calling out the names of jurymen, sir, as I was about to begin the assizes, Flavius Archippus started to apply for exemption as a philosopher. (2) Some people said he should not be freed from the obligation of jury service, but removed entirely from the ranks of jurymen, and sent back to suffer the punishment from which he had escaped by breaking out of his fetters. (3) A judgment of the proconsul Velius Paulus was read out, from which it was demonstrated that Archippus had been condemned

to the mines on a charge of forgery: he was unable to produce anything by which he could show that his status had been festered; however, he advanced as evidence of his restoration both a petition submitted by himself to Domitian and epistles of the latter which had a bearing upon his reputation, as well as a resolution of the people of Prusa. To these he also added letters which you had written to him, he added both an edict and an epistle of your father's, in which he had confirmed the favours bestowed by Domitian. (4) Accordingly, although such serious charges were laid against this man, I thought no judgment should be reached until I consulted you about this matter, which seemed to me to be worthy of your decision. I have appended to this letter the documents which were read out on either side.

(5) *Epistle of Domitian to Terentius Maximus*

Flavius Archippus the philosopher has prevailed upon me to give instructions for the purchase of an estate worth up to 100,000 sesterces for him in the area of Prusa, his native city, on the income from which he can support his dependents. I wish this to be bestowed upon him. You will charge the full cost to my generosity,

(6) *Of the same person to Lappius Maximus*

I should wish you, Maximus my friend, to treat the philosopher Archippus, a good man whose character lives up to his profession, as a man recommended by me, and to show him your full kindness in those requests he may respectfully make of you.

(7) *Edict of the deified Nerva*

Some things, citizens, the very happiness of our age proclaims for certain by edict, nor does a good emperor need to be waited for in matters where it is enough for him to be understood, since the confidence of my fellow-citizens can be assured, even without being explicitly told, of this fact, that I have placed the safety of all before my own tranquillity, in order that I might both grant new favours and confirm those conceded before my reign. (8) In order, however, that neither the uncertainty of those who obtained favours nor the reputation of him who conferred them should introduce any element of hesitation into the public rejoicing, I have judged it alike necessary and delightful to anticipate their doubts by my generosity. (9) I wish no man to suppose that what he has obtained in the reign of another emperor, whether as an individual or as a member of a community, would be revoked by me, for this reason at any rate, that he should be indebted for it to me instead. Let these favours be confirmed and secure, nor should the joy of anyone on whom the good fortune of the empire has looked with a kind face require renewed prayers. Let them permit me to keep my time free for new favours, and let them know that only those things which they do not possess need to be asked for.

(10) Epistle of the same person to Tullius Iustus

Since the arrangement of all matters which have been begun and completed in earlier times is to be respected, then one must also abide by the epistles of Domitian.

59. C. Plinius to Traianus Imperator

Flavius Archippus begs me in the name of your well-being and eternal fame to send you the memorandum which he has given to me. I decided that, since he has asked in this way, this request must be granted, on condition, however, that I made it known to the woman who is his accuser that I was going to send it. A memorandum which I have received from her in her turn I have attached to these epistles, that you may the more easily, having as it were listened to both parties, consider what you think should be decided.

60. Traianus to Plinius

(1) Domitian could, it is true, have been unaware of what the status of Archippus was at the time when he wrote so much that had a bearing upon his reputation; but it is more in accordance with my character to believe that support was given to his status by the emperor's intervention, especially since the honour of having his statue put up was voted to him on so many occasions by those who were not unaware of the judgment which the proconsul Paulus had delivered against him. (2) This, however, my dearest Secundus, does not imply that, if anything in the way of a fresh accusation is laid against him, you should suppose that less notice is to be taken of it. I have read the memoranda from his accuser Furia Prima, and also from Archippus himself, which you had attached to your second letter.

61. C. Plinius to Traianus Imperator

(1) You are indeed most far-sighted, sir, in your anxiety in case the lake, if linked to the river and so to the sea, drains away; I, however, believe that, being on the spot, I have found a means of forestalling this danger. (2) For the lake can be brought as far as the river by means of a canal, yet not be let out into the river, but, by leaving a bank as it were, it can be at the same time both brought together and kept separate. In this way we shall ensure that it is not deprived of its water by being mingled with the river, yet that it should be in the same position as if it were mingled. For it will be easy to transport to the river loads brought down on the canal across the very narrow strip of land which will lie in between. (3) It will be carried out in this way, if necessity forces us, and (I hope) it will not force us. For the lake is both deep enough in itself and at present pours a river out in the opposite direction. If the outlet is closed off on that side and turned aside in the direction we wish, it will only discharge the amount of water

it carries at present, without any loss to the lake. Moreover streams ran across the tract through which the canal will have to be dug; if these are carefully collected together, they will increase the supply of water which the lake will have provided. (4) Again, if it is decided to extend the canal further and, by cutting it deeper, to bring it to the level of the sea, and to let it out, not into the river, but into the sea itself, the counter-pressure of the sea will protect and push back whatever comes out of the lake. If the nature of the ground did not permit us any of these schemes, yet it would be practicable to restrain the flow of the water by means of sluice-gates. (5) However, a surveyor, whom you certainly should send out, sir, as you promise, will investigate and assess these and other schemes with far more skill. For the project is one worthy both of your greatness and your concern. I in the meantime have written, on your authority, to that most distinguished man Calpurnius Macer, to send as capable a surveyor as possible.

62. Traianus to Plinius

It is evident, my dearest Secundus, that you have spared neither forethought nor effort in the matter of that lake of yours, seeing that you have worked out so many devices to ensure that it would not be in danger of being drained and would be of greater use to us for the future. Choose therefore the scheme which the actual situation especially recommends. I believe that Calpurnius Macer will see to it that he supplies you with a surveyor, and those provinces of yours are not lacking in these experts.

63. C. Plinius to Traianus Imperator

Your freedman Lycormas has written to me, sir, to detain until his arrival any embassy which might have come from the Bosporus in order to make its way to the city. And in fact no embassy has yet come, at any rate to the city where I am myself staying, but a letter-carrier from king Sauromates has come. I decided to take advantage of the opportunity which chance had offered me and to send him along with the letter-carrier who arrived in advance of Lycormas on his journey, in order that you should be able to learn at the same moment from Lycormas' and the king's epistles news about which you should perhaps be informed at the same moment.

64. C. Plinius to Traianus Imperator

King Sauromates has written to me that there are some matters about which you ought to be informed as soon as possible. For this reason I have assisted with a pass the speedy journey of a letter-carrier whom he has sent to you with epistles.

65. C. Plinius to Traianus Imperator

(1) Sir, there is an important dispute, and one which affects the whole province, concerning the status and the costs of rearing of those whom they call "foster-children". (2) I myself, after having heard decisions of emperors on this matter read to me, because I could not find any local rule or any general one which should be applied to the Bithynians, decided that I must consult you about what rule you wish to have followed; and I did not think that, on a matter which called for your authority, I could be satisfied with precedents. (3) In fact there was read out in my presence an edict relating to Achaia which was said to be one of the deified Augustus'; there were also read out epistles of the deified Vespasian to the Spartans, and of the deified Titus to the same people and to the Achaeans, and of Domitian to the proconsuls Avidius Nigrinus and Armenius Brocchus, and likewise to the Spartans. I have not sent these texts to you for this reason, because they seemed to me to be both inadequately corrected and, in some cases, of doubtful authenticity, and because I believed that the genuine and corrected texts were in your archives.

66. Traianus to Plinius

(1) That dispute, which is concerned with those persons who, born free, have been put out to die and then rescued by certain individuals and reared in slavery, has often been discussed, and there is no rule to be found in the registers of those who were emperors before me which was laid down for all the provinces. (2) There are, it is true, epistles of Domitian to Avidius Nigrinus and Armenius Brocchus, which ought perhaps to be respected: but Bithynia is not among those provinces about which he wrote in reply; and for that reason I do not think that the right to free status should be refused to those who will be proved to be entitled to freedom on grounds of this kind, nor should they have to buy back their actual freedom by paying for the costs of their rearing.

67. C. Plinius to Traianus Imperator

(1) When the ambassador of king Sauromates had waited of his own accord for two days at Nicaea, where he had found me, I did not think, sir, that he ought to experience a longer delay, in the first place because it was still uncertain when your freedman Lycormas was going to arrive, in the second because I was myself on the point of setting out for a distant part of the province at the pressing call of my duties. (2) I considered that I must bring these facts to your attention, because I had only just written that Lycormas had asked me to detain any embassy which might have come from the Bosporus until his arrival. No satisfactory reason has presented itself to me for doing so any longer, especially since it seemed likely that Lycormas' epistles, which, as I told you earlier, I did not want to hold back, would arrive from here several days in advance of the ambassador.

68. C. Plinius to Traianus Imperator

Certain persons have asked me to allow them, in accordance with the precedent set by the proconsuls, to transfer the remains of their relatives to some site or other either because of damage caused by the passage of time or because of the flooding of a river and other reasons similar to these. Because I knew that in our city it is the custom for application to be made to the college of pontiffs in a case of this kind, I decided that I must consult you, sir, as supreme pontiff, about what course you wish me to follow.

69. Traianus to Plinius

It is harsh to enforce upon provincials an obligation to apply to the pontiffs, should they wish to move the remains of their relatives from one site to another for some proper reasons. It is therefore the precedents set by those who have governed that province before you which ought rather to be followed by you, and permission ought to be granted or refused in accordance with the reason each person gives.

70. C. Plinius to Traianus Imperator

(1) When I was investigating whereabouts in Prusa the bath-house for which you had given permission could be built, the best site seemed to be one on which there was once a house, a beautiful one, so I am told, but which is now unsightly with ruins. For by this means we shall ensure that a most foul blot upon the city is beautified and that at the same time the city itself is enhanced without any buildings being demolished, but that those which have crumbled away with age are enlarged and improved. (2) Now the circumstances of this house are as follows: Claudius Polyaenus had bequeathed it to Claudius Caesar and directed that a temple to him should be built in the courtyard, while the rest of the house was to be let. For a while the city collected income from it; then, little by little, in part through being looted, in part through being neglected, the whole house along with the courtyard fell into ruin, and by now almost nothing of it is left except the ground. Whether you, sir, make a gift of it to the city or give orders for it to be sold, the city will consider it a very great service because of the convenience of the site. (3) I myself, if you give your permission, am thinking of siting the bath-house on the unoccupied ground, but of enclosing the actual place where the buildings stood with a recess and colonnades and dedicating them to you, through whose favour a handsome building, and one worthy of your name, will be put up. (4) I have sent you a copy of the will, although it is defective: from it you will learn that Polyaenus bequeathed many items for the embellishment of the same house, which, like the house itself, have disappeared, but which will be hunted out by me as far as will be possible.

71. Traianus to Plinius

We can use that ground at Prusa with the ruined house, which you say in your letter is unoccupied, for the building of the bath-house. You did not however make this quite clear, whether a temple was put up to Claudius in the courtyard. For, if it was put up, even though it may have fallen down, its religious influence has filled the site.

72. C. Plinius to Traianus Imperator

Certain persons are requesting that I should myself exercise jurisdiction in cases of children being acknowledged and having their freeborn status restored, in accordance with an epistle of Domitian written to Minicius Rufus and with the precedents set by the proconsuls. I have looked at the resolution of the Senate relating to the same kinds of cases, which talks only about those provinces which have proconsuls as governors; and for that reason I have left the matter undecided until you, sir, direct me about the principle you wish me to follow.

73. Traianus to Plinius

If you send me the resolution of the Senate which has given you pause, I shall judge whether you ought to exercise jurisdiction in cases of children being acknowledged and having their true birth-status restored.

74. C. Plinius to Traianus Imperator

(1) Appuleius, sir, the soldier who is stationed at the military post in Nicomedia, wrote to me that an individual named Callidromus, when he was being kept under duress by Maximus and Dionysius, bakers to whom he had hired out his services, had taken refuge at your statue, and that, when he was brought before the magistrates, he had revealed that he had at one time been the slave of Laberius Maximus and been taken prisoner by Susagus in Moesia and sent by Decibalus as a gift to Pacorus the king of Parthia, and that he had been in his service for many years, and then escaped, and so had come to Nicomedia. (2) I had him brought before me; when he had told the same story, I decided that he should be sent to you; I have done so somewhat belatedly, while I sought to find a jewel bearing a likeness of Pacorus and the things which he was wearing, which he claimed had been taken away from him. (3) For I wished to send this also at the same time, if it could be found, just as I have sent the small lump of ore which he said he had brought from a Parthian mine. It has been sealed with my ring, the device on which is a four-horse chariot.

75. C. Plinius to Traianus Imperator

(1) Iulius Largus, sir, from Pontus, a man I had never seen and not even heard of (no doubt he put his faith in your good judgment) has entrusted me with the disposal and management of an act of devotion towards you. (2) For in his will he has asked me to accept and enter upon his estate, and then, after fifty thousand sesterces have been set aside as a prior legacy, to hand over all the residue to the cities of Heraclea and Tium, with the provision that it should be in my power to decide whether I thought buildings should be put up which would be dedicated in your honour or quinquennial competitions should be founded which would be known as the Trajanic. I decided that this should be brought to your attention, mainly for this purpose, that you may consider which I ought to choose.

76. Traianus to Plinius

Iulius Largus settled upon your good faith as if he had known you well. So choose for yourself what will particularly conduce to the perpetuation of his memory, in accordance with the circumstances of each place, and follow the course which you decide is the best.

77. C. Plinius to Traianus Imperator

(1) You acted with the greatest forethought, sir, in that you instructed that most distinguished man Calpurnius Macer to send a legionary centurion to Byzantium. (2) Consider whether you think the interests of the people of Iuliopolis should also be provided for by a similar plan. Their city, although it is very small, bears very heavy burdens and suffers injuries which are the more serious by reason of its greater weakness. (3) Moreover, whatever help you give to the people of Iuliopolis will also be of advantage to the entire province. For they lie at the edge of Bithynia, and provide passage for very many persons who travel through it.

78. Traianus to Plinius

(1) The situation of the city of the Byzantines, with a throng of travellers flooding into it from every direction, is such that we thought it right, following the practice of earlier periods, that its magistrates should be supported by the protection of a legionary centurion. (2) If we decide that the people of Iuliopolis should be helped in the same way, we shall be burdening ourselves with a precedent: for more cities will seek the same help to the extent that they are weaker ones. I have such confidence in your conscientiousness that I feel sure you will employ every means to ensure that they are not exposed to injuries. (3) If any individuals conduct themselves in violation of my discipline, let them be punished at once; or, if they commit acts too serious for it to

be enough for them to be punished summarily, if they are soldiers, you shall make it known to their commanding officers that you have arrested them, or, if they are persons on their way back to the city, you shall write to me.

79. C. Plinius to Traianus Imperator

(1) It is prescribed, sir, in the Pompeian law which was laid down for the Bithynians, that no one should hold a magistracy or be a member of a senate who was under thirty years of age. In the same law it was provided that those who had held a magistracy should be members of a senate. (2) Next there followed an edict of the deified Augustus in which he allowed men to hold lesser magistracies from the age of twenty-two. (3) The question is therefore raised whether a man under thirty years of age who has held a magistracy can be enrolled in a senate by the censors, and, if he can, whether those who have not held a magistracy can also, under the same construction, be enrolled as senators from that age at which they have been allowed to hold a magistracy; furthermore this is asserted to have been the practice hitherto and to be necessary, because it is far better that the sons of honourable men should be admitted to the senate-house than that commoners should be. (4) I myself, when asked what my opinion was by the censors-elect, thought that men under thirty years of age who had held a magistracy could indeed be enrolled in a senate both according to the edict of Augustus and according to the Pompeian law, since Augustus had allowed men under thirty years of age to hold a magistracy and the law had wanted anyone who had held a magistracy to be a senator. (5) But about those who had not held one, although they were of the same age as those who had been allowed to hold one, I was in doubt. Hence I have been led to consult you, sir, about what principle you wish to have followed, I have appended to this letter the chapters of the law, and the edict of Augustus.

80. Traianus to Plinius

I agree with your construction, my dearest Secundus: that the Pompeian law was amended to this extent by the edict of the deified Augustus, that men who were not younger than twenty-two years of age could indeed hold a magistracy and that those who had held one might enter the senate of each city. However, I do not think that those who are under thirty years of age can be enrolled in the senate of each place without having held a magistracy, just because they can hold a magistracy.

81. C. Plinius to Traianus Imperator

(1) While I was attending to official business, sir, in my lodgings at Prusa by Olympus, on the same day that I was intending to leave, the magistrate Asclepiades reported that an appeal had been made to me by Claudius Eumolpus. When Cocceianus Dion at a

session of the council requested that a building, the supervision of which he had undertaken, should be handed over to the city, at that moment Eumolpus, acting as counsel for Flavius Archippus, said that the accounts of the building should be demanded from Dion before it was transferred to the community, because he had behaved otherwise than he ought to have done. (2) He further added that your statue had been placed in the same building as well as the bodies of persons who had been buried, the wife and the son of Dion, and he requested that I should hear the case in open court. (3) When I had said that I would do this at once and that I would postpone my departure, he asked me to give him a longer period to put his case together, and to hold the hearing in another city. I answered that I would hear the case at Nicaea. (4) When I had taken my place on the bench there in order to hold the hearing, this same Eumolpus began to apply for an adjournment on the grounds that he was not fully prepared, while Dion in response demanded that the case should be heard. Many things were said on either side, some of them also about the case. (5) When I had decided that an adjournment should be granted and that you must be consulted on a matter which involved a precedent, I told both sides to supply memoranda of their pleadings. For I wanted you to learn the arguments which had been advanced as far as possible from their own words. (6) And Dion in fact said that he would supply this. Eumolpus replied that he would include in a memorandum the claims he was making for the community, but that, as far as the buried bodies were concerned, he was not the plaintiff but counsel for Flavius Archippus whose instructions he had been carrying out. Archippus, for whom Eumolpus was acting as counsel just as he had at Prusa, said that he would supply a memorandum. However, neither Eumolpus nor Archippus, despite being waited for for very many days, has yet supplied me with the memoranda; Dion has supplied one which I have attached to this epistle. (7) I have been to the spot myself and seen your statue also which has been placed in the library, and the site where Dion's son and wife are said to be buried, which lies in open ground which is enclosed by colonnades. (8) I ask you, sir, to deign to guide me especially in this kind of case, since there is in addition great public interest, as is inevitable with an issue which is both not contested and is defended by precedents.

82. Traianus to Plinius

(1) You could have been in no uncertainty, my dearest Secundus, about that matter on which you decided that I should be consulted, since you were very well aware of my determination not to obtain respect for my name through inspiring men with fear or terror or through charges of treason. (2) Accordingly that charge which I should not allow even if it were supported by the precedents should be dropped; rather let the accounts of the building carried out under the supervision of Cocceianus Dion be examined, since the interest of the city requires it and Dion does not object, nor ought he to object.

83. C. Plinius to Traianus Imperator

Having been requested, sir, by the people of Nicaea as a community, in the name of those things which are and ought to be most sacred to me, that is in the name of your eternal fame and your well-being, to pass on to you their petition, I did not think it right to refuse and I have attached to this letter the memorandum which I have received from them.

84. Traianus to Plinius

You will be obliged to give a hearing to the people of Nicaea who maintain that the right to claim the property of their fellow-citizens who die intestate was conceded to them by the deified Augustus. Collect together all the persons involved in this same business and summon as your advisers the procurators Virdius Gemellinus and Epimachus my freedman, in order that, after also assessing the arguments which are maintained on the opposite side, you may jointly reach the decision which you will jointly believe to be the best.

85. C. Plinius to Traianus Imperator

Having found by experience, sir, that your freedman and procurator Maximus, during the whole period we have been together, is upright, hardworking and conscientious, and as completely devoted to your interests as he is faithful in observing your discipline, I am very pleased to send him on his way with my recommendation to you, in that good faith which I owe to you.

86A. C. Plinius to Traianus Imperator

Having found by experience, sir, that Gavius Bassus the prefect of the Pontic shore is honourable, upright, hardworking, and besides this most respectful towards myself, I send him on his way with my prayers as well as my support, in that good faith which I owe to you.

86B. C. Plinius to Traianus Imperator

… a man trained by his military service in your company, to whose discipline he is indebted for the fact that he is deserving of your generosity. Both soldiers and civilians, by whom his fairness and his kindness have been closely examined, have vied with each other in bearing witness to him before me, both as individuals and as communities. I bring this fact to your attention, in that good faith which I owe to you.

87. C. Plinius to Traianus Imperator

(1) I had Nymphidius Lupus, the former chief centurion, as a comrade in arms, sir, when I was a tribune and he a prefect: then I began to feel a close affection for him. Later these feelings strengthened with the long duration of our mutual friendship. (2) Therefore made my claim on his retirement and required him to help me with his advice in Bithynia. This he in a most friendly way has already done and will continue to do, having set aside the usual consideration of leisure and old age. (3) For these reasons I count his relatives as my own, especially his son, Nymphidius Lupus, an upright, hard-working young man, and most worthy of an excellent father. He will be well qualified to receive your generosity, as you can learn from the first trials you have made of him, since he has earned as prefect of a cohort the fullest commendation of those most distinguished men Iulius Ferox and Fuscus Salinator. You will crown my happiness and my satisfaction, sir, by conferring an honour on the son.

88. C. Plinius to Traianus Imperator

I pray, sir, that you may celebrate both this and very many other birthdays in as much happiness as possible and that with eternal fame … the flourishing glory of your merit … [probable lacuna] which, safe and strong, you will increase by achievements upon achievements.

89. Traianus to Plinius

I acknowledge your prayers, my dearest Secundus, in which you beg that I may celebrate very many most happy birthdays with our commonwealth in a prosperous condition.

90. C. Plinius to Traianus Imperator

(1) The people of Sinope, sir, are short of water; this, it appears, both good and plentiful, can be brought to them from the sixteenth milestone. However, there is ground which is suspect and soft, just by the source, a little more than a mile away. In the meantime I have given orders for it to be investigated, at little expense, to see whether it can take and support a structure. (2) Money, collected under our supervision, will not be wanting, if you, sir, permit this kind of building which will contribute both to the health and the attractiveness of a very thirsty colony.

91. Traianus to Plinius

Investigate thoroughly, dearest Secundus, just as you have begun to do, whether the ground which you consider suspect can support the structure of an aqueduct. And I do not think there should be any hesitation about bringing water to the colony of Sinope, provided only that it can in fact carry the work through out of its own resources, seeing that this project will contribute very greatly both to its health and its pleasure.

92. C. Plinius to Traianus

The free arid allied city of the Amiseni employs its own laws through the benefit of your generosity. I have appended to this letter a memorandum concerning *eranoi* which was handed to me in this city, in order that you, sir, may consider what you think should be forbidden and to what extent they should be allowed.

93. Traianus to Plinius

If the Amiseni, whose memorandum you had attached to your epistle, are permitted by their own laws, which they employ through the benefit of a treaty, to have an eranus, we cannot stand in the way of their having one, all the more readily if they use contributions of this kind not on crowds and unlawful assemblies, but to support the poverty of the humbler people. In the other cities, which are bound by our law, anything of this kind is forbidden.

94. C. Plinius to Traianus Imperator

(1) I have long, sir, included that most upright, honourable and learned man, Suetonius Tranquillus, among my friends, having admired both his character and his learning, and I have begun to love him all the more now that I have had a closer insight into his character. (2) Two reasons make it necessary for him to be awarded the rights of a parent of three children; for he both earns the good opinion of his friends and has had rather an unfortunate experience of marriage, and he must obtain from your kindness through our agency that which the hostility of fortune has denied him. (3) I know, sir, how great is the favour for which I apply, but I am applying to you, and I have experience of your generosity in all my requests. For you can infer how greatly I want this from the fact that I should not be asking for it when not face to face with you if I only wanted it to a moderate degree.

95. Traianus to Plinius

You are certainly aware, my dearest Secundus, of how sparing I am in granting these favours, since I am in the practice of stating in the Senate itself that I have not exceeded the number which I declared in the presence of that most noble order would be large enough for me. However, I have agreed to your request and have given orders for an entry to be made in my registers that I have given Suetonius Tranquillus the rights of a parent of three children, subject to that proviso which I have been in the habit of making.

96. C. Plinius to Traianus Imperator

(1) It is my custom, sir, to bring before you everything about which I am in doubt. For who can better guide my uncertainty or inform my ignorance? I have never been present at trials of Christians; for that reason I do not know what the charge usually is and to what extent it is usually punished. (2) I have been in no little uncertainty about whether any distinction should be made between different ages or whether, however young they may be, they should be treated no differently from the more mature ones; whether pardon should be granted for repentance or whether it is of no help to the man who has been a Christian at all to have given it up; whether it is the name itself, if it is free from crimes, or the crimes associated with the name which are being punished. Meanwhile, in the case of those who were prosecuted before me on the charge of being Christians, I followed this procedure. (3) I asked the people themselves whether they were Christians. Those who admitted that they were I asked a second and a third time, warning them of the punishment; those who persisted I ordered to be executed. For I was in no doubt that, whatever it might be that they were admitting to, their stubbornness and unyielding obstinacy certainly ought to be punished. (4) There were others of a similar madness whom I have listed as due to be sent on to the city, because they were Roman citizens.

Subsequently, through the very course of dealing with the matter, as usually happens, the charge spread widely and more forms of it turned up. (5) An anonymous pamphlet containing the names of many persons was posted up. Those who denied that they were or had been Christians, after they had called upon the gods when I dictated the formula, and after they had made offerings of incense and wine to your statue which I had ordered to be brought in along with the cult-images of the gods for this purpose, and had in addition cursed Christ, none of which acts, it is said, those who are truly Christians can be compelled to perform, I decided should be discharged. (6) Others, named by an informer, said that they were Christians and then denied it; they said that they had in fact been Christians but had given it up, some three years before, some more years earlier than that, and a few even twenty years ago. All these also both paid homage to your statue and to the cult-images of the gods and cursed Christ. (7) Moreover they maintained that this had been the sum of their guilt or error, that they had been in the habit of gathering together before dawn on a fixed day, and of singing antiphonally a hymn to Christ as if to a god, and of binding themselves by oath, not to some wickedness, but not to commit acts of theft or robbery or adultery, not to break faith, not to refuse to return money placed in their keeping when called upon to do so. When these ceremonies had been completed, they said it had been their custom to disperse and to meet again to take food, but food that was ordinary and harmless; they said that they had given up doing even this after my edict, in which, in accordance with your instructions, I had banned secret societies. (8) So I believed it to be all the more necessary to ascertain what the truth was from two slave women, who were called deaconesses, and under torture. I found nothing other than a depraved and extravagant superstition. (9) Accordingly I postponed the hearing and hastened to consult you. For the matter seemed to me to be worthy of your consideration, especially on account of the number of people who are endangered. For many persons of every age, of every rank, of both sexes, are being brought and will be brought into danger. The infection of this superstition has spread, not only through the towns, but also through the villages and the countryside; it seems possible for it to be checked and put right. (10) At any rate it is well established that temples which just now were almost abandoned have begun to be thronged, and customary rites which had long been suspended to be renewed, and the flesh of sacrificial victims, for which until recently very few buyers were to be found, to be sold far and wide. From this it is easy to conjecture what a host of people could be reformed, if room were given for repentance.

97. Traianus to Plinius

You followed the procedure which you ought to have followed, my dear Secundus, in examining the cases of those who were being prosecuted before you as Christians. For no rule with a universal application, such as would have, as it were, a fixed form, can be laid down. (2) They should not be sought out; if they are prosecuted and proved to be guilty, they should be punished, provided, however, that the man who denies that he is a Christian and makes this evident by his action, that is by offering prayers to our gods, shall obtain pardon for his repentance, however suspect he may be with regard to the past. However, pamphlets posted up without an author's name ought to have no place in any criminal charge. For they both set the worst precedent and are not in keeping with the spirit of our age.

98. C. Plinius to Traianus Imperator

(1) The elegant and finely built city of the Amastrians, sir, has among its outstanding structures a most beautiful and also very long street; by the side of this, along its entire length, there stretches, what is by name a stream, but in reality a most foul sewer, and, just as it is disgusting in its most filthy appearance, so it is injurious to health in its most revolting stench. (2) For these reasons it is just as much in the interest of health as of beauty that it should be covered over; this will be done, if you permit it, and we will ensure that money also is not lacking for a project both grand and necessary.

99. Traianus to Plinius

There is good reason, my dearest Secundus, for that stream which flows through the city of the Amastrians to be covered over, if, left uncovered, it is a danger to health. I feel certain that with your usual diligence you will ensure that money is not lacking for this project.

100. C. Plinius to Traianus Imperator

The vows, sir, undertaken last year, we have eagerly and joyfully fulfilled and we have again undertaken new ones, with my fellow-soldiers and the provincials vying with each other in devotion. We prayed to the gods that they would keep you and the commonwealth prosperous and safe with that kindness which you have earned, apart from your great and numerous merits, by your outstanding purity and reverence and honour to the gods.

101. Traianus to Plinius

I was delighted to learn from your letter, my dearest Secundus, that my fellow-soldiers in most joyful unanimity with the provincials have fulfilled, with you dictating the formula to them, the vows to the immortal gods for my preservation, and renewed them for the future.

102. C. Plinius to Traianus Imperator

We have celebrated with due observance the day on which guardianship of the human race was passed on to you in a most happy succession, recommending both our public vows and our rejoicings to the gods who are the authors of your rule.

103. Traianus to Plinius

I was delighted to learn from your letter that the day of my accession was celebrated with due joy and observance by my fellow-soldiers and the provincials, with you dictating the formula to them.

104. C. Plinius to Traianus Imperator

Valerius Paulinus, sir, having excluded Paulinus, has bequeathed to me his rights over his Latin freedmen; for the time being I ask you to grant three of these the rights of Roman citizens. For I fear that it may be presumptuous to appeal on behalf of all of them at once to your generosity which I am obliged to use the more sparingly, the fuller my experience of it is. Those for whom I am making the request are in fact C. Valerius Astraeus, C. Valerius Dionysius, C. Valerius Aper.

105. Traianus to Plinius

Since you most honourably wish to make prudent provision through me for the interests of those who were entrusted to your good faith by Valerius Paulinus, I have in the mean time given orders for an entry to be made in my registers that I have granted the rights of

Roman citizens to those on whose behalf you have made a request this time, and I shall do the same in the case of all the others on whose behalf you make a request.

106. C. Plinius to Traianus Imperator

Having being asked, sir, by P. Accius Aquila, centurion of the sixth mounted cohort, to send on to you a petition in which he appeals to your generosity on behalf of the status of his daughter, I thought it harsh to refuse, since I knew how much patience and kindness you were in the habit of showing to the appeals of soldiers.

107. Traianus to Plinius

I have read the petition of P. Accius Aquila, centurion of the sixth mounted cohort, which you sent on to me; moved by his appeal, I have granted Roman citizenship to his daughter. I have sent you the petition with its rescript, for you to hand over to him.

108. C. Plinius to Traianus Imperator

(1) I ask, sir, that you write back about what rights you wish the cities both of Bithynia and of Pontus to have in recovering sums of money which are owed to them from leases or from sales or for other reasons, I have discovered that the right of prior claim was granted to them by very many of the proconsuls, and that this has come to have the force of law. (2) I think, however, that by your forethought some rule ought to be decided upon and laid down through which their interests may be safeguarded for ever. For the practices which have been introduced by them, even though they may have been wisely conceded, are nevertheless short-lived and precarious, if your authority does not uphold them.

109. Traianus to Plinius

What rights the cities of Bithynia or Pontus ought to exercise in respect of those sums of money which, for whatever reason, will be owed to the community, must be determined in accordance with the law of each city. For, if they have a privilege by which they take priority over all the other creditors, it should be protected, but if they do not have one, it will not be appropriate for this to be granted by me to the detriment of private persons.

110. C. Plinius to Traianus Imperator

(1) The public advocate of the city of the Amiseni, sir, was suing Iulius Piso before me for around forty thousand denarii which had been granted to him from public funds twenty

years ago with the agreement of the Council and the Assembly, and he cited in support your instructions in which grants of this kind are forbidden. (2) Piso in response said he had made very many gifts to the community and had nearly spent his entire fortune. He also pointed out the lapse of time and begged that he should not be compelled to repay what he had received in return for many gifts and a long time ago, to the ruin of what was left of his standing. For these reasons I thought that the case should be left undecided, in order that I might ask your advice, sir, about what course you think should be followed.

111. Traianus to Plinius

Although the instructions do forbid gifts to be made from public funds, yet, in order that the security of many persons may not be undermined, those that were made some time ago must not be reconsidered or claimed to be invalid. Let us therefore disregard whatever was done for this reason twenty years ago. For I wish the interests of individuals in each place to be safeguarded, no less than those of public funds.

112. C. Plinius to Traianus Imperator

(1) The Pompeian law, sir, which the people of Bithynia and Pontus observe, does not order those who are enrolled in a council by censors to pay money; but those whom your generosity has allowed some of the cities to add over and above the lawful number have paid one or two thousand denarii each. (2) Later the proconsul Anicius Maximus ordered those who were enrolled by censors to pay as well, but only in a very few cities, and different sums in different cities. (3) So it remains for you yourself to consider whether in all the cities all those who will henceforward be enrolled as councillors ought to pay some fixed sum for their admission. For it is fitting that that which will remain permanently in force should be determined by you to whose deeds and words eternal fame is due.

113. Traianus to Plinius

No general rule can be laid down by me about whether or not all those who become decurions in every city in Bithynia should pay a fee for their decurionate. So I think that the law of each city should be followed, something which is always the safest course, but indeed I am sure that those who become decurions by invitation will so act that they outstrip [sic] all the rest in generosity.

114. C. Plinius to Traianus Imperator

(1) Under the Pompeian law, sir, the Bythinian cities are allowed to enroll any persons they choose as honorary citizens, provided that none of them come from those cities

which are in Bythinia. In the same law it is laid down for what reasons men may be expelled from a senate by censors. (2) And so some of the censors decided that they should consult me about whether they ought to expel a man who came from another city. (3) I myself, because the law, although it forbade a foreigner to be enrolled as a citizen, yet did not order a man to be expelled from a senate for that reason, and because, moreover, I was assured that in every city there were very many councillors from other cities and that the result would be that many men and many cities would be thrown into confusion by that part of the law which had long since become a dead letter by a kind of general agreement, thought it necessary to consult you about what course you think should be followed. I have appended the chapters of the law to this letter.

115. Traianus to Plinius

You had good reason to be uncertain, dearest Secundus, about what you ought to write in response to the censors who consulted you about whether those who were citizens of other cities, but came from the same province, ought to remain in a senate. For the authority of the law and a custom which had been long established in violation of the law could have pulled you in different directions, I have decided on the following resolution of this issue, that we should make no change in respect of what was done in the past, but that citizens of whatever cities, although they were enrolled in violation of the law, should remain; for the future, however, the Pompeian law should be observed. Should we wish to maintain the force of the law retrospectively as well, it is inevitable that many things would be thrown into confusion.

116. C. Plinius to Traianus Imperator

(1) Those who put on the toga of manhood or celebrate a wedding or enter upon a magistracy or dedicate a public building are in the habit of inviting the whole council and no small number from the commons as well and to give them two denarii or a single denarius apiece. I ask you to write to say whether you think this celebration should be held and on what scale. (2) For my own part, while I believe that this kind of right of invitation should be allowed, especially for the customary reasons, yet I am afraid that those who invite a thousand people, and sometimes even more, may be thought to be going beyond the bounds and to fall into a type of bribery.

117. Traianus to Plinius

You have good reason to fear that an invitation would turn into a type of bribery, if it is one which goes beyond the bounds in the matter of numbers and gathers people together for customary gifts in organised bodies, as it were, not as separate individuals on the basis of personal acquaintance. But it was for this purpose that I chose a man of your wisdom, that you might exercise control over shaping the habits of that province and lay down those rules which would be of benefit for the permanent tranquillity of the province.

118. C. Plinius to Traianus Imperator

(1) The athletes, sir, think that the rewards which you established for triumphal games are due to them from the very day on which they were crowned; for, they say, it is not the date on which they made a triumphal entry into their native city which matters, but the date when they were victorious in the games, as a result of which they can make a triumphal entry. I myself, on the other hand, seriously doubt whether it should not rather be the time at which they made their entry which ought to be observed. (2) These same men are applying for allowances in respect of that contest which was made triumphal by you, although they won their victories before it was so made. For they say that it is fitting that, just as allowances are not paid to them in respect of those games which ceased to be triumphal after they won their victories, they should likewise be paid in respect of those which began to be triumphal (after they won their victories). (3) On this point also I have the gravest doubts, whether consideration should be given to anyone retrospectively and whether that which was not due to them when they won their victories should be paid to them. So I ask you to deign to guide my uncertainty yourself, that is to clarify your own benefactions.

119. Traianus to Plinius

It seems to me that a triumphal reward first begins to be due at that time when any man himself has made his entry into his own city. The allowances in respect of those games which I have decided are to be triumphal are not due retrospectively, if they were not triumphal previously. Nor does the fact that they have ceased to receive allowances in respect of those games which I decided should not be triumphal after they won their victories support the claim of the athletes. For, although the status of the games has been changed, the allowances which they had collected before that are nevertheless not being reclaimed.

120. C. Plinius to Traianus Imperator

(1) Up to this time, sir, I have not provided anyone with passes nor have I sent anyone off on any business but yours. A kind of necessity has broken down this permanent rule of mine. (2) For I thought it harsh to deny the use of these passes to my wife who, after hearing of her grandfather's death, was anxious to hasten to her aunt's side, since the value of a service of this kind depends on speed, and I knew that you would

approve of the reason for a journey the motive for which was family affection. I have written to you about this, because I considered that I should be quite ungrateful, if I had concealed the fact that, in addition to your other kindnesses, I was also indebted to your generosity for this particular fact, that I did not hesitate, in my confidence in that generosity, to take action as if I had consulted you, since, if I had consulted you, I should have acted too late.

121. Traianus to Plinius

You were right to feel confidence in my attitude, dearest Secundus, nor should there have been any doubt whether you should have waited until you could consult me about whether your wife's journey ought to be expedited by the passes which I provided for your official duties, seeing that your wife was under an obligation to enhance the gratitude felt by her aunt for her arrival by its promptness as well.

Alexander the Quack Prophet

By Lucian

Translated by Lionel Casson

In Abonoteichus on the south shore of the Black Sea, an obscure town in a remote corner of the Roman Empire, a certain Alexander gained a great reputation in Lucian's day as mouthpiece of a new god of prophecy.

Lucian despised all oracles and rarely passed up a chance for a joke or sneer at their expense (cf. pp. 140, 225, 322). But this was no joking matter. This was no shrine going back to hoary antiquity and famous in song and story but one that had been founded in his own lifetime by a man of intelligence and vast ability, one that, moreover, was doing an active and very profitable business. So, when a person high among the Epicureans, who were implacable enemies of anything that smacked of the supernatural, asked Lucian to do a brief life of Alexander, he went at the task with gusto.

This memoir reads as if it had burst white-hot from a pen burning with righteous indignation. As a matter of fact, it was written at least fifteen years after the events, described here so vividly they seem to have happened yesterday, took place. This immediacy is part of Lucian's artistry, another stroke of the brush on this portrait in tar that he deliberately set out to make. For Lucian the rationalist it was enough that Alexander was passing himself off as a prophet: it gave him carte blanche to go after the man with no holds barred.

You must, therefore, not believe every word you read here. Alexander very likely was neither a pederast nor an oversexed ravisher of women; this is the sort of mud ancient pamphleteers slung at their pet hates as a matter of course. He certainly was no Greek Rasputin with a sinister influence pervading the entire Roman Empire; this is Lucian the spellbinding rhetorician at work. The dramatic tale of a face-to-face encounter with Alexander, the bitter vignette of the Epicurean barely saved from stoning, the exciting story of the attempted murder—this is Lucian the master of narrative at work; they may or may not be true, Alexander the Quack Prophet *is not a documented tract against superstition; it is a creative work of art.*

That there was such a person who ran such an oracle cannot be doubted. We have incontrovertible proof: the Abonoteichans, proud of the shrine, embellished their coins with a likeness of Alexander's new god; specimens can be seen in many a museum today. Lucian says it was Alexander who got the emperor's permission to mint these, and he may very well be telling the truth. And he must be telling the truth when he names a high-ranking Roman official as one of the fish Alexander caught—and hooked so securely he was able to marry off his daughter to the fool.

Alexander's customers came from almost all the key provinces—as Roman administrative districts were called—of Asia Minor. The ones Lucian names are: Bithynia and Pontus (where Abonoteichus was located) along the south shore of the Black Sea; Galatia and Paphlagonia (which, very near to Abonoteichus, supplied the bulk of the clientele) in the interior behind; Asia (including the region of Ionia) and Cilicia on the Mediterranean coast to the west and south.

You may be under the impression, my dear Celsus, that you've given me a minor and trivial assignment in asking me to compose and send you an account of the life, schemes, brazen effrontery, and hocus-pocus of Alexander, the quack of Abonoteichus. Actually, if a man were to do a detailed study, it would be no less a project than composing a life of Alexander the Great: the one was as great a villain as the other a hero. However, if you will read with indulgence and fill in from your own imagination the gaps in my narrative, I'll take on the job. I'll try to clean up this Augean stable—If not all of it, at least as much as I can; I'll haul out a few basketfuls of dung, enough to give you an idea of how vast and unspeakable was the total accumulation that three thousand head of cattle had been able to pile up over all those years.[1]

I feel a sense of shame for both our sakes, yours as well as mine. Yours because you're willing to let the memory of a damned scoundrel be committed to writing and so preserved, mine because I'm spending so much time and energy on such a topic, on the acts of a man who ought not be a subject for the educated to read about but an object for the masses to behold being torn to bits by foxes and apes in some vast theater. However, if anyone criticizes me for what I am doing, I have the following to offer as precedent Arrian, Epictetus' disciple, an outstanding Roman and a man who devoted a lifetime to culture, can come to my defense as well as his own.[2] He did the same thing; he was willing, for example, to draw up a biography of Tilliborus the bandit. I'm doing a memoir of a much more vicious bandit—mine didn't do his plundering in forests and on mountainsides but in cities and, in his marauding, didn't range over merely Mysia and Ida and a few of the more barren areas of Asia Minor but, in a sense, saturated the entire Roman Empire with his brigandage.

First I want to paint for you a word picture of the man, making as exact a likeness as I can, though I'm not much of a literary portraitist. In physical appearance, to give you an idea of that as well, he was tall and had good looks with a genuine godly quality about them. His skin was white, his beard was long but not shaggy, and his flowing locks were partly real and partly a wig he wore, but one so well matched that few people were aware his hair wasn't all his own. His eyes were piercing and had an inspired gleam, his voice very soft, yet at the same time perfectly clear.

That was his outward appearance and, in all of it, there isn't a single flaw to be found anywhere. But that soul and mind of his! O Heracles the Protector, O Zeus the Guardian, O Castor and Pollux the Saviors! Throw a man in with his worst enemies, and keep him away from someone like Alexander! You see, in brains and shrewdness and keenness there wasn't anybody like him. Energy, grasp, memory, a natural aptitude for learning—he had more than his due of each. But he used these endowments for the worst possible ends. Though he had such a wealth of noble talents, he lived in a way that outdid all the notorious evildoers of history—he was worse than the Cercopes, worse than Eurybatus or Phrynondas or Aristodemus or Sostratus.[3] Once, in a letter to his son-in-law Rutilianus, when he was being modest about himself, he claimed he could be compared with Pythagoras. With all due respect for Pythagoras, who was a wise man with an inspired mind, had he been a contemporary of this fellow, believe me, he would have looked like a child in comparison. Now, in the name of all three Graces, don't imagine for a moment that I say this to insult Pythagoras or because I'm trying to pair the two men for having achieved similar ends. If you were to take the vilest actions Pythagoras' detractors have attributed to him to ruin his good name—actions I, for one, don't believe are true, but no matter—if they were all lumped together, the whole batch would amount to only a minuscule part of Alexander's ingenious scheming. All in all, you must conceive of, you must conjure up in your mind, a soul composed of the most varied ingredients, one that blended deceit, trickery, lying, sharp practices, carelessness, nerve, recklessness, and tirelessness in carrying out plans with trust, reliability, and the knack of acting a better role, of looking white when the end in view was black. As a matter of fact, everyone who met him for the first time left with the impression that this was the finest and most decent person alive, even the most simple and naïve. On top of all this, he was a man whose ideas were on the grand scale: he never paid attention to anything small but always kept his mind on the big things.

When a young boy Alexander was extremely good-looking—not only could you hear this from people who told his story but you could see for yourself the traces left in the grown man. He made an out-and-out prostitute of himself: he went to bed with whoever wanted him and would pay. Among the many lovers who took him on was some quack, one of those who offer magic, miracle-working incantations, charms to snare a lover, tricks to defeat an enemy, places to dig for buried treasure, and ways to inherit a fortune. This fellow observed that the youngster not only had a natural talent and all the qualifications to be of help in his business but that the boy was as much in love with his dirty tricks as he was with the other's blooming youth. He took the youngster under his wing and used him constantly as servant, attendant and assistant. He himself had been a government doctor supposedly and, like the wife of Thon of Egypt, knew the

Brewing of many a potion most healthful and many most harmful.[4]

To all this Alexander became sole heir. His teacher-lover, a native of Tyana, belonged to the circle of Apollonius of Tyana and knew all the ins and outs of the act Apollonius used to put on.[5] You see now the school that produced the subject of this memoir!

Our friend from Tyana died just when Alexander was of an age to grow a beard. He was left penniless, and at the same time the good looks by which he could have made a living lost their bloom. But he no longer had his mind on anything small. Instead he went into partnership with a worse scoundrel than himself, someone from Byzantium who used to cast horoscopes for contestants in the games held on festival days—"Nutsy," I think he was nicknamed. The two of them went around masquerading as magicians, pulling off swindles, and fleecing the "fat-heads," as the public is called in the magicians' argot. Among their victims was a wealthy woman named Macetis who had outlived her attractiveness but still had the urge to be alluring to men. Once they had discovered her, they made a very good thing out of it and followed in her tracks when she left Bithynia to go back to Macedonia. She came from Pella which long ago, during the days of the kings of Macedon, was a flourishing spot but today has the merest handful of miserable inhabitants. Here their eye was caught by certain enormous snakes which were perfectly gentle and tame—they were fed by the women, slept with the children, allowed themselves to be stepped on, didn't turn fierce when petted, and took milk from the breast just like any infant. These serpents are extremely common there, a fact that very likely gave rise, in bygone days, to the story about Olympias when she became pregnant with Alexander;[6] I imagine that one such snake had been sleeping with her. The partners bought one of these creatures, the finest available, for a few pennies, and, to quote Thucydides, "this was the starting point of the war."[7]

As you'd expect of a pair of out-and-out rascals who were ready to stoop to anything and stop at nothing and who had gotten together for the same ends, it didn't take them long to figure out that two all-important factors, hope and fear, tyrannize every man's life and that anyone able to make use of either for his own good could become rich overnight. They saw that what both the fearful and the hopeful needed and wanted the most was knowledge of the future, that this was the reason Delphi and Delos and Clarus and Didyma had ages ago become rich and famous:[8] men, because of the two tyrants I mentioned, hope and fear, were forever coming to these shrines and asking to know the future, and, in payment, they sacrificed whole hecatombs and donated ingots of gold. After turning this discovery over in their minds and pondering it, the partners laid plans to set up an oracle, a seat of prophecy. They hoped, if things went well, to become prosperous and wealthy in short order; what actually occurred far surpassed their initial expectations and was much greater than anything they had ever looked for.

Next they took up two questions: first, where to locate their enterprise, and, second, how to launch and operate it. "Nutsy" voted for Chalcedon[9] as a likely spot since it was a commercial town near to both Thrace and Bithynia and, in addition, wasn't far from Asia and Galatia and all the peoples in the hinterland. Alexander, on the other hand, was in favor of his home town. His point—a perfectly valid one—was that, in its initial stages, they needed "fatheads" and boobs to fall for such an operation as this, and, he claimed, the natives of Paphlagonia who lived beyond Abonoteichus, superstitious—and well-heeled—yokels for the most part, were ideal; all a man had to do was come along, at his heels someone tootling a flute or beating a drum or clashing cymbals, and offer to tell fortunes with a sieve,[10] as the saying goes, and the next minute all their jaws would drop and they'd stare at him like a god from heaven.

After a bit of a squabble over this Alexander finally won out. They first went to Chalcedon—in spite of their decision they felt the city could serve a useful purpose. Here, in the sanctuary of Apollo, the oldest in Chalcedon, they planted some bronze tablets with an inscription to the effect that Asclepius and his father Apollo were moving forthwith to Pontus and were going to settle down in Abonoteichus.[11] The opportune unearthing of these tablets spread the news for them the length and breadth of Bithynia and Pontus with no effort on their part. The first place it reached was Abonoteichus, whose townspeople promptly voted to erect a temple and started at once to dig the foundations. At this point "Nutsy" was left behind in Chalcedon, busily turning out ambiguous, equivocal, and enigmatic oracles. Not long after that he died, of snake bite I think.

Alexander went on ahead. By now he had long, flowing locks, wore a white-trimmed purple shirt with a white mantle over it, and carried a scimitar à la Perseus, whom he had added to his genealogy as a maternal ancestor. The Paphlagonians, poor devils, though they knew perfectly well that both his parents were low-class nonentities, willingly believed the oracle that said:

> Hail the descendant of Perseus, the dearly beloved of Apollo,
> > Heir to the great Podalirius' blood—Alexander the godly! (Podalirius,[12] I take it, was so oversexed and woman-crazy he produced an erection which reached from Tricca to Alexander's mother in Paphlagonia.) By now Alexander had also come up with an oracle according to which the Sibyl purportedly had long ago prophesied that:
> > > Near to Sinope upon the long shore of the Pontus Euxinus,
> > > Born will there be by a Tow'r, in the days of the Romans, a prophet,
> > > One who will show, first, the primary unit, then a decade thrice over,
> > > Followed by five other units, then twenty plus twenty plus twenty;
> > > Numerals four which add up to the name of a man to defend us![18]

So, after a long absence, Alexander descended upon his home town accompanied by all this fanfare. There he made himself a celebrity and leading light by pretending to have fits of madness and even managing to froth at the mouth at times. For him there was nothing to it—he simply masticated soapwort root, the plant dyers use—but to the onlookers this foam was something fearful from heaven. There was also ready for use—it had been made up a while back—a linen mask in the form of a serpent's head with a more or less human face. It was all painted over to look most lifelike; its mouth, rigged with horsehair strings, opened and closed, and a black forked tongue like a serpent's could be made to stick out, also by means of strings. The snake from Pella was there, too, being cared for in his house until the moment when it would be revealed to the public and assigned a role—or rather the leading role—in the act.

It was by now time to get under way. The scheme he worked out was this. One night he stole out to the excavation that had just been dug for the foundations of the new temple. There was a puddle of water standing in it which was either the result of a rainstorm or had seeped in by itself from somewhere. He had with him a goose egg that, emptied of its contents, now carried inside a newly hatched snake. He set it down, buried it deep in the mud, and took off. At the crack of dawn into the main square he tore, wearing not a stitch of clothes except a G string of gold brocade over his genitals (but carrying his scimitar, of course) and tossing that head of hair around as wildly as a fanatic collecting money for Cybele. Clambering up on a high altar, he launched into a speech congratulating the city on the visit it was very soon to receive from the god in person. His audience—practically the whole town, women, old men, children and all, had collected there—was dumfounded; they all fell on their knees and began to pray. Then he mouthed some gibberish—Hebrew or Phoenician words perhaps—which left them awe-struck: they had no idea of what he was saying; all they could catch were the "Apollos" and "Asclepiuses" he slipped in everywhere. The next minute he was off like a shot for the site of the new temple. Coming to the excavation with its oracular spring already in place, he jumped into the puddle and, in a loud voice, sang some hymns to Asclepius and Apollo and called on the god to "Come to the city and bring it blessings." Then he asked for a sacrificial saucer; somebody handed him one; he dipped it in and, presto, in a bowlful of mud and water hauled up his god-bearing egg, the crack where he had opened it sealed carefully with white wax and white lead. Picking it up, he announced that he now held Asclepius in his hands. Everybody, already overwhelmed by the discovery of the egg a moment ago, waited, goggle-eyed, for what would happen next. When he cracked the shell and let the tiny snake fall into the palm of his hand, and they saw it wriggle and curl about his fingers, they raised a cry to heaven, welcomed the god, congratulated the city, and, to a man, began praying their hearts out, begging this deity for money, health, and every other kind of blessing. Our sprinter then dashed off to his house, taking with him his fledgling Asclepius, who

Twice had been born whereas once is the lot of us other poor mortals,

and not from a Coronis, not even from a crow, but from a goose.[15] The mob followed him en masse, everyone in a frenzy and crazed with expectations.

Alexander kept to his house for a few days and hoped. He was not disappointed: the word got around, and most of the population of Paphlagonia promptly came to him on the run, leaving their hearts and brains behind and looking not like "men who eat of the fruits of the earth"[16] but, in everything save shape, exactly like a flock of sheep. When the city was filled to bursting with them, he dressed himself up like a god, seated himself on a couch in some small room, and took his Asclepius from Pella to his bosom. The snake, an enormous and magnificent specimen as I mentioned, he wound about his throat, except for the tail which was so long it streamed over his breast and dragged for part of its length on the ground. The head alone he hid, keeping it under his arm—all this the creature put up with—and, in its place, beside his beard he displayed that linen mask, making it look for all the world as if it belonged to the body everyone could see.

Now picture in your mind a dim cell with insufficient light and a motley, excited mob, already overawed on arrival and floating in air with hope. Naturally, when they entered the whole affair seemed like a miracle: the snake, a tiny infant a few days ago, had, in so short a span, grown into this enormous serpent, one that was tame and had the face of a man in the bargain. And the next minute, before they had time to get a good look, they were shoved toward the exit and pushed out by the unbroken stream of spectators entering. You see, he had had an exit cut in the wall opposite the doorway, the way we're told the Macedonians did in Babylon during Alexander the Great's illness, when he was failing and everyone was standing around the palace, anxious for a last look and word. According to reports, the scoundrel put on this act not once but a number of times, particularly when fresh arrivals from the ranks of the wealthy came along.

To tell the truth, my dear Celsus, in all this we can't be too hard on those poor people from Paphlagonia and Pontus for being taken in. They were uneducated "fatheads"; they actually touched the snake—this privilege Alexander extended to whoever wanted it—and in a dim light they saw what was presumably the head with the mouth opening and closing. To see through such a set-up would have taken the brains of a Democritus or of Epicurus himself or of Metrodorus or of anyone else who had a mind that was adamant against this sort of thing, someone who would be instinctively suspicious and either guess at what was involved or, if he couldn't discover the trick, would at least be convinced that it was some magician's stunt he couldn't fathom, that it was all a hoax and simply couldn't be true.[17]

Before long all Bithynia, Galatia, and Thrace poured into the place; I'm sure everybody who brought back the news went on record that he had seen the god born and then, had touched it when, a few days later, it had grown into an enormous serpent with a man's face. Next came pictures, models, and statuettes, in silver as well as bronze, and the giving the god a name. He was dubbed Glycon as the result of a command which Heaven delivered in meter. Alexander proclaimed that:

Glycon am I, of Jove's blood once removed, and a light unto mortals.

Now came the big moment, the culmination of all his scheming: to follow the lead of Amphilochus in Cilicia and supply oracles and prophecies for whoever wanted them.

Amphilochus, you see, after his father Amphiaraus' death and disappearance in Thebes, had been banished from his home town; he made his way to Cilicia and there came out of it all very nicely by going into oracle making himself and foretelling the future for the Cilicians at a charge of seventy-five cents per prediction.[18] Taking his cue from him, Alexander announced to all visitors that the god was going to prophesy on such and such a day. He instructed them to write down whatever wishes they had or whatever they most wanted to know on a scroll, to tie it up, and to seal it with wax or clay or the like. He would take the scrolls and go into the inner sanctum—by now the temple was up and he had a stage setting at his disposal—listen to what the god had to say, have an announcer and an assistant prophet call in the clients in order, and hand back each scroll with seal absolutely intact and response added below (the god delivered an individual answer to each question). It was a trick which, to someone like yourself or, if it's not presumptuous to say so, someone like myself, was obvious and simple to understand, but to those poor slobs it was a miracle, something beyond belief. You see, since he had figured out all sorts of techniques to open the seals, he simply read each question, appended whatever answer he thought best, then rolled the scroll up again, sealed it, and handed it back, to the vast amazement of the recipient. Time and again you'd hear, "How could he have known what I gave him sealed tight under seals that couldn't be counterfeited unless he really is a god who knows everything?"

"What were those techniques of his?" you may ask. Listen then, so you can be in a position, to expose this kind of thing yourself. The first, my dear Celsus, was the one everybody knows. He would remove the seal by cutting through the wax beneath it with a hot needle; then, after he had read the contents, with the same needle he'd warm the wax under the string and on the under side of the seal and, with no trouble at all, stick the two together again. Another way involved what is known as collyrium plaster, a preparation made from south Italian pitch, bitumen, powdered glass, wax, and mastic. After making up the plaster from all these ingredients, he would warm it over a fire, smear the seal with saliva, then apply the compound to the seal and make a mold of it. Since this hardened instantly, he would go right ahead and break the seal, read the contents, then smear on wax and, using his mold just like a seal-stone, make a new impression that looked exactly like the original. Here's still a third method. He would add marble dust to bookbinder's glue, make a paste out of it, apply it when still moist to the seal, and then remove it. This would instantly dry harder than bone or even iron, and he would use it to make a new impression. He had thought up a good many other tricks to handle the problem, but I needn't mention them all—I don't want to seem to be overdoing it, particularly since you've gone into the subject sufficiently and presented far more material than this in that exposé of magicians you wrote, an excellent and most useful work which should pound some sense into whoever opens it.

So Alexander gave out oracles and made prophecies, using a great deal of resourcefulness and combining guesswork with inventiveness. To some questions he delivered enigmatic and ambiguous answers, to others absolutely unintelligible ones; this, he felt, had the proper oracular touch. Some people he encouraged or discouraged, depending on which course he guessed was the best to take; for other people he prescribed therapy or diets since, as I mentioned at the outset, he knew a good many useful drugs. His favorites were his "cytmides," a name he coined for a cure-all he compounded from a base of goat grease. However, hopes and improved prospects and the inheriting of fortunes he invariably put off into the future, adding the statement that "All this will come to pass when I so wish, and Alexander my prophet pleads and prays in your behalf." The fee he charged was two dollars and thirty cents per oracle. Don't imagine for a moment, my dear friend, that this brought him any small or modest income. With customers avid enough to put in for ten to fifteen oracles each, his total annual receipts ran between a hundred and fifteen and a hundred and thirty thousand dollars. What he took in he didn't spend solely on himself or put away for his own private fortune; by this time he had a large staff—assistants, servants, investigators, oracle writers, oracle recorders, secretaries, seal makers, interpreters—and he gave each whatever share he deserved.

Pretty soon Alexander was even sending agents into neighboring lands to spread the word about his oracle among various peoples. These men advertised that he offered general prophecy, recovery of runaway slaves, detection of thieves and bandits, discovery of buried treasure, healing of the sick, and, on occasion, raising of the dead. The result was a stampede from all sides plus sacrifices and offerings—with double allotments for the prophet and disciple of the god. You see, among the oracles he issued was this one:

> Honor, I bid you, my servant, the one who gives voice to my sayings;
>   Care have I none for possessions, all my care is reserved for my servant.

By this time a good many men of sense, as if coming out of a drunken stupor, got together to attack him, particularly the followers of Epicurus, of whom there were quite a number. In the cities they gradually unmasked all his hocus-pocus and the act he was putting on. When this happened, Alexander began a campaign of intimidation against them. He announced that Pontus was full of atheists and Christians who had the effrontery to utter the worst possible slanders about him, and he ordered everyone who wanted to stay in the good graces of his god to stone the offenders. And this is the oracle he issued when someone asked how Epicurus was faring in the underworlds.

In filthy slime he sits with leaden shackles on his ankles. (Do you wonder that that shrine of his was able to reach the heights when you see how intelligent and informed the clientele's questions were?) In a word, it was war to the death against Epicurus. And no wonder—what man had a better right to be the bitter enemy of a quack who loved humbug and loathed truth than Epicurus, the one who delved into the nature of things, the only one who discerned the truth in it all? The Platonists and Stoics and Pythagoreans were Alexander's friends; between them and him a profound peace reigned. But the "unmitigated" Epicurus, as Alexander called him, was his worst enemy and rightly so—Epicurus had laughed at everything the man stood for and treated it as child's play. That's why, of all the towns in Pontus, Alexander hated Amastris the most: he found out that Lepidus and his disciples and sympathizers, a sizable group in all, lived there.[19] He never prophesied for people from Amastris. Once he took a chance and gave out an oracle to the brother of one of its aldermen and he ended up a laughingstock. He couldn't make up the right oracle himself or find anybody able to turn one out on the spur of the moment; he wanted to tell the man, who was complaining of a pain in the stomach, to eat pig's foot cooked with mallow, and it came out:

> Mallow of pig in a trough that is holy besprinkle with cummin.

As I mentioned before, he often displayed the snake to people who asked to see it. He didn't expose it all but chiefly the tail and the rest of the body, keeping the head out of sight in his robe. But he wanted to impress his public even more, so he issued a promise that he would have the god deliver prophecies in person without any intermediary. Whereupon, with no trouble at all, he joined together some cranes' windpipes and fitted one end into the artificial head, making it all look very natural; in answer to the questions, a confederate outside bellowed into the tube, and the voice issued from the linen Asclepius. Oracles of this sort he labeled "self-spokens." They were not given out indiscriminately to everyone but were reserved for the notable, the rich, and the openhanded. For example, the one given to Severianus about his march into Armenia was a "self-spoken." The oracle, encouraging him to make the attempt, went:

> After thy spear has laid low both Iran's and Armenia's peoples,
>   Home wilt thou go to the city of Rome and the Tiber's bright waters,
>   Decked on thy brow with a garland of victory rayed like a sunburst.

That numbskull from Gaul was convinced and launched an attack. When he ended up cut to ribbons, he and his whole army, by Chosroes, Alexander removed the above from the records and inserted this instead:

> March not thy men—for it augurs not well—'gainst Armenia's peoples.
>   Lest by a man in the garb of a woman be shot the fell arrow
>   Fated to sever thy soul from its life and thine eyes from the daylight.[20]

As a matter of fact, this was a very shrewd idea of his, these ex post facto oracles to help out bad predictions that had missed the mark. Time and again he would prophesy recovery for the sick before their end and then, when they died, have his recantation all ready in a second oracle:

> Seeketh no longer for succor against the dread scourge of thy sickness—
>   Now is thy destiny manifest, gone every chance to escape it.

He found out that the priests at Clares, Didyma, and Mallus enjoyed a great reputation for the same brand of divination as his. So he made friends with them and sent them a good many of his clients by giving such responses as:

Now unto Clarus begone, to give ear to the voice of my father,

or

Wendest thy way to the shrine of Didyma and list to its prophet,

or

Get thee to Mallus. 'Tis there that Amphilochus tells of the future.

Up to now he had stayed within the borders of Ionia, Cilicia, Paphlagonia, and Galatia. But soon the fame of his shrine made its way to Italy and descended on Rome. Every soul there, one on the heels of the other, hurried either to go out in person or to send an envoy, particularly the most influential and important personages in the city. The leader and prime figure in this movement was Rutilianus.[21] Rutilianus, in every other respect a fine and cultured man and a proven public servant in many a Roman governmental post, was, when it came to religion, a serious mental case willing to accept on faith the most outlandish claims. All he had to do was see somewhere a stone smeared with holy oil or crowned by a wreath, and down on his knees he would go, making obeisance, and then stand there for hours, praying to it and beseeching it for blessings. He heard about the shrine and practically threw up his current public office to fly off to Abonoteichus; as next best thing he sent off one envoy after another. The people he used, ordinary servants who were no trouble at all to fool, came back with paeans of praise: they reported not only what they had seen but what they thought they had seen or heard—and then increased the dimensions all around for good measure in order to raise themselves in their master's estimation. They had the poor fellow on fire; they whipped him up into a mad frenzy. He then made the rounds of the city's notables, most of whom were in his circle of friends, and told them what he had heard from his envoys plus some trimmings of his own. He filled the city with talk of Alexander and threw it into an uproar. He got the people at the emperor's court so worked up most of them promptly rushed out to hear something about their own futures. Alexander greeted all comers with great cordiality, won them over with lavish hospitality and expensive gifts, and sent them home not only with the answers to their questions but ready to sing the praises of his god and fabricate miracles on behalf of the shrine and himself.

All this led the damned scoundrel to concoct a canny scheme well beyond the capacity of any ordinary swindler. As he opened and read the scrolls sent him, if he came across any in which something indiscreet or risky had been asked, he didn't hand them back—he held on to them. The idea was to throw a scare into the senders, who remembered very well what their questions were, and thereby get them under his thumb and practically make slaves of them; you know yourself the sort of inquiries the rich and powerful are likely to make. Plenty of blackmail came his way from the victims; they knew he had them trapped.

Let me tell you about some of the oracles he gave Rutilianus. Rutilianus had a son by his first marriage who was the right age to start higher education. So he asked the oracle which teacher he should select for the boy's studies. The answer was:

Choose thou Pythagoras. Choose the great poet and teacher of battle.

Then, just a few days later, the boy died. Alexander was stymied and had nothing to say to his critics: his oracle had been refuted right on the heels of its delivery. But Rutilianus, that goodhearted soul, rushed to its defense. He explained that the god had predicted precisely what had come to pass in that he had ordered him to choose for the boy, not any living teacher, but Pythagoras and Homer, who had both been dead for ages and with whom the youngster was probably studying at that very moment down in Hades. How can you blame Alexander for deciding to devote his time to such pathetic creatures as the likes of this? On another occasion Rutilianus asked, "Whose soul have I inherited?" The answer was:

First as Achilles thou entered the world, and thou next wert Menander,
  Third came the man thou art now, and in time thou shalt shine in the heavens.
  Eighty more years shalt thou live, when thou once hast completed a hundred.

Actually he died of manic depression when he was seventy, without waiting to make good the god's promise. And this oracle was a "self-spoken," no less. Once he asked about marriage; he was told in no uncertain terms:

Marry the daughter that goddess Selene has borne Alexander.

Alexander had long ago given out the story that the mother of the one daughter he had was Selene: she had once seen him when he was asleep and had been overcome with love for him—it's her tradition, after all, to fall in love with sleeping beauties.[22] Rutilianus, that epitome of wisdom, didn't hesitate a minute. He promptly sent for the girl, celebrated the wedding—the groom was now sixty—and lived with her, making up to his mother-in-law Selene with whole hecatombs and regarding himself as officially entered into the ranks of the heavenly host.

Once Alexander had gained a foothold in Italy, his ideas grew ever bigger and bigger. He sent his oracle agents to all the cities of the Roman Empire with a warning to be on guard against plagues, fires, and earthquakes; he then offered to furnish assistance guaranteed to keep any city safe from such things. One particular oracle—a "self-spoken"—he sent to every area that had been hit by the plague.[23] It was just a single verse:

Long-tressed Apollo it is who protects against plague's blighting shadow.

This line you could see written on doorways everywhere, as a charm, against the plague. In most cases things turned out the other way around: through some quirk of fate the households that had put up the inscription were the ones wiped out. Now don't think I'm trying to say they were destroyed on account of the verse. It just worked out that way. Perhaps most of them, overconfident because of their line of poetry, took things easy and were careless and did nothing to help the oracle combat the disease, figuring they had all those metrical feet fighting for them plus long-tressed Apollo keeping the plague off with his magic bow.

In Rome itself Alexander stationed a good number of his accomplices to serve as undercover agents. They sent him reports about the character of all clients and gave him advance notice of what they were going to ask and what they wanted most. Envoys found him all ready with the answers—they had been composed even before the questions arrived.

Also aimed at the Italian trade was the following scheme. He worked up a mystery ceremony of his own, complete with torchbearers and presiding priests. It lasted three whole days in a row. On the first there was, as at Athens, an initial proclamation. Here it took the form: "If any atheist, Christian, or Epicurean has come here to spy, let him be gone. And may the true believers of the god conduct their rites with heaven's blessing." Immediately thereafter the ceremony led off with an expulsion ritual. Alexander opened it with the words, "Christians, begone!" and the crowd responded with one voice, "Epicureans, be gone!" Then came the acting out of Leto in labor, of the birth of Apollo, his mating with Coronis, and the birth of Asclepius. On the second day there was the birth and presentation of the god Glycon. On the third day came the marriage of Podalirius and Alexander's mother; this was called Torch Day, so torches were burned. The finale was Alexander's love affair with Selene and the birth of Rutilianus' wife. Alexander alias Endymion was torch-bearer and officiating priest. He lay in the center of the scene, ostensibly asleep. Flying down to him from the roof, as if from heaven, came, not Selene, but Rutilia, a beauty married to one of the imperial procurators. She was actually in love with Alexander and he with her, so there, with everybody around, before her poor husband's very eyes, the pair exchanged kisses and embraces. And, if there hadn't been lots of torches burning, Alexander probably would have carried on some under-the-dress lovemaking as well. A little later he reappeared in the officiating priest's regalia and, amid a dead silence, cried in a loud voice, "Hail, Glycon!" Whereupon the garlic-reeking Paphlagonian clodhoppers who were presumably his Eumolpidae and Ceryces responded with, "Hail, Alexander!"[24]

At frequent intervals during the torchlight parades and mystic jigging he made sure his thigh was bared so everyone could see it was golden; apparently he had wrapped around it a piece of gilded leather which glittered in the lamplight. A pair of brainless academes once undertook to do research on whether his golden thigh meant he actually had Pythagoras' soul or one similar to it.[25] They brought the problem to Alexander himself, and Lord Glycon settled all difficulties with an oracle:

> Sometimes the soul of Pythagoras waxeth and sometimes it waneth.
>> Prophets however, are blessed with a fragment of heavenly spirit
>> Sent by the father of gods as an aid to all god-fearing mortals.
>> Homeward to Zeus doth it hasten when Zeus's swift thunderbolt strikes it.

Alexander used to issue warnings to the public to refrain from pederasty on the grounds that it was a sin. Yet he himself, noble soul, worked out the following scheme. He ordered the cities in Paphlagonia and Pontus to send choirboys who for a three-year period would be quartered at his house and sing for the god. They were to be carefully screened, and only those judged perfect in family qualifications and age, and unrivaled in looks, were to be sent. Alexander kept those boys behind closed doors and used them like so many slaves, sleeping with them and behaving like a drunken degenerate with them. He had made it a general rule never to greet anyone over eighteen on the lips or welcome them with a kiss. They got his hand to kiss; his mouth was reserved for the fresh flowers, to whom he gave the official title "Receivers of the Kiss." Such were the pleasures he enjoyed at the expense of the poor dupes about him; life was a continuous round of ruining young women and sleeping with young boys. All husbands without exception considered it a most desirable mark of distinction to have the prophet notice their wives, and, if he decided they were worth a kiss, the poor devils were sure their households would be swamped by a wave of good fortune. Many of the wives boasted of having had children by him—and their own husbands were willing to testify they spoke the truth.

I'd like to quote for you a dialogue that took place between Glycon and a certain Sacerdos from Tium,[26] whose intellectual capacity you'll gauge from the questions he asked. The whole thing was inscribed in letters of gold on a wall of Sacerdos' house in Tium, which is where I read it:

> "Tell me, Lord Glycon, who are you?"
>> "I am the new Asclepius."
>> "What do you mean? Different from the former one?"
>> "You are not allowed to know that."

"How many years will you remain with us and give us your prophecies?"

"One thousand and three."

"Then where will you go?"

"To Bactria and the lands there. For foreigners, too, must reap the benefits of my presence among them."

"Does your forefather Apollo still abide in the other seats of prophecy, at Didyma and Claras and Delphi, or are the oracles now issued from there all false?"

"Do not seek to know this either. It is forbidden."

"What will I become after this life?"

"A camel, then a horse, and then a wise man and prophet as great as Alexander."

This was the dialogue that took place between Glycon and Sacerdos. The god, knowing Sacerdos was a friend of Lepidus', ended up with an oracle in meter:

Trust not in Lepidus—ill-fated doom is his constant companion.

You see, as I mentioned before, Alexander was terribly afraid of Epicurus as a professional rival and counteracter of all his hocus-pocus. One Epicurean, for example, who had the courage to show him up in front of a large crowd, he placed in a position of mortal danger. The man had gone up to him and said in a loud voice, "Alexander, you talked so-and-so of Paphlagonia into bringing his servants up for the death penalty before the governor of Galatia on the grounds that they had murdered his son in Alexandria where the boy was attending school. But the son is alive, he has returned in the flesh—and you have already had those servants handed over to the wild beasts and destroyed." What had happened was this. The boy sailed to Egypt and pushed on to Suez; here a ship was just leaving for India and he was persuaded to go along. Since he took a long time getting back, his poor servants, convinced he had drowned in the Nile or been captured by pirates—they were rife at the time—went home and reported his disappearance. Then came the oracle, the trial, and, after that, the boy's reappearance with the explanation of his absence. The man spoke his piece. Alexander's reaction was to fly into a rage at being exposed—the rebuke was true, and that was what he couldn't take. He shouted to the audience that, if they didn't stone the fellow, he would put them under a curse and brand them all Epicureans. Just as everybody began throwing, a certain Demostratus, a prominent citizen of Pontus who was in town on a visit, threw himself in front of the man and barely saved him from being stoned to death. But he deserved to die! What right did he have to take advantage of Paphlagonia's imbecility and be the only person with sense among all those madmen?

So much for what happened to one Epicurean. For the others there was this. The clients for oracles used to be presented one by one the day before the prophesying took place, and the announcer would ask, "Do you have a prophecy for this man?" If the answer from within was, "A curse on him!" then nobody would ever again receive the rejected applicant under his roof or share fire or water with him—he was to be hounded from one land to the next; he was unclean; he was godless; he was—the most horrible epithet of all—an Epicurean.

As a matter of fact, Alexander did one extremely silly thing in this connection. He came across a copy of Epicurus' *Principal Doctrines,* his finest work, as you know, and the one that embraces the key tenets of his philosophy. Alexander carried the book into the main square and burned it on a pyre of fig logs, presumably feeling he was destroying the author in the fire. The ashes he dumped into the sea, adding an oracle for good measure:

Hear my command: to the flames with the thoughts of a visionless dotard.

The damned fool had no conception of the great benefits that book holds for all who open it, how much peace and calm and freedom it builds up in the reader by ridding him of the fear of specters and portents, of vain hopes and excessive desires, by implanting in him understanding and a feeling for the truth, by cleansing his mind for real, not with torches and squills and such nonsense, but with honest thought and truth and candor.

Of all the acts of colossal nerve the filthy rascal pulled the greatest was this. Through Rutilianus, who stood so high there, he had easy entree to the palace and court. When the war in Germany was in full blaze and the late Emperor Marcus Aurelius had already come to grips with the Marcomanni and Quadi,[27] Alexander forwarded an oracle. It stated that two live lions should be thrown into the Danube along with a lot of expensive spices and other sacrificial offerings. But I'd better quote it verbatim:

Into the churning and eddying stream of the rain-swollen Danube
    Cast, I do bid you, a pair of the beasts that are Cybele's servants,
Mountain-bred lions. And cast in the plants and the sweet-smelling blossoms
Nourished in India's climes. Whereupon there shall come in an instant
Victory, glory abounding, and with it the peace we so cherish.

His instructions were carried out. The first result was that the lions swam for the enemy shore where the barbarians, taking them for gods or a new kind of wolf, finished them off with clubs; the second was that there "came in an instant" the greatest loss our forces sustained, the destruction en masse of close to twenty thousand men. This was followed by the campaign around Aquileia in which the town escaped capture by a hair. To explain what happened, Alexander coolly produced for his defense the Delphic oracle and its answer to Croesus: the god had simply prophesied a victory without specifying whether it was to be Rome's or the enemy's.[28]

By now droves of people were pouring in. The city was bursting at the seams with the crowds coming in to consult the oracle, and there wasn't enough food to go round. So Alexander hit upon the idea of "nocturnals," as he called them. Taking the scrolls, he slept on them, so he said, and the answers he gave were ostensibly what he had heard in a dream from the god. They certainly weren't very clear; the majority were enigmatic and confused, particularly when the prophet noticed that a scroll had been sealed with extra care. Alexander, you see, was running no risks: he would write down the first thing that popped into his head, since he considered material of this sort as suitable as any other for oracles. Special interpreters were on hand who collected a nice fee from the recipients of "nocturnals" for solving and elucidating them. This concession they enjoyed cost money: each interpreter paid Alexander ten thousand dollars.

Every now and then, to dumfound the brainless, he would issue a response to someone who hadn't submitted a question either in person or through an envoy and who, as a matter of fact, didn't exist at all. Here is an example:

> Who is it, all unbeknownst to thyself, on the bed in thy chamber
>   Layeth fair Calligeneia, thy wife? Dost thou want me to name him?
>   Know 'tis Protogenes, know 'tis the slave thou implicitly trusted,
>   *Thou* got thy loving from him, wherefore *he* turns for his to thy madame.
>   Such is the recompense, paid thee in kind, for the insults he suffered.
>   Horrible drags have been brewed by these two in their battle against thee,
>   Potions that close both thine eyesight and mind to the things they are doing.
>   These thoult discover against the back wall underneath thine own. Bedstead
>   Near to the head. And Calypso, thy handmaid, has been their accomplice.

Wouldn't even a Democritus have been disturbed at hearing the specific names and places?[29] But then, a minute later, realizing it was all just a scheme, he'd have been revolted.

Here's another instance. He issued, in prose, not verse, the following injunction to return home: "This very day he who sent you has fallen by the hand of his neighbor Diocles in league with the bandits Magnes, Celeras, and Bubalas, who have already been arrested and thrown into jail." No recipient was around and, in fact, no recipient existed.

Very often, when people submitted questions in a native tongue, Syrians or Galatians, for example, Alexander would prophesy in a foreign language, going to a great deal of trouble to locate among the visitors in town fellow nationals of the clients. Because of this there was quite a lapse between the handing in of such scrolls and the delivery of the response, an interval long enough to give him plenty of time to unseal the questions safely and find people able to provide letter-perfect translations. Here is an oracle, for example, that he gave to some Scyth:

Morphi ebargulis eis skien chnenchikrank leipsei phaos.

Let me tell you about a few of the oracles he gave me. Once, making it obvious that I had sealed my scroll carefully, I asked whether Alexander was bald. I got back a "nocturnal":

Sabardalachu malach Attis was different.

Another time I submitted two separate scrolls under two different names but with the same question on both: "Where was Homer born?"[30] Taken in by my servant—Alexander asked the boy why his master had sent him and was told, "To find how to treat a pain in the side"—to one of them he gave the answer:

Rub it, I bid, with a "cytmis" plus foam from the mouth of a race horse.

To the second, since we had let him overhear another piece of information, that the sender wanted to know whether it was better for him to sail to Italy or go on foot, he gave this answer—and it had very little to do with Homer:

Ships I forbid thee—the way across land with thy feet shalt thou follow.

Yes, I personally played lots of tricks of this kind on him. Here's another example. I submitted a scroll with a single question. On the outside, for the brief customary identification, I wrote "Request for Eight Oracles from So-and-So," adding a false name. I enclosed eighteen dollars plus the change and sent it all off. He took on faith the amount of money I had forwarded and the information on the scroll and, in answer to my single question—it was: "When will Alexander the quack magician be caught?"—sent me eight oracles, every one of which was unintelligent, unintelligible, and totally unconnected with anything under heaven or on earth, as the saying goes.

When he later found out not only about all this but that I had tried to dissuade Rutilianus from his marriage and from leaning on the bright prospects offered by the oracle, naturally he hated me and considered me his worst enemy. Rutilianus once submitted a question about me; the answer was:

Colloquies whispered at night does he relish, and vicious liaisons.

All in all, I was, as you'd expect, his worst enemy.

When he got word that I was in his city and found out that I was *the* Lucian—I even had an escort of two soldiers, a spearman and a pikeman, assigned by the governor of Cappadocia, who was a friend of mine, to accompany me as far as the nearest seaport—he promptly sent me a very cordial and most friendly invitation. On my arrival I found him with a considerable crowd standing around. By a stroke of luck I had my soldiers with me. He stretched out his hand for me to kiss, as he did with his public, but I, bending over as if to kiss it, gave it one beauty of a bite that practically crippled it. At that the crowd closed in to throttle me and beat me up as a sacrilegious desecrater; I had raised their hackles even earlier by addressing him as Alexander instead of "Prophet." He bore up under it all nobly. He held back the mob, assuring them he would have no trouble taming me and demonstrating Glycon's greatness, the god who turns even the bitterest enemies into friends. Then, sending everybody off to the side, he argued his case before me. He told me he knew all about the advice I had given Rutilianus and he asked, "Why did you do this to me? I could have made you stand very high with that man." In view of the dangerous spot I had gotten into, I was glad by that time to accept this overture. A few minutes later I stepped forth his fast friend. The ease with which I had been converted seemed no mean miracle to all beholders.

Then, since I had elected to go by sea—I was alone with Xenophon at the time; my father and the rest of the family I had sent ahead to Amastris—Alexander, along with a load of souvenirs and gifts, sent an unsolicited offer to supply a boat and rowers to take me home. I took it as a straightforward, friendly gesture. But when, in the middle of the crossing, I noticed that the captain, with tears in his eyes, was arguing with the crew, my hopes for the future sank: they had received orders from Alexander to 'heave me over the rail into the sea. Had it gone off as planned he'd have had an easy end to his war against me. The captain's tears, however, convinced the men not to do me any harm or wrong. "Im sixty years old, as you can see," he told me, "a man with a wife and children. I've always led a clean, decent life and, at this point in it, I wouldn't like to filthy my hands with a murder." And he confessed to me the reason he had taken me aboard and the orders he had gotten from Alexander. He set me ashore at Aegiali, a town even the noble Homer has mentioned, and turned back. There I came on some men from the Bosporus who were sailing along the coasts a delegation from King Eupator en route to Bithynia for the delivery of their annual levy, and I explained to them the danger I was in.[31] Luckily I had fallen in with decent people: I was taken aboard and, after coming so close to death, arrived safely at Amastris.

From that moment on I was up in arms against Alexander, and I moved heaven and earth in my desire to get even with him. Even before this plot of his I had hated the man and looked on him with loathing because of his despicable character. We set out to file charges against him, I and a large group of co-plaintiffs, particularly people from the circle of Timocrates, the philosopher from Heraclea.[32] However, Avitus, the governor of Bithynia and Pontus at the time, put a stop to it by practically getting down on his knees and beseeching me to give it up. He was on good terms with Rutilianus and because of that, he claimed, he wouldn't be able to punish the man even if he caught him red-handed.[33] So my attempt was cut short, and I stopped pounding the table since it served no purpose in front of a judge who felt that way.

Here is an act of brazen nerve that stands out even among all his others: Alexander requested the emperor to change the name of Abonoteichus to Ionopolis and to issue a new coin, one side to be engraved with the likeness of Glycon, the other with himself holding the insignia of his grandfather Asclepius and that famous scimitar of his maternal ancestor Perseus.[34]

Although he once predicted in an oracle about himself that he was destined to live for a hundred and fifty years and then be killed by the thunderbolt's stroke, he came to a miserable end, and before he had reached even seventy. The son of Podalirius died because his leg *(poda-)* was alive with maggots and had rotted through and through right up to the groin. It was then that we found out he was bald: he was in such pain he let the doctors put wet compresses on his head, which they couldn't do without removing his wig.

Such was the finale of Alexander's act, the denouement of his whole drama. Even though it happened totally by chance you could almost believe it had been somehow prearranged that way. And he was to have a funeral contest worthy of his career: a struggle over the oracle arose among the leading lights in that pack of accomplices and fellow quacks he had. They came to Rutilianus for a decision: he was to pick one of them to inherit the shrine and assume the crown of priest and prophet. The group included even Paetus,[35] a doctor by profession and a grayish little man, who never in his life did anything worthy of a doctor or a graybeard. Referee Rutilianus sent them all home uncrowned and preserved the office intact for the soul of the defunct.

The above, my dear Celsus, just a few instances out of many, will serve as samples. I felt it right to put them in writing for two reasons. The first was the wish to give pleasure to a dear friend and comrade, a man whom I have admired above all others for his wisdom, love for the truth, gentleness, decency, serene way of life, and warmth toward those about him. The second, more important reason, one that will appeal to you even more than to me, was to avenge Epicurus, a man who was *genuinely* holy and possessed of a divine nature, who alone perceived the truly beautiful and passed his knowledge on, and who became thereby the emancipator of those who were his disciples. But all who read this account will, I think, find it useful, as much for the encouragement it gives to men of good sense as for the exposures it makes.

NOTES

1. Cleaning these stables had been one of Heracles most disagreeable labors.
2. A well-known Roman historian of the early second century A.D. A number of his writings have been preserved, but this life of Tilliborus failed to survive.
3. The Cercopes were thieving imps who robbed Heracles in his sleep. Eurybatus and Phrynondas were proverbial evildoers. Aristodemus and Sostratus may possibly be identical with two figures lampooned by Aristophanes for immorality.
4. *Odyssey* 4.230.

5. Apollonius, born at Tyana in southeastern Asia Minor around the beginning of the Christian Era, acquired a great reputation for wonder-working and clairvoyance.

6. Olympias was Alexander the Greate's mother. The story had it that Zeus visited her in the form of a serpent and her celebrated son was the product of the union.

7. Thucydides 2.1.

8. Sanctuaries of Apollo that were famous seats of prophecy. Delphi was in Greece, Delos on an isle in the Aegean, Claras and Didyma in Asia Minor,

9. Chalcedon lay just across the Bosporus from modern Istanbul. The province of Thrace corresponded roughly to what is today Turkey in Europe.

10. Coscinomancy, a very simple, everyday way of telling fortunes, enjoyed a great vogue in the ancient (and medieval) world.

11. Apollo was the god of oracles par excellence (cf. p. 152). It was one of Alexander's master strokes to turn the son Asclepius, usually only a god of healings into a source of prophecy as well.

12. One of the two doctors attached to the Greek army during the Trojan War (*Iliad* 11.833). He was a son of Asclepius and lived in Tricca in north Greece.

13. This gibberish all works out to the greater glory of Alexander. "Born by a Tow'r," i.e., a fortified spot, refers to Abonoteichus; the second element in the name, -*teichus,* means "wall." The four numbers in the second and third lines—1, 30, 5, 60—in Greeks which used letters of the alphabet to represent numerals, would be written A,L,E,X. And "a man" *(andr-)* + "to defend" *(alex-)* = Alexander.

14. The cult of Cybele, the mother-goddess, was one of the most violent in the ancient world. The goddess's cart was drawn by lions, her priests practiced self-castration, and her followers went in for bouts of frenzy.

15. The quotation is a parody of *Odyssey* 12.22. Coronis was Asclepius' mother. There is a pun here: the Greek word for "crow" is *corone.*

16. *Odyssey* 9.191.

17. Three philosophers. For Democritus, see p. 332, n. 8; Epicurus, p. 333, n. 12; Metrodorus, p. 169, n. 24.

18. Amphiaraus had been a seer during his lifetime. After a mysterious death (Zeus clove the ground in front of his chariot and he was swallowed up), he continued prophesying from a famous shrine in central Greece. The son's oracle was located in the town of Mallus.

19. Tiberius Claudius Lepidus was a local notable and apparently a dedicated Epicurean, Amastris was a city on the coast west of Abonoteichus.

20. Marcus Sedatius Severianus, of Gallic extraction was governor of Cappadocia. In 161 a serious war broke out between Rome and Parthia. Severianus marched into Armenia to meet the enemy, and Chosroes, commanding the Parthians,

wiped the expedition out. Chosroes is given the "garb of a woman" because, in Greek and Roman eyes, all oriental costume seemed effeminate.

21. Publius Mummius Sisenna Rutilianus was a well-born, prominent Roman whose long and successful career in the imperial service included the governorship of several provinces.

22. See p. 54, n. 5.

23. From 165 to 168 A.D. a great plague ravaged most of the Roman Empire.

24. Alexander's homemade mystery religion was modeled on the famous Eleusinian Mysteries (cf. p. 169, n. 32) which began with an expulsion ritual to rid the congregation of foreigners, homicides, and the like, and then presented a dramatized version of the life of Demeter and Persephone. The Eumolpidae and Ceryces, ancient and distinguished families, had the hereditary right to supply priests for the cult.

25. Cf. p. 210, n. 7.

26. Tium lay on the southwest shore of the Black Sea, west of Amastris and Abonoteichus.

27. Between 167 and 169 A.D.

28. See p. 147.

29. Democritus (cf. n. 17 above) was the proverbial hard-headed skeptic.

30. See p. 41.

31. The little kingdom of the Bosporus (i.e., the Cimmerian Bosporus, the modern Crimea) maintained its independence by paying tribute to the empire, delivering it apparently to the governor of Bithynia. Tiberius Julius Eupator ruled ca. 154–171 A.D. Aegiali lay somewhat west of Amastris.

32. Timocrates was a distinguished philosopher and teacher. Heraclea was an important city on the southwest shore of the Black Sea.

33. Lucius Lollianus Avitus, governor of Bithynia in 165 A.D.

34. A good example of the coin and a bronze statuette of Glycon (cf. p. 277), both from the collection of the Boston Museum of Fine Arts, are pictured in F. Allinsori's *Lucian, Satirist and Artist* (Boston, 1926), opposite p. 108. The town's name actually *was* changed; it's called Ionopolis on the coins, and the modern Turkish village on the site is Ineboli.

35. Paetus is otherwise unknown.

Apuleius' *Metamorphoses* (Book 11)

𒀭𒀭𒀭𒀭𒀭𒀭𒀭𒀭𒀭𒀭𒀭𒀭𒀭𒀭

By Apuleius
Translated by Jack Lindsay

BOOK THE ELEVENTH

About the first watch of the night I was aroused by sudden panic. Looking up I saw the full orb of the Moon shining with peculiar lustre and that very moment emerging from the waves of the sea. Then the thought came to me that this was the hour of silence and loneliness when my prayers might avail. For I knew that the Moon was the primal Goddess of supreme sway; that all human beings are the creatures of her providence; that not only cattle and wild beasts but, even inorganic objects arc vitalized by the divine influence of her light; that all the bodies which are on earth, or in the heavens, or in the sea, increase when she waxes, and decline when she wanes. Considering this, therefore, and feeling that Fate was now satiated with my endless miseries and at last licensed a hope of salvation, I determined to implore the august image of the risen Goddess.

So, shaking off my tiredness, I scrambled to my feet and walked straight into the sea in order to purify myself. I immersed my head seven times because (according to the divine Pythagoras) that number is specially suited for all ritual acts; and then, speaking with lively joy, I lifted my tear-wet face in supplication to the irresistible Goddess:

'Queen of Heaven, whether you are fostering Ceres the motherly nurse of all growth, who (gladdened at the discovery of your lost daughter) abolished the brutish nutriment of the primitive acorn and pointed the way to gentler food (as is yet shown in the tilling of the fields of Eleusis); or whether you are celestial Venus who in the first moment of Creation mingled the opposing sexes in the generation of mutual desires, and who (after sowing in humanity the seeds of indestructible continuing life) are now worshipped in the wave-washed shrine of Paphos; or whether you are the sister of Phoebus, who by relieving the pangs of childbirth travail with soothing remedies have brought safe into the world lives innumerable, and who are now venerated in the thronged sanctuary of Ephesus; or whether you are Proserpine, terrible with the howls of midnight, whose triple face has power to ward off all the assaults of ghosts and to close the cracks in the earth, and who wander through many a grove, propitiated in divers manners, illuminating the walls of all cities with beams of female light, nurturing the glad seeds in the earth with your damp heat, and dispensing abroad your dim radiance when the sun has abandoned us—O by whatever name, and by whatever rites, and in whatever form, it is permitted to invoke you, come now and succour me in the hour of my calamity. Support my broken life, and give me rest and peace after the tribulations of my lot. Let there be an end to the toils that weary me, and an end to the snares that beset me. Remove from me the hateful shape of a beast, and restore me to the sight of those that love me. Restore me to Lucius, my lost self. But if an offended god pursues me implacably, then grant me death at least since life is denied me.'

Having thus poured forth my prayer and given an account of my bitter sufferings, I drowsed and fell asleep on the same sand-couch as before. But scarcely had I closed my eyes before a god-like face emerged from the midst of the sea with lineaments that gods themselves would revere. Then gradually I saw the whole body (resplendent image that it was) rise out of the scattered deep and stand beside me.

I shall not be so brave as to attempt a description of this marvellous form, if the poverty of human language will not altogether distort what I have to say, or if the divinity herself will deign to lend me a rich enough stock of eloquent phrase. First, then, she had an abundance of hair that fell gently in dispersed ringlets upon the divine neck. A crown of interlaced wreaths and varying flowers rested upon her head; and in its midst, just over the brow, there hung a plain circlet resembling a mirror or rather a miniature moon—for it emitted a soft clear light. This ornament was supported on either side by vipers that rose from the furrows of the earth; and above it blades of corn were disposed. Her garment, dyed many colours, was woven of fine flax. One part was gleaming white; another was yellow as the crocus; another was flamboyant with the red of roses. But what obsessed my gazing eyes by far the most was her pitch-black cloak that shone with a dark glow. It was wrapped round her, passing from under the right arm over the left shoulder and fastened with a knot like the boss of a shield. Part of it fell down in pleated folds and swayed gracefully with a knotted fringe along the hem. Upon the embroidered edges and over the whole surface sprinkled stars were burning; and in the centre a mid-month moon breathed forth her floating beams. Lastly, a garland wholly composed of every kind of fruit and flower clung of its own accord to the fluttering border of that splendid robe.

Many strange things were among her accoutrements. In her right hand she held a brazen sistrum, a flat piece of metal curved like a girdle, through which there passed some little rods—and when with her arm she vibrated these triple chords they produced a shrill sharp cry. In her left hand she bore an oblong golden vessel shaped like a boat, on the handle of which (set at the most conspicuous angle) there coiled an asp raising its head and puffing out its throat. The shoes that covered her ambrosial feet were plaited from the palm, emblem of victory.

Such was the goddess as breathing forth the spices of pleasant Arabia she condescended with her divine voice to address me.

'Behold, Lucius,' she said, 'moved by your prayer I come to you—I, the natural mother of all life, the mistress of the elements, the first child of time, the supreme divinity, the queen of those in hell, the first among those in heaven, the uniform manifestation of all the gods and goddesses—I, who govern by my nod the crests of light in the sky, the purifying wafts of the ocean, and the lamentable silences of hell—I, whose single godhead is venerated all over the earth under manifold forms, varying rites, and changing names. Thus, the Phrygians that are the oldest human stock call me Pessinuntla, Mother of the Gods. The aboriginal races of Attica call me Cecropian Minerva. The Cyprians in their Island-home call me Paphian Venus. The archer Cretans call me Diana Dictynna. The three-tongued Sicilians[1] call me Stygian Proserpine. The Eleusinlans call me the ancient goddess Ceres. Some call me Juno. Some call me Bellona. Some call me Hecate. Some call me Rhamnusia. But those who are enlightened by the earliest rays of that divinity the sun, the Ethiopians, the Arii, and the Egyptians who excel in antique lore, all worship me with their ancestral ceremonies and call me by my true name, Queen Isis.

'Behold, I am come to you in your calamity. I am come with solace and aid. Away then with tears. Cease to moan. Send sorrow packing. Soon through my providence shall the sun of your salvation arise. Hearken therefore with care unto what I bid. Eternal religion has dedicated to me the day which will be born from the womb of this present darkness. Tomorrow my priests will offer to me the first fruits of the year's navigation. They will consecrate in my name a new-built ship. For now the tempests of the winter are lulled; the roaring waves of the sea are quieted; and the waters are again navigable. You must await this ceremony, without anxiety and without wandering thoughts. For the priest at my suggestion will carry in the procession a crown of roses attached to the sistrum in his right hand; and you must unhesitatingly push your way through the crowd, join the procession, and trust in my good will. Approach close to the priest as if you meant to kiss his hand, and gently crop the roses. Instantly you will slough the hide of this beast on which I have long looked with abhorrence.

'Fear for no detail of the work to which I once put my hand. Even at this moment of time in which I appear before you, I am also in another place instructing my priest in a vision what is to be brought to pass. By my command the crush of people will open to give you way; and despite all the gay rites and ferial revelries not one of my worshippers will feel disgust because of the unseemly shape in which you are incarcerated. Neither will any one of them misinterpret your sudden metamorphosis or rancorously use it against you.

'Only remember, and keep the remembrance fast in your heart's deep core, that all the remaining days of your life must be dedicated to me, and that nothing can release you from this service but death. Neither is it aught but just that you should devote your life to her who redeems you back into humanity. You shall live blessed. You shall live glorious under my guidance; and when you have travelled your full length of time

---

1   'Three-tongued Sicilians': The islanders changed from Sicilian to Greek to Latin. The Arii are of Parthian Aria.

and you go down into death, there also (on that hidden side of earth) you shall dwell in the Elysian Fields and frequently adore me for my favours. For you will see me shining on amid the darkness of Acheron and reigning in the Stygian depths.

'More, if you are found to merit my love by your dedicated obedience, religious devotion, and constant chastity, you will discover that it is within my power to prolong your life beyond the limits set to it by Fate.'

At last the end of this venerable oracle was reached, and the invincible Goddess ebbed back into her own essence. No time was lost. Immediately snapping the threads of sleep, and wrung with a sweat of joy and terror, I wakened. Wondering deeply at so direct a manifestation of the Goddess's power, I sprinkled myself with salt water; and eager to obey her in every particular, I repeated over to myself the exact words in which she had framed her instructions. Soon the sun of gold arose and sent the clouds of thick night flying; and lo, a crowd of people replenished the streets, filing in triumphal religious procession. It seemed to me that the whole world, independent of my own high spirits, was happy. Cattle of every kind, the houses, the very day, all seemed to lift serene faces brimful with jollity. For sunny and placid weather had suddenly come upon us after a frosty yesterday; and the tuneful birdlets, coaxed out by the warmths of the Spring, were softly singing sweet hymns of blandishment to the Mother of the Stars, the Producer of the Seasons, the Mistress of the Universe. The trees also, both those that blossomed into fruit and those that were content to yield only sterile shade, were loosed by the southerly breezes; and glistening gaily with their budded leaves, they swished their branches gently in sibilant sighs. The crash of storm was over; and the waves, no longer mountainous with swirling foam, lapped quietly upon the shore. The dusky clouds were routed; and the heavens shone with clear sheer splendour of their native light.

By this time the forerunners of the main procession were gradually appearing, every man richly decked as his votive fancy suggested. One fellow was girded about the middle like a soldier; another was scarfed like a huntsman with hunting-knife and shoes; another, wearing gilt sandals, silken gown, and costly ornaments, walked with a woman's mincing gait; another with his leg-harness, targe, helm, and sword, looked as if he had come straight from gladiatorial games. Then, sure enough, there passed by a man assuming the magistrate with fasces and purple robe, and a man playing the philosopher with cloak, staff, wooden clogs, and goat's beard; a fowler with bird-lime elbowing a fisherman with hooks. I saw also a tame she-bear dressed as a matron and carried in a sedan-chair; an ape with bonnet of plaited straw and saffron-hued garment, holding in his hand a golden cup and representing Phrygian Ganymede the shepherd; and lastly, an ass with wings glued on his back ambling after an old man—so that you could at once have exclaimed that one was Pegasus and the other Bellerophon, and would have laughed at the pair in the same breath.

Into this playful masquerade of the overflowing populace the procession proper now marched its way. Women glowing, in their white vestments moved with symbolic gestures of delight. Blossomy with the chaplets of the Spring, they scattered flowerets out of the aprons of their dresses all along the course of the holy pageant. Others, who bore polished mirrors on their backs, walked before the Goddess and reflected all the people coming-after as if they were advancing towards the Image. Others, again, carrying combs of ivory, went through the various caressive motions of combing and dressing the queenly tresses of their Lady; or they sprinkled the street with drops of unguent and genial balm.

There was a further host of men and women who followed with lanterns, torches, waxtapers, and every other kind of illumination in honour of Her who was begotten of the Stars of Heaven. Next came the musicians, interweaving in sweetest measures the notes of pipe and flute; and then a supple choir of chosen youths, clad in snow-white holiday tunics, came singing a delightful song which an expert poet (by grace of the Muses) had composed for music, and which explained the antique origins of this day of worship. Pipers also, consecrated to mighty Serapis, played the tunes annexed to the god's cult on pipes with transverse-mouthpieces and reeds held sidelong towards the right ear; and a number of officials kept calling out, 'Make way for the Goddess!'

Then there came walking a great band of men and women of all classes and ages, who had been initiated into the Mysteries of the Goddess and who were all clad in linen garments of the purest white. The women had their hair anointed and hooded in limpid silk; but the men had shaven shining polls. Terrene stars of mighty deity were these men and women; and they kept up a shrill continuous tingle upon sistra of brass and silver and even gold. The chief ministers of the ceremony, dressed in surplices of white linen tightly drawn across the breast and hanging loose to the feet, bore the relics of the mighty gods exposed to view. The first priest held on high a blazing lamp—not at all like the lamps that illumine our evening suppers; for its long bowl was gold, and it thrust up from an aperture in the middle a fat flame. The second priest was similarly vestured, but he carried in both hands model altars to which the auxiliary love of the supreme Goddess has given the fitting title of Auxilia. The third priest grasped a palm-tree with all its leaves subtly wrought in gold, and the wand of Mercury. The fourth priest displayed the Symbol of Equity; a left hand moulded with open palm (since the left hand seemed to be more adapted to administer equity than the busier, craftier right hand). The same man also bore a vessel of gold rounded into the shape of a woman's breast, from which he let milk trickle to the ground. The fifth priest had a winnowing-fan constructed with thickset sprigs of gold; and the sixth priest had an amphora.

After these came the Gods themselves (deigning to walk before our eyes on the feet of men). First we saw the dreadful messenger of the gods of heaven and hell, Anubis, with his face blackened on one side and painted gold on the other, lifting on high his dog's head and bearing his rod in his left hand. Close upon his heels followed a Cow (emblem of the Goddess that is fruitful mother of all) sitting upright upon the proud shoulders of her blessed worshipper. Another man carried the chest that contained the Secret Things of her unutterable mystery. Another bore in his beatified bosom a venerable effigy of Supreme Deity, which showed no likeness to any bird or beast (wild or tame) or even to man, but which was worthy of reverence because of its exquisite invention and originality: a symbol inexpressible of the true religion that should be veiled in Deep Silence. This effigy was of burnished gold, made as follows: a small urn was delicately hollowed out with a round bottom: the strange hieroglyphs of the Egyptians covered its outside; the spout was shaped rather low but jutting out like a funnel; the handle on the other side projected with a wide sweep; and on this stood an asp, stretching up his scaly, wrinkled, swollen throat and twining round the whole length.

At last the glorious moment which the presiding Goddess had promised me was at hand. For the priest, adorned exactly as she had described, neared with the instrument of my salvation. In his right hand he carried the Goddess's sistrum and a crown of roses. Ah, by Hercules, a crown indeed it was for me, since by the providence of the overmastering gods, after so many toils of experience, I was now to find my efforts crowned with victory over Fortune, my cruel foe.

However, though shaken with up-bubbling joy, I did not dash immediately forwards; for I did not want the peaceful order of the holy procession to be disturbed by an unruly beast. Instead, I nosed through the crowd with a polite all-but-human tread and a sidelong twist of my body; and, as the people (clearly by the Goddess's dispensation) disparted to let me through, I slowly approached the flowers. But the priest (as was obvious to me) recollected his admonitory vision of the night. He at once stopped stock-still; and spontaneously raising his right hand, he held the bunch up to my mouth. Trembling, with a thudding heart, I seized the crown in which some fine rose blooms were brightly woven; and greedily I masticated the whole lot.

Nor did the heavenly promise fail. At once my ugly and beastly form left me. My rugged hair thinned and fell; my huge belly sank in; my hooves separated out into fingers and toes; my hands ceased to be feet and adapted themselves to the offices of my erected state; my long neck telescoped itself; my face and head became round; my flapping ears shrank to their old size; my stony molars waned into human teeth; and my tail (the worst cross of my ass-days) dimply disappeared.

The populace stood in blinking wonder; and the devotees adored the Goddess for the miraculous revelation of her power in a metamorphosis which partook of the shifting pageantry of a dream. Lifting their hands to heaven, with one voice the beholders rendered testimony to the loving-kindness of the Goddess thus signally declared. As for me, I remained nailed to the spot in mute stupefaction; for my wits were scattered by the shock of joy, and I was quite at a loss. What was the right utterance with which to begin my new life? Where was my voice to come from? How was I most auspiciously to employ my newborn tongue? What phrases could I choose to express my gratitude to so great a Goddess?

But the priest (who by advertisement knew the whole tale of my misfortunes) though wonderstruck at the miracle recovered himself so far as to signify with gestures that I should be handed a linen garment. For from the moment that the ass stripped me of his wretched skin I had been doing my naked best to hide my privities with the sole naturally-supplied veil (the hand), while compressing my thighs. At once one of the initiated pulled off his upper tunic and wrapped me in it; and then the priest, smiling kindly but still staring at my quite-human countenance, thus addressed me:

'At last, Lucius, after the long days of disaster and the heavy storms of fortune you have reached the haven of peace and the altar of mercy. Neither your high lineage, nor your pride of place, nor your learning, profited you one jot. You gave yourself to the slavery of pleasure in the lewdness of hot-blooded youth; and you have reaped the reward of your improspering curiosity. Nevertheless, blind Fortune, persecuting you with horrors and snares, has led you in her shortsighted malice to this beatitude of release. Let her go now and rage as madly as she will; but let her seek another object for her hate. For terror and calamity have no power over him whose life the majesty of our Goddess has claimed for her service.

'What benefit has furying Fortune gained from the robbers, from the wild beasts, from the servitude, from the unending hardships of the way, from the daily fears of death? You are now received into the protection of Fortune, but of Fortune who is open-eyed and who lightens even the other gods with the splendours of her light. Let your face be joyous therefore. Let it be such a face as accords with that white gown you wear. Follow in the train of the Goddess your Saviour with steps of triumph. Let the scoffer behold. Let him behold and be shamed, saying in his heart:

'"Lo, here is Lucius who rejoices in the providence of mighty Isis. Lo, he is loosed from the bonds of misery and victorious over his fate."

'Yet, that you may be the safer and the surer, enrol your name in this army of' holiness, to which you were but a short time past pledged by oath. Dedicate yourself to the service of true religion, and voluntarily bend your neck to the yoke of this ministry. For when you have begun to serve the Goddess you will feel the full fruitfulness of your liberty.'

When the worthy priest, labouring hard to breathe under the pressure of inspiration, had concluded this speech, I joined the ranks of the religious and followed the procession. All pointed or nodded at me, and cried aloud: 'This day has the august power of Almighty Goddess restored him that you see there to human form. Happy, by Hercules, thrice blessed is he who by the purity and faith of his past life has merited such particular patronage from above! For it is as though he had been set apart from the moment of his second birth for the ministry of heaven.'

Among these ejaculations and the hum of happy prayers, we moved slowly on till we approached the sea. The spot chosen was the very beach where on the preceding day (while yet an ass) I had stabled myself. First, the images of the gods were orderly disposed; and then the high priest dedicated and consecrated to the Goddess a nobly built boat (scribbled all over with the peculiar Egyptian marks) after purifying its torch, flame, egg, and sulphur, and pouring solemn prayers from his sanctified lips.

The shining-white sail of this blessed ship bore a broidered inscription repeating the words of the prayer for this year's prosperous navigation. The mast, when raised, was seen to be a rounded pine-tree of great height with a glittering top that drew all eyes. The prow was curved to represent a goose-neck[2] and covered with flaming gold-plates, while the whole of the polished keel consisted 'of rich citronwood.

All the people (initiate or lay) zealously piled up winnowing-fans with aromatic scents and other such offerings, and threw libations of milk mixed with crumbs into the sea, until the ship, cargoed with plentiful gifts and auspicious devotions, was let slip from her anchoring ropes. She put out to sea with a mild breeze; all her own; and after she had sailed out of sight into the distance on her course, the bearers of the holy things reassumed their burdens and began a lively return journey to the temple in the same order and propriety as they had come.

On arrival at the temple, the high priest, those who bore the divine figures, and those who had been admitted into the inner light of the cult, collected in the sanctuary of the Goddess. First they put back the breathing images into their right places; then a man (whom all entitled the scribe) took his stand in a high pulpit before the doors, and the Society of the Pastophori[3] (such is the name of the sacred college) was convoked. The scribe thereupon read out of a book a set of patriotic prayers for 'the great Prince, the Senate, the Equestrian Order, the Roman people, and all sailors and ships which come under the jurisdiction of Rome.' After that he pronounced in the Greek tongue and manner the words '*Laois aphesis*.' The people were dismissed.

The shout that followed showed the popular approval of the day's proceedings; and the congregation began to file out, beaming with joy, carrying boughs of olive and other votive wreaths, and garlanded with flowers. As they left the precincts, they one and all stopped to kiss the feet of a silver image of the Goddess that stood on the steps. But my emotions would not allow me to stir a single inch away from the place. With my eyes fixed upon the image I brooded over my past miseries.

Winging rumour, however, let no moss grow on her feathers. The tale of the Goddess's adorable goodness and of my curious adventures very soon had reached my native city; and my servants, friends, and those near to me in blood, at once discarded the sorrow into which the false tidings of my death had plunged them. Overjoyed and surprised, they hastened to visit me with various gifts, looking upon me as a man divinely raised up out of death. I who had shared their grief now shared their pleasure but gratefully refused their gifts, particularly as my servants had luckily taken care to bring me more than enough of clothes and money. Therefore, after I had met these acquaintances politely and told them the full story of my past pains and present prospects, I once more returned to what had become my chief source of delight: the contemplation of the Goddess. Renting a temporary apartment within the temple enclosure I took part

---

2 'Goose-neck': The goose was sacred to Isis.
3 'Pastophori': The priests that carried the shrines of the gods.

in all the services, frequenting the company of the priests and becoming a constant worshipper at the shrine. Nor did a single night pass without some vision visiting my sleep and commanding me to be initiated into the priesthood, to which vocation I had long since been destined.

But though I profoundly desired to take this step, yet a religious qualm held me back. For after careful inquiry I had learned that a consecrated life was full of snags, that the requisite chastity was difficult to observe, and that only the most unrelenting discipline could save the priest from casual pollutions. Turning these doubts over and over in my mind, I kept delaying my initiation, though every day brought me closer to the final decision.

One night I had a dream, I thought that the high priest came to me with his bosom full of something or other. I asked him what he was offering me, and he answered, 'presents from Thessaly, for that Snowy Servant of yours has arrived from that province.'

When I awoke I pondered over the meaning of this vision, especially as I was sure that I had never had a servant of that name. However, I concluded that something to my advantage was portended by the priest offering me presents. Thus, worried and yet hopeful, I awaited the opening of the temple in the morning. At last the white curtains were drawn, and we offered up our prayers before the holy face of the Goddess. The priest went the round of the altars, performed the sacred ceremonial with solemn supplications, and poured out libations of water from the sanctuary-spring. When all these rites were completed, the worshippers saluted the rays of dawn and announced in clear voices that the day had begun.

Then lo, some men who had been in my employ arrived from Hypata, where I had left them on the day when Fotis by her wicked error fitted me for a halter. Accosting them I found that they had brought back my old horse, which had been recovered after changing hands several times and which I indentified by a mark on his back. At once I realized how admirably prophetic was my dream; for not only had it foretold gain in a general way but it had actually described the recovery of the horse, my snowy servant.

After this I applied myself even more diligently to attendance on the temple-services; for I considered that the Goddess had vouchsafed sure token of future blessings by her present benignity. Besides, my desire to enter the priesthood increased by bounds every day. Accordingly I had frequent interviews with the high priest, during which I earnestly besought him to initiate me into the mysteries of the Holy Night. But he, a serious-minded man who was noted for his strict observance of his unevangelical religion, checked my implorations with gentle friendliness, as parents get rid of children who come bothering at the wrong moment. At the same time he was careful to soothe me with hopes for the future.

For (he said) the initiation date for each aspirant was given by direct sign from the Goddess; and the officiating priest was selected by the same process—as also the precise sum to be expended on the ceremony. All these details must be awaited with uncomplaining patience, since it was necessary on every count to avoid either forwardness or contumacy, and neither to be slothful when called nor precipitate when not called. Not indeed that there was a single man among them who was so lost to common sense or so foolhardy that he would dare in rank blasphemy to undertake the ministries of the Goddess, which without her consent would be an invocation of destruction. For the gates of shadow as well as the bulwarks of life were under the Goddess's control; and the act of initiation had been compared to a voluntary death with a slight chance of redemption. Therefore the divine will of the Goddess was wont to choose men who had lived their life to the full, who were coming near to the limits of waning light, and who yet could be safely trusted with the mighty secrets of her religion. These men by her divine providence she regenerated and restored to strength sufficient for their new career. Consequently I must await the celestial token, although I had already been manifestly indicated as destined for the blessed ministry. Meanwhile I should abstain from all profane or forbidden foods like the other devotees, that I might hasten the more uprightly into the secret bosom of the faith.

Thus spoke the priest; nor did impatience fret my obedient days. For I ambitiously performed the daily tasks of the ministry, intent upon preserving a serenity of soul and a laudable silence. Nor did the mindful love of the Goddess desert me or nail me on a cross of long delay; for there was no darkness in the visions that admonished the darkness of my sleep. She appeared and told me that the day of my desire had arrived, the day which would fulfil my dearest wishes. She also stated the sum of money to be spent on the ceremonial, and appointed the high priest Mithras to preside over my initiation; for (she said) he and I had our destinies mingled by a conjunction of our stars.

Elated by these and other divine commandments of the supreme Goddess, I threw off the coverlet of my sleep, although light was just greying. Hastening straightway to the retreat of the high priest I greeted him just as he was leaving his bedchamber. I had resolved to press my initiation as a thing now due; but the moment that he saw me he began speaking:

'O Lucius, what a happy and blessed man are you, whom the august deity has selected for such direct honours. O why,' he cried, 'do you stand there idle? Why do you delay a moment? The day that you have so constantly desired is come. You are to be initiated into the holy mysteries by these hands of mine in accordance with the divine mandate of the many-titled Goddess.'

Thereupon the old man took me by the hand and led me towards the spacious temple; and after he had duly performed the rituals of opening the doors and of making the morning-sacrifice, he produced from the secret recesses of the shrine certain books written in unknown characters. The meaning of these characters was concealed, at times by the concentrated expression of hieroglyphically painted animals, at times by wreathed and twisted letters with tails that twirled like wheels or spiralled together like vine-tendrils—so that it was altogether impossible for any peeping profane to comprehend. From these books the high priest interpreted to me the matters necessary for my mystic preparation

That done, I set about purchasing, partly at my own cost and partly with the aid of friends, all the required commodities. This I did on a larger scale than I had been bidden; and then, at the time that the priest had appointed as most suitable, I was led to the Baths, surrounded by a crowd of devotees. There, after I had taken the usual bath, Mithras himself washed and sprinkled me with pure water, invoking first the pardon of the gods.

Then he led me back once more into the temple and sat me down at the very feet of the Goddess. Two parts of the day had now gone; and after giving me some secret charges (too holy to be uttered) he bade me aloud to fast for the next ten days, eating no flesh and drinking no wine. This fast I reverently observed; and then at last the day arrived when I was to pledge myself to heaven. The sun swung down and drew the evening on; and lo, hosts of people came eagerly from every direction, each man honouring me with various gifts according to the ancient rite. Then, after the uninitiated had withdrawn to a distance and I had donned a new linen gown, the priest grasped my hand and conducted me into the Holy of Holies.

Perhaps, curious reader, you are keen to know what was said and done. I would tell you if it were permitted to tell. But both the ears that heard such things and the tongue that told them would reap a heavy penalty for such rashness. However, I shall not keep you any longer on the cross of your anxiety, distracted as you doubtless are with religious yearning. Hear therefore and believe what I say to be truth.

I approached the confines of death. I trod the threshold of Prosperine; and borne through the elements I returned. At midnight I saw the Sun shining in all his glory. I approached the gods below and the gods above, and I stood beside them, and I worshipped them. Behold, I have told my experience, and yet what you hear can mean nothing to you. I shall therefore keep to the facts which can be declared to the profane without offence.

Morning arrived; and after the due solemnities I came forth sanctified with twelve stoles, an habiliment of deep religious import, but which the bonds of my obligation do not keep me from mentioning, as I was seen by many bystanders. For, by order of the priest, I climbed a wooden pulpit which stood in the middle of the temple before the image of the Goddess. I wore a vestment of linen embroidered with a flower-pattern; a costly cope hung down from my shoulders to my ankles; and from whatever angle you inspected me you saw interesting new animal-shapes among the decorations—here Indian serpents, there Hyperborean griffins (which the Antipodes incubate like birds). This latter garment was what the priests commonly call an Olympic Stole. In my right hand I held a lighted torch; and a comely chaplet was wound round my head, from which the palm-tree leaves jetted like rays of the sun.

Thus decorated like the sun and draped like a statue (the curtains being whisked away) I was suddenly revealed to the gaze of the multitude. After this I celebrated the festal day of initiation (as if it were a birthday) with a sumptuous feasting and merry converse; and the third day was taken up with similar ceremonies, with a ritual-breakfast and the consummation of my priesthood.

Lingering about the temple for several more days, I was granted the delight of viewing the Holy Face: a benefit that no grateful services can ever repay—till at length, after humbly thanking the Goddess (not as she deserved but as I was able), I received her admonition to depart home; and I reluctantly made my preparations. But I could hardly bear to break the ties of intense affection that bound me to the place. Prostrating myself before the Goddess and watering her feet with my tears, I addressed her, gulping back the sobs that disturbed my articulation:

'Most holy and everlasting Redeemer of the human race, you munificently cherish our lives and bestow the consoling smiles of a Mother upon our tribulations. There is no day or night, not so much as the minutest fraction of time, that is not stuffed with the eternity of your mercy. You protect men on land and sea. You chase the storms of life and stretch out the hand of succour to the dejected. You can untwine the hopelessly tangled threads of the Fates. You can mitigate the tempests of Fortune and check the stars in the courses of their malice. The gods of heaven worship you. The gods of hell bow before you. You rotate the globe. You light the sun. You govern space. You trample hell. The stars move to your orders, the seasons return, the gods rejoice, the elements combine. At your nod the breezes blow, clouds collect, seeds sprout, blossoms increase. The birds that fly in the air, the beasts that roam on the hills, the serpents that hide in the earth, the monsters that swim in the ocean, tremble before your majesty.

'O my spirit is not able to give you sufficient praises, nor have I the means to make acceptable sacrifice. My voice has no power to utter what I think of you. Not a thousand mouths with a thousand tongues, not an eternal flow of unwearied declaration, could utter it.

'Howbeit, poor as I am, I shall do all that a truly religious man may do. I shall conjure up your divine countenance within my breast, and there in the secret depths I shall keep divinity for ever guarded.'

I thus offered my prayer to the supreme Goddess. Then I embraced the priest Mithras (my father in Her); and clinging upon his neck and kissing him oft, I begged his forgiveness that I could not recompense him adequately for the benefits he had heaped upon me. After expressing my sense of obligation at full length, I left him and prepared to revisit my ancestral home from which I had been so long absent.

So, a few days later (as the Goddess admonished), after hastily packing my luggage I went on shipboard and set sail for Rome. Safely and swiftly carried by a favouring breeze, we soon reached the port of Augustus. There I disembarked; and travelling by post-chariot I arrived at the Holy City on the evening of the day before the Ides of December. Nothing now mattered to me so much as to supplicate daily the supreme godhead of Queen Isis (who is propitiated in this city with the deepest veneration as Campensis:[4] a

---

4 'Campensis': In-the-Fields—the Campus Martius.

name derived from the site of her temple). In short, I became an unslackening worshipper, a newcomer to this church of hers, but indigenous to her religion.

Now the strong-thewed Sun had passed through all the signs of the circling zodiac, and the year was ended. But the loving insistence of the Goddess once more broke in upon my sleep, once more strongly speaking of mysteries and holy rites. I wondered what was the meaning of this, and what even was foreshadowed. How should I not? For I had thought myself fully initiated already.

After I had re-examined all my religious doubts in the privacy of my own conscience, I consulted a priest. I then learned a new and disturbing thing: that I was initiated into the mysteries of the Goddess, but that I knew nothing of the rites of the mighty God, the supreme Father of the Gods, unconquerable Osiris.

For though there is amity and even unity to be found between the two essences and their religious statement, yet the approach to knowledge of them is by different tracks. So now what I had to do was to await a summons from the great God to his service. Nor was I left long in doubt. During the next night I saw in a dream one of his devotees clad in linen and bearing ivied thyrsi and other objects (which I may not name). He placed his load before my Household Gods; and then, seating himself in my chair, he recited to me the articles necessary for a splendid religious feast—and, in order that I might know him again, he showed me how the heel of his left foot was somewhat hurt, giving him a slight hobble. All the mists of my doubt were cleared away by such a manifest sign of the will of the gods.

Therefore, as soon as my matins were finished, I carefully noted the priests, to see if any of them walked like the man in my dream. There he was, the very man. One of the Pastophori closely resembled my midnight visitor in stature and looks as well as in gait. His name, I later found, was Asinius Marcellus (a name asininely suggestive of my late plight). I at once approached the priest, who was not at all surprised at what he heard me say; for he had been similarly admonished as to my initiation into the mysteries of Osiris. On the preceding night, while dressing the garlands on the statue of the Great God, he imagined that the Mouth (which pronounced the dooms of all mankind) spoke to him. The message said that a native of Madaura was being sent to him and that he must impart to this man, poor as he was, the sacraments of the God—whereby through the God's providence the one would be glorified for his religious exercises and the other greatly profited.

Thus affianced to religion I was yet held back from the full consummation of my desire through the slenderness of my means. For the travel expenses had wasted the remnant of my estate; and the cost of living in Rome was far ahead of that in the provinces. My poverty thus kept interfering with my plans; and I was left stranded (as the saying goes) between the altar and the block.

Yet the mandates from the God did not weaken their pressure. They continued to goad me till I became very troubled; and then as the commands grew more incisive, I sold the clothes off my back and scraped up enough to carry on. This indeed was the course prescribed; for the God said to me: 'If you were hot after some trifle of pleasure, would you hesitate to throw your clothes away? And now, on the brink of initiation, do you shrink from a poverty that can bring no repentance?'

Everything was thus fully prepared; and now once more I abstained for ten days from eating flesh. Then, admitted with shaven head to the nocturnal orgies of the Lord of Gods, I resorted to the ceremonies with the full confidence that knowledge of a kindred ritual evoked. This occurrence consoled me for my sojourn in a foreign city and also gave me a better chance of earning my livelihood. For, favoured by the god Good-Luck, I managed to subsist on the small fees I gained in the Forum pleading causes in the Latin tongue.

But shortly afterwards I was once more molested by unexpected visionary commands; and a third time[5] I found myself yearning towards a mystery. This left me in an oppressively shaken and perplexed state of mind, uncertain what could be the significance of this new and peculiar expression of celestial will and what could remain incomplete in my dual initiation. Surely (thought I) the instructions given me by the two priests must have been either incorrect or fragmentary; and, by Hercules, I began to suspect them of bad faith. While, however, I was drifting on these stormy tides of doubt and driven to the verge of distraction, the benign figure of the God appeared in dream once more.

'To no end,' said he, 'are you frightened by the continued series of religious rites, as if something had been previously omitted. Rather, you should take heart because the deities repeat the tokens of their love for you. You should exult that you will thrice achieve that which is scarcely even once given to others. And you may rightly conjecture from the number Three that you will remain eternally blessed. Moreover, you will find the ceremony indispensable if you will but realize that the stole of the Goddess with which you were invested in the province is still kept in the temple there. You are thus unable to supplicate at Rome in your stole or to be distinguished by that auspicious garment when you are bidden to don it. Therefore let my command be as glory, happiness, and health to you. Once more joyously become initiated, with the mighty gods for your sponsors.'

Thus far did the persuasive majesty of the divine vision announce what I must profitably do so I did not neglect or weakly postpone the matter. At once I related to a priest what I had seen; and I not only submitted to the yoke of abstinence from meat but voluntarily extended the period beyond the ten days ordained by everlasting law. Then I bought all the necessary articles, considering more the measure of my piety than the narrowness of the regulations. Nor, by Hercules, was I ever sorry for my trouble and expense. And why should I? For now by the generous aid of the gods I was being decently repaid for my forensic labours.

---

5 'Third time': This initiation was into the mysteries of the Roman Isis—the first having been into those of the Achaian Isis.

At length, after the lapse of a few days, the Lord Osiris, the most powerful of the great gods, the highest of the greater, the greatest of the highest, and the ruler of the greatest, appeared to me in the night, now no longer disguised by deigning to speak to me in his own person and with his own divine voice. He declared that I should rapidly come to the forefront of the legal profession at Rome and that I should not fear the slanders of the malevolent who naturally disliked me on account of the learning I had studiously acquired.

In addition, to enable me to mingle with the throng of devotees and duly serve his mysteries, he appointed me a member of the College of Pastophori—and more, one of the five-yearly decurions; and so, with tonsured crown, I set about joyfully executing my duties in that most ancient society (which had been founded in the period of Sylla), not shading or hiding my baldness but freely exposing it where-ever I went.

Printed in the United States
218059BV00001B/2/P